Twentieth-Century Italy

A Social History of Europe

General Editor: Raymond Pearson

Twentieth-Century Italy is the fifth volume to be published in this major Longman series. Wide-ranging both geographically and chronologically, it will explore the history of the peoples of Europe in an ambitious programme of analytical surveys, each examining a nation, state or region in a key phase of its development. The books will be written by leading experts; and each, while synthesizing the latest scholarship in the field, will be invigorated by the findings and preoccupations of the author's original research.

The series is designed for a wide audience: the volumes will be necessary reading for serious students and fellow scholars, but they are also written to engage and interest the non-specialist coming to the subject for the first time.

Inaugurated by the late Harry Hearder, the series is under the General Editorship of Professor Raymond Pearson, Professor of European History at the University of Ulster at Coleraine.

Titles available in the series:

A Social History of the Russian Empire 1650–1825
Janet Hartley

France, 1800–1914
Roger Magraw

French Society 1589–1715
Sharon Kettering

Spanish Society 1400–1600
Teofilo Ruiz

Forthcoming titles in this series:

French Society 1700–1810
Gwynne Lewis

Modern Spanish Society 1939–2000
Michael Richards

A Social History of the Russian Empire 1810–1917
David Saunders

Twentieth-Century Italy: A Social History

Jonathan Dunnage

Longman

An imprint of **Pearson Education**

London · New York · Toronto · Sydney · Tokyo · Singapore · Hong Kong · Cape Town
Madrid · Paris · Amsterdam · Munich · Milan

PEARSON EDUCATION LIMITED

Edinburgh Gate
Harlow CM20 2JE
Tel: +44 (0)1279 623623
Fax: +44 (0)1279 431059
www.pearsoned.co.uk

First published in Great Britain in 2002

The right of Jonathan Dunnage to be identified as Author
of this Work has been asserted by him in accordance
with the Copyright, Designs and Patents Act 1988.

ISBN-10: 0-582-29278-6
ISBN-13: 978-0-582-29278-9

British Library Cataloguing in Publication Data
A CIP catalogue record for this book can be obtained from the British Library

Library of Congress Cataloging in Publication Data
A CIP catalog record for this book can be obtained from the Library of Congress

10 9 8 7 6 5 4 3
10 09 08 07 06

Typeset in 9.5/12.5pt Stone Serif by Graphicraft Limited, Hong Kong
Printed and bound in Malaysia

The Publishers' policy is to use paper manufactured from sustainable forests.

Contents

General editor's preface

For far too long 'social history' was regularly, even routinely, defined dismissively and negatively along the lines of 'history with the high politics, economics and diplomacy left out'. Over the latter decades of the twentieth century, however, a virtual revolution in the sub-discipline of 'social history' gathered momentum, fuelled not only by historians but also by specialists from such established academic disciplines as anthropology, economics, politics and especially sociology, and enriched by contributors from burgeoning cultural, demographic, media and women's studies. At the cusp of the twenty-first century, the prime rationale of the recently launched 'Social History of Europe' series is to reflect the cumulative achievement and reinforce the ripening respectability of what may be positively yet succinctly defined as nothing less than the 'history of society'.

Initiated by the late Professor Harry Hearder of the University of Wales, the 'Social History of Europe' series is conceived as an ambitious and open-ended collection of wide-ranging general surveys charting the history of the peoples of the major European nations, states and regions through key phases in their societal development from the late Middle Ages to the present. The series is not designed to become necessarily either chronologically or geographically all-embracing, although certain pre-eminent areas and periods will demand a systematic sequence of coverage. Typically, a volume covers a period of about one century, but longer (and occasionally shorter) time-spans are proving appropriate. A degree of modest chronological overlap between volumes covering a particular nation, state or region is acceptable where justified by the historical experience.

Each volume in the series is written by a commissioned European or American expert and, while synthesizing the latest scholarship in the field, is invigorated by the findings and preoccupations of the author's original research. As works of authority and originality, all contributory volumes are of genuine interest and value to the individual author's academic peers.

Even so, the contributory volumes are not intended to be scholarly monographs addressed to the committed social historian but broader synoptic overviews which serve a non-specialist general readership. All the volumes are therefore intended to take the 'textbook dimension' with due seriousness, with authors recognizing that the long-term success of the series will depend on its usefulness to, and popularity with, an international undergraduate and postgraduate student readership. In the interests of accessibility, the provision of notes and references to accompany the text is suitably restrained and all volumes contain a select bibliography, a chronology of principal events, a glossary of foreign and technical terms and a comprehensive index.

Inspired by the millennial watershed but building upon the phenomenal specialist progress recorded over the last quarter-century, the eventually multi-volume 'Social History of Europe' is dedicated to the advancement of an intellectually authoritative and academically cosmopolitan perspective on the multi-faceted historical development of the European continent.

Raymond Pearson
Professor of Modern European History
University of Ulster

Acknowledgements

I am highly indebted to Gino Bedani, Giuseppe Vatalaro, Doug Thompson, Bruce Haddock, Mirco Dondi, Philip Cooke and Howard Moss for reading and commenting on parts of the manuscript.

Italy: Regions and Provinces (late twentieth century)
© David Hine, 1993. Reprinted from *Governing Italy: The Politics of Bargained
Pluralism* by D. Hine (1993) by permission of Oxford University Press.

Introduction: between tradition and modernity

At the start of the twenty-first century Italy appears as a nation in which tradition and modernity exist side by side sometimes in a baffling variety of combinations. Italy is one of the most powerful world economies. Yet, much of the strength of this economy lies in a flourishing sector of small and medium-sized family-based companies founded on old artisan traditions. In both the private and public sectors, job appointments still depend to a great extent on family connections, while the socially and culturally backward forces of the *Mafia* continue to control large areas of economic life in the South. In spite of a national health system deprecated for its inefficiency, cancer survival rates are far higher in Italy than in the United Kingdom. Most Italians are trained in the use of computers and own mobile phones, yet they continue to respect ancient traditions and family values more than most other Western nations. Celebrations of saints' days or harvest festivals linked to Italy's peasant tradition are still important. Italians continue to respect the ritual of family gatherings around the table and attach great importance to eating high-quality local produce. There is much debate today concerning levels of civic and national consciousness among Italians. They are generally mistrustful of authority and their own government and administration; hence there are high levels of tax evasion. They display an equal sense of local and national identity. Local dialect is still widely spoken alongside standard Italian. They are often suspicious of foreigners and their customs but more pro-European than most other European Union partners. And they are capable of extraordinary acts of solidarity.

Italy has long been known for its regional economic, social and cultural disparities. The North–South divide dominating the history of post-unification Italy is yet to be fully overcome, though major inroads have been made over the last hundred years. Such regional disparities clearly account for low levels of national consciousness and the difficult relationship between government and governed that followed unification. This relationship was most problematic in Southern Italy, where at the moment of unification during the 1860s Piedmontese administrators faced the hostility and incomprehension of a highly illiterate peasant population. Yet, as current historiography of the South is arguing, the 'unifiers' of Italy had from the very start failed to see these lands as anything more than 'dark' territories to be conquered and civilized. They had never considered the South as being able to contribute in any way towards their model of a unified Italy.

Following unification Italy was ruled by highly centralized and potentially authoritarian forms of government, reflecting an innate fear on the part of Italy's 'unifiers' of the 'subversive' tendencies of their subjects. Such fear was to dominate rule in Italy for much of the twentieth century and had earlier resulted in the frequent imposition of restrictions on personal liberty, facilitating the establishment of a Fascist dictatorship. Italian public life has historically been characterized by frequent episodes of internal conflict between citizens and representatives of the state. Well into the seventies the number of citizens killed by the police during strikes and demonstrations remained tragically high. Yet, such authoritarian expedients betrayed a state that was in reality aware of its own vulnerability. This was partly a product of the existence since unification of a system of administration that was strongly consumed by clientelistic practices and often failed to cater for the needs of the populace as a whole. There is little wonder that, in the face of misgovernment and state repression, national consciousness was slow to develop in a country that had only recently been politically unified. However, misgovernment was not merely imposed 'from above'. The clientelistic system that was responsible for a highly inefficient and mismanaged administrative machinery, and that would culminate in the *Tangentopoli* corruption scandals of 1992 and 1993, though clearly perpetuated and manipulated from the centre, was rooted in the subversion of the state 'from below' by the backward-looking social and cultural remnants of Italy's feudal era.

In the absence of efficient state institutions, the Italian family has always provided a basis of solidarity for its members. Foreign observers often envy, for example, the willingness of Italian families to care for their elderly relatives. 'Familistic' survival strategies are currently being debated. Are they to be blamed for the low levels of civic consciousness the Italians are often labelled with, given their direct link to the clientelistic system dominating social, economic, cultural and political relations? Have they stood in the way of the development of healthy institutions? Or have they, as has recently been posited, on the contrary actually assisted processes of civic modernization, as well as directly seeing to the welfare of their members? It would be fair to say that Italian family life was nowhere as socially and culturally backward as superficial observation would lead us to believe. Although reputed to be behind other Western countries in the adoption of birth control methods, for example, many Italian families began to contracept from the end of the nineteenth century onwards, in spite of the opposition of the state and the Catholic Church.

Today no social history is complete without an analysis of the role of women. Contrary to what one might imagine, by the beginning of the twentieth century a large number of Italian women were in employment.

Even though economic necessity was the main reason for this, the phenomenon demonstrates the start of a decline in patriarchal authority within the family in Northern and Central Italy. It is true that in Southern Italy strict codes of family honour discouraged women from working outside the home. It is equally true that an article in the criminal code in force until 1981 more or less condoned male 'crimes of honour'. Yet, in practice the number of such crimes committed was relatively low. And Southern Italian women, even if acting within a strongly patriarchal subculture, besides running the family household, often played a key social role in establishing kinship relations with other families in the community. The second half of the twentieth century saw a notable improvement in female status within the family and society at large. However, levels of equality achieved by Italian women today still fall short of those of most other Western countries, for reasons that will be described in this volume.

In writing this social history, I have taken a chronological approach. Each chapter focuses on the ways in which Italians lived against the background of state policy and major historical events affecting them. In looking at specific areas of social study, such as the family and gender relations, health and demography, work and education, leisure and consumption, I pay particular attention to the impact on the individual, the family or the community of state policy in these areas. I feel this is particularly appropriate to the study of a nation in which 'localist' values, lack of national consciousness and mistrust of authority remain strong. The social, economic and political modernization programme of the new highly centralized Italian nation state was not easily accepted and was often rejected if not subverted by 'local' forces. Italy is uniquely characterized by the fact that the key to acceptance of the 'new' lay precisely in the mediating ability of such grass-roots institutions as the family or the Church, even though this often involved compromise and allowed the perpetuation of 'backward-looking' tendencies that could in the long run be counterproductive to the modernization process.

The chapter that follows, intended as an extended introduction to an analysis of Italian society in the twentieth century, examines life in Italy during the period spanning the national unification of the 1860s and the outbreak of the First World War in 1914. It focuses on the effects on the Italian population of the social and economic upheaval brought by the unification process and the role of the state in managing the serious tensions created as a consequence, whether through law and order enforcement or the provision of welfare and education. In doing this, the chapter also identifies and discusses in depth those social, cultural and political characteristics accounting for the particular development of Italian society that will be addressed throughout the volume.

Chapter 1

Italian society in the wake of the *Risorgimento*, 1860–1914

The difficult unification of the Italians

The *Risorgimento*, the name given to the process of unification of Italy during the nineteenth century, saw the joining together of states of varying levels of political enlightenment.[1] The Kingdom of the Two Sicilies (making up the South and Sicily) had been ruled by backward-looking dynastic powers. In Piedmont, the leading state in the unification process, the monarchy had ceded some of its powers to the middle classes following popular and nationalist insurrections throughout Italy in 1848. Other parts of the Italian peninsula had been subjected to foreign dominion, as in the case of Austrian-controlled Veneto and Lombardy. Much of Central Italy had been ruled by the Papacy. The unification process represented, therefore, both an act of national redemption, as Italians were liberated from foreign rule, and a Liberal revolution against absolutist rule and temporal power.

However, it was not easy to generate support for the *Risorgimento* among the mostly peasant peoples of Italy. It has been estimated that in 1861 between 2.5 per cent and 10 per cent of the population were able to use standard Italian, with the majority of Italians speaking local dialect only.[2] This did little to create a sense of national consciousness among them. Many remained loyal to the dynastic powers from which the Liberal forces wished to liberate them. Others were opposed to the dynasties but equally opposed to new forms of rule. Their loyalties often varied according to region or province and on occasion veered between support for progressive and reactionary forces, particularly in the Kingdom of the Two Sicilies. Adrian Lyttelton notes that Calabria, for example, was the centre of anti-Borbon risings in 1848 but following unification gave strong support to counter-revolutionary brigandage. The Abruzzi, on the other hand, were consistently pro-Borbon: 'Even to generalize about single provinces is rash; southern peasant communities were remarkably autarchic and their mutual jealousies were another source of conflicting political allegiances'.[3]

Because of their frequent mobilization in the cause of counter-revolution, the fathers of the *Risorgimento* mistrusted the masses to the extent that, while prepared to make use of them for revolutionary purposes, they were reluctant to concede power to them. Even figures like Giuseppe Mazzini, one of the main inspirers of Italian unification, belonged to an enlightened middle class and aristocratic élite that was not prepared to overturn economic injustice or consider redistribution of the land, with the result, according to Roger Absalom, that it was 'impossible realistically to tap the revolutionary potential of the peasantry, which formed the vast majority of the population'.[4] This attitude was maintained by the Piedmontese Liberals leading the unification process under Count Camillo di Cavour with the support of the monarchy. Even the Republican hero of the *Risorgimento*, Giuseppe Garibaldi, whose legendary 'Expedition of the Thousand' to liberate Sicily from Borbon rule caused Cavour and King Victor Emanuel II to fear a radical democratic revolution throughout Italy, did not hesitate to put down social uprisings in Sicily.

During the 1860s the rule of the Liberal Right (*Destra Storica*) often appeared to take on the characteristics of a dictatorship rather than a politically enlightened power. Popular participation in the life of the new nation state was limited by the restriction of the electorate to 2 per cent of the population, representing half a million male Italians out of a population of 32 million. The Liberals' fear of conceding too much power to the people was also reflected in their adoption of police and criminal codes – inherited from the Piedmontese *ancien régime* and Napoleon's occupation of the peninsula at the beginning of the nineteenth century – severely limiting personal freedom.[5] In the South in particular, where unification was perceived by many as little more than a foreign invasion, law and order was often maintained through the imposition of martial law. The strong tensions characterizing the rule of the *Destra* in the South were partly a result of the failure of the unifiers to understand the broad cultural differences between themselves and those they were supposed to have liberated. Northern Italian civil servants fed with Northern cultural models felt that Southern inhabitants unjustly rejected the 'civilization' that they were bringing.[6]

However, more than an indication of disregard for the principles of Liberal democracy, the authoritarian expedients that the *Destra Storica* employed to maintain order were often a result of a sense of vulnerability and powerlessness in the face of serious opposition to the unification process. Though the centralized system of administration and policing over the provinces under the command of the prefects (of Napoleonic inspiration) was potentially oppressive, in practice local forces were easily able to undermine the power of the central government. According to a recent study of Sicily by Lucy Riall, 'many prefects, when surveyed in 1869 over proposals to increase local autonomy, argued that their capacity to direct local government was severely limited'.[7] Similarly, authoritarian methods of rule in the South were also justified on account of widespread brigandage. While, according to official figures, between 1861 and 1865 5,212 brigands were executed or killed in action against the Italian army, casualties among troops sent to fight them were equally serious. Though few were killed in action, thousands died of malaria and typhus.[8]

Though often interpreted as a justified resistance against a 'military invasion', brigandage saw an intertwining of social, political and purely criminal motives, bringing together peasants, bandits and members of the ex-Borbon state. As Lyttelton notes, peasant support of the brigands was strong because law breakers were not disliked 'in societies which had their own methods of resolving conflict which were at odds with the official system of law enforcement'.[9] Peasant support of forms of rebellion throughout Italy was also due to the consent if not open support of representatives of the Church that were angered by the state's confiscation of their lands and imposition of new restrictions on their privileges. The 1869 riots in Emilia and Romagna against a tax on grain were partly encouraged by the Catholic clergy. Lack of popular support for Liberal policies was exacerbated by the Vatican's *non-expedit*, following the annexation in 1870 of Rome and the removal of the temporal power of the Papacy. According to this Papal edict, practising Catholics were barred from participating in political activities. Stirred up by discontent over high taxes and enforced military conscription, the peasantry were also drawn into acts of rebellion promoted by Radical, Socialist and Republican movements advocating social revolution and the overthrow of the monarchy.

The above conflict and tensions formed the root of the divide between what is known as *paese reale* (real Italy) and *paese legale* (legal Italy), expressing the difficulty experienced by the great majority of Italians in identifying with the aspirations of the Liberal political class, which appeared not to take account of their needs and to deny them citizenship of the new nation state. This naturally hindered the development of national consciousness among the Italian masses. Such a divide, which has dominated Italian life for much of the twentieth century, was a consequence of not only high levels of indifference towards unification but also the devastating effects of economic unification on some regions and sections of the population. During the immediate post-unification period a positive response to the idea of a united Italy had not been lacking. This clearly emerges in the desire of each community to be put on the national communications network as the railways developed during the 1860s. It was the subsequent economic policies of the Italian state – discussed in the following section – which encouraged many Italians to look back nostalgically to their former rulers.[10]

The economic unification of Italy

At the moment of political unification Italy was a poor and overpopulated country in which the majority of inhabitants lived by agriculture. The main crops produced were cereals, grapes, oil, fruit, cheese, silk, hemp and flax. However, Italy was not self-sufficient in food. This was a consequence of the scarcity and misuse of capital and the fact that large areas of land were unfit for cultivation as a result of erosion and flooding. Yet, there were strong regional contrasts in farming forms and levels of productivity. Northern agriculture was the most advanced, particularly in the plains, showing high levels of diversification, productivity and commercial development and strong links with manufacturing. Many farms were equipped with irrigation and drainage systems. The sharecropping systems present in much of Central Italy were less commercially developed. Southern agriculture was particularly disadvantaged by erosion (owing to excessive deforestation), summer droughts, malaria and earthquakes. With its poor lines of communication, it was mainly characterized by commercially backward large estates, *latifondi*, producing cereals or rearing livestock. Some coastal areas of the South produced luxury goods, including wine, oil and citrus fruits. In Sardinia the main economic activity was sheep farming. A large proportion of those who worked the land – whether for the most advanced capitalist farmers in the Po Valley or the *latifondisti* in the South – were landless day labourers (*braccianti*) who lived in dire poverty as a result of low wages and the fact that they were not guaranteed work all the year round. Those peasants that owned or rented land often grew crops for subsistence only. A lack of resources together with an inward-looking mentality prevented the development of more efficient farming methods in most areas. Industrial activity of any significance was more or less restricted to the North-West of Italy (mainly metal and textiles) with pockets of industrial development in Veneto, Tuscany and Naples and a sulphur-mining industry in Sicily.[11]

As Denis Mack Smith notes, manufacturing was strongly linked to agriculture, as is illustrated by the strength of cottage industries, especially in the textile field, which were gradually replaced by factories employing agricultural workers seasonally. A census of 1861 calculated that, while 8 million Italians were employed in agriculture, only 3 million were employed in craftsmanship and manufacture of which the majority were part-time female workers. Limited industrial development in Italy may be attributed to a lack of raw materials like coal which had to be imported, an abundant but unskilled labour force, a reliance on expensive industrial machinery from abroad and limited lines of communication and energy sources. Industrial development was more or less limited to the North-West because of the development of sources of hydro-electric power, good transport facilities, accessible markets and a stronger industrial tradition. Perhaps most significantly there existed in Italy an archaic mentality that disfavoured industrial development and entrepreneurial activities, such that many industries were financed by foreign developers.[12]

The government of the Liberal Right has been credited with completion of the process of economic and administrative unification of Italy with the creation of single tax, administrative and judicial systems, the abolition of customs barriers, land reform and the building of a road and rail network. Yet, the immediate consequences of such policies were often devastating, reflecting the narrow social basis and lack of economic vision of the ruling class. The Southern economy was unable to compete with that of the North, now that it was no longer protected, while less developed Northern industries proved to be equally fragile. Although one of the primary objectives of the *Destra* was the complete privatization of the land, the results were far from beneficial to society as a whole. The number of smallholdings grew with the sale of church and common lands. However, while peasants were able to buy small plots of land, there were no structures to assist them, hence property sold often contributed to the enlargement of already existing properties. Crucially, the government failed to invest in a new Southern peasant property-owning class in line with Liberal laissez-faire ideology, because it was forced to sell land at high prices to the emerging middle class and post-feudal nobility in order to pay for military expenses incurred during the unification process.[13] As another example of the narrow social vision of the Liberal ruling class, military costs were also met through the taxation of a population that was already economically burdened. According to Absalom, taxes were 'uniformly regressive so that the poorest paid the highest proportion of their income'. Between 1862 and 1880 tax revenue more than doubled. Italians became the most heavily taxed in Europe for the least in return.[14]

The development of heavy industry and modern forms of agriculture did not take place before the late 1880s, when under the government of the Liberal Left (*Sinistra Storica*), which succeeded the *Destra* in 1876, protectionist measures were introduced in order to cope with an agricultural crisis caused by the flooding of the economy by cheap grain from Russia and America. Northern Italian agriculture was more easily able to cope with the effects of world market slumps than the South. According to Anthony Cardoza, between 1870 and 1900 privately and publicly financed land reclamation projects in the Po Delta and the Piedmontese rice-growing areas allowed the development of a capitalist system of production on new land, characterized by commercial farms specializing in rice and industrial crops. The huge profits made as a result of the introduction of a grain tariff in 1887 allowed agrarians to invest in more modern systems of cultivation, as they were drawn into intimate relations with suppliers of chemical fertilizers and farm machinery and food-processing firms. State-assisted travelling chairs of agriculture (*cattadre ambulanti*) provided laboratories for the evaluation of soils, seeds and fertilizers, and experimental fields to determine the most productive factors for local conditions. However, agricultural rationalization measures threatened the stability and well-being of the peasantry. New forms of mechanization together with fertilizers reduced the need for labour. It became far more efficient for farmers to rely on landless day labourers rather than share-croppers (*mezzadri*).[15]

Protectionist policies, while allowing for Northern economic development, perpetuated Southern economic difficulties. As a result of the grain tariff of 1887, Northern farmers were able to increase their grain production between 1885 and 1898 by 38 per cent in Lombardy and 28 per cent in Emilia. By contrast the South saw a fall in agricultural production by 42 per cent. Many *latifondisti* overcame the crisis by scaling down production, upgrading the quality of products and reducing the work force. The undiplomatic attitude of Francesco Crispi – prime minister during the late 1880s and much of the 1890s – over protectionist policies brought further poverty when he provoked tariff wars with Italy's principal importers, with the result that the South was unable to export luxury goods that had not benefited from the protection measures. France raised tariffs on wine, oil and liquorice. Russia imposed a 300 per cent tariff on citrus fruits.[16]

State protectionist measures at the end of the 1880s allowed a significant development of heavy industry, particularly in the iron, steel, engineering and shipbuilding sectors, though this was confined to the North-West and even there sustained industrial growth did not take place until the very end of the century. Donald Bell notes that Milan was until the 1890s a centre of commerce and light manufacturing, specializing in goods, while many of its industries were directly linked to the agriculture of its hinterland (silk, for example). The opening of the St Gotthard Pass over the Alps in 1882, facilitating the supply of imported raw materials, together with the provision of new hydroelectric energy sources at the end of the 1890s, allowed the development of heavy industry in the Lombard capital, which became the focus of steel production and a centre of finance. The 1890s saw the transfer of industry from the heart of the city to peripheral areas, due also to the increase in size of manufacturing establishments, such that Milan grew outwards along the railway lines and roads (particularly northwards along lines of communication with European markets). This led to the growth of zones of industrial concentration in engineering and textiles (to the North-West), chemicals (to the North) and steel and heavy machinery centred upon the fast-growing town of Sesto San Giovanni (to the North-East).[17]

Most economic historians agree that the initial phase of the Italian industrial revolution took place between the very end of the nineteenth century and the outbreak of the First World War. This more or less coincided with the rule of Giovanni Giolitti, prime minister for most of 1901–14. Between 1899 and 1910 industrial production almost doubled with the annual rate of growth increasing from 1 per cent during the 1880s to 7.5 per cent between 1897 and 1907. Production in the iron and steel, mechanical, chemical and electrical industries grew from 11.3 per cent to 26.3 per cent of value added in manufacturing between 1896 and 1916. Exports also increased at an annual rate of growth of 4.5 per cent. Between 1901 and 1911 the number of industrial workers increased from 2.5 to 4.5 million. These impressive figures were the result of a number of factors: the end of the tariff war with France, increased wages and fairer negotiations in labour disputes (discussed below), technological advancements, increased use of electrical power, greater financing of industrial investment by the state and banks and an increase in agricultural production, particularly in the North.[18]

The Giolittian period was also characterized by more decisive state intervention in the Southern economy. This centred around the policies of the Liberal economist, Francesco Saverio Nitti, assisted by engineers, agronomists and financial experts. Nitti believed that Italian unification had been achieved at the expense of the South, preventing it from developing independently through its own energies, and felt that state intervention was required in order to redress the resulting imbalance with the rest of the country. Intervention in the South included the special law of 1904 which sought to stimulate industrial growth in Naples, leading to the construction of the Bagnoli steel industry, and the building of a hydroelectric plant at Volturno, which provided electricity for Campania. The Giolittian government also attempted more decisive intervention in land reclamation than its predecessors (which had only benefited the Po valley). Of particular importance were the laws on Basilicata (1904) and Calabria (1906) allowing hydroforestal reconstruction, public works for the construction of aqueducts, farmhouses and drains, and tax incentives and loans for encouraging private participation. This was boosted by legislation for the extension and consolidation of state forestry (1910) and the reclamation of mountain basins (1911).[19]

In spite of state intervention in the South, regional economic divisions were actually reinforced during this period. According to statistics for 1911, the industrial triangle of Milan, Genoa and Turin accounted for 55 per cent of industrial income, the North-East and Centre 29 per cent and the South only 16 per cent. While the industrial triangle saw the greatest concentration of technologically advanced plants, many industries in the North-East and Centre were characterized by artisan methods of production and poor levels of technology. Within the North-West of Italy itself, there were strong contrasts in levels of industrial development. Smaller size artisan-based industries were damaged by protective tariffs which were of benefit to larger producers (for example, in the metal and engineering sectors) and industrial development was consequently slower in smaller centres such as Brescia where small-time entrepreneurs were unable to compete with larger firms in Milan. Though Brescia underwent industrial growth and modernization from 1890 onwards, it was badly affected by the world financial crisis of 1907. Sustained industrial development in these smaller towns did not take place before the First World War.[20]

The 'Southern question'

The economic disadvantages that Southern Italy faced over the rest of the country were the consequence of several factors. Geographical isolation, an inward-looking mentality and high levels of illiteracy were frequently blamed for entrepreneurial backwardness. Problems of land erosion, frequent droughts, earthquakes and disease also disadvantaged the South. In this sense malaria was highly significant, as Frank Snowden shows: though few Italian provinces were free of it, the Southern epidemics were more acute and regular. In 1887, for example, statistics showed 21,000 deaths from the disease, of which over 18,000 were in the South. According to Snowden, the 'apathy' characteristic of much of Southern life 'had in fact an overwhelming medical foundation'.[21] Ever since unification the South has been the object of study of politicians, anthropologists and scholars obsessed with the need to overcome not only its economic weaknesses but also what the Liberal statesman, Leopoldo Franchetti, presented during the 1870s (in referring to the Neapolitan provinces) as 'a perverse realm of social disorder and moral degradation in which human existence cannot be conceived of according to the standard measure of European civilization'.[22] The nineteenth-century *meridionalisti* (the term given to experts on the 'Southern question'), were divided between those who believed that the South was incapable of managing itself on its own, and was therefore in need of correction through state intervention, and those who challenged this assertion in their belief that the centralized state administrative system was a corrupting influence on local government which needed to develop on its own strengths.[23]

The South has traditionally been seen as lacking any entrepreneurial ability or self-propelling capacity. This was because Southern Liberals were represented by the landowning élite who, rather than sharing the Liberal ideology of their Northern counterparts, merely wished to increase their privileges. According to the well-known interpretation of the founder of the Italian Communist Party, Antonio Gramsci, the South witnessed no middle-class revolution involving the peasantry. In its place a 'passive revolution' occurred without social upheaval. This formed the basis of an alliance in a context of limited suffrage between advanced Northern industrialists and backward Southern landowners, in which the latter were absorbed into hegemony of the former. The Northern economy was able to draw off capital from the South through taxation and exploit the internal imbalance of trade to its own advantage. After unification the relatively narrow Southern bourgeoisie, the professional, bureaucratic and intellectual classes, were easily attracted to Cavour's state programme, which provided an important basis for the continued exercise of Northern influence rather than the development of a strong Southern middle class of merchants, bankers and entrepreneurs in its own right.[24]

Some of the difficulties in overcoming the North–South divide lay in the rejection, often among the *meridionalisti* themselves, of the idea that the South might contribute culturally or economically to the unification process. It was seen as lacking the features of an ideal nation and therefore excluded from the model upon which Italy was to be built (that of the Medieval city states, Dante, Palladio and the Medici), effectively becoming the end of civilization, an image bolstered by photographs of hanged brigands. More recent research argues, however, that a constant tendency to compare the economies of North and South has resulted in the latter being eternally interpreted as backward and uniform, while it did have an economic system in its own right, which if anything was weakened by Liberal state intervention. Moreover, it is argued that a modernizing Southern middle class did exist and that there were, for example, a variety of farming forms, many of which demonstrated positive adaptation to new market forces. The claims of the *meridionalisti* that the South was dominated by estates owned by absentee landlords generating income for status maintenance rather than maximizing profits, and investing in the immediate returns of wheat rather than more suitable Mediterranean crops, while plausible for Western Sicily, ignored the cattle-rearing *latifondi* of Latium and the more rationally managed estates of the mainland.[25]

Until recently a concept of backward landownership surrounding the great estates was seen as accounting for a weaker Southern economy. It was argued that the great estate was not a source of production but a basis for the exploitation of the needs and poverty of a fragile peasant economy, as was evidenced by the Jacini government inquiry of the 1880s. Pino Arlacchi's sociological case study of farming systems around Crotone (Calabria) argues that the entrepreneurial success of the *latifondo* lay precisely in such backwardness, however. The Northern capitalist agricultural enterprises reinvested profit into machinery and plants, so reducing the need for labourers. The Southern *latifondisti* invested profit in more land, landed monopoly being a measure of status and well-being. Consequently, wage labour remained the exclusive protagonist of production. The *latifondista* was able to rely on a dense local proletariat of landless labourers to ensure high levels of productivity (the taxable income of which was greater than all Piedmont). Aided by the coercive methods of his private guards, he kept local workers in a perpetual state of subordination and competition to this end, importing workers from other areas when the greatest number of hands was required during harvests, to prevent the development of worker solidarity.[26]

Familism, clientelism and the *Mafia*

Even today it is difficult not to stress the importance of the Italian family as a haven of solidarity and a vehicle for adaptation to the effects of social, political, cultural and economic upheaval. As Paul Ginsborg states:

In Italy, the oft-stressed solidarity between generations, not by any means limited to the extended families of rural Central Italy in the nineteenth century, contrasts stridently with the frequent pattern of isolation and even abandonment of older relatives in Northern European countries, and the corresponding absence of contact between grandparents and grandchildren.[27]

In nineteenth-century Italy family households varied in form according to geographical area as well as the inheritance and economic systems governing them. Urban areas were mainly inhabited by nuclear families, while a high proportion of multiple peasant families characterized rural areas of Northern and Central Italy. In Northern Italy landless day labourers tended to form nuclear households in urban settlements, as did most of the Southern peasantry. This may be attributed to the fact that peasant day labourers contracted work in the town squares. Where Southern peasants owned land, lack of good hygienic conditions and water in the countryside encouraged them to walk miles from the town where they lived to their plots. Most importantly, however, their land was usually insufficient to feed their families, hence they needed to supplement this by working as day labourers. The risks of malaria also accounted for the lack of farm settlements in the Southern countryside.[28]

The key role of the Italian family as a vehicle of solidarity in the face of transformation is demonstrated by its ability in some parts of Italy to partially inhibit the break-up of the multiple household and the urbanization and proletarianization of its members brought about by modernization processes. As the research of Anna Cento Bull and Paul Corner demonstrates, when from the end of the eighteenth century in the hills and mountains of Lombardy landowners turned their back on the sharecropping system by relying on dependent workers in order to intensify wheat production, sharecropping families avoided disintegration by specializing in other activities. Women and children were able to supplement the family income by working in the local silk industry so as to remain on the land as sharecroppers, rather than being turned into day labourers. While the silk crisis of the 1890s broke this newly established equilibrium, forcing many destitute families to emigrate to Milan, on other farms individual family members, usually the sons, began to take jobs in industry by commuting to the Milan hinterland, as lines of communication improved, in order to maintain the holding.[29]

Migration constituted one of the main strategies of Italian families for survival in the face of crisis produced by the economic transformations of the nineteenth century. Since the eighteenth century many regions had witnessed annual migrations for seasonal work, usually the harvesting of crops, sometimes across the French, Swiss and Austrian borders too. In line with the urbanization and industrialization process, a phenomenon of more permanent migration took place from the 1870s onwards, with many cities doubling in population by the First World War as they filled up with immigrants from the surrounding countryside. As a result of the dramatic effects of the agricultural crisis and the inability of a late-developing Italian industry to absorb the large number of peasants expelled from the land, from the 1880s many Italians emigrated abroad, at first mainly from Northern Italy to Europe and Latin America but from the turn of the century increasingly from the South to the industries of North America. Italian emigration was traditionally seen as being of a uni-directional movement, transforming peasants from a rural world in crisis into proletarians at the service of the rapidly developing industrial Western world.

More recent research argues that this theory can no longer stand on its own. The phenomenon of emigration is now seen as the broadening out of already existing family strategies of survival and self-improvement. Temporary migration, whether abroad or within Italy, served to 'lighten' the weight of the family during a moment of economic crisis, subsequently allowing new fortunes in its place of origin through, for example, the buying of land. From the turn of the century emigration abroad was temporary in most cases and envisaged returning to the community of origin in Italy, to which all earnings from the host country were destined. Between 1881 and 1900 4,710,000 people left the country, 52.5 per cent permanently. Though between 1900 and 1910 as many as 6,030,000 Italians emigrated, only 16.9 per cent never returned. Economic historians have emphasized the important role played by the huge amount of earnings of emigrants abroad in bringing finance and development to their communities of origin and improving the livelihood of their families. Undoubtedly, emigration solved problems of local unemployment and low wages, while emigrants sent money to the families they had left behind. On returning to their native communities, emigrants brought with them higher levels of education and more progressive ideas about employment and political rights which they gained from living in politically and culturally more progressive parts of Italy or beyond. The question remains whether this compensated for less positive social consequences of emigration, as communities were increasingly populated by women and the elderly as the men went off, if only temporarily, in search of work.[30]

The primacy of the Italian family as a vehicle for survival has been strongly associated with widespread practices of patronage and clientelism and seen as an obstacle to the development of civic consciousness and horizontal solidarity, particularly in Southern Italy. The American sociologist, Edward Banfield, introduced the term 'amoral familism' during the late fifties, to describe the tendency of Southern nuclear family units to 'look after their own', so preventing the development of horizontal peasant solidarity against the landed élite.[31] In the South most inter-family alliances created, for example, through Godfathering (*comparaggio*) were between families of different social standing, as part of a system of patronage in which limited resources such as work were obtained through loyalty to those holding positions of power and influence. According to Robert Putnam, Southern landowners, along with members of the urban professional classes who had acquired Church and common lands, used private violence and their privileged access to state resources to reinforce 'vertical relations of dominion and personal dependency' and to discourage the development of horizontal solidarity.[32]

Yet, the assumption that kinship ties were stronger in the South than elsewhere and that familism and patronage automatically impeded the development of horizontal solidarity has recently been questioned. Anna Cento Bull argues that even today family and friendship ties remain strong in Northern Italy. Yet, this has not prevented the development of horizontal associations. What is significant is that 'it is often the family which is the springboard for wider social participation, as well as political values and attitudes'.[33] It is possible that the 'familistic' strategies of the multiple families of rural Northern and Central Italy actually facilitated the development of horizontal solidarity. Paolo Macry suggests that strong kinship ties in themselves were not the cause of limited associationism, rather, the capacity of kinship ties to give way to horizontal solidarity was determined by the type of family and the farming and inheritance systems governing it. Strong kinship ties in the North – characterized by high levels of collaboration within and between families as is exemplified by the sharecropping system – encouraged trust and collaboration and were therefore conducive to the development of horizontal solidarity. In the South conflict between nuclear family units generated mistrust and rivalry. As Macry notes: 'It was . . . unusual in the South for brothers to cooperate, whereas in the share-cropping regions this was an essential prerequisite for getting a farm. In the South brothers were from the start competitors for their father's inheritance while their destinies were not brought together by living under the same roof or working together on the same land'.[34]

Likewise, patronage relationships did not automatically prevent the development of horizontal solidarity. David Moss argues that it was the quality of such relationships that was the determining factor. In Central Italy, for example, the intense relationship between sharecroppers and landlords and the resultant circulation of information concerning the reputations of individual patrons (the landlords) and clients (the sharecroppers) increased the possibilities of successful collective action by the latter. Moreover:

> Equally valuable information could be elicited in the course of conflict, individual or collective, between patrons and clients. The participants had the opportunity to observe each other's behaviour under pressure and to assess the response; more accurate calculations could thus be made about the distribution of the readiness to take risks and the trustworthiness of others.[35]

Moss goes on to argue that in Southern Italy the conditions for similar circulation of knowledge and reputation were lacking, given high levels of landlord absenteeism and the short-term nature of tenancies.

15

Attempts by the central government at controlling and bringing innovation to Southern Italy were frustrated as local government rule was contested by individual families and their supporters. Moreover, with the rise to power in 1876 of the Liberal Left (*Sinistra Storica*), and in order to compensate for an increase in the electorate from 2 per cent to 7 per cent of the population (and 11 per cent for local elections), the system of patronage came to dominate and paralyse central politics and administration as a result of *trasformismo* ('transformism'), by which members of the Chamber of Deputies (lower house of parliament) gave their support to unstable government majorities in return for favours rather than on the basis of party affiliation. Thus Liberal politics became the private issue of select groups with little sense of ideology, public responsibility or representation of collectivity. The key figure in this process was the prefect who had the job of maintaining links of support between centre and periphery, which he achieved by doling out administrative favours to government-supporting politicians and their electors. In the South political corruption was endemic, and prefects were even expected to turn a blind eye to violence employed to ensure that government supporters were returned to power at elections. What is more, the ensuing jobs-for-votes system 'Southernized' the national civil service and reinforced administrative corruption and technical incompetence. In Northern Italy, however, the ills of *trasformismo* were partly contested as local systems of patronage gradually gave way to the development of mass political movements and parties (described below). This limited the power of state officials to adopt underhand methods during elections.[36]

In parts of the South (particularly Western Sicily, Naples and Southern Calabria) the system of patronage was managed by the *Mafia*, which exacted protection payments, ran election campaigns and used violence against anyone who challenged its position. According to socio-cultural interpretations, the *Mafia* developed in a society traditionally based on power feuds between the ruling barons in an environment in which the natural concept of power was founded on the arbitrary exercise of force in defence of personal interests and in which each man sought the support of and protection from the strongest in the absence of legitimate authority. The *Mafia* exerted authority because it was at one with the cultural norms of society, where violence was used to incite fear, to obtain revenge and to gain respect, and where the official state was mistrusted. According to Henner Hess, the position of the *mafioso* 'is legitimated in popular morality, and its peculiar consolidation is due to the fact that his activity serves not only the satisfaction of his own needs, but performs a function (a protective and intermediary function) for the entire sub-cultural system'.[37]

Recent historiography contests sociological visions of the *Mafia* as being at one with the community in which they existed. Given the uniformity of the anthropological characteristics of the South (mistrust of the state, self-justice, clientelism, a sense of honour and familism), Salvatore Lupo asks why the *Mafia* only spread throughout Sicily, Calabria and Campania, and to Apulia for the first time ever, after the Second World War, if it was considered an integral part of Southern culture.[38] It is more realistic to suggest, therefore, that where it existed, the *Mafia* was able to exploit certain anthropological aspects of Southern life, including the practice of *omertà*, a conspiracy of silence, which made it difficult for the authorities to identify the authors of crimes. Anton Blok argues that: 'Through their manipulation of this complex cultural code and the social control it entailed, *mafiosi* tried to isolate the local population from external rival powers.'[39]

Recent analysis sees the *Mafia* above all as a vehicle for adaptation to social, political and economic transformations brought by the unification process. With reference to the Sicilian *Mafia*, Judith Chubb states:

> To understand the development of the mafia in the 19th and 20th centuries, it is necessary to place the mafia in the context of the economic, social and political arrangements within which it emerged and thrived. Recent scholarly analyses of the origins of the mafia depict it not as a residue of a feudal past, but rather as a product of the disintegration of the feudal system and the penetration of the market and modern state into the Sicilian countryside in the 19th century – a situation of transition in which traditional relationships of economic and political power were breaking down but not fully replaced by the impersonal structures of the market and the state.[40]

In a highly competitive and unregulated market situation where positions of monopoly could only be achieved by force, the strength of the *Mafia* lay in its ability to act as an intermediary between external modernizing forces and local society. The figure of the *mafioso* in its earliest form was represented by the farm estate foreman (*gabelloto*), effectively a 'middle-class' figure in the agricultural hierarchy, who after the abolition of feudalism was able to play off the peasantry against the landowners using threats and violence to acquire wealth and become a dominant figure in the local power structure. *Mafiosi* occupied other intermediary or middle class professions, such as carters, animal herders, merchants, doctors, lawyers and pharmacists. They oversaw legal transactions, organized protection rackets and controlled the transportation and marketing of local produce. In the political sphere, the *mafioso* either acted as a mediator between the local politician and the electorate, overseeing election campaigns on his behalf, or, as a local coun-cil leader or parliamentary deputy, controlled the administration of state resources to the local population.

The inability of the Italian state to repress the *Mafia* may be attributed to its failure to establish a firm basis of authority in much of the south of the peninsula and Sicily following unification, a situation compounded by the politics of *trasformismo* which led to complicity between *mafiosi*, politicians and civil servants. A strongly under-represented Italian state often delegated to *Mafia* organizations the task of controlling society in order to maintain the supremacy of the landowning élites, repress political deviation and to reduce brigandage and common crimes in areas under its control. This does not mean that the *Mafia* stood for order in the absence of the state. Recent research emphasizes the *Mafia*'s ability to use violence and extortion to generate the conditions required to force people to recognize it as the main centre of power. According to Paolo Macry, the Neapolitan Camorra was, for example, a criminal organization that obtained wealth through the running of illegal entrepreneurial activities (prostitution, gambling, smuggling) involving widespread extortion. Although the state presence was weak, private protection and public order services were effectively manufactured through the deliberate creation of disorder with the complicity of local state representatives. The Camorra system, therefore, gave rise to (rather than originating in) a public lack of trust in the state.[41]

The development of the working-class movement and mass politics

As the above analysis has demonstrated, the economic upheaval brought by processes of modernization threatened the livelihood of large numbers of agricultural workers. Yet, the industrialization process did not automatically bring prosperity to make up for their impoverishment. Industrial workers were concentrated in the factories for long hours, often in dust-infested, stifling conditions. Salaries were very low for women and children (respectively making up 27 per cent and 17 per cent of the industrial work force in 1901[42]) and not much higher for unskilled men. Without a system of social security, periods of illness or unemployment often threw families well below the bread line. Between 1880 and 1910 the population of many cities increased dramatically. That of Milan, for example, nearly doubled from 322,000 to 579,000 inhabitants. This led to serious housing difficulties for the working classes. The housing census of 1881 revealed a national average of 1.65 inhabitants per room, with higher figures for cities like Genoa, Naples, Rome, Turin and Milan. In Milan the situation subsequently worsened, so that by 1911 the number varied between 2 and 3.78, according to district.[43] Sanitary conditions were often bad as workers' families had to share a common lavatory and draw water from a communal well in the courtyard of their tenement block. There was no proper state provision for the cure of disease. Public health, placed under the jurisdiction of the prefects and mayors after unification, was perceived more as a problem of public order than a socio-cultural issue, so that Italy remained distant from the most developed European countries in the cure of diseases such as typhus, rickets, pellagra, cholera, smallpox and syphilis.[44]

18

From the 1880s onwards, Italian economic life was increasingly dominated by organized struggles for better pay and working conditions. The origins of the Italian working-class movement lay in the development during the second half of the nineteenth century of mutual aid organizations to alleviate the social and economic hardships of urban artisans. Many ran co-operative retail stores for their members, undertook social insurance and organized educational activities for their benefit, and they very quickly spread to the countryside. By 1871 there were 1,500 such organizations. By 1904 they numbered 6,535 with over 900,000 members.[45] Mostly confined to the North and Centre of Italy, these organizations were initially politically neutral in character. Indeed, employers often contributed money to them, since they saw them as a means of limiting labour unrest. However, severe economic crisis during the last two decades of the nineteenth century gradually turned them into militant leagues (*leghe di resistenza*) of political inspiration that declared war on the employers, demanding better pay and working conditions. Socialist organizations were particularly strong in industrial areas and parts of the countryside, while Catholic workers' organizations were most successful in rural areas, particularly in the North-East of Italy and Lombardy. Anarchists also played a significant role in worker agitations, particularly in Central Italy.

The speed with which mutual aid societies became instruments of class war depended on myriad factors. The attitude of employers was particularly important. In Milan, for example, a large number of engineer entrepreneurs were concerned to promote a culture of interclass collaboration at the work-place in an attempt to prevent the development of union associationism. By contrast the entrepreneurs of the shipbuilding and steel industries, inspired by Nationalist and imperialist ideology, rejected paternalistic strategies in favour of a more aggressive approach to labour relations. In Veneto, Lombardy and Tuscany during the first years of industrial development many Catholic entrepreneurs attempted to reduce social tensions, by running small-size factories in the countryside and guaranteeing workers a range of services, including sickness benefits, nurseries, professional schools and savings banks.[46] With regard to agriculture, in Veneto and Emilia there was from the 1880s a strong incentive to destroy the sharecropping system, owing to the opportunities for capitalist farming in those regions, and this led to class conflict. In Tuscany, by contrast, landowners resisted this process in order to prevent class conflict that would inevitably develop from the impoverishment and proletarianization of the peasantry.[47]

Union organization also required time to take root as a result of the attitude of peasants and industrial workers themselves. In the South associations of horizontal solidarity failed to develop substantially, whether Catholic or Socialist. Society was too highly factionalized between client and patron, rather than classes, except in Apulia, which saw the development of political protest from the turn of the century. Even among the urban proletariat of the North, however, there were difficulties. Socialist labour activism was rooted in the mutualist and co-operative tradition of the artisan professions, which was brought to the factories with the aim of instilling in lesser skilled pro-letarianized workers a sense of hierarchy, regard for specialization and a code of independence and mutual support. Political militancy partly aimed to achieve a higher level of integration of workers into the developing industrial society. Overcoming problems of illiteracy and the teaching of work discipline, for example, gave workers the necessary tools for such integration.[48]

Yet, the success of the above policies in a situation in which many workers lived and worked in precarious conditions is questionable. In this regard, recent research suggests that the social and political homogeneity of Italian urban working-class districts has been over-stressed in the past. As Louise Tilly states with reference to Milan:

> The city's manufacturing workers were themselves a heterogeneous group, and they lived and labored alongside a high proportion of service workers. Milan's labor force was divided as well by the place of birth and gender of its members, by the scale of their workplaces, and by the type of production – consumer or producer – in which they were engaged.[49]

Much of the working-class population of urban areas was migrant or of recent migration from the surrounding rural areas and overcame hardships, such as redundancies, by returning to the countryside, rather than becoming involved in union activities.

In the countryside, the *braccianti* had little to lose by joining union organizations. The conservative peasant 'middle classes' were initially more difficult to win over. According to Snowden, while the sharecropping con-tract allowed the landowners to exploit the tenant and interfere in such private matters as the education and marriages of his sons and daughters, any impulse towards rebellion was blunted by the advantages of landlord paterna-lism. Moreover, the multiple sharecropping family of up to 120 members was physically and psychologically isolated from knowledge and political awareness, the head of family (*capoccia*) becoming a 'buffer between lordly power and peasant discontent', fostering division within the family rather than between it and the landlord.[50] Even where 'middle-class' peasant families came into contact with union militancy as a result of supplementary work in the factories, family authority often stood in the way. In the silk factories of Northern Lombardy, for example, women labourers could not always engage in collective activity, since there was little support from the male heads of the sharecropping families from which they came. Indeed, indus-trial employers preferred to take on workers from peasant families precisely in order to prevent the development of occupational solidarity in the factory. Only the experience of migration by individual family members brought radical ideas to peasant families.[51]

The Catholic Church played a prominent role in promoting union activities but in doing so endeavoured to contain social conflict. This allowed it to regain influence in society after the general decline in its hegemony following unification. According to Snowden:

> Whereas the parish church had once been a focus for the few great occasions in peasant life, in Liberal Italy the multiplication of contacts and occasions of a commercial, political and lay character diminished the awe and importance of the church and created other rival repositories of attention, loyalty and hope – the town hall, the party, even the market place. By the propagation of a secular culture and ideology, united Italy weakened the esteem in which the clergy were held.[52]

The Church was, however, able to capitalize on the general unpopularity of the Liberal state. Towards the end of the nineteenth century it attempted to regain influence within society and offset the effects of Socialist ideology through the creation of its own institutions. These included banks and workers' associations, Catholic Action (*Azione Cattolica*), which ran a wide range of religious and social activities, and the parish and diocesan committees of the *Opera dei Congressi*, which co-ordinated charity and welfare activities. Such developments in social and political Catholicism were inspired by Pope Leo XIII's 1891 encyclical *de Rerum Novarum*, which looked to deal with social problems and lifted the *non-expedit* for administrative elections, turning the parish into a political focal point. According to John Molony, by the late 1890s there were 4,000 parish groups and 700 Catholic workers' societies backed by 24 daily papers and 155 periodicals.[53] From the start of the twentieth century the Catholics also began to win municipal power.

However, the extent of influence that the Catholic movement was able to exercise varied from region to region. In the South the ideological power of the Church was less strong and incisive since the centre of power at the community level was not the parish but the clientelistic structure dominated by the landowning elite. In North-Eastern Italy and Lombardy, Catholic ideology was particularly strong. The existence of a Catholic subculture helped to promote class collaboration, with Catholic associations and initiatives defending the structure of local society. The Church also acted as a mediator between landlords and peasants in the purchase of holdings. According to John Earl, the influence of the clergy in systems of credit benefiting the peasantry was fundamental from the moment that the parish priest was able to judge the morality and creditworthiness of parishioners requesting loans.[54]

Socialist-led worker protest became more effective with the founding from 1890 of Chambers of Labour (conciliatory labour exchanges) in the main Northern cities, Rome and Naples, and the creation of union category federations to defend workers' interests, alongside their representation in parliament and local government by politicians. Socialist labour battles were often highly confrontational. Originally influenced by the Anarchist ideas of

Bakunin, even after the creation of a Reformist-based Socialist Party (*Partito Socialista Italiano* – PSI) in 1892 by Andrea Costa, the Socialist movement was prone to periods of dominance by Revolutionary factions, which exacerbated levels of confrontation with not only employers but also non-unionized workers or those belonging to rival associations, not infrequently resulting in violence. Union militancy is partly explained by the strong middle-class character of the Socialist Party, resulting from restrictions on the right to vote, which prevented the development of strong linkages with the workers' movement.[55] Nevertheless, it is important to distinguish between Northern-based labour struggles, which were for the most part controlled by party and union leaders, and the purely rebellious and spontaneous action of the peasantry of the South where union presence was limited, typified by the storming of municipal offices or *Carabinieri* barracks and the looting of food reserves. It is no surprise that only the extreme left-wing Anarcho-Syndicalist movement, calling for 'direct' action against employers, managed to take root in the South, especially Apulia.[56]

As indicated above, rival political and union organizations did not co-exist peacefully. In particular the Socialists were antagonized by the willingness of Catholic organizations to accept lower wages, with the result that their workers were favoured by employers. Such rivalry was also reflected in deeper subcultural divisions. As is demonstrated by Donald Bell in his study of Sesto San Giovanni, Catholics and Socialists identified with specific types of dress, recreational activities, meeting places and even marriage and funeral services (religious or secular). This often involved imitation, as was evident in the Socialists' adoption and adaptation of Catholic rituals (the singing of religious anthems, flag-flying, processions, funerals, etc.). The heights that such cultural and ideological rivalry could reach were evident on religious feast days when Socialist and lay marchers hurled abuse against Catholics and burned their flags.[57]

State control in Liberal Italy: repression, welfare and education

The opposition of Liberal governments also limited the achievements of the Italian workers' movement. Moreover, the earlier experience of popular rebellion against Piedmontese rule shaped the attitude of the Liberal leaders for decades to follow. Much of the contents of emergency legislation set up to deal with brigandage during the 1860s, for example, was introduced into the 1865 Public Security Law on a regular basis. The powers of the police to impose restrictions on the movements of individuals (*ammonizione*) or send them to exile (*domicilio coatto*) on remote islands or distant areas of the peninsula were used against not only vagabonds, prostitutes and habitual criminals but also political opponents of the Liberal government and trade union leaders. The 1890s in particular were characterized by frequent declarations of states of military rule to deal with mass anti-government protests. In October 1894 all Socialist and Anarchist associations were closed. In 1897 the activities of Catholic organizations were restricted and the following year widespread social unrest culminated in the military repression of riots in Milan, which saw the killing of 85 protesters on 8 May. This was followed by the suspension of numerous newspapers, the closure of thousands of Catholic and Socialist organizations and the arrest of opposition party leaders.

The extent of state repressive measures was partly a consequence of the sense of vulnerability of the Liberal ruling class. Awareness of the limited efficiency of the police and armed forces at the end of the century, rather than purely anti-Liberal sentiments, may well have accounted for moments of particularly harsh forms of repression and restrictions upon civil liberties. Such attitudes also demonstrated the tendency of the ruling class to ascribe economic protest to revolutionary designs without a thought for the dramatic effects of state policies on the livelihood of the populace. The social conflict of the 1890s was very much a product of the attitude of Francesco Crispi, prime minister for much of that period, who pushed for imperialist expansion in Africa – which culminated in the humiliating defeat at the battle of Adowa, Ethiopia, in 1896 – at the cost of neglecting serious domestic problems. The rebellion of 1893 of the short-lived mutual aid societies and leagues of the *Fasci Siciliani*, resulting in the imposition of military rule, was also a consequence of Crispi's aggressive tariff war against France, which had the effect of reducing the Sicilian sulphur workers and peasants to destitution. The riots and demonstrations of 1897 and 1898, while certainly encouraged by the parties of the Left, were in fact an expression of intense economic hardship caused by a tax on the price of flour which pushed up the price of bread.[58]

In contrast to the 1890s, the following decade saw an attempt under the government of Giolitti to limit the use of force in dealing with worker protests. This was part of a broader strategy inspired by the idea that improved worker–management relations would speed the pace of industrialization. In the aftermath of the assassination of King Umberto I by an Anarchist the previous year, he was also aware that repression alone would not prevent social revolution, especially when the grievances of the masses were often justified. Giolitti also raised the electorate from 3 to 8 million in 1912, granting the vote to all males over the age of thirty and paving the way towards the development of mass parties. He argued that political groups potentially representing a threat to the Liberal ruling class such as the Socialists, the Radicals and the Catholics should be integrated into the political framework rather than opposed as subversive. This was clearly the idea behind his alliance with the Socialist Party (1901–3), as a result of which the Reformist leader, Filippo Turati, pledged parliamentary support of the government in return for which Giolitti ordered his prefects not to prevent peaceful, economically based strikes, which they should attempt to solve through mediation.

From the end of the nineteenth century the process of economic modernization was accompanied by state welfare and sanitary initiatives. While health care and insurance were originally the object of the paternalistic policies of some employers, the onus on their provision increasingly became the responsibility of the state, as is illustrated by the introduction of sickness, accident and pension schemes and the raising of the minimum working age for children to twelve and the setting of a maximum number of working hours. This coincided with general hospital reform and developments in medicine, such as the curing of tuberculosis, typhus and malaria and the development of aspirin and antiseptics allowing more complicated surgery and improvement of hygiene. Between 1885 and 1902 the number of those cured annually in hospitals increased by 50 per cent and the number of beds available increased by 58 per cent between 1885 and 1914. New medical cures allowed an improvement in the nutrition and lifestyles of the peasantry of many Northern regions, so reducing cases of pellagra. Between 1861 and 1913 the average life expectancy increased from 30 to 47 and the mortality rate went down from 31 per cent to 18.7 per cent (and that of infants in their first year from 223 per 1,000 to 138) such that on the eve of the First World War Italy was safely on a level with other countries. This was partly a result of successful economic strikes from the turn of the century.[59]

In spite of a general improvement in the Italians' standard of living from the end of the nineteenth century onwards, several social categories continued to live below the bread line. These included *braccianti* and factory workers. *Braccianti* were badly off on account of being likely to earn no more than 200 days' wages per year, while other peasant categories were able to survive hard times through strategies of family solidarity. Factory workers, though earning more than *braccianti*, had to spend more money on food and accommodation because of a higher cost of living in urban areas. Though there were 'worker aristocracies', especially in the metal-mechanical sector, enjoying a higher standard of living than other workers, there was a wide gap between their wages and those of white-collar workers and professionals. In 1910, for example, the average annual wage of a factory worker of 688 lire compared unfavourably with the average teaching salary of 2,440 lire. Although the new insurance schemes for workers may have seemed impressive, they did not immediately cater for all categories and most of them remained voluntary.

The rule of Giolitti also helped to improve education provision and literacy levels in a country in which the majority of people spoke local dialect only. The attitude of the post-unification Liberal political class to mass education had in many respects been progressive for its time, though distinction needs to be made between policy and practice. The desire of the *Destra Storica* to provide professional education for the Italians lay in the need for socialization of the masses according to Liberal ideals, overcoming a legacy of previous control over education by the Church. This was the ideology behind the Casati Law of 1859, which made the first two years of primary education obligatory. In spite of such legislation, it was difficult to overcome high regional imbalances. A census of 1870 showed illiteracy among 69 per cent of Italians. By regional breakdown 80 per cent of the population above the age of six in the South was illiterate, followed closely by Tuscany and Latium (68 per cent) and Veneto (65 per cent). This was contrasted by Piedmont (42 per cent), Lombardy (45 per cent) and Liguria (56 per cent). Primary education provision varied from 26 schools per 10,000 inhabitants in Piedmont to six in Sicily and Basilicata. There were also evident imbalances in illiteracy between the city and the country (49/72 per cent) and males and females (62/76 per cent).[60]

Under the *Sinistra* the Coppino Law of 1877 reiterated compulsory schooling from ages six to nine, the duty of municipal councils to supply schools and, in opposition to traditional religious hegemony in education, the need to teach youngsters their rights and duties as citizens of a Liberal nation state, though again without achieving the desired ends. One of the main causes of high levels of illiteracy lay in the attitude of local governments, to whom the provision of education was entrusted. While notables running Southern municipalities, for example, were able to claim that insufficient funding prevented the enforcement of obligatory primary education, in reality such attitudes may be attributed to their fears that education would encourage subversion and revolution. Education was seen as superfluous for women given their primarily domestic role within society and among the lower classes the imperatives of family survival through labour often prevented children from being sent to school. Moreover, for peasant children access to schooling often required the permission of the landowner. The growth rate of primary education was notably restrained during periods of economic expansion which increased the need for child labour.

From the turn of the century, however, partly as a result of the passing of responsibility for primary education from the municipal councils to the central state, there was a general improvement in literacy levels throughout Italy. The 1911 census showed a drop in levels of illiteracy to a national average of 37.6 per cent, though the North–South divide was broadened if one is to consider that the lowest figures regarded Piedmont (11 per cent), Liguria (17 per cent) and Lombardy (13.4 per cent) and the highest Calabria (69.6 per cent), Basilicata (65.3 per cent) and Apulia (59.4 per cent). Regions of the North-East and Centre showed intermediate figures ranging from 25.2 per cent in Veneto to 50.7 per cent in the Marches. Improvements in the South may also be attributed to an increase in the number of state schools, though still well behind the national average of 18.35 per 10,000 inhabitants by

1907–8. Literacy levels still compared unfavourably with those of other Western European countries, however. While the imbalance between the city and the country remained marked, the number of literate females in proportion to males improved with higher levels of female over male literacy in parts of the North-West of Italy.[61]

The Italian sociologist, Marzio Barbagli, has identified the lack of a positive link between education and economic development in Italy with the result that growth patterns in education were particularly evident during moments of economic crisis. Notably, the South, while registering a lower rate of primary and lower secondary enrolment than elsewhere, showed a higher rate of upper secondary and university enrolment, partly thanks to the Casati Law, which favoured the influx of a relatively high number of students to university in comparison with other more industrially developed countries. Consequently, the Italian educational system 'produced a relative quantity of intellectual labor higher than or equal to that of the other European countries. Considering that Italy also had the lowest level of socio-economic development, and consequently presented, in all likelihood, the lowest demand for this type of labor, it is not hard to imagine how difficult it was for graduates of the Italian university to find work.'[62]

The process of modernization and urbanization that parts of Italy underwent from the end of the nineteenth century had direct implications on the ways in which Italians spent their free time. In rural areas leisure activities were still formed around the centuries-old peasant traditions of gathering around the kitchen fire or in the barn during the evenings (*la veglia*), especially during the winter period, the café or tavern (*osteria*) for the men, and the occasion of weddings, fairs and religious festivals. But the towns and cities increasingly offered modern pastimes to their citizens as they became better off. Theatre and opera-going was no longer restricted to the social élite. More Italians watched or participated in a greater variety of sports activities. If gymnastics, fencing, shooting and mountaineering had been the main physical activities of a restricted élite after unification, during the Giolittian period several new sports, including football (imported from Britain), cycling, and motor racing came on to the scene, the latter two in line with new technological developments. From the second half of the nineteenth century onwards, an increasing number of middle-class Italians were able to afford summer holidays. In imitation of well-established practices in Britain and Northern Europe, and aided by the construction of the railways, Italy saw the development of several seaside resorts, including Rimini on the Adriatic Coast and San Remo on the Italian Riviera. The invention of the motor car, marked in Italy by the founding of the Fiat motor industry in Turin in 1899 (followed by Lancia in 1906 and Alfa in 1910), also increased the mobility of the Italians, though there were far fewer cars on the road than in Great Britain and France.

Yet, in the development of modern pastimes Italy remained behind other European countries. With regard to sport, for example, with the exception of cycling, levels of popularization comparable to Great Britain were not reached until after the First World War. Similarly, most working-class categories were too poor and worked too many hours to be able to enjoy much free time or take holidays. Class divisions in the use of urban space for leisure were evident in the designation of cafés in the main streets and squares of the cities for a middle- and upper-class clientele, while workers would frequent the taverns (*osterie*) – reputed as the seedbeds of political subversion and alcoholism – in the outer districts. Nevertheless, from the turn of the century the arrival of variety theatre and, most significantly, the cinema, which was initially snubbed by the social élite, provided the urban working and lower-middle classes with the first forms of truly modern entertainment.[63]

The extent to which greater wealth, literacy and welfare helped to neutralize union militancy is questionable, especially since many peasant and worker categories did not benefit. As would be expected in a climate of greater freedom, the workers' movements continued to grow after the turn of the century. While total Socialist union membership reached a peak of well over 500,000 in 1902, numbers only receded a little in subsequent years and increased again in the middle of the decade. During 1901–2 national union federations linked to the Socialist Party were formed, the largest of which, the Federation of Agricultural Workers (*Federterra*), represented 240,000 peasants. In 1906 the Socialists brought together the union federations under the General Confederation of Labour (*Confederazione Generale del Lavoro* – CGL). In the Catholic camp there were 374 workers' organizations with 104,600 members by 1910. Giolitti's initial willingness to respond positively to worker grievances was demonstrated by the particularly high number of strikes in 1901. In 1900 there had been 383 industrial strikes and only 27 agricultural strikes. The following year saw 1,042 industrial strikes and 629 agricultural strikes.[64]

A decrease in the number of strikes in 1902 may have been a consequence of Giolitti's unwillingness to support industrial action when it threatened production levels, as suggested by an economic recession which the employers blamed on the previous year's strikes. Giolitti also took measures to ban public service strikes called by Revolutionaries within the PSI who were disillusioned with the party's collaborative alliance with the government. Giolitti also failed to remove the traditionally repressive and pro-employer mentality of the prefects and of the police, whose conduct was of paramount importance where a political agreement was founded on the need for greater tolerance of the working-class movement. Since the 1880s the Italian police forces had been plagued by low resources and poor-quality personnel. Many policemen were recruited among the semi-literate Southern peasantry. As a result of failure on the part of Giolitti to adequately upgrade the quality of policemen and provide better working conditions, strikes often ended in conflict because badly trained policemen felt more vulnerable than ever before, now that they were expected to be tolerant of large crowds of demonstrators.[65]

Giolitti's policies were also affected by his need to maintain a parliamentary majority and depended on the willingness of the Socialist organizations to co-operate with him. When in 1903 his alliance with the Reformist Socialists ended, Giolitti looked to the political forces of the Right to form a new government, as a result of which there was an increase in employer intransigence towards labour relations supported by the police and army. Between 1904 and 1907 Revolutionary Syndicalists took over the union organizations, exacerbating levels of confrontation during labour disputes. In the belief that Turati in allying with Giolitti had betrayed the workers' cause, they frequently declared general strikes, which they saw as the only arm capable of creating a social revolution. During such strikes the police often lost their nerve, opening fire on demonstrators. On occasion, such incidents created a vicious circle by sparking off further protest strikes which in turn ended in tragedy. Conflict during agricultural strikes increased in the Po valley, when *Federterra*, though remaining Reformist, began a strategy of fierce boycotts of non-union workers and land occupations. The success of Giolitti's policing strategy was even more limited in the Southern regions, where the government relied on parliamentary support from landowners and notables in return for continued authoritarian control of the masses. This is reflected in the large number of *eccidi proletari* (police massacres) occurring during strikes and protests, and the violence characterizing election campaigns.[66]

If the working-class movements often accused Giolitti of failing to respond to their grievances adequately, the employer class accused him of having given in to the demands of the Left, such that they could no longer count on the support of the police and army in the maintenance of law and order. Towards the end of the first decade of the twentieth century social conflict heightened as the employers increased their intransigence and the Socialist movement returned to the control of the Revolutionaries, marked by the appointment of the young Benito Mussolini as Party leader in 1912. In many cases the employers took the law into their own hands. On the large farms of the Po valley, for example, capitalist farmers with Nationalist sympathies began to hire gangs of armed strikebreakers to make up for the inability of the police to oppose land occupations.

The above conflict was also reflected in broader social divisions, which partly revolved around Italy's international status. A significant minority of Italians felt that under Giolitti Italy's imperial potential had been insufficiently exploited because of excessive government spending on welfare benefits for the working classes. This group was strongly Nationalist and opposed to Giolittian democracy, which it considered corrupt and backward-looking. Giolitti's tortuous and costly invasion of Libya in 1911 failed to weaken the influence of the Nationalists. Such divisions were also evident at the cultural level and are well depicted in Bosworth's account of the May Day celebrations of 1911 in Venice in which young members of the middle classes and Nationalists celebrated the fiftieth anniversary of the unification of Italy with sports events, processions and band music, while the Socialist youth organizations, in their refusal to accept Italy united in the *Risorgimento*, held their own congress and sang the *Internazionale*.[67]

Civil conflict intensified in some areas of Italy during 'Red Week' in June 1914 when, following the killing of anti-militarist demonstrators by the police in Ancona, violent working-class demonstrations took place in many parts of the peninsula. In the Marches and Romagna there was full-scale insurrectionary action as whole towns and villages were taken over and Red republics were set up without the authorities being able to intervene. In Bologna, which to the indignation of the middle and upper classes saw the inauguration of a left-wing city council during the same month, the 'parties of order' reacted to Socialist protest demonstrations by organizing counter-demonstrations and ordering the national flag to be flown from all balconies. When workers attempted to have the flags removed, Nationalist supporters violently dispersed them.[68]

Marriage, demographic strategies and the status of women

While Italian society is often seen as highly backward-looking and patriarchal in terms of family relationships and relations between the sexes, there is strong historical evidence of closer alignment with Northern European countries from the end of the nineteenth century, though the pace of modernization varied between regions and between urban and rural areas. Traditionally, for example, Italian marriages were arranged by families on the basis of interest rather than sentiment. Referring to the isolated community of Nissorini in Sicily, Rudolph Bell notes that: 'Even *braccianti*, who literally had only the labor power of their arms, assessed a potential spouse's family for evidence of sexual purity, industriousness, common sense, resourcefulness and good health.'[69] The value of the bride's dowry also constituted an effective demonstration of the advantage that a family stood to gain from the marriage of one of its sons. Often marriages were the result of lengthy cultivation of mutual interest between families. Passion and love between youngsters were seen as a threat to the perpetuation of the family rather than a basis for marriage, though, as Bell argues, a shift in marital choice from *interesse* to *amore* took place as society was modernized, especially in urban areas which contained more meeting places for young people outside the control of the family, whether the church, the main square or the café. As a result of greater individual choice, women began to marry later and to men closer to their age (instead of to older men, as typical of arranged marriages).

The patriarchal character of the Italian family was determined by the civil code of 1865, according to which the husband was the head of the household with full rights over his wife and children (including their choice of marriage). In practice, however, the exercise of absolute male authority within the Italian family depended on the type of household and decreased as Italy underwent processes of industrialization and modernization. Statistics compiled by Barbagli concerning women born between 1890 and 1910 suggest, for example, that in urban families husband and wife often took joint decisions and had joint authority over the family budget. Only in the families of industrialists was there a rigid patriarchal hierarchy. In the multiple families of the countryside patriarchal authority was more emphasized. There was a similar contrast between urban and rural areas regarding the participation of husband and wife in leisure activities. In rural areas men went out in the evenings to friends, the café, the tavern or the party recreation centre while women would visit friends or relatives on Sunday afternoon only, staying in during the evenings. In urban areas there was a greater tendency for husbands and wives of the middle and upper classes to go out together (to the theatre or cinema). Among urban working-class couples roles were similar to those of rural areas.[70]

An overview of family demographic policies in Italy at the end of the nineteenth century reveals a mixture of old and new practices too. According to Lyttelton, well before unification:

> Peasant families in most of the North and Centre (excluding wage labourers) shared the general European tendency towards late marriage. In the South this check on population expansion was lacking, except in a few privileged coastal areas. This was as much a consequence of proletarianisation as a cause; where the conditions for a stable peasant agriculture existed, marriages were delayed.[71]

With few exceptions overall fertility levels were higher in the South than in the rest of Italy. The country as a whole began to witness a fertility decline during the last decades of the nineteenth century. This was particularly marked in Piedmont, Liguria and Tuscany, but did not seriously affect other regions of the North and Centre before the First World War and the South between the two World Wars. The overall rate of population increase fell from 6.9 per cent to 6.5 per cent between 1871 and 1911.[72]

The adoption of modern birth-control methods in Italy was partly inhibited by the persistence of traditionalist attitudes towards the role of women and relations between the sexes clearly linked to Catholic teachings. The strength of religious hegemony may partly account for a total lack of sex education and misconceptions – supported by anthropological and medical research – about female sexuality being purely linked to maternity, though from the turn of the century women's magazines and Socialist journals put forward more progressive ideas and published information on modern forms of birth control. Nevertheless, recent research has suggested that independently of the influence of the Church, family planning practices other than migration and late marriage began to take place throughout Italy, though initially restricted to the wealthier classes. Even in the South members of the social élite began to practise *coitus interruptus* in order to limit the size of their families.[73]

The myth that Italian women were for the most part confined to the home has been somewhat shattered by the reality of widespread female employment. Though figures of 1900 show that a third of women aged between 14 and 65 worked, with Italy becoming the fourth industrial nation with the highest proportion of female employment, it needs to be emphasized that this was usually a result of necessity, rather than a desire for emancipation.[74] Levels of female employment varied geographically, however. As a demonstration of the strength of patriarchal values in rural Italy, female prestige lay in working for one's own family, not those of others, though in parts of Northern and Central Italy this attitude gave way to the imperatives of survival as female members of the household began to work outside the home. By contrast, according to Macry, in the South: 'The importance attached to women's honour meant . . . that they could play no independent role in social or political life and were largely confined to the home (where women's roles and values of femininity were of great importance), and tasks were rigidly differentiated by sex.'[75]

The Catholic Church was also opposed to female employment. In particular the 1891 papal encyclical *de Rerum Novarum* expressed its fear of the effects of the process of industrialization on the family, as it sent women out of the home to work in the factories and threatened their maternal capacity. Similarly, the arrival of legislation protecting women and children, and the setting up of a national maternity leave fund in 1910, was founded more on the need to protect women's subordinate status, than to enhance possibilities for their emancipation. According to Silvana Patriarca:

> An image of women that stressed their dependence and maternal roles dominated the rhetoric of those who supported these reforms, and was evident even in the Socialist Party which had changed its strategy in 1900 to make the protection of women workers part of its program. . . . The debate that preceded the introduction of the law [protecting women workers] showed that groups within the Italian middle classes and government elites were imposing their ideas of female domesticity on working-class women at a moment when women workers had shown they could be as militant as men.[76]

The first movements for female emancipation did not develop until the 1890s because of high levels of economic backwardness and widespread female illiteracy. Those that did were too closely tied to the major protests of the Italian labour organizations and limited to the towns of the North. As Victoria

31

De Grazia notes, only with the growth in economic prosperity of the Giolittian era did women's movements become more widespread, developing into Socialist, Catholic and middle-class lay currents, which, however, were ideologically divided. The main feminist thrust came from the lay movement, which rejected radical egalitarianism in favour of 'maternalist' feminism. Its exponents demanded to be recognized not as equals to men but as indispensable to the social order as mothers. The Liberal government remained fearful of the female vote, however, and showed little appreciation of the social services rendered by women to 'cure social ills and calm working-class unrest through philanthropic undertakings'.[77]

The Italian civil code governing family relations, which was not seriously revised until 1975, supported differential treatment of men and women in marriage for much of the twentieth century. The absolute authority of a father was exercised with regard to both natural and illegitimate children, such that even after his death the courts could limit his widow's rights in respect of the education of children and the administration of property. Differential treatment between the sexes also existed over separation rights. With regard to adultery, for example, a woman could only obtain legal separation if her husband invited his lover to live in the family home, whereas it was enough for her to commit adultery for her husband to be able to obtain separation. A man faced a maximum of three years' imprisonment only for a 'crime of honour', according to an article of the Italian criminal code which remained in force until 1981.[78] Nevertheless, as this volume shows, the survival of such legislation was often more indicative of the failure of the state institutions to keep up with the modernization of Italian society than a reflection of the persistence of a traditionalist culture.

Conclusion

By the eve of the First World War Italian society had undergone a considerable process of economic modernization, which had been accompanied by an increase in mass participation in the life of the new nation state, particularly under Giolitti. Nevertheless, economic, cultural and social imbalances characterizing Italy remained difficult to overcome and levels of national consciousness low. This was partly because the modernization process had been concentrated in the North-West of the peninsula, and had actually worsened the imbalance between North and South. Indeed, John Dickie sees this as emblematic of the non-national nature of many of the historical transformations Italy underwent.[79] As discussed in the following chapter, the experience of the First World War undoubtedly speeded processes of modernization and enhanced national unity, but in the long run it also exacerbated pre-existing social and political divisions that would lead to severe conflict and eventually dictatorship.

The rise of Fascism represented, among other things, an aggressive response to previous failures in nation-building and low levels of national consciousness. However, such deficiencies were in part a product of that very frustration. During the nineteenth and twentieth centuries historians, journalists and politicians frequently put forward negative images of Italy and of Italians and this was not limited to the South. They lamented Italy's 'inferiority' compared with other nations (particularly with regard to her military failures) and the 'weak' national character (traditionally seen as corrupt, opportunist, servile, individualistic and anarchic). They referred to Italy's past greatness – epitomized, for example, in the Renaissance and the *Risorgimento* – but forever expressed the idea that 'something had gone wrong' in subsequent processes of national development. Moreover, Italian historiography was characterized by serious ideological divisions, as Radical, Liberal, Marxist and Catholic historians put forward their own particular views of history with questionable objectivity. Not infrequently did this lead to confrontation and controversy.[80] Although such pronouncements on Italy and the Italians may have been intended as a means of overcoming a deficiency in national consciousness, the question remains whether in practice they made popular identification with a national culture all the more difficult.

Notes

1. For studies of the *Risorgimento*, see Derek Beales, *The Risorgimento and the Unification of Italy* (2nd edn, London: Longman, 1981); John Gooch, *The Unification of Italy* (2nd edn, London: Routledge, 1989); Harry Hearder, *Italy in the Age of the Risorgimento, 1790–1879* (London: Longman, 1983); Denis Mack Smith, *The Making of Italy, 1796–1870* (2nd edn, London: Macmillan, 1988); Lucy Riall, *The Italian Risorgimento: State, Society and National Unification* (London: Routledge, 1994).
2. Anna Laura Lepschy, Giulio Lepschy and Miriam Voghera, 'Linguistic Variety in Italy', in Carl Levy (ed.), *Italian Regionalism. History, Identity and Politics* (Oxford: Berg, 1996), 69–80(73–4).
3. Adrian Lyttelton, 'Landlords, peasants and the limits of Liberalism', in John A. Davis (ed.), *Gramsci and Italy's Passive Revolution* (London: Croom Helm, 1979), 104–35(123).
4. Roger Absalom, *Italy since 1800. A Nation in the Balance?* (London: Longman, 1995), 23.
5. For detailed analysis of difficulties encountered by the Italian state in maintaining order in post-unification Italy, see John A. Davis, *Conflict and Control. Law and Order in Nineteenth-Century Italy* (Basingstoke: Macmillan, 1988), Part II; Richard Bach Jensen, *Liberty and Order: The Theory and Practice of Italian Public Security Policy, 1848 to the Crisis of the 1890s* (New York: Garland, 1991).
6. Gabriella Gribaudi, 'Images of the South', in Jonathan Morris and Robert Lumley (eds), *The New History of the Italian South* (Exeter: University of Exeter Press, 1997), 83–113(89).

7. Lucy Riall, *Sicily and the Unification of Italy* (Oxford: Clarendon Press, 1998), 139–40.
8. Jensen, *Liberty and Order*, 18.
9. Lyttelton, 'Landlords, peasants and the limits of Liberalism', 124.
10. Giorgio Fiocca, 'Viva la patria, abbasso lo Stato. Le molteplici appartenenze delle classi dirigenti', *Passato e presente*, 43, 1998, 35–59.
11. Discussed in Denis Mack Smith, *Modern Italy. A Political History* (New Haven, CT: Yale University Press, 1997), 4–6, 41–3; Vera Zamagni, *The Economic History of Italy, 1860–1990. Recovery after Decline* (Oxford: Clarendon Press, 1993), 12–25, 72–3.
12. Mack Smith, *Modern Italy*, 43–7.
13. Zamagni, *The Economic History of Italy*, 66–9.
14. Absalom, *Italy since 1800*, 51.
15. Anthony Cardoza, 'Agrarians and industrialists: the evolution of an alliance in the Po Delta, 1896–1914', in Davis (ed.), *Gramsci and Italy's Passive Revolution*, 172–212(172–8).
16. For figures, and an analysis of the effects of protectionist measures on a Southern great estate, see Marta Petrusewicz, 'The Demise of the Latifondo', in Morris and Lumley (eds), *The New History of the Italian South*, 20–41.
17. Donald Howard Bell, *Sesto San Giovanni: Workers, Culture and Politics in an Italian Town, 1880–1922* (New Brunswick, NJ: Rutgers University Press, 1986), 10–13.
18. Facts and figures in this section relating to economic growth during the Giolittian period – unless indicated otherwise – are from Giovanni Balcet, *L'economia italiana. Evoluzione, problemi e paradossi* (Milan: Feltrinelli, 1997), 23–4; Zamagni, *The Economic History of Italy*, 117–26. For the size and composition of the industrial working class, see Nicola Lisanti, *Il movimento operaio in Italia, 1860–1980. Dall'unità ai nostri giorni* (Rome: Editori Riuniti, 1986).
19. Discussed in Gribaudi, 'Images of the South', 98; Zamagni, *The Economic History of Italy*, 50–1, 167.
20. Alice A. Kelikian, 'From liberalism to corporatism. The province of Brescia during the First World War', in Davis (ed.), *Gramsci and Italy's Passive Revolution*, 213–38 (214–18).
21. Frank M. Snowden, ' "Fields of death": malaria in Italy, 1861–1962', *Modern Italy* 4(1)(1999), 25–57(26–7, quote from 37).
22. Nelson Moe, 'The Emergence of the Southern Question in Villari, Franchetti and Sonnino', in Jane Schneider (ed.), *Italy's Southern Question. Orientalism in One Country* (Oxford: Berg, 1998), 51–76(63).
23. Discussed in detail in Gribaudi, 'Images of the South', 91–4.
24. Discussed in John A. Davis, 'Introduction: Antonio Gramsci and Italy's Passive Revolution', in Davis (ed.), *Gramsci and Italy's Passive Revolution*, 11–30.
25. For misrepresentations of the South, see Jonathan Morris, 'Challenging *Meridionalismo*', 1–9, (5–6), and Gribaudi, 'Images of the South', in Morris and Lumley (eds), *The New History of the Italian South*; John A. Davis, 'Casting off the "Southern Problem" ', in Schneider (ed.), *Italy's Southern Question*, 205–24. See also John Dickie, *Darkest Italy: The Nation and Stereotypes of the Mezzogiorno, 1860–1900* (Basingstoke: Macmillan, 1999).
26. Pino Arlacchi, *Mafia, peasants and great estates. Society in traditional Calabria* (Cambridge: Cambridge University Press, 1983), chapter 3.

27. Paul Ginsborg, 'Italian Political Culture in Historial Perspective', *Modern Italy*, 1(1), 1995, 3–17(5).
28. For further analysis of Italian family forms, see Marzio Barbagli, 'Marriage and the family in Italy in the early nineteenth century', in John A. Davis and Paul Ginsborg (eds), *Society and Politics in the Age of the Risorgimento* (Cambridge: Cambridge Unviersity Press, 1991), 92–127(99–106); Marzio Barbagli, 'Three Household Formation Systems in Eighteenth and Nineteenth Century Italy', in David I. Kertzer and Richard P. Saller (eds), *The Family in Italy from Antiquity to the Present* (New Haven, CT: Yale University Press, 1991), 250–70(258–9). For the role of malaria in determining settlement patterns, see Snowden, ' "Fields of Death" ', 33.
29. Anna Cento Bull and Paul Corner, *From Peasant to Entrepreneur: The Survival of the Family Economy in Italy* (Oxford: Berg, 1993), chapters 2 and 3.
30. Zamagni, *The Economic History of Italy*, 203–4. For Italian emigration, see also Ercole Sori, *L'emigrazione italiana dall'Unità alla seconda guerra mondiale* (Bologna: Il Mulino, 1979) and Franco Ramella, 'Emigrazioni', in Bruno Bongiovanni and Nicola Tranfaglia (eds), *Dizionario storico dell'Italia unita* (Bari: Laterza, 1996), 297–307.
31. Edward Banfield, *The Moral Basis of a Backward Society* (London: Collier-Macmillan, 1958). For a critical discussion of Banfield's work and interpretations of it, see Gribaudi, 'Images of the South', 106–9.
32. Robert Putnam in *Making Democracy Work: Civic Traditions in Modern Italy* (Princeton, NJ: Princeton University Press, 1993), 145.
33. Anna Cento Bull, *Social Identities and Political Cultures in Italy. Catholic, Communist and 'Leghist' Communities between Civicness and Localism* (Oxford: Berghahn, 2000), 29.
34. Paolo Macry, 'Rethinking a stereotype: territorial differences and family models in the modernization of Italy', *Journal of Modern Italian Studies*, 2(2), 1997, 188–214(206).
35. David Moss, 'Patronage revisited: the dynamics of information and reputation', *Journal of Modern Italian Studies*, 1(1), 1995, 58–93(74).
36. For *trasformismo*, see Christopher Duggan, *A Concise History of Italy* (Cambridge: Cambridge University Press, 1994), 161, 163–5. For the role of the prefects, see Robert C. Fried, *The Italian Prefects: A Study in Administrative Politics* (New Haven, CT: Yale University Press, 1963), 121–5.
37. Henner Hess, *Mafia and Mafiosi: The Structure of Power* (2nd edn, New York: New York University Press, 1998), 13.
38. Salvatore Lupo, *Storia della mafia: dalle origini ai giorni nostri* (Rome: Donzelli, 1993), 11–12.
39. Anton Blok, *The Mafia of a Sicilian Village, 1860–1960: A Study of Violent Peasant Entrepreneurs* (2nd edn, Cambridge: Polity Press, 1988), 212.
40. Judith Chubb, *The Mafia and Politics: The Italian State under Siege* (Ithaca, NY: Cornell University Press, 1989), 7. See 7–12 for a general discussion.
41. Paolo Macry, 'The Southern Metropolis: Redistributive Circuits in Nineteenth-Century Naples', in Morris and Lumley (eds), *The New History of the Italian South*, 59–82(72–5).
42. Lisanti, *Il movimento operaio in Italia*, 59.
43. The population of Turin increased from 254,000 to 427,000 and that of Rome from 300,000 to 542,000 over the same period. Data from B.R. Mitchell, *European*

35

Historical Statistics (London: Macmillan, 1978), A4. For housing census, see Zamagni, *The Economic History of Italy*, 185.

44. Giorgio Cosmacini, 'Sanità', in Bongiovanni and Tranfaglia (eds), *Dizionario Storico dell'Italia unita*, 792–803(792–4).

45. Mutual aid organizations are discussed in Daniel L. Horowitz, *The Italian Labour Movement* (Cambridge, MA: Harvard University Press, 1963), 12–17; Maurice F. Neufeld, *Italy: School for Awakening Countries. The Italian Labor Movement in its Political, Social, and Economic Setting from 1800 to 1960* (Westport, NY: Greenwood Press, 1974), 358–9; Putnam, *Making Democracy Work*, 145–6.

46. Discussed in Zamagni, *The Economic History of Italy*, 103–9.

47. Lyttelton, 'Landlords, peasants and the limits of Liberalism', 113–14, 117–18.

48. Bell, *Sesto San Giovanni*, chapter 2; Stefano Musso, 'Operai', in Bongiovanni and Tranfaglia (eds), *Dizionario storico dell'Italia unita*, 654–66(658–9); Lyttelton, 'Landlords, peasants and the limits of Liberalism', 125. For Apulia, see Frank M. Snowden, *Violence and Great Estates in the South of Italy. Apulia, 1900–1922* (Cambridge: Cambridge University Press, 1986).

49. Louise A. Tilly, *Politics and Class in Milan, 1881–1901* (Oxford: Oxford University Press, 1992), 50. See also Maurizio Gribaudi, *Mondo operaio e mito operaio. Spazi e percorsi sociali a Torino nel primo novecento* (Turin: Einaudi, 1997).

50. Frank M. Snowden, 'From sharecropper to proletarian: the background to fascism in rural Tuscany, 1880–1920', in Davis (ed.), *Gramsci and Italy's Passive Revolution*, 136–71(143–7).

51. Cento Bull and Corner, *From Peasant to Entrepreneur*, 31–2, 49–53.

52. Snowden, 'From sharecropper to proletarian', 159.

53. John N. Molony, *The Emergence of Political Catholicism in Italy. Partito Popolare 1919–1926* (London: Croom Helm, 1977), 25. For the origins of Catholic unions and party politics, see also Horowitz, *The Italian Labor Movement*, 96–102; Neufeld, *Italy: School for Awakening Countries*, 355–8.

54. John Earle, *The Italian Co-operative Movement. A Portrait of the Lega Nazionale delle Cooperative e Mutue* (London: Allen & Unwin, 1986), 15–16. See also Lyttelton, 'Landlords, peasants and the limits of Liberalism', 120. For the South, see Carlo Tullio-Altan, *La nostra Italia. Arretrattezza socioculturale, clientelismo, trasformismo e ribellismo dall'Unità ad oggi* (Milan: Feltrinelli, 1986), 94.

55. James Miller, *From Elite to Mass Politics. Italian Socialism in the Giolittian Era, 1900–1914* (Kent, OH: Kent State University Press, 1990), 36–41.

56. The different attitudes of worker movements according to geographical location are discussed in Tullio-Altan, *La nostra Italia*, 89–90.

57. Bell, *Sesto San Giovanni*, 54–63.

58. The repression of the 1890s is discussed in detail in Jensen, *Liberty and Order*, chapters 4–11 and Jonathan Dunnage, *The Italian Police and the Rise of Fascism. A Case-Study of the Province of Bologna, 1897–1925* (Westport, NJ: Praeger, 1997), chapters 1 and 2. For Crispi's policies, see Absalom, *Italy since 1800*, 62–5.

59. Data cited on health and living standards in this section is from Zamagni, *The Economic History of Italy*, 187–91, 197–202.

60. For facts and figures on education in Liberal Italy, see Ester De Fort, 'Istruzione' in Bongiovanni and Tranfaglia (eds), *Dizionario storico dell'Italia unita*, 475–86.

61. Ester De Fort, *Scuola e analfabetismo nell'Italia del'900* (Bologna: Il Mulino, 1995), chapter 2.

62. Marzio Barbagli, *Educating for Unemployment. Politics, Labour Markets and the School System. Italy 1859–1973* (New York: Colombia University Press, 1982), 15.
63. The leisure activities of Italians are analysed in detail in Stefano Pivato and Anna Tonelli, *Italia Vagabonda. Il tempo libero degli italiani dal melodramma alla pay-tv* (Rome: Carocci, 2001); Fiorenza Tarozzi, *Il tempo libero. Tempo della festa, tempo del gioco, tempo per sé* (Turin: Paravia, 1999).
64. Figures from Horowitz, *The Italian Labor Movement*, 58–63, 110–15.
65. For further details, see Dunnage, *The Italian Police and the Rise of Fascism*, chapter 3.
66. The effect of Giolitti's policies on the South is discussed in Frank M. Snowden, *Violence and Great Estates in the South of Italy. Apulia, 1900–1922* (Cambridge: Cambridge University Press, 1986), 136–42.
67. R.J. Bosworth, 'Venice between Fascism and international tourism, 1911–1945', *Modern Italy*, 4(1) (1999), 5–23(7–10).
68. Dunnage, *The Italian Police and the Rise of Fascism*, 65–6.
69. Rudolph Bell, *Fate and Honour, Family and Village* (Chicago, IL: University of Chicago Press, 1979), 90. See 90–9 for a general discussion of marriage arrangements.
70. Marzio Barbagli, *Sotto lo stesso tetto. Mutamento della Famiglia in Italia dal XV al XX Secolo* (Bologna: Il Mulino, 1984), 439–43, 462–6.
71. Lyttelton, 'Landlords, peasants and the limits of Liberalism', 122.
72. Massimo Livi-Bacci, *A History of Italian Fertility during the Last Two Centuries* (Princeton: Princeton University Press, 1977), 61–9; Zamagni, *The Economic History of Italy*, 29.
73. This is the conclusion reached in Jane and Peter Schneider's case study of a Sicilian community, *Festival of the Poor: Fertility Decline and the Ideology of Class in Sicily, 1890–1980* (Tucson, AZ: University of Arizona Press, 1996), 143, 211–14. For matters of female sexuality and relations between the sexes, see Michela De Giorgio, *Le italiane dall'unità a oggi: modelli culturali e comportamenti sociali* (Bari: Laterza, 1992).
74. Victoria De Grazia, *How Fascism Ruled Women: Italy, 1922–1945* (Berkeley, CA: University of California Press, 1992), 168.
75. Macry, 'Rethinking a stereotype', 205–6.
76. Silvana Patriarca, 'Gender trouble: women and the making of Italy's "active population", 1861–1936', *Journal of Modern Italian Studies*, 3(2), 1998, 144–63(155).
77. De Grazia, *How Fascism Ruled Women*, 20–5. See also Cecilia Dau Novelli, *Sorelle d'Italia. Casalinghe, impiegate e militanti nel novecento* (Rome: AVE, 1996) and De Giorgio, *Le italiane dall'unità ad oggi*.
78. Legal factors determining the nature of the Italian family and relations between the sexes are discussed in detail in Lesley Caldwell, *Italian Family Matters: Women, Politics and Legal Reform* (London: Macmillan, 1991), 55–6, 71–3.
79. John Dickie, 'The notion of Italy', in Zygmunt G. Baranski and Rebecca J. West (eds), *The Cambridge Companion to Modern Italian Culture* (Cambridge: Cambridge University Press, 2001), 17–33(21–2).
80. For academic and journalistic attitudes towards Italy's past and the Italian character, see Silvana Patriarca, 'Italian neopatriotism: debating national identity in the 1990s', *Modern Italy*, 6(1), 2001, 21–34. For the characteristics of Italian historiography, see Martin Clark, *Modern Italy, 1871–1995* (2nd edn, London: Longman, 1996), 4–7.

Chapter 2

Social fragmentation and violence in Italy, 1915–25

Introduction

This chapter examines life in Italy during a particularly turbulent period spanning the First World War and the development of a right-wing dictatorship under Benito Mussolini. In its analysis of the dramatic events of the period, the chapter aims to stress as much as possible their impact on the lives of the Italian people, paying particular attention to regional variations and the different social classes. Italy's participation in the First World War quickened the pace of economic modernization in Northern and Central Italy. The experience of the war increased levels of national consciousness. Though the war itself was characterized by greater concentration of power in fewer hands, in the long run it brought a larger number of Italians into the public arena, as is evident in the dramatic development of mass party politics and the labour movement immediately following the conflict. This in turn brought greater economic wealth and opportunity to the lower classes. On the other hand the war also brought to a head serious political tensions that had been developing since the beginning of the century. These were closely connected to the longer-term question of how Italy's irredentist and colonial aspirations could be reconciled with the need for social emancipation of the masses. In the aftermath of an experience which encouraged violent solutions to problems and in the context of severe economic crisis such tensions quickly manifested themselves in acts of high-handedness, intimidation and physical confrontation that threatened the newly won gains of the masses and greater sense of national unity that the war had fostered.

The intervention crisis

The crisis surrounding the question of Italy's participation in the First World War brought to a head divisions that had been growing in Italian society since the turn of the century. Italy's initial response to the outbreak of the First World War in August 1914 was a declaration of a state of neutrality.[1] Between the fall of 1914 and the signing of the Treaty of London in May 1915, by which Italy officially joined the war on the side of France, Britain and Russia, political groups fought out the question of intervention both in parliament and on the streets of Italy's major urban centres. If those in favour of intervention claimed to represent the majority of Italians, the opposite was true. There were varying reasons for lack of enthusiasm for joining the European conflict. At the moment of the outbreak of war, Italy was an ally of Austria and Germany as a result of the Triple Alliance of 1882 (renewed for the third time in 1912). However, entering the war on the Austrian side against Britain and France would have meant betraying Italian patriotic aspirations, given that Italy laid claim to territories belonging to the Austro-Hungarian Empire. Moreover, many Italians harboured strong cultural sympathies for France and the industrialists were opposed to the idea of fighting Great Britain since she was the principal supplier of Italy's coal. The possibility of intervention against Austria on the side of France and Britain was equally unwelcome to many sections of Italian society, despite the prospects of territorial gains, which meant very little to vast sections of the Italian masses, represented by both the political parties of the Left and the Church (which did not want a war against Catholic Austria). The middle classes were happy with the prospect of economic gains from a neutralist position. Moreover, as Giolitti, the main promoter of neutrality, recognized, the army was still very much occupied in Libya, following the invasion of 1911, and not sufficiently equipped or manned for such a large-scale conflict, nor were the country's finances adequate.

Division over intervention was linked to historical political tensions concerning the question of Italy's colonies and the resolution of internal social problems. Most Italians, represented politically by the Giolittian Liberals, the Catholics and the Socialists, were content with modest imperial successes in North Africa marked by the recent Libyan invasion or were quite simply indifferent. They gave greater importance to the solving of urgent domestic problems. On the other hand, a significant nationalistic minority felt that under Giolitti Italy's imperial potential had been insufficiently exploited because of excessive government spending on welfare benefits for the working classes. They saw the war as an opportunity for fulfilling their aspirations, for completing the *Risorgimento* process through acquisition of such territory as Trento and Trieste, South Tyrol, Istria and Dalmatia. The Interventionists were made up of Nationalists, several avant-garde cultural groups, including Futurists, together with a number of dissident Liberals, Socialists, Anarchists and Revolutionary Syndicalists.

The spring of 1915 saw frequent demonstrations for or against the war, which were not unconnected to the above tensions. The prefects reported Neutralist groups attempting to prevent the movement of trains carrying troops and Interventionists holding hostile demonstrations in front of German and Austrian consulates. In Northern and Central Italian cities there were frequent scuffles between the two sides, which were not unconnected to civil conflict witnessed during 'Red Week' in June 1914. Indeed, the anti-Interventionist Left, made up of the Socialist Party and trade union movement, whose neutralist rhetoric was easily misrepresented as anti-patriotic, bore the brunt of Interventionist attacks. By May the Interventionists were gaining the upper hand. This was partly a result of the reluctance of the prefectoral authorities to stand in their way, in view of the commitment to intervention of the government, which had secretly signed the Treaty of London at the end of April. Many policemen were not unhappy to see Socialist leaders attacked. Nor did they want to be seen as oppressing patriotic fervour. In Rome on 12 May, three days before the official declaration of war, students invaded the Chamber of Deputies and attempted to attack Giolitti's house following a provocative speech by the Nationalist poet, Gabriele D'Annunzio. Though the Interventionists stood for a minority of Italians, they were believed to represent a far greater number on account of their loud and violent behaviour. This strongly influenced the decision of the Chamber of Deputies to vote in favour of joining the war at the last moment in spite of its officially Neutralist majority.

The Interventionist experience was a useful lesson in the effectiveness of intimidatory force. The battles of what became known as 'Radiant May' were a dress rehearsal for the far more explosive launching of the Fascist movement in 1919. Yet, precisely because of the manner in which Italy's entry to the war was determined, lack of popular consensus shaped the whole manner in which it was conducted. Whereas in France, Great Britain and Germany the departure of the troops for the Front caused huge patriotic demonstrations, in Italy the Interventionists had through their confrontational methods failed to create a climate of national solidarity. This had if anything increased divisions which would culminate in a passive and resigned attitude on the part of many. This led to incidents of defeatism among both civilians and soldiers, especially once it was clear that the conflict would continue for much longer than had been believed at first. Only after the military defeat at Caporetto in October 1917 and consequent greater willingness on the part of the government to adopt a more humanitarian approach to both soldiers on the battlefields and peasants and factory workers on the home front did a more genuine sense of national solidarity develop.[2]

Mobilization for war: life at home and at the Front

While the majority of industrialists had originally been against entry to the war, they moved over to the idea of intervention when it became clear that they would not gain any economic benefits by remaining neutral. Their hopes of being able to take advantage of the conflict to arm the belligerent countries were dashed by the realization that they would lose access to raw materials on the international market. An alliance with Great Britain and France on the other hand would guarantee Italy sufficient raw materials for arming which would be financed by state orders. The production demand created by the need for weapons and clothing to fight the war had the effect of enlarging and modernizing many industrial plants, particularly in the chemical and engineering sectors of the industrial triangle of Milan, Turin and Genoa. Developments stimulated by mobilization for war were of greatest benefit to companies already of considerable size and technological advancement, which were in a position to exert political pressure on the government in order to secure production contracts. The war enabled the Ansaldo steel company, for example, to grow in prominence, producing over 46 per cent of Italy's artillery, more than 3,000 planes, 1,574 start motors, 96 warships and 10 million pieces of ammunition. The wartime success of the Fiat motor car company of Turin lay in its adoption of strategies of diversification with the production of aeroplane motors, boat engines, bullets and machine guns. It created its own metal plants and started the construction of a new plant at Lingotto. The military production demand also allowed the expansion of small but highly specialized companies, such as the Alfa Romeo motor car company at Milan whose workers increased from 200 to 4,130 after it turned to the production of ammunition, motors and grenades. The significant economic growth stimulated by the war is demonstrated by the huge number of workers employed in the 1,976 auxiliary factories producing for the armed forces. The number of workers employed by Ansaldo, for example, grew from 6,000 before the war to 56,000, and Fiat saw a ten-fold increase in workers to 40,000.[3] Consequently, the main industrial cities grew rapidly as many workers were drafted in from the countryside. The population of Milan, for example, increased from 579,000 to 836,000 between 1910 and 1920, while that of Turin grew from 427,000 to 502,000.[4]

In many plants the war brought the reorganization of the manufacturing process with the introduction of assembly lines and the intensification of already developing processes of work rationalization, though this had the negative effect of undermining the status of skilled labourers. The modernizing effects of the war economy on working practices and relations within the factory quickly became evident. The town of Brescia in Lombardy provides an example of how a weak and productively archaic metal and engineering industry was boosted by government contracts during the war, with the result that the nature of its productive basis was radically altered. According to Alice Kelikian, in 1910 only 6 out of 52 iron and steel shops employed more than 100 labourers each. Only with war mobilization did the predominance of factories over workshops become established. The number of workers engaged in the metal industry swelled from 8,059 in 1915 to 20,534 by the second half of 1916, bringing relief to chronic unemployment.[5] As demonstrated in the following section, however, not all firms took advantage of the opportunity for long-term investment and modernization that mobilization for war brought, and this would partly account for serious economic difficulties once peacetime production resumed.

41

State finance and contracts also helped to reinforce the productive capacity of the less industrially developed regions of Northern and Central Italy, though the South of Italy remained without the investment received during the Giolittian period, with the result that its economic distance from the rest of the country grew further. In Bologna, for example, the necessity for increased production helped to expand and mechanize the chemical, machine, wood and textile industries, allowing the employment of unskilled workers for mass production, as in the industrial triangle. Several industries were converted into auxiliary gun-cartridge factories. The wartime factories employed between 20,000 and 25,000 workers, many of whom came from the countryside, attracted by the prospect of a safe wage. The war brought full employment to the province and in order to meet the continual requirement for labour a significant number of women (about 6,000 in the state and auxiliary industries) were employed. The number of children working in Bologna's factories also increased from 1,148 in 1914 to 1,803 in 1915.[6]

Illustrating greater centralization of government in contrast to Giolitti's cautious democratization policies, Italy's entry into the war allowed the government to place restrictions on political and union activities in order to maximize production and morale. Special legislation passed in 1915 and 1916 gave the military greater powers of interference in civilian life, particularly in the war zones of North-Eastern Italy closest to the conflict. Public assemblies were prohibited, censorship tightened and the activities of political associations restricted, in an effort to prevent left-wing activists from lowering morale on the home and military fronts with anti-militarist propaganda. In the economic sphere legislation empowered the authorities to move workforces according to local requirements. The authorities were also ordered to encourage the employment of women and oblige farmers to share farm vehicles and animals to prevent the loss of valuable crops. In the industrial sector emergency legislation placed restrictions on the freedom of employees of firms involved in important military production. All male workers in the auxiliary factories were militarized, becoming subject to strict disciplinary procedures under the jurisdiction of the military penal code such that if they abandoned their posts they were considered deserters.

Though the entry of Italy into the war placed restrictions on union power, the relative industrial peace characterizing the war years cannot be attributed to state repression alone. While the PSI was the only Socialist Party among the main European belligerent countries to oppose the war, its policy of 'neither adherence nor sabotage' marked internal divisions that were also reflected in contrasting attitudes towards the Party line when it came to practical issues of the war effort. Though many activists were involved in anti-war propaganda campaigns, the positive response of some Party and union leaders was undoubtedly motivated by the desire to achieve both immediate concessions and the future legitimization of the workers' movement. Anthony

Cardoza notes that, in areas where the Socialist municipalities, unions and co-operatives were efficiently organized, their co-operation had to be obtained through concessions, if mass mobilization for war was to be effective. In exchange for a promise not to strike, the Bologna Federation of Agricultural Workers, for example, came to an agreement with the agrarian employers whereby the latter would only hire Socialist workers.[7] Wage increases and the institution of arbitration commissions to solve disputes also encouraged peaceful labour relations.

Nevertheless, strikes did occur during the war years, though on a much smaller scale than in the preceding period. They were usually economically motivated in view of serious material difficulties suffered by workers and peasants as a result of wartime inflation, long working hours and food short- ages, though PSI activists sometimes tried to turn them into anti-war pro- tests. By 1916 workers at Fiat, for example, faced a 75-hour week. For all industrial workers pay rose regularly but did not keep up with the cost of living, so that by 1917 real wages had fallen to 73 per cent of 1913 levels. Food shortages were caused by both the short-sightedness of government policy and the lack of co-operation of agricultural producers. Only from 1916 did the government authorize harvest requisitions and introduce fixed prices for cereals. Bread and pasta rationing was introduced as late as September 1917. Such initiatives did not prevent black-market speculation and wastage, while low requisition prices discouraged agricultural production.[8]

Economic hardship was not the only cause of strike action, however. In rural areas the employers often provoked labour disputes by violating agreements. In particular, they avoided employing Socialist union members in favour of less troublesome Catholic or non-union workers, and, towards the end of the conflict, less costly prisoners of war. Moreover, the arbitration commissions set up to deal with disputes tended to come down on the side of the employers. One of the myths surrounding the First World War that would later play a role in the rise of Fascism was founded on the conviction that the PSI and working-class movement had sabotaged the war effort. Yet, the commercial and employer classes showed little sense of patriotism in their concern for profit-making and speculation, as revealed by their constant violation of labour pacts and their general refusal to make economic sacrifices in line with the rest of the nation. In July 1917 the Prefect of Bologna criti- cized the so-called 'law abiding citizens' not only for their incapacity to match Socialist anti-war propaganda, choosing the 'politics of silence' instead of demonstrations of patriotism, but also for their economic selfishness. Agricultural employers, he claimed, abandoned the cultivation of non- profit-rendering crops and shopkeepers profited from the war with price increases of up to 100 per cent.[9]

As the strikes demonstrate, in spite of restrictions imposed on union activit- ies, working-class solidarity was far from removed during the war. It was merely experienced in new forms. Women, who made up a prominent part of the workforce in view of military call-ups, played an important role in strike activities and protests. Though they were affected by policies of militarization, in practice women strikers could not be sent to the Front (unlike their male work companions) and employers were afraid of denouncing workers for fear of losing them. Because of the shortage of labour, women were able to make repeated demands for wage increases and play a prominent role in the organization of strikes against the war. Donald Bell notes, with regard to his case-study of Sesto San Giovanni, that, where union powers were restricted, workers turned to community traditions and institutions in order to overcome wartime strife and continue oppositional activities: 'In the midst of the war, such organizations as workers' circles, youth groups and sports and leisure associations provided a setting for oppositional activities, while less formal meeting places – most notably the bar and the *trattoria* – also served as centers of discussion and dissent'.[10]

Towards the end of the conflict, the authorities, while continuing to send the most militant activists to the Front in order to avoid industrial disruption, were prepared, often with the support of factory owners, to tolerate strikes and demonstrations, which PSI leaders were expected to prevent from getting out of hand, and willing to offer concessions to end them. Repression was not always avoidable, however, as was demonstrated by the deaths of 50 people under the fire of the army during bread riots in Turin in August 1917. After military defeat the following October when the Austrians broke through the Italian line at Caporetto the government was concerned to encourage national solidarity by taking the economic grievances of workers more seriously while the PSI and CGL responded in a more patriotic vein to the enemy invasion.

If life on the home front was harsh, that of the 5 million Italians called up was far worse. Of those conscripted 60–70 per cent were peasants. Many of them were torn away from their native region for the first time with little understanding of the motives for which the war was being fought and with limited patriotic enthusiasm. They accounted for 60 per cent of the 600,000 Italians who were killed.[11] The horrors of a war were compounded by extremely harsh treatment of conscripts. This was partly a result of the attitude of political leaders who, realizing that the peasant masses had permanently been denied proper integration into national life, now feared that they would not be able to count on their loyalty. Such fears were exacerbated by the presence in Italy of an influential Socialist organization that was opposed to war. While it is true that a widespread attitude of defeatism was partly behind the military defeat at Caporetto in October 1917, bad military leadership and training were equally to blame. Defeatist attitudes were encouraged by the government's total lack of concern for the welfare of those called up, who suffered inadequate food rations and low pay for much of the period of conflict, as well as often ruthless treatment by their commanders.

Between May 1915 and September 1919 almost 290,000 soldiers were tried by courts martial for crimes of insubordination, usually desertion. Yet, demonstrating the paranoia of military leaders, 120,000 were acquitted, while most of the remainder were amnestied in 1919. Four thousand soldiers received the death sentence, of which it was carried out on 750, while 200 or more faced summary executions, compared with far lower figures for France, which had a larger army. The military leadership saw capture by the enemy as equally cowardly. The 600,000 soldiers imprisoned by the Austrians and Germans were more or less abandoned by the government, which neglected to send them aid. One hundred thousand died in captivity (compared with only 20,000 out of the same number of French prisoners). Soldiers' families were excluded from the horror of their experiences owing to the censorship of letters and to the official press and propaganda, which kept the country under illusions, turning the most squalid situations into episodes of romantic heroism. The fantastical air and sea raids invented by the poet Gabriele D'Annunzio were miles away from the day-to-day existence of the ordinary conscript.[12]

After Caporetto, the government showed greater concern for the troops, with better food provisions and more periods of leave. It also stepped up a propaganda campaign to maintain popular support for a continued war effort with the promise of land to the peasants and of the right to vote, and this would partly account for its leniency towards working-class demands during the post-war period. Common experiences at the Front went some way towards creating a greater sense of national consciousness among Italians of different regions and dialects and encouraged more awareness of the need to fight for political rights and democratic representation. This would also give workers and peasants greater powers in their post-war negotiation with employers. As Mack Smith notes: 'Many workers had acquired novel standards of comparison; many could write and add, so that they could check the *mezzadria* [sharecropping] accounts with the *padrone* [boss]'.[13]

However, the unifying experience of the First World War should not be overstressed. Indeed, it is more likely that regional and class divisions were accentuated, contributing to social and political fragmentation and conflict during the immediate post-war years. Southern conscripts and officers were over-represented on the front line, while more technically trained Northern workers were needed in the artillery and engineering corps, with Northern officers serving in technical or mobile units further away.[14] The large number of peasant conscripts had grievances against not only the government but also the PSI and the industrial working classes on account of their exemption from being drafted, grievances also shared by middle-class officers who developed a strong sense of comradeship during the war years. It was not only at the Front that Italians from different regions were brought together for

45

the first time. During the final year of the war Austrian troops occupied Friuli and parts of Veneto, causing a large exodus of homeless refugees to provinces further south. While in some instances this may have heightened patriotic feeling and a sense of national consciousness, the accounts of many refugees suggest that they often felt discriminated against by the host community on account of their cultural differences.[15]

Other opportunities brought about by mobilization were also missed on account of social and political divisions. During the war women played an increasingly prominent role in production and public life, taking the place of men who had been drafted into the army. Yet, as Victoria De Grazia points out, work divided them socially and politically and this prevented the crea-tion of a united front able to improve female status. While middle-class women were involved in the running and working of the hospitals and the Red Cross, forming associations with strong patriotic connotations, working-class women worked in the factories and remained loyal towards the PSI. Upper and middle-class women also founded groups to help veterans, widows and orphans. While the war experience could have created a force capable of obtaining the vote, equal work opportunities, and the revamping of family law, their forces were irreversibly divided as a result of political divisions which pervaded Italian society as a whole.[16]

Economic crisis and worker militancy, 1918–20

Social fragmentation was enhanced by contrasting economic gains made during the war. The industrialists had undoubtedly benefited most, making huge profits out of state-financed military production contracts. A lot of money had also gone into the hands of war profiteers who had speculated on wartime inflation and shortages of basic items. The urban middle and working classes had suffered badly, hit by inflation, which had seen the cost of living index rise from 100 in 1914 to 264 in 1918.[17] The value of real wages had fallen to 64.6 per cent of 1913 levels, dramatically reducing the purchasing power of families. In the Milan area, for example, an average daily wage of 7 lire in 1918 went nowhere near to meeting the 75 lire required for the basic necessities of a family.[18] In the countryside the war had failed to stimulate an increase in production and there had been no investments or technical improvements. Wartime inflation was advantageous to those who earned their income through the sale of products, while dam-aging to those who gained their income through rent payments, which were frozen. In particular, the leaseholder class of the Po Valley benefited both from the increase in output demand and from wartime rent freezes which pushed down real rents in the face of dramatic levels of inflation, to the detriment of the landowners, many of whom were forced to sell up to them. Some members of the peasant middle classes gained considerably from the

European conflict. A number of sharecroppers and tenant farmers had made enough money to buy their own plots of land, pointing towards the post-war emergence of a new class of small peasant owners. The number of smallholdings doubled, slowing down a long-term process of urbanization, proletarianization and nuclearization of the family in Italy and setting a trend that would in part continue under Fascism. Such gains contrasted, however, with the poverty of the day labourers and most sharecroppers. These categories had suffered most from the effects of inflation, military conscription and the violation of agrarian pacts.[19]

The economic hardships suffered by many Italians during the war were exacerbated as a result of a post-war economic crisis. The government had short-sightedly relied on spending and borrowing to finance the war without increasing the tax burden, so that by 1917–18 war costs absorbed a third of the GNP. As a result of borrowing from savers and her war allies, particularly the United States and Great Britain, Italy's budget deficit had reached 108 per cent of the GNP by 1920. While money circulation had quadrupled during the war, causing inflation, it continued to grow in 1919 and 1920 resulting in an exchange devaluation and further inflation so that the values of working-class wages and of pensions and salaries in the public service sector continued to fall. For many Italians the end of the conflict also meant job redundancies, as many industries went into crisis when state orders for arms ceased. By November 1919 unemployment had reached a peak of 2 million.

In many areas of Northern Italy the war had provoked a rapid but precarious expansion of industry, which, during the post-war period, had to face problems of industrial rationalization and concentration that state support had allowed to be eluded for the duration of the war. Smaller unmodernized industries were able to adapt back to a pre-war economy, but those that had been directly linked to war production left thousands unemployed. In Tuscany, Snowden notes, the post-war crisis in the textile and steel industries, which had been considerably boosted by mobilization, was provoked by concern, during the war period, for quick profits alone without any attempt to invest in new equipment or cost-reducing methods of production or to think about the long-term requirements for a peacetime economy. In Prato's wool factories: 'Production was simply increased to the maximum consonant with the existing plant and existing production methods'.[20] People of rural origins, who had worked in industry during the war and were now redundant, often had difficulty returning to the countryside, where a crisis in agriculture had reduced the demand for labour. In the long run, however, the war reinforced the industrial basis of the Milan–Genoa–Turin triangle and to some extent that of Emilia, Veneto and Tuscany. This was only possible, however, through government financing of saving operations and the introduction, in 1921, of more universally applied protectionist measures, in order to compensate for the failure of Italian goods to command markets abroad.

   The immediate post-war years saw an intensification of working-class militancy and the development of a revolutionary political mood as a result of
both economic crisis and the promises for greater freedom made by government leaders during the war.[21] This is demonstrated by the explosion of work
stoppages occurring during the years 1919 and 1920, referred to as the *Biennio
Rosso* ('Two "Red" Years'). During 1919 there were 1,663 strikes in industry,
involving 1,049,000 workers, and 208 in agriculture, involving 505,000 peasants. This contrasted with the involvement of 385,000 industrial workers and
80,000 peasants in labour disputes in 1913. In 1920 the figures were even
higher with 1,881 strikes in industry, involving 1,268,000 workers. Though
the number of agricultural strikes decreased to 189, more than double the
number of peasants (1,046,000) were involved compared with the previous
year.[22] If during the war the converging economic interests of workers and
employers had prevented prolonged disputes, the demobilization process
reduced willingness on both sides to find compromises. But there was also a
greater tendency towards militancy as a direct result of the experience of the
previous four years, whether in the factory or at the Front. The end of restrictions on union and party activities, the emancipating effects of conscription
and the promises the government had made during the war for land raised
people's expectations of material reward for the sacrifices they had made.
   The increase in strikes went hand in hand with the dramatic growth of the
workers' movement. Membership of CGL increased from 250,000 in 1918 to
2 million by late 1920. The Catholic union movement, which had grown
during the war, also made notable gains: The Italian Confederation of Labour
(*Confederazione Italiana del Lavoro* – CIL), founded in 1919, had over a million
members by the following year, mostly sharecroppers, tenant farmers, small
farm owners, as well as textile workers, from Liguria, Lombardy and Veneto.
The Socialist agricultural union, *Federterra*, dramatically increased its membership to almost half a million by the autumn of 1919 and 900,000 in 1920,
growing not only in its traditional strongholds, Emilia and Apulia, but also
among previously non-unionized peasant categories, such as the sharecroppers
of Tuscany and Umbria.
   It was not only industrial workers and peasants who were involved in labour
disputes during the *Biennio Rosso*. Public employees, including railway workers
and clerical workers, many of whom joined the Socialist unions, and several
middle class categories, including magistrates, also went on strike. The unions'
success during the first months of 1919 in obtaining a minimum wage, an
eight-hour working day and official recognition of factory grievance committees known as internal commissions (*commissioni interne*) lay not only in
the weakness of the employers' organizations after the war but in the fact
that the government had strongly encouraged them to start post-war production in a climate of collaboration with their employees. This was matched
by the attitude of many prefects who hoped to reduce labour militancy by

taking as many steps as possible to alleviate hardships suffered as a result of demobilization. As a consequence of post-war industrial action, the index of real wages, which by 1918 had fallen to 65 per cent of 1913 levels, had reached 114.4 per cent in 1920 and increased further to 127 per cent by 1921. Wage increases were matched by welfare initiatives by the state. In April 1919 compulsory old-age and disability insurance was provided. The following month parliament set new standards of factory hygiene. In October 1919 legislation ensured compulsory employment insurance and introduced a national system of employment offices.

Many parts of rural Italy also saw labour disputes during the *Biennio Rosso*. At the beginning of 1920 the Socialist leagues launched a particularly fierce strike offensive in the Po valley. *Federterra* demanded recognition of Socialist labour exchanges and guarantees of a fixed number of workers per hectare of land (*imponibile*). Moreover, an increase in the cost of hiring *braccianti*, which the sharecroppers could no longer afford, motivated the formation by *Federterra* of a *braccianti*–sharecropper front. The contracts that Federterra secured in the fall of 1920, as a result of the success of strikes, obliged the farmers to recognize the federation's employment offices as the exclusive suppliers of labour, imposed employment quotas and improved sharecropping pacts. In the hill areas of Northern Italy and parts of the Po valley the Catholic unions, sometimes in conflict with the Socialists, attempted to achieve more favourable conditions for peasants of a mainly middling order, promoting more favourable rents for tenant farmers, better sharecropping contracts and the sale or co-management of land. They also fought for an eight-hour working day for textile workers in Lombardy.

In the sharecropping regions of Tuscany and Umbria the peasants hoped to gain a greater share of produce, safer contracts and greater independence over the management of land. Tuscany in particular saw for the first time the development of large-scale class conflict led by the Socialists. The experience of the war brought the peasants together, showing them that militancy could achieve things, and giving impetus to a slowly developing collective conscience. The extent of post-war sharecropper militancy shocked both the landlords and the Socialist Party. After a strike in July 1920 the Tuscan sharecroppers won a new contract giving them over 50 per cent of the proceeds of production and transferring a higher proportion of production costs on to the landlord, together with security of tenure and a say in how their farms were run. As Frank Snowden notes: 'The great socialist strike of 1920 revealed a peasant solidarity throughout the region that was wholly without precedent. Even by Emilian standards the agitation was impressive as 500,000 sharecroppers (72,000 families) out of the total of 710,800 Tuscan *mezzadri* took part.'[23]

In the South the *Biennio Rosso* manifested itself in occupations of uncultivated land belonging to the *latifondisti*. They were not automatically motivated by desire for landownership. Snowden argues that in Apulia: 'In the majority of cases . . . the occupation was primarily a means to combat the acute crisis of unemployment. The occupiers normally planted the uncultivated fields and then demanded payment.'[24] According to Morgan, with the exception of Latium and Apulia, the Socialist presence at the scene of land occupations in Southern Italy was limited. They were more often led by war veterans and sometimes by the Catholic peasant leagues. In general they resulted in rental and lease agreements rather than peasant ownership, while the promotors were absorbed into the 'clientelistic fabric of local Southern politics':

> The occupations of 1919–20 were rolled back or contained effectively enough by the combined repressive and mediating actions of the police and prefects. Their action was facilitated by the readiness to negotiate and compromise of the improvised veterans' co-operatives. This stance reflected the PPI [Catholic Party]'s inter-class approach and composition, and the continuing hold of the old clientelistic relationship between landlord and peasant.[25]

In a period that had seen revolutionary turmoil in many parts of Europe, many proponents of the working-class movement and their political enemies believed that Italy was following the same path. This feeling was bolstered by the rhetoric of the Maximalist (i.e. Revolutionary) leadership of the Socialist Party and the fact that the government frequently appeared to give way to union demands, one consequence of the increased influence that the new proportional representation system brought to mass-party politics. At the general election of November 1919 the PSI gained 156 seats in the Chamber of Deputies, mainly representing Northern constituencies. PSI membership dramatically increased from 23,000 in 1918 to over 200,000 in 1920. At the election the first mass Catholic Party, the Italian Popular Party (*Partito Popolare Italiano* – PPI), founded in 1919 by the Sicilian priest, Luigi Sturzo, also received nearly 1,200,000 votes, allowing it to take 100 seats representing localities south of Rome and rural areas of Lombardy, Veneto and Piedmont. The increased strength of mass parties meant that, though the old Liberal class continued to govern, in order to survive it had to take into account the demands of both the PPI and the PSI.

The Liberal government was all too aware of the disastrous state in which the police and armed forces had emerged from the First World War. Not only were they ill-prepared to face labour militancy but the overwhelming proletarian composition of the lower ranks of the army brought about through war mobilization left its commanders in fear of acts of subversion, easily encouraged by Anarchist and Maximalist anti-militarist propaganda. Consequently, the authorities attempted to reduce potential economic causes of militancy, on occasion supporting workers' grievances and condemning employer obstinacy. Despite such intentions, conflict was not always avoidable. This was particularly evident during cost-of-living strikes throughout

Italy in July 1919 characterized by widespread looting and the setting up of 'Red' republics in some towns. In several places the police opened fire on crowds of looters, killing demonstrators. Yet, in order to avoid a repetition of these events, mayors and prefects, aided by the local Socialists, set up food committees to requisition stores and reduce prices.

The authorities were equally hesitant in the face of the militancy of both the Catholic and Socialist leagues in the Po valley. Acts of violence and intimidation and illegal land occupations often took place without resistance on the part of the police or army, which in many rural areas lacked the resources to prevent them. Indeed, in the summer of 1920 the newly appointed prime minister, Giolitti, ordered prefects to negotiate with the agricultural leagues with a view to allowing the occupation of uncultivated land and enforcing the requisition of crops, ignoring the protests of employers. This attitude undoubtedly misled party and union leaders into believing that revolution was imminent. In the 'Red' provinces of Emilia the Socialist leagues often took control over who could be hired and conditions of work. They were able to impose fines on agricultural employers for pact violations. Many league leaders tried to dictate the everyday life of their fellow villagers on such issues as church-going and the politics of the newspapers they read. The situation was particularly tense on account of the growing prominence and wealth of those belonging to the middle ranks of the peasantry, who were opposed to league action. In Bologna, for example, during the summer of 1920 the *Federterra braccianti*–sharecropper alliance was threatened by sharecropper dissidence. Supported by the Socialist municipal administrations, special league tribunals ordered indiscriminate boycotts against anyone who did not join the strike. According to Cardoza: 'The victims of the strike faced virtually total isolation. A subsequent parliamentary commission reported that "the boycotted peasants were not only denied any manual labour, but they could not purchase food or clothing, they could not sell their produce, and in some cases . . . they and their families were denied medical assistance." '[26]

While the Fascist movement (described in the following section) would base its legitimacy on the need to defend citizens from 'Red' terror, the extent of political violence characterizing the *Biennio Rosso* is open to debate. With regard to the post-war peasant movement, for example, Paul Corner argues in his case study of the province of Ferrara that true and proper acts of violence at the incitement of the leagues were limited:

> It has to be recognized that the two principal weapons of the leagues, the boycott and the fine, were non-violent weapons. Intimidation and extortion they might be, but only when they were backed up by rick-burning, the maiming of animals, or physical assault, can they be viewed as violent actions. Often the pressure of violence was not necessary; a rigid boycott could achieve the desired ends, if a little more slowly.[27]

Guido Crainz on the other hand suggests that peasant action was character-ized by a more widespread phenomenon of violence than that suggested by Corner, over which union leaders had limited control. This, he argues, was often the product of a more general sense of rebellion resulting from the experience of war, which taught individuals to solve problems by means of force. In areas where before 1915 the peasantry had been reasonably docile, such as Veneto, returning conscripts ended their traditional deference towards the employer class. This was the case in the province of Padua where peasants, who before the war had been willing to emigrate to other pro-vinces as blackleg labour, now demanded to be given work without having to emigrate. While the violence betrayed the anger and desperation of ex-conscripts in the face of chronic post-war unemployment, there was also a clear sense of vengeance on account of particularly harsh treatment suffered at the front. In many parts of Veneto the peasantry reacted to employer intransigence by invading and ransacking their property and in some cases the whole community (including women and children) took part.[28]

Any possibility of exploiting post-war rebelliousness to achieve revolution-ary ends was, however, doomed by the lack of a clear unifying strategy and internal divisions within the labour movement. As the above analysis has suggested, in agriculture unity among the peasantry was not always sustain-able as a result of conflicting ideals. Though, for example, sharecroppers were receptive to the improvement policies of the Socialist leagues, they did not want to become part of a rural proletariat, desiring ultimately to be able to buy land. Friction between Socialist and Catholic unions over the organ-ization of middle-class peasants was not infrequent. In the cities the ability of the workers' movement to capitalize on the proletarianization process induced by the war also has to be questioned. It did not always succeed in mobilizing the new but more marginal members of the industrial popula-tion, many of whom had come from the countryside to work in the factories during the conflict. Nor did it bring together the urban and rural movements during moments of large-scale mobilization.

In the factories skilled workers, often of an older generation and attached to the artisan-based traditions of the smaller workshops, were not always in agreement with their younger less skilled work companions, perhaps of rural origin, working on the newer assembly lines of the larger factories, over the aims and forms of labour struggles. Such differences were often mirrored by ideological divisions between Reformists, Maximalists, Anarchists and Revolutionary Syndicalists. The refusal on occasion of Catholic workers to go out on strike alongside their Socialist colleagues, reflecting the PPI's tendency to collaborate with the government, also caused fierce resentment. Following the strike of state postal and telegraph workers in January 1920, for example, CIL members, who had not taken part, were forced to transfer to other posts in the agency after former strikers refused to work beside them.[29]

The revolutionary experiment centred around the creation of factory councils modelled on the Russian Soviets, the first of which were born at Fiat in September 1919, largely failed as a result of the reluctance of Socialist leaders to put their rhetoric into practice. In April 1920 a general strike throughout Northern Italy in defence of the councils, following a lockout by Turin employers, ended in defeat because of lack of support from both the PSI and the CGL leadership. The question of worker factory control came to a head during the occupation, in September 1920, of engineering and metal factories and shipyards throughout Northern Italy, called by the metalworkers' union (*Federazione Italiana Operai Metallurgici* – FIOM). The occupation, which originated in Turin, under the leadership of Antonio Gramsci, represented an attempt at worker management of production. Elsewhere there was little support and this only in the form of economic demands. Such confusion of aims was demonstrated at the leadership level of the Socialist Party and union. Notably the PSI and CGL leaders played an ambivalent role in proclaiming the occupation as revolutionary while stressing purely economic goals.[30]

The occupations did, nevertheless, demonstrate high levels of worker solidarity at the local level. The offensive, though not truly revolutionary, represented a newly found unity between skilled and unskilled workers throughout the steel and metal works of Lombardy, Liguria and Emilia. As Bell's case-study of Sesto illustrates, the whole of the worker community played an important role of solidarity, with women and children bivouacking outside the factories and supplying their men with food, workers heavily guarding the factories with any weapon possible (lances, revolvers, rifles), and the organization of factory councils to co-ordinate production, maintain discipline and organize defence. An important role was played by the Red Guards (*Guardie Rosse*), Maximalist paramilitary organizations patterned on former Soviet militia formations, in both preventing looting and sabotage and defending the factories from outside intervention. Working-class cultural organizations and the Chamber of Labour co-ordinated the occupations with the planning of defence, provisioning of occupying workers and circulation of information through their press.[31]

In spite of unity at the local level, the national agreement between the industrialists' association, Confindustria, and the FIOM to end the occupations was the object of dispute and division among the workers. It was accepted overall, though only by a narrow majority in Turin. The agreement, which led to a pay increase and formal recognition of the principles of trade-union control in the factories, effectively marked the failure of the revolutionary experiment. The question of worker control of production never reached discussion in parliament. Disunity within the working-class movement should also be considered in the broader context of the dramatic growth in influence of the two mass parties and the missed opportunity for joint government. Internal divisions within the PSI and PPI prevented the formation of a majority coalition that would have ousted the old Liberal ruling class from power. James Miller notes that, though the PPI and PSI with their unions and cultural and educational associations brought Italy's masses into active political participation: 'Their mutual mistrust paralyzed parliament and opened the way for an extreme mass movement to seize power.'[32]

The Fascist movement

Throughout the period of the *Biennio Rosso* any chance the Socialists had of coming to power within the existing system was sacrificed in the name of a revolution to which in reality they were not willing to commit themselves. More crucially, however, the employers took the revolutionary rhetoric seriously. They were outraged when, in September 1920, Giolitti allowed the factory occupations, ordering the police and armed forces to avoid conflict with those involved. Little did they appreciate that, by doing this, the Prime Minister was taking steps to ensure that any risk of insurrection was minimized. Social prejudice among the ruling classes also played a role in distorting the effective power of the 'Red' enemy. In Ferrara, for example, as Corner illustrates, there was much resentment by the prefect and the landowners and urban middle classes that the party of the 'people', which had recently gained control over the city council, should hold power. Moreover, they found it difficult to tolerate the fact that the Socialists 'invaded' territory that was traditionally theirs, taking over the municipal headquarters, housed inside the city castle, which became a centre for union meetings and had 'Long live Socialism!' painted over its walls. Corner notes: 'Convinced that social revolution was on the way, they became incapable of distinguishing between the real and the imagined situation.'[33]

In economic terms the property-owning and middle classes felt that the lower classes had made economic and social gains at their expense. The high level of union protests resulting from the economic crisis had led to a gradual transfer of income away from them to *braccianti*, industrial workers, sharecroppers and state employees. They had been hit by increased tax pressure in the post-war years, while the government had been afraid to end bread subsidies for the poor. Extra tax withdrawals on capital and the confiscation of war profits also antagonized them.[34] Not immediately, however, were these social categories politically united. In Bologna, for example, the middle classes of shopkeepers, artisans, public and private employees, teachers and small-scale industrialists and employers began to form associations to represent their economic needs. They felt that they had been worse affected by the crisis than the large-scale industrial and agricultural employers. The government, they claimed, favoured big business as well as the working classes, while they were hit by price reductions imposed by the Socialist council, with the assent of the Prefect.[35]

Middle-class resentment was also evident in the failure of post-war governments to provide jobs in the state and professional sectors. The First World War had seen an abnormal increase in secondary school and university enrolments. The number of university graduates in the 1919–20 academic year had doubled in comparison with that of 1913–14. This factor added difficulties to the post-war employment situation, leading to high levels of intellectual unemployment and a general loss of status among professionals. In 1920 more than 40,000 primary school teachers qualified, for example, while only 11,000 posts were available to be filled. The situation was partly blamed on the fact that the labour market had been flooded by an increased number of educated individuals from working-class backgrounds.[36] There was even bitterness about the recent gains of women as a result of wartime mobilization, which post-war governments were accused of prolonging to the detriment of male workers. As De Grazia points out, soldiers returning from the Front were led to believe that women had stolen their jobs during their absence, though in reality the jobs women had taken were often new. Women faced prejudice from their male colleagues, who unrealistically saw them as shirking owing to female problems (such as their menstrual period) and spending wages on sweets and perfume rather than basic necessities. The Sacchi Law of 1919, moreover, increased areas in which women could work (with the exception of the judiciary, military defence and the exercise of political power and executive authority in government).[37]

In the eyes of patriotic Italians the Liberal governments' conciliatory attitude towards strikes went hand in hand with their apparent inability to defend Italy's territorial claims in reward for her part in the First World War. They were incensed by the banning of demonstrations in protest at the Treaty of Versailles (which awarded Italy Trento, Alto Adige and the port of Trieste and Istria but denied her territories in Africa, Asia Minor and Dalmatia), while 'revolutionary' demonstrations were seen to be permitted. A division came to the fore between those, represented by Giolitti and Turati, who recognized the Wilson agreement on self-determination and were therefore prepared to renounce previous claims on non-Italian speaking regions and those who, like the poet D'Annunzio, believed that independent of ethnic and linguistic considerations territories like Dalmatia belonged to Italy by divine right.[38]

The Fascist movement developed as a result of these resentments, representing a culmination of a pattern of social conflict, which can be traced back to the Nationalist-inspired strike-breaking episodes of the Giolittian period and was also manifest during 'Red Week' in June 1914, and the intervention crisis of 1915. The first paramilitary 'Fascist' groups were strongly connected to the Interventionist movement of 1915 and the development of war mobilization committees. They were boosted, during the latter half of the war, when following the military defeat at Caporetto there were many defections from the Neutralist to the Interventionist camp, strengthening the resolve of the latter that Socialism, which was seen as responsible for the military disaster on account of its anti-war propaganda, should be destroyed. Since before the end of the war these paramilitary organizations, founded on the experience of the military front, had the support of army veterans and active members of the military forces, especially the officer class. On frequent occasion they occupied the streets of Italian cities, attacking workers and disturbing left-wing demonstrations. In Bologna, for example, as early as May 1918 war veterans, many of them disabled, attempted to storm the Socialist city council headquarters.

Rising to prominence among the above groups were the *Fasci di Combattimento*, the first of which was launched in Milan in March 1919 by the one-time Revolutionary Socialist leader, Benito Mussolini, and was quickly imitated in other Northern cities. Expelled from the Socialist Party in 1914 for rejecting neutrality, Mussolini was converted to the belief that revolution should be carried out in the national interest as a result of his experiences at the Front during the war. The *Fascio* was a strongly heterogeneous group with a programme that was highly patriotic and anti-Socialist but not insensitive to the needs of workers. Prominent among the first 'Fascists' were First World War shock troops known as *Arditi*, army officers, Futurists and students, but there were also Catholics, Radicals, Republicans and Revolutionary Syndicalists. On several occasions the provincial authorities unofficially employed these groups to help them police major working-class demonstrations. During the general strike of July 1919, called in protest at the sending of British, French and Italian troops to Russia and Hungary to combat revolutionary movements, members of these paramilitary organizations, including the Milan *Fascio di Combattimento*, collaborated with the police in order to prevent violence. There were similar initiatives in other cities, though the ambivalence of such 'policing' activities is shown by the fact that the so-called 'men of order' employed by the authorities often assaulted left-wing demonstrators, including parliamentary deputies.

Closely linked to the 'Fascist' phenomenon, in September 1919 two thousand patriotic volunteers, on the initiative of the poet, D'Annunzio, marched on the half-Italian, half-Croat-speaking port of Fiume on the Istrian peninsula in protest at Italy's limited territorial rewards for her part in the war (though in fact Fiume had never been included among the territories mentioned in the Treaty of London). The attitude of Liberal governments towards this initiative once again displeased patriotic Italians. During the autumn of 1919 the prime minister, Francesco Nitti, ordered prefects to prevent the recruitment and departure of volunteers, though he was initially unwilling to test the loyalty of the army by ordering D'Annunzio's eviction because of clear military support for the adventure. Only in December 1920 did Nitti's successor, Giolitti, send troops to expel the occupiers. Ironically, the eviction of

D'Annunzio, whose popularity had gradually waned during the 15-month period of occupation, was a present to Mussolini, who had only formally supported D'Annunzio's initiative, since it meant that a dangerous rival over the leadership of a future right-wing government had been virtually eliminated.[39]

The political gains of Mussolini's *Fasci* were initially insignificant, as was demonstrated by their miserable defeat at the general election of November 1919 and their temporary disappearance from the political scene. They were, however, quickly able to capitalize on the growing impatience of a large number of citizens on account of the Liberal governments' apparent acquiescence towards the working-class organizations and their inability to maintain law and order, as was evidenced by the fact that some rural areas were under the complete control of the 'Reds'. From the spring of 1920 onwards the urban middle classes began to join forces with the industrialists and agricultural employers in their growing determination to stand up to labour militancy. On the occasion of general strikes in April and May 1920 many of them joined committees mobilized to oppose strike action and maintain public services. Polarization among different categories of factory employees during these strikes also facilitated growing opposition to union militancy. Engineers, for example, rather than aligning with the workers against their employers, engaged in strike-breaking activities. This phenomenon was matched by a return to the traditional practice of employing anti-league strike-breaking squads in the countryside, though on a much larger scale than ever witnessed before. From the autumn of 1920 a second more solidly right-wing, less politically heterogeneous Fascist movement was born in the context of such activities.

Not everywhere were the Fascist action squads founded on opposition to working-class gains alone. Indeed, the first Fascist political victory occurred in Trieste and Venezia–Giulia, where national and social issues were inextricably linked. According to Lyttelton: 'In April–May 1920 the paramilitary organization of the squads was already well developed, on the pretext both of aiding D'Annunzio and of responding to a possible *coup de main* by Slavs and Communists acting in confederation against Trieste'.[40] However, the main launch of the second Fascist movement coincided with preparation for the local elections of the autumn of 1920 in which patriotic associations turned to the *Fasci* requesting their support against the mass parties. At the elections the PSI won over a quarter of the 8,000 local councils. While most of the cities were won by anti-Socialist coalitions, in the provincial capitals and smaller towns of Northern and Central Italy the Socialists were very successful. The Catholics won majority control in 1,650 communes. The prospect of Socialist or Catholic municipal control was daunting to many, since, according to Clark, it 'meant that only union leaders and their friends would get local government jobs and subsidies, public works would be entrusted only to peasant leagues and to Socialist or Catholic co-operatives, and party propaganda would be subsidized from the rates – which would rise sharply'.[41]

The electoral results only heightened the resolve of the 'losers' to intensify their support of Fascist squads that started to engage in gratuitous acts of violence against workers and their leaders, frequently ransacking Socialist and Catholic party, union and press headquarters and publicly burning their flags and newspapers. Mayors representing the PSI and PPI were often intimidated to the point of resignation. During the autumn of 1920 *fasci* were founded in the provincial cities of the Po valley, Liguria, Tuscany and Umbria. Made up of middle-class employees, students, professionals and in some cases blackleg workers, they were employed by local industrialists and manufacturers to allow them to violate previous contracts at will and to intimidate workers into joining Fascist unions, from which they promised to hire workers in return for lower wages and longer working hours. However, violence was not always necessary to obtain support. While many middle-class employees had initially backed the CGL over wage increases and the eight-hour working day, a large number of them subsequently defected to the Fascists of their own free will.

The main thrust of Fascist action lay, however, in the movement's penetration of the countryside, from early 1921, to come to the aid of agricultural employers in their opposition to the Socialist and Catholic leagues. A rural *Fascio* was founded – sometimes under the direct leadership of the agrarians themselves or their sons – when local employers called on the nearest town *Fascio* for help. Truckloads of *squadristi* (squad members), wearing black shirts and carrying cudgels and firearms, invaded villages to carry out 'punitive expeditions' in which union and political leaders were beaten and union headquarters and co-operatives ransacked. In the Po valley provinces rural *squadrismo* was employed by the capitalist farmers in order to split the *braccianti*–sharecropper front through the forced disbanding of their unions. Under the slogan, 'land to those who work it', agrarian Fascism advocated the regimentation of the masses through their own unions and the development of a conservative class of peasant proprietors, which would reduce the number of *braccianti* and so eliminate the power of rural Socialism.

In view of the prospect of lower wages, desertions to Fascist unions were mainly obtained through relentless violence and fear of unemployment. Some of the success of the Fascists has, however, been attributed to the fear that the Socialists had previously instilled in the minds of many peasants to whom the Fascist slogans, promising land and protection from league persecution, appealed. Moreover, increasing economic difficulties from 1921 reduced the attraction of the working-class organizations. In the lower Po valley provinces rural *Fascio* membership was heterogeneous in view of the partial support given by the dissident members of the working classes. According to Cardoza, in the small town of San Giorgio di Piano in the province of Bologna, for example, the *Fascio* consisted of ten agrarians, four merchants and manufacturers, seven white-collar workers, five public-service employees, fifteen factory workers, eighty-two *braccianti* and sharecroppers, and eighteen from the professional classes. Rural *Fasci* were divided into two sections: young *squadristi* formed the action group for punitive expeditions, while the older members were responsible for such administrative jobs as the organization of transport and information.[42]

The success of *squadrismo* lay not only in the financial support it enjoyed from local élites, but in the indifference if not co-operation of the police and the *Carabinieri*, who, in spite of orders from the government to prevent violence, saw Fascism as a positive means of re-establishing order where they had lost control of whole areas of territory. Additionally, many policemen had fought alongside the future Fascists during the First World War and on many occasions they carried out punitive expeditions together. Arms were supplied by the military, given its frequent contacts with the *squadristi*. Even when the authorities attempted to maintain order, they found themselves up against well-armed groups that were able to move around the countryside at great speed in motor vehicles supplied by the employers and that were often difficult to identify on account of their provenance from other provinces. In any case, the police were inhibited in their repression by the ambiguous attitude of the Liberal governments, which attempted to appease Fascism through the politics of *trasformismo*. This was most evident in Giolitti's inclusion of Fascist candidates on his coalition list in the general election of May 1921, such that official instructions to the authorities to prevent Fascist violence during the election campaign were mostly ignored. Where Fascists were arrested and brought to trial for acts of violence, witnesses were often too frightened to come forward and local magistrates ensured their acquittal, while in the case of the prosecution of Fascist leaders huge rallies were organized denigrating the provincial authorities for their 'limited sense of patriotism'. With the support of the local judiciary the agrarians were also able to exploit the peasants' fear of Fascist violence in order to violate the terms of previous contracts and punish league leaders for past acts of violence and intimidation. Many were prosecuted for organizing boycotts and the use of fines, though such instruments had usually been stipulated in contracts and had not, therefore, been illegal.[43]

The ascendancy of the Fascist movement is easier to understand if placed in the context of a historical culture of acceptance of political violence in Italy, characterized by the involvement of representatives of the Italian state with organized crime, as demonstrated, for example, by a permanent state of *Mafia* control over certain geographical areas. In an administrative system influenced by patronage, state officials became used to giving priority to political concerns over and above the impartial enforcement of the law.[44] Though some *squadristi* saw themselves as revolutionaries changing society, political ideas were often limited to vague patriotic ideals. Inevitably the squad action was characterized by a sense of vengeance, often at a personal level, as a result of the humiliation suffered under the 'Reds'. Emblematic in this sense was the killing in Medicina (Bologna), in 1921, of a Socialist labourer and the injuring of his father by relatives of two armed guards killed during a land occupation the previous year. The son of a landowner, who had suffered league boycotts, also took part in the punitive expedition.[45] Where personal vendetta was not involved, a strong driving force for many *squadristi* lay in the cult of violence, which had its roots in the recent experience of warfare. A high percentage of the squad membership was also adolescent, representing the need to fulfil fantasies of youth heroism, a sense of rebellion against authority and family tradition, as well as a means of earning money.

In many areas of Italy the appeal of the Fascist movement was more limited. In Tuscany and parts of Veneto and Lombardy, for example, although Fascism made notable political gains, it remained an instrument of the agricultural employers. It was less able to attract a popular following because of the homogeneity of the peasant system. In these areas there was no rural proletariat whose interests could be played off against those of an intermediate peasant class as in the Po valley. The proletarian composition of some urban centres was too strong to allow the launch of the Fascist movement in the violent and dynamic form it took in the Po valley provinces. There the success of the Fascists partly depended on the attitude of the industrialists. Many large entrepreneurs of Piedmont and Lombardy, including Olivetti and Agnelli, the owner of Fiat, avoided overt support of Fascism. A recession from late 1920 onwards was sufficient to reduce labour demands. More significantly, as Morgan argues: 'Their violent and crude methods of restoring industrial peace were anyway often seen as undermining the continuity of production and destructive of good relations with the workers and their unions in the factory.'[46] The case of Liguria was rather different, as Lyttelton illustrates. Initially the *Fasci* had a strong working-class backing demonstrating the autonomist position of the regional Socialists and trade unions, who had supported the war. In particular, the Seamen's Union, which had its headquarters in Genoa, was presided over by Giovanni Giulietti, who financed D'Annunzio's occupation of Fiume. In 1920 the *Fasci* were reorganized with the financial backing of the industrialists. In the face of unemployment, which hit the armaments industry with particular severity, they were able to function as employment agencies for them. In the city of Genoa, however, until the summer of 1922 the *Fasci* were less tied to the industrialists, maintaining contacts with Giulietti.[47]

In the South, Fascism made far less of an impact before it became the party of government. This was partly because of the limited threat posed by the working-class movement, which had only significantly developed in Apulia, which experienced a full squadrist counter-offensive. Even in Apulia Fascism did not have a populist following. The lines of class division were too clearly drawn between the *latifondisti* and the great mass of day labourers without the presence of a traditional peasantry, 'whose ambiguous relationship with the unions could be developed into a system of class alliances in defence of property'.[48] In many urban centres of the South, Fascism of a kind was made up of heterogeneous groups of young urban middle-class members, many ex-servicemen, of interventionist, avant-gardist, Nationalist, Syndicalist, even Socialist inspiration which was above all opposed to the traditional static Liberal establishment. Many areas of the South had been characterized by the violent exercise of arbitrary power well before 1922 and remained relatively uninfluenced by *squadrismo*. As Jonathan Steinberg notes, in the Crotone area of Calabria with its great estates employing large numbers of landless day labourers landowners did not require the help of the Fascists since they had always maintained social control through the use of armed guards.[49]

The extent of resistance against Fascism varied from region to region. In the Po Valley the Fascist onslaught was so dynamic that the working-class movement had little chance of organizing any proper form of defence. The Fascists had an advantage over both their political opponents and the forces of law and order in their being well-armed and able to move quickly from province to province. Several hundred workers, peasants and union leaders were killed in Fascist attacks between 1920 and 1922, and many more were injured, while the figures for deaths and injuries among the Fascists were much lower. The institutional support that the Fascists received is plainly evident in the practice of selective arrests. Indeed, it was not unusual for the victims of Fascist punitive expeditions to be arrested when the police arrived on the scene. Bearing these factors in mind, it is difficult to talk realistically of a civil war between Socialists and Fascists, the term often referred to by prefects in describing the state of law and order in their provinces – and used in order to justify the fact that little was being done to repress Fascist violence. The working-class movement was too consumed by internal divisions to put up an effective united front against the Fascists. Not long after the start of the Fascist onslaught and in a moment of economic recession, the splintering off in 1921 of the far left of the PSI to form the Italian Communist Party (*Partito Comunista Italiano* – PCI) under the leadership of Gramsci weakened the movement and the working-class community as a whole.

This is not to say that the workers and peasants did not try to defend themselves. This was particularly evident in Romagna where punitive expeditions often met the armed resistance of Socialists, Communists and Anarchists.[50] Self-defence was usually locally, if not individually organized, however, revealing the inability of an increasingly divided working-class movement to co-ordinate a proper resistance. Emblematic in this sense is the development of the *Arditi del Popolo*, a left-wing paramilitary organization founded to defend the working classes from Fascist attacks. If they were outlawed by the

61

central government as an armed association (while this qualification was not given to the Fascist squads), the Communist and Socialist Parties in naively agreeing to a Pact of Pacification with the Fascists in the summer of 1921 (which was eventually rejected by the latter) refused to sanction their activities too. Similarly, continued divisions between the Catholic and Socialist worker movements played to the advantage of the Fascists. The attempt, for example, to arrange a mutual defence pact between Socialist and Catholic peasants of the province of Cremona against the particularly violent assaults of the Fascists of Roberto Farinacci failed because the PPI and PSI leaders repudiated it.[51] Pockets of resistance would continue, however, well into the first years of Fascist government, characterized by the refusal, even at the cost of unemployment, hunger and beatings, to join Fascist unions. This was the case in the rural centre of Molinella, in the province of Bologna, where resistance had to be forcibly ended in 1926, with the removal of over 200 families.

By mid-1922 most Northern and Central provinces had extensive Fascist organizations amounting to 250,000 *squadristi*. It was above all the psychologically devastating effect of the dynamism of the movement, which was able to carry out military-style occupations of Northern cities in the summer of 1922 without the local authorities being able to prevent them, that accounted for the Liberal government's increasing reluctance to oppose it. When squads from all over the Po valley and even further afield concentrated in Bologna at the end of May, in protest at what they saw as the anti-Fascist policies of the Prefect, Cesare Mori, the government preferred to negotiate an end to the occupation by promising that Mori would be removed. This only encouraged the resolve of the Fascists and discouraged the authorities from opposing the occupation of other cities. In August 1922 an Alliance of Labour, which brought together the main left-wing trade union bodies and parties, declared a general strike in a final attempt to rally support against an imminent Fascist seizure of power. This backfired as few workers came out on strike. Consequently, the Left was further discredited to the advantage of the Fascists, who volunteered to maintain public services and even resorted to brutal reprisals against individuals who had stayed away from work. In some instances they assaulted workers in their own homes, after they obtained their addresses from their employers.

The failure of the 'Alliance of Labour' strike heightened disunity within the Left and secured Fascist participation in government. The March on Rome, by which Mussolini came to power in October 1922, was not a true act of revolution, though it would subsequently be hailed as such in Fascist textbooks and literature. Although 30,000 blackshirts converged in three formations on the capital, contemporaneously Mussolini's prime ministership was negotiated with the Liberal government, so that they could walk through military roadblocks straight into the city. Nevertheless, the first stage of the operation had involved an attempt at occupying the main Italian cities. Though the military authorities prevented this in Bologna, Milan, Turin and Genoa, many other cities and smaller towns surrendered – or formally permitted occupations – and this inevitably weakened the resolve of the government of Luigi De Facta and King Victor Emanuel III to put the army to the test by declaring a state of martial law.[52]

It is likely, however, that had that decree been signed and had the government given unequivocal orders to prevent the occupations, the armed forces would have responded positively. It was one thing to support the squads in crushing the working-class movement. It was quite another openly and collectively to surrender the power of the state to them. The success of the March on Rome lay in the ability of the Fascists, during the previous summer, to create the impression that the provincial armed forces were disloyal to the Liberal government, when in point of fact the passiveness of the former had more often than not been provoked by the ambivalent behaviour of the latter in their vain attempt to buy off Mussolini politically, through the politics of *trasformismo*.

The road to dictatorship, 1922–26

Between 1922 and 1926 the future of Fascism was uncertain. After the March on Rome Mussolini was invited to preside over a coalition government and many political obstacles had to be overcome before he obtained full powers. While the Liberal parliamentary system remained in existence the Fascist Party (*Partito Nazionale Fascista* – PNF), which had replaced the Fascist movement in November 1921, was still open to possible electoral defeat. Mussolini's dictatorship was set up through a combination of continued squad violence and legal measures. In November 1923 a new electoral law, named after the Fascist deputy, Giacomo Acerbo, who proposed it, granted two-thirds of seats in the Chamber of Deputies to the electoral list gaining the most votes (provided that it gained more than 25 per cent of the total number). However, this change in the electoral system proved unnecessary. At the general election of April 1924 the very high percentage of the vote the Fascists and their conservative and Nationalist flankers won depended to a large degree on traditional clientelistic tactics and prefectoral intervention, as well as blackshirt violence. The *listone* of Fascists won nearly 65 per cent of the vote and 374 seats (of which 60 per cent belonged to genuine Fascists). Squad intimidation ensured that majorities were gained in Emilia and Tuscany. And in the South and the islands majorities were gained, too, as Liberal politicians joined the Fascist bandwagon. Majorities over other electoral lists were not, however, achieved in Piedmont, Liguria, Lombardy and Veneto.[53] The election result allowed a huge Fascist parliamentary majority to vote in favour of new legislation which disbanded the democratic institutions of the

Liberal state, abolished non-Fascist political parties and unions, banned the right to strike and enforced strict newspaper censorship.

As part of the process of establishing a dictatorship, between 1923 and 1926 Mussolini also had to deal with internal divisions and infighting within the PNF between 'intransigents' and 'moderates'. The very manner in which Mussolini seized power – in which a combination of intimidation and negotiation rather than true revolutionary force were the key denominators – demonstrates how such divisions had developed well before the March on Rome. During the summer of 1921 internal differences had become apparent as provincial *squadrismo*, in its desire for a system of terror, fought to maintain supremacy over more conservative Fascists closer to the leadership who had made their entrance to parliament following the election of 35 Fascist deputies on Giolitti's coalition list the previous May. The sheer dynamism of the provincial movements and the extreme loyalty of their members to local leaders (*ras*), who had created true and proper fiefdoms, constituted a threat not only to the Liberal state but to the position of Mussolini himself, who felt that, once the power of the 'Reds' had been reduced, continued excesses would have a negative influence on public opinion.

The battle for supremacy, between the Fascist government and the provincial *ras*, continued after the March on Rome, as the latter pushed for completion of a Fascist revolution in which the PNF would play a key role. The struggle was partly prolonged because government policies towards provincial Fascism were ambivalent. After coming to power, it was Mussolini's intention that the job of crushing the political opposition be entrusted to the state organs. Prefects intensified police raids against opposition unions and parties and were empowered to dissolve their associations and arrest their leaders on public security grounds. They were officially ordered not to tolerate violence, whatever quarter it came from, as part of Mussolini's desire for respectability. Yet, in practice the government also continued to rely on the support of the squads to destroy the remnants of the working-class movement and move into areas where Fascism had not yet taken power, suggesting that the police forces, which underwent a notable cut in resources immediately after the March on Rome, were not sufficiently equipped to do so.

The creation of the Fascist Militia (*Milizia Volontaria per la Sicurezza Nazionale* – MVSN) in January 1923, of which all *squadristi* were made members, was seen as one way of bringing provincial Fascism under control. The Militia were to work parallel to the other armed forces and could be called upon by prefects for policing operations. In reality Militia members were often indistinguishable from the squads and many of them maintained their loyalty to former squad leaders. Indeed, the fact that they wore a uniform effectively immunized them from punishment for acts of violence. On the occasion of the general election of March 1924, for example, while the Militia were officially employed to ensure correct voting procedures, in practice they were able to resort to violence to ensure a Fascist victory without the government interfering to stop them. This contradiction is partly explained by the Italian revisionist historian, Renzo De Felice, who argues that as men of government Mussolini and his ministers wanted order at all costs, but as Fascists they could not fail to understand the psychological motivations of grassroot Fascism in its desire to eliminate dissidence and suffocate political opposition. In this sense law and order could only be formally respected.[54] It is equally likely that tolerance of violence was motivated by fear of an anti-Fascist resurgence during a period in which a long-term Fascist government was far from certain.

Closely linked to the above tensions within Fascism, Mussolini also had to deal with friction between employers and syndicalist Fascists over the question of workers' rights. Such conflict revealed the dangers inherent in the founding of alternative union organizations for the working classes within a movement, become government, increasingly relying on the support of the property-owning classes. The National Confederation of Syndicalist Unions (*Confederazione Nazionale delle Corporazioni Sindacali*) had been founded in January 1922 to unite the 250,000 members of locally organized Fascist unions under the leadership of Edmondo Rossoni. Organized into corporations of occupational groups, by January 1923 the Confederation claimed 850,000 members when membership of the CGL had fallen to little over 200,000. The following year the Fascist government endorsed the eight-hour working day and a policy of collaboration between the Fascist unions and employers, in the national interest. However, Rossoni's desire to extend his organizational network over the employers through a system of mixed syndicates, failed in December 1923 when, following a meeting between representatives of the Fascist unions and the employers' associations, the Palazzo Chigi Pact established that separate organizations for workers and employers would be maintained. In practice the employers often showed little consideration for workers' rights. They were able to reduce wages as prefectoral decrees abolished more advantageous labour pacts signed during the *Biennio Rosso*. They often imposed wage cuts well exceeding those officially stipulated. Fascist syndicalists started to make more radical demands upon the employers, such as recognition of the *imponibile* in agricultural employment, once it became clear that employers were only formally prepared to guarantee respect of Fascist labour agreements. This even resulted in episodes of squad warfare between agrarian and syndicalist factions.[55]

The weak position of the Fascist unions came to the fore during the political crisis of the summer and autumn of 1924, surrounding the abduction and murder of the Socialist deputy, Giacomo Matteotti (described below). During this period power had to be temporarily restored to the syndicalist Fascists as a means of countering a possible Socialist resurgence. In August, for example, the Prefect of Bologna, Arturo Bocchini, warned the government

65

that attempts by the local brick industry management to disrupt negotiations with the Fascist unions were causing serious tensions among the
syndicalist Fascists, particularly since many brickworkers were turning to the
CGL once again. During this period the Fascist unions were frequently caught
off their guard by CGL strike initiatives and this forced urban Fascist unions
in many parts of Italy to stage cost-of-living strikes in the autumn of 1924.
In March 1925, Rossoni and the PNF leader, Farinacci, permitted metalworkers' strikes though, as Morgan notes, the strike only took hold because
the CGL-affiliated metalworkers' union (FIOM) called out the bulk of workers
remaining loyal to the non-Fascist unions. The Fascist government remained
only lukewarm in its support of the syndicalists, who were gradually isolated. Though the Palazzo Vidoni Pact of October 1925, between the Fascist
Unions and Confindustria, confirmed a full Fascist union monopoly on
industrial syndicates and abolished elective factory councils on which
Communist and Socialist representatives stood, the councils were not replaced
by shop-floor union presence, with the result that Fascist union power was
seriously reduced in the face of management authority.[56]

As the next chapter demonstrates, the social class that had financed the
squads would continue to play a role in the institutional framework of a
conservative type of Fascism, paying lip-service to the empty edifice of the
Corporate State, while maintaining its autonomy and privileges. In the
absence of strong union influence, Fascist economic policies sought to move
wealth gained during the *Biennio Rosso* from the lower classes back to the
upper and middle classes. According to Zamagni, they had, however, partly
been anticipated by the Liberal government which had removed bread
subsidies in February 1921 and suspended post-war tax measures that had
most antagonized the owner and middle classes. Yet, it is clear that many
lower-middle-class categories whose support had been crucial in bringing
Fascism to power would not necessarily benefit from Fascist economic policies.
After the March on Rome the Fascist government sacked many public
employees, as part of continued public spending cuts, and introduced income
tax for rural categories hitherto exempted, including sharecroppers, small
farm owners and contract workers.[57]

The growing conservative character of Fascism is also demonstrated by
transformations it underwent in the South. After October 1922, Southern
intransigent and syndicalist Fascists had wanted to use Fascism to destroy
clientelism and regenerate society, but this clashed with Mussolini's reliance
on the support of the traditional agrarian élite, a problem which was solved
by the fusion of the Nationalists with the PNF and the consequent isolation
of the syndicalist faction in 1923. Areas of the South which had not seen a
Fascist movement before the March on Rome hurried to set up Party sections
once Fascism was in government, as part of the traditional tendency to gain
as many benefits as possible by supporting governing factions and in many

cases local Fascist institutions quickly fell into the hands of partisan groups or families, reinforcing their arbitrary powers rather than bringing the social and economic renewal that Fascism had promised. Local agrarian notables, often with *Mafia* connections, were relied upon for their consent for Fascism in return for being able to maintain their personal powers at the local level. For this reason, the general election of April 1924 saw a huge triumph of the Fascist vote in the South.[58]

The public uproar and consequent political crisis during the second half of 1924 provoked by the murder by Fascist thugs of the Socialist deputy, Giacomo Matteotti, for his outspoken denunciation of Fascist violence during the recent election campaign, brought to a head the government's dilemma over the extent to which it should tolerate Fascist extremism. While defeat by the opposition forces, which under the name of the Aventine Secession abandoned parliament in protest, was prevented by the failure of the conservative forces and the monarchy to lend their support to the initiative, it was obvious to Mussolini that a process of 'normalization', in which manifestations of violence were prevented and revolutionary tendencies were eradicated, would have to take place if his future power was to be secured. However, by the end of 1924, many Militia leaders were in a state of revolt after their corps had been placed under greater control of the army and, supported by violent demonstrations in several cities, they demanded an all-out Fascist revolution.

At the beginning of 1925 Mussolini decided to satisfy the demands of the 'intransigents' in such a manner as to neutralize their powers in the long term, allowing the creation of a dictatorship in which the PNF was sub-ordinated to the state. On 3 January, in his famous parliamentary speech, the Prime Minister assumed personal responsibility for previous acts of violence committed. On the same day a circular to the prefects ordered the dissolution of clubs and associations posing a threat to state security, the arrest of subversives suspected of criminal activities and the confiscation of illegally held arms. Such measures were backed up over the following two years by legislation – easily passed by a large Fascist parliamentary majority – which strongly limited the rights of association and concentrated executive power in the hands of Mussolini, allowing the government the permanent right to govern by decree, limited the freedom of the press, abolished elective municipal and provincial councils and gave prefects greater powers. Following several assassination attempts on the Fascist leader, the death penalty was reintroduced for attempts on the life of members of the royal family and the head of government, while the power of the police to place restrictions over citizens was increased to the point of practically eliminating civil rights as judicial guarantees against abuse of power were removed.[59]

The squads were initially unleashed as part of the intensified measures of repression, in spite of the fact that on 4 January 1925 the PNF secretary, Farinacci, had officially ordered the Fascists to end their violence on the grounds that such behaviour would obstruct the work of the government and play to the advantage of their political opponents. It is likely that in the absence of sufficient resources the police either continued to rely on the collaboration of the squads in their repression or were simply unable or unwilling to control them. However, the government became increasingly intolerant of their excesses, which it could not always hide from the public, no matter what powers of press censorship it had at its disposal. Between 1925 and 1927 state supremacy over provincial and Party Fascism was achieved through the removal of the intransigent Farinacci, the reaffirmation of the power of the prefect over Party federals, the replacement of elective municipal councils by government-appointed *podestà*, the increased power of the Fascist cabinet (known as the Fascist Grand Council – *Gran Consiglio Fascista*) over Fascist provincial organizations, and the abolition of elections inside the Party.[60]

Conclusion

The above processes were part and parcel of the creation of a strongly conservative dictatorship, yet falling far short of the totalitarian model. As the next chapter demonstrates, the Fascist regime's reliance on the support of such institutions as the Catholic Church, the monarchy, the police and the army precluded the possibility of setting up a proper system of terror and of enforcing a thorough process of 'Fascistization' of society. Yet, the elimination of *squadrismo* remained incomplete. According to Lyttelton:

> Crimes of violence, in fact, diminished in number from 1926 on, reflecting a general stabilization and lessening of the acute tensions of the postwar period. But in rural districts and in some working class areas the squads remained as an instrument of intimidation directly or indirectly controlled by the employers: and in the smaller *fasci* some local leaders continued to use the squads as a prop for arbitrary personal power.[61]

These words indicate the continued presence, however subdued, of an extremist element within Fascism that would be unleashed once again during the final years of Mussolinian rule against the background of the military defeats of the Second World War and the setting up of the Italian Social Republic in Nazi-occupied Northern and Central Italy (discussed in Chapter 4).

Notes

1. For further reading on the events leading to the entry of Italy to the First World War, see Clark, *Modern Italy*, 180–5; Mack Smith, *Modern Italy*, 255–67; Christopher Seton-Watson, *Italy from Liberalism to Fascism, 1870–1925* (London: Methuen, 1967), 413–50.

2. The attitude of Italian troops is discussed in Giovanni Carpinelli, 'Guerra mondiale, prima' in Bongiovanni and Tranfaglia (eds), *Dizionario storico dell'Italia unita*, 406–22.
3. Data and analysis from Zamagni, *The Economic History of Italy*, chapter 7.
4. Population data from Mitchell, *European Historical Statistics*, A4.
5. Alice A. Kelikian, 'From Liberalism to Corporatism', 218–19. See also Bell, *Sesto San Giovanni*, 87.
6. Angela De Benedictis, 'Note su classe operaia e socialismo a Bologna nel primo dopoguerra', in Luciano Casali (ed.), *Movimento operaio e fascismo nell'Emilia Romagna, 1919–1923* (Rome: Editori Riuniti, 1973) 69–134(71–2).
7. Anthony L. Cardoza, *Agrarian Elites and Italian Fascism: The Province of Bologna, 1901–1926* (Princeton, NJ: Princeton University Press, 1982), 222–3.
8. For the living and working conditions on the home front, see Clark, *Modern Italy*, 192–3; Neufeld, *Italy: School for Awakening Countries*, 363; Zamagni, *The Economic History of Italy*, 214–17.
9. Dunnage, *The Italian Police and the Rise of Fascism*,77.
10. Bell, *Sesto San Giovanni*, 91–3. See also Cento Bull and Corner, *From Peasant to Entrepreneur*, 62–4, for a discussion of the role of peasant women in organizing strikes and demonstrations during the First World War.
11. Figures from Cento Bull and Corner, *From Peasant to Entrepreneur*, 60.
12. Figures taken from Clark, *Modern Italy*, 187–8; Carpinelli, 'Guerra mondiale, prima'. See also Mario Isnenghi, 'La grande guerra' in Mario Isnenghi (ed.), *I luoghi della memoria. Strutture ed eventi dell'Italia unita* (Bari: Laterza, 1997), 273–309, for a general account of the effects of war on the lives of conscripted Italians and the civilian population as a whole.
13. Mack Smith, *Modern Italy*, 291.
14. Clark, *Modern Italy*, 186–7.
15. Isnenghi, 'La grande guerra', 295–7.
16. De Grazia, *How Fascism Ruled Women*, 27–8.
17. For the state of the Italian economy during and after the First World War (and relevant figures), see Zamagni, *The Economic History of Italy*, chapter 7; Balcet, *L'economia italiana*, 29–34.
18. Horowitz, *The Italian Labor Movement*, 142; Bell, *Sesto San Giovanni*, 88.
19. Cardoza, *Agrarian Elites*, 230–4. The effect of changes in landownership on the form of the Italian household is discussed in Barbagli, *Sotto lo stesso tetto*, 108–10.
20. Frank M. Snowden, *The Fascist Revolution in Tuscany, 1919–1922* (Cambridge: Cambridge University Press, 1989), 108. See also 129–30.
21. For the gains of the rural and urban working-class movements (and relevant figures), see Clark, *Modern Italy*, 207–13; Horowitz, *The Italian Labor Movement*, 115–54; Philip Morgan, *Italian Fascism, 1919–1945* (Basingstoke: Macmillan, 1995), 23–8; Neufeld, *Italy: School for Awakening Countries*, 365–82.
22. Strike statistics from Horowitz, *The Italian Labor Movement*, 141; Neufeld, *Italy: School for Awakening Countries*, 363.
23. Snowden, 'From sharecropper to proletarian', 163; see also Morgan, *Italian Fascism*, 25.
24. Snowden, *Violence and Great Estates in the South of Italy*, 165.

25. Morgan, *Italian Fascism*, 24.
26. Cardoza, *Agrarian Elites*, 284.
27. Paul Corner, *Fascism in Ferrara, 1915–1925* (Oxford: Oxford University Press, 1975), 96.
28. Guido Crainz, *Padania. Il mondo dei braccianti dall'Ottocento alla fuga dalle campagne* (Rome: Donzelli, 1994), 157–82.
29. Neufeld, *Italy: School for Awakening Countries*, 374–5. For a discussion of problems of worker unity, see Kelikian, 'From Liberalism to Corporatism', 222–33; Bell, *Sesto San Giovanni*, 95–106.
30. For the factory occupations of September 1920, see Paolo Spriano, *The Occupation of the Factories* (London: Pluto Press, 1975); Gwyn Williams, *Proletarian Order: Antonio Gramsci, Factory Councils and the Origins of Italian Communism, 1911–1921* (London: Pluto Press, 1975); Bell, *Sesto San Giovanni*, chapter 6.
31. Bell, *Sesto San Giovanni*, 108–20.
32. Miller, *From Elite to Mass Politics*, 207.
33. Corner, *Fascism in Ferrara*, 83.
34. Discussed in Zamagni, *The Economic History of Italy*, 210–12, 238–40.
35. Tarozzi, 'Dal primo al secondo fascio di combattimento: note sulle origini del fascismo a Bologna (1919–1920)', in Casali (ed.), *Bologna 1920*, 93–114(96–9).
36. The status and attitude of professional employees is analysed in detail in Barbagli, *Educating for Unemployment*, 110–24.
37. Discussed in De Grazia, *How Fascism Ruled Women*, 170–2.
38. The attitude of Italians towards the 1919 peace settlements is discussed in Mack Smith, *Modern Italy*, 276–82.
39. For details on the Fiume adventure and the relationship between Mussolini and D'Annunzio, see John Whittam, *Fascist Italy* (Manchester: Manchester University Press, 1995), 25–8.
40. Adrian Lyttelton, *The Seizure of Power: Fascism in Italy, 1919–1929* (London: Weidenfeld & Nicolson, 1973), 53. The rise of Fascism is also discussed in Clark, *Modern Italy*, 213–21; Morgan, *Italian Fascism*, 34–59.
41. Clark, *Modern Italy*, 210.
42. Cardoza, *Agrarian Elites*, 316, 320.
43. The role of the police and judiciary in the rise of Fascism is discussed in detail in Dunnage, *The Italian Police*, chapter 6.
44. The origins and motivations of Fascist violence and its social acceptance are discussed in Adrian Lyttelton, 'Cause e caratteristiche della violenza fascista. Fattori costanti e fattori congiunturali' in Casali (ed.), *Bologna 1920*, 33–55. See also Cardoza, *Agrarian Elites*, 345.
45. Crainz, *Padania*, 180.
46. Morgan, *Italian Fascism*, 40. See also Snowden, *The Fascist Revolution*, 207.
47. Lyttelton, *The Seizure of Power*, 68–70.
48. Snowden, *Violence and Great Estates*, 180.
49. Jonathan Steinberg, 'Fascism in the Italian South: The Case of Calabria' in David Forgacs (ed.), *Rethinking Italian Fascism: Capitalism, Populism and Culture* (London: Lawrence and Wishart, 1986), 83–109(94). See also Marinella Chiodo, 'Il "fascismo delle origini" e le origini del fascismo in Calabria', *Bollettino dell'Istituto*

Calabrese per la Storia dell'Antifascismo e dell'Italia Contemporanea, 9, 1990, 14–20.

50. Crainz, *Padania*, 194–6. For the difficulties encountered by the Fascist movement in Romagna, see Pietro Alberghi, *Il Fascismo in Emilia Romagna. Dalle origini alla marcia su Roma* (Modena: Mucchi, 1989), 297–304, 475–6.
51. Molony, *The Emergence of Political Catholicism in Italy*, 98–9.
52. The March on Rome is discussed in detail in Lyttelton, *The Seizure of Power*, 87–90.
53. Morgan, *Italian Fascism*, 73; Duggan, *A Concise History of Italy*, 209.
54. Renzo De Felice, *Mussolini il fascista*. Vol. 1, *La conquista del potere, 1921–1925* (Turin: Einaudi, 1966), 444–5.
55. For Fascist unions, see Neufeld, *Italy: School for Awakening Countries*, 384–7; David D. Roberts, *The Syndicalist Tradition and Italian Fascism* (Manchester: Manchester University Press, 1979), 213–41; Cordoza, *Agrarian Elites*, 410–13; Morgan, *Italian Fascism*, 67–8.
56. Morgan, *Italian Fascism*, 88.
57. Zamagni, *The Economic History of Italy*, 217–18, 244–6.
58. Lyttelton, *The Seizure of Power*, 118–20; Morgan, *Italian Fascism*, 71–3.
59. For a detailed description of the laws forming the basis of the Fascist regime, see Doug Thompson, *State control in Fascist Italy. Culture and conformity, 1925–1943* (Manchester: Manchester University Press, 1991), 6–12.
60. Lyttelton, *The Seizure of Power*, 293–5.
61. Ibid., 287–8.

Chapter 3

The experience of Fascism, 1925–39

Introduction

This chapter considers the impact of the Fascist dictatorship on Italian society. The first part of the chapter analyses the quality of life of the Italians in the context of Fascist policies concerning the economy, welfare and education and the effects of the world economic depression. The second part of the chapter considers the means by which the Mussolinian dictatorship attempted to create a new Fascist order within Italian society. In the first instance this was to be achieved by means of repression and coercion. After the democratic system was disbanded, the regime needed to be vigilant against underground forms of resistance, preventing political activists from having contact with those sections of the population, particularly the working classes, most hostile towards it. The regime also made use of its dictatorial powers in an attempt to 'Fascistize' Italian society, organizing citizens' daily lives, whether at work, in school or during their free time. Paradoxically, the most radical Fascist leaders believed that as a result of this one day Italians would consent to Fascism of their own free will without the need for coercive forms of government. Yet, the effectiveness of the 'Fascistization' programme has to be questioned in view of the limited totalitarian character of the Mussolinian regime resulting from the compromises at the root of its creation. Indeed, much of the consent that was generated for Fascism was passive and lacking in ideological fervour, based as it was on the satisfaction of material need and largely conservative, at most authoritarian and nationalistic, political aspirations.

The quality of life of the Italians under Fascism

The Fascist economy

Fascist economic policies were distinguished by the totalitarian idea of 'permanent war' that was applied to them as part of Mussolini's quest to free Italy from foreign dominion. As John Whittam states: 'Like most dictators Mussolini believed more in will power than economic theories and sought to solve intractable problems concerning the currency or the grain supply by waging "battles".'[1] This idea was evident in the pursuit of policies which in the face of rising inflation and balance of trade and payments deficits aimed to achieve economic independence and self-sufficiency, most clearly exemplified by the 'battle for grain' and the 'battle for the lira' (by which the lira was re-valued at 90 to the pound sterling, also known as *Quota 90*). Yet, once such policies were stripped of the rhetoric and propaganda surrounding them, it becomes clear that Fascism continued to function within the Liberal economic framework. This partly reflected Mussolini's fear of alienating big business and the agrarians. As Martin Blinkhorn argues:

> The ground rules of what passed for fascist economic policies were laid by such dominant characteristics of the Italian economy, clearly visible even before the war, as the close bonds between state and heavy industry, the selective favouring by governments of some interests at the expense of others, and a weak consumer sector caused by the state's attempts to divert personal incomes, through taxation, into industrial investment.[2]

During the thirties protectionist and regulatory intervention by the Italian state in the wake of the world depression, characterized by the creation of state and para-state holding companies to rescue private firms from bankruptcy, was in many respects an example of continuation of Italian economic tradition. The Institute for Industrial Reconstruction (*Istituto per la Ricostruzione Industriale* – IRI), set up in 1933, increasingly took over from private banks the task of investing in industrial development. By the mid-thirties Italy had the highest percentage of state-owned enterprise outside the Soviet Union, though managers and former owners continued to run them as private companies. Yet, as Carl Levy notes, state intervention 'deepened the already existing promiscuous relationship between mostly family based industrial empires, state owned industries and capital and politicians'. Moreover, the considerable increase in state-owned industry did not improve or modernize Italian society, because, 'as a trading nation locked into a protectionist alliance and with depressed domestic demand caused by the poverty of its rural population, the resulting margins for real growth were tight indeed'.[3]

Post-depression economic recovery was boosted from the mid-thirties onwards as the state-financed programme moved towards a war economy in line with Mussolini's imperialist designs, representing a convergence of interests between the regime and industry and finance. Many old wartime industries including Ansaldo and the Genovese steel company, ILVA, once rescued by IRI, were reconverted to war production, while private companies like Fiat greatly benefited from military orders. As a result, the gross national product increased by 5.2 per cent per year between 1935 and 1937, with an increase of 3.7 per cent in agricultural production and of 7.5 per cent in industrial production.[4] The much publicized Fascist drive for autarchy, which intensified following the imposition of international sanctions against Italy for invading Ethiopia in 1935, was directly linked to Mussolini's war politics too. It resulted in new research in the use of synthetic materials and national raw materials (including aluminium, zinc, alcohol and brown coal), the founding of a national petroleum industry, and an increase in chemical and electrometallurgical production, centred round new industrial zones, such as Porto Marghera (Venice). Yet, Italy's natural resources were limited and autarchy experiments costly. This, together with an international economic situation unfavourable to the export industry, did little to relieve a wide balance of trade deficit.

Nevertheless, during the thirties Italy was firmly transformed into an industrial economy. In 1933 for the first time ever, industrial value added was higher than that of agriculture.[5] Many light industries also developed in technology and organization, partly to meet the need for self-sufficiency, and these developments were often outside the industrial triangle (particularly Veneto, Emilia, the Marches and Tuscany). They enabled old artisan traditions to survive and formed the basis of the post-war success of the clothes, leather and woodwork industries. But the North–South divide was further accentuated, in spite of increased state investment in the steel industry at Bagnoli (Naples) and in the shipbuilding and aeronautic industries of Taranto and Bari. Most Southern industry (accounting for only 18.4 per cent of industrial workers) remained in the form of small factories with low levels of mechanism and productivity.[6] If by 1938 industrial production was back at 1929 levels, this was achieved at the cost of a huge budget deficit, higher taxation and spiralling inflation. Moreover, a lack of raw materials and large companies with modern assembly lines prevented Italian industry from sustaining a total war, as was illustrated by military disaster during the Second World War. Vera Zamagni argues, however, that in the long term war production did have a positive effect on the Italian economy: 'Despite the nation's heavy military defeats, the war effort was to leave a significant mark on the Italian industrial framework. . . . This new industrial capacity was to furnish the basis for the reconstruction in the post-Second World War period'.[7]

Labour relations and the Corporate State

The rural and urban working classes paid for the high costs of protectionist policies and autarchy experiments with salary cuts and redundancies. With opposition political parties and trade unions outlawed and strikes and lockouts banned, there was little that they could do to defend themselves. Though Fascism officially catered for their well-being within the framework of the Corporate State, there was a great distance between propaganda and reality. Several foreign economists and political observers were fascinated by the introduction of a corporatist economic system based on the idea of the bonding together of different classes in the service of the nation, a system engulfing all forms of productive activity with political as well as economic functions that would one day, as Mussolini boasted, replace the Chamber of

Deputies, a system in which workers and employers were equally represented. Provision was made by the Ministry of Corporations, created in 1926, for the formation of bodies dealing with each area of production. However, such bodies were not full-fledged corporative organizations, since they did not bring workers and employers together, but placed them in separate associations. During the thirties the National Council of Corporations united workers and employers in corporations representing different production categories. However, the balance of power was clearly in favour of the employers.[8]

The economic and social principles of corporativism were outlined in the Fascist Labour Charter of 1927, which promoted reconciliation between the interests of employers and those of the workers through their subordination to the highest interests of production. In practice, however, the state rarely intervened over and above private initiative in the sphere of production. Where agreements were brokered by the Fascist Party or the Ministry of Corporations, employers' demands always took precedence over workers' needs, such that the first acts of the workers' organizations were the endorsement of wage reductions, so that production costs could be accommodated to the new value of the lira. In spite of propaganda claims about the role of the Corporate State in national economic planning, the government did not entrust the post-depression recovery programme to the corporations, with the main decisions being taken through IRI, which had no links with them. Parallel to the corporations there existed other bodies and consortia operating in all spheres of the economy outside their control and often with wider powers. In the end the Corporate State amounted to a new but inefficient bureaucracy, which duplicated operations carried out by the civil service and served above all to create safe jobs which would guarantee the regime a certain amount of consent.

Though the Labour Charter established the creation of labour courts for solving disputes, they were without effective worker representation. The failure of Fascist unions to represent and defend the working class is well documented by the anti-Fascist Radical, Gaetano Salvemini. Writing in exile in 1936, Salvemini noted that, whereas in Liberal Italy union officials could be dismissed by members, in Fascist Italy each union official was 'a miniature Mussolini within the limits of his jurisdiction' who could decide who was allowed to become a member and who had to be expelled as morally or politically undesirable. While no one was forced to join a union, every worker had to pay annual dues to it. Meetings of local and provincial organizations were called only when the government deemed them opportune and public demonstrations were considered unnecessary. While meetings held on premises remained legal, press representatives were not allowed to be present and debates were brought to the attention of the public through reports issued by the unions themselves. Salvemini continued:

Meetings and congresses are held chiefly for ceremonial purposes. A more or less important Fascist personage delivers a harangue exalting Mussolini and the regime; some secretary reads a report; occasionally there is the barest semblance of a discussion, but more usually not even that; and the acts of the secretary are approved by acclamation. Were anyone to be so bold as to ask an awkward question, he might expect a visit next morning from a militiaman, to reduce him to 'reason'; or he might be expelled from his union as 'undesirable from the national standpoint'.[9]

The Italian working classes were notably impoverished as a result of Fascist economic policies, given also the inability of the Fascist trade unions to defend their members. Although during some periods prices fell as a result of deflationary policies, between 1928 and 1936 the value of real wages dropped by over 7 per cent. In 1927 blue-collar workers' wages were reduced by between 10 per cent and 20 per cent with the justification that revaluation of the lira would provoke a fall in the cost of living. In practice reductions were often in excess of the official percentage. The main effect of *Quota 90* on the livelihood of industrial workers was an increase in levels of unemployment as many companies virtually collapsed, since goods were practically unexportable. The world depression led to further official wage cuts in 1930 and 1934 that were accompanied by sackings. Industrial unemployment between 1931 and 1935 was officially estimated at between 11.4 per cent and 15.5 per cent of the work force, but may have been as high as 35–40 per cent.[10]

Overt dismissals were avoided in some companies through exploitation of the possibilities of shift work or a shortened working week. In 1934 a 40-hour week was introduced in order to reduce unemployment, though this meant a further drop in earnings for workers, which in turn meant that despite a lower cost of living during the mid-thirties the buying power of monthly wages remained practically the same. Even when there were economic up-turns redundant workers often found themselves substituted by younger ones. Employers found other ways of reducing labour costs at the expense of workers' livelihood. It was not unusual for them to sack workers in order to rehire them at the minimum hourly wage, if they had risen above it, or at a lower grade. The effects of Fascist economic policies and the depression on a single industrial community are illustrated by the case of the Brescia province, where 67 firms went bankrupt following revaluation. Consequently, the number of unemployed metal workers increased almost seven times, while 33,713 textile workers were sacked. By December 1932 49 per cent of industrial workers were unemployed.[11] White-collar workers to some extent benefited from Fascist economic policies, though they too faced salary cuts in 1930 and 1934. They recuperated the consumer power lost during the First World War and the *Biennio Rosso*, while sections of the middle and lower middle classes on fixed incomes, such as public employees and teachers, initially benefited from the deflationary effects of *Quota 90*, which restored their traditional status over blue-collar workers. In 1935, for example, a specialized worker's wage of between 300 and 400 lire per month compared unfavourably with 800 lire taken home by a well-qualified middle-class employee.[12]

Fascist agricultural policy and the plight of the peasantry

Contrary to propaganda claims, Fascism did little to modernize Italian agriculture and bring wealth to the countryside. Fascist agricultural policies were designed to meet the difficulties that the Italian economy faced from 1925 without sacrificing the industrial sector. The agrarian employer class clearly benefited from the banning of strikes and state-imposed wage controls, such that labour costs were drastically reduced. Though Fascist ruralist rhetoric hailed the peasantry as the 'pillar of the nation', and exalted their moral and physical health for demographic ends, the main purpose of such propaganda was to hide the peasant's worsened lot as a result of the need to shift the nation's economic burdens towards agriculture, without adversely affecting the agrarian élite. State intervention in the social structure of the Italian peasantry did not help agriculture in the long term either. While Fascism favoured the defence of rural tradition through the absorption of the proletariat into growing middle classes of sharecroppers, leaseholders and owners, this was in direct contradiction to processes of increased productivity, which depended on capitalist-based large farms employing day labourers.

In practice, however, adverse economic conditions prevented the development of a dynamic small landowning class. In his detailed analysis of Fascist agrarian policy, Paul Corner writes:

> Relatively little land changed hands as a result of the fascist land programme. Far from that division of holdings which the first fascist agrarian programme had encouraged many people to expect, the early years of fascism saw a gradual strengthening of the intermediate categories in agriculture – sharecroppers and small leaseholders – and a fresh increase in the number of fixed contract labourers and other dependent labourers.[13]

These words are confirmed by statistical information. Under Fascism there was a notable reduction in the use of day labourers that by 1936 made up 27.2 per cent of those employed in agriculture, compared with 43.8 per cent in 1921. But the fall in the number of day labourers was compensated not by an increase in the number of smallholders but by an increase in the number of tenant farmers (from 7 per cent to 18 per cent of those employed in agriculture) and sharecroppers (from 15 per cent to 19 per cent).[14] As Corner shows, many day labourers became fixed-contract labourers (*obbligati*), while sharecropping contracts were frequently down-graded, so that the agrarians could make up for a fall in prices and investment from 1925 and survive the

77

world depression more or less unscathed. Agricultural workers lost any possibility of self-defence in the face of more disadvantageous working conditions and the abolition of the Socialist leagues.

Agricultural protectionism introduced in 1925, under the name of the 'Battle for Wheat', which aimed at making Italy self-sufficient in the production of foods, may like *Quota 90* have carried a certain propaganda value for the regime but was of limited help to agriculture or internal consumption. It had the effect of placing undue importance upon wheat production, to such an extent that other more specialist areas of agriculture, such as fruit, wine and olives, were disadvantaged, with particularly disastrous effects for small peasant farmers. If the battle was a success in terms of quantity (with annual production rising from around 58 million quintals in 1926 to 63 million in 1931 and over 80 million by 1938), Italian wheat was far more expensive than American-produced wheat, which was imported in much reduced amounts, and consequently more Italians starved. Annual grain consumption per inhabitant dropped from an average of 180 kg during the twenties to a low of 138 kg in 1934 rising back up to only 146 kg by 1940.[15] Similar to the effects of the introduction of the grain tariff towards the end of the nineteenth century, as a result of the 'Battle for Wheat' the gap between capitalist forms of agriculture in the North and non-capitalist forms in the South widened. The main beneficiaries were the commercial farmers of the Po Valley who were increasingly able to employ machines instead of men and switch from cash crops to the protected grain market. However, much land was turned over to the production of wheat, even though it was unsuitable and thus marginally productive, because of state subsidies and the guaranteed market. The dairy and small beef industry suffered greatly as a result of this.

Another of the regime's policies from which agriculture was supposed to benefit was the much-vaunted reclamation of land. Though ruralist propaganda on state intervention in agriculture claimed that hundreds of thousands of rural homes had been restructured or replaced and that modern facilities including electricity and tarred roads had been brought to the countryside, in reality intervention of this kind was limited. Legislation of 1924, which provided for the drying of land and the construction of waterways, irrigation systems, roads and drinking water, was a continuation of post-war liberal policies of reform in which absentee owners had been threatened with expropriation if they were not compliant with the modernization programme. Though the reclamation went ahead under Fascism, its most innovative aspects, which would have transformed farming in the South particularly, were more or less abandoned, and any threats of expropriation were dropped. Statistics of 1946 suggest that, while 58 per cent of basic reclamation work was completed, only 32 per cent of planned irrigation systems were finished. Only 16 per cent of improved lands had been genuinely transformed according to the original proposals. The main reason for this failure, especially in the South, was that the landowners themselves were entrusted with selecting land for reclamation and overseeing the process. Though land reclamation was mostly restricted to the North, a significant improvement was made to the area of the Pontine Marshes south of Rome and limited areas of the South. Increases in agricultural yield were minimal, but malaria levels were substantially reduced (as described below).[16]

Throughout Italy, however, rural poverty was compounded by the disastrous effects of the world depression, wage cuts of 20–40 per cent during the early thirties, and, during the second half of the decade, autarchy policies in which industry was favoured at the cost of agriculture. Consequently many Italians moved away from the countryside. After the First World War emigration had started again but this was reduced from the early thirties as a result of immigration restrictions imposed by the United States in 1921 and 1924 and the intolerance of the Fascist government. The number of Italians leaving the country during the thirties dropped to around 702,000, compared with over one million (mainly to other European countries and south America) between 1926 and 1930 alone. However, within Italian territory there was a notable increase in migratory movement as individuals and families moved from the rural parts of the Southern, Central and North-Eastern regions of Italy mainly to the industrial triangle and to Rome with its expanding tertiary and public sectors. The population census of 1931 showed that 7.4 out of every 1,000 Italians lived in a different region from that in which they were born (compared with 4.9 in 1921, 4.8 in 1911 and 4.2 in 1901). The regime partly attempted to prevent a rural exodus through programmes of colonization of newly reclaimed land and Italian territories in Africa. Though it passed a series of laws to prevent internal migration from the country to the cities, backed up by ruralist propaganda, which exalted the values of peasant life, in practice the authorities did little to prevent it. It is likely, however, that because of restrictions on migration, many of those who did reach the cities were without formal work contracts or only semi-employed and, therefore, badly paid. The migration northwards of Southerners during the Fascist period represented an anticipation of the more dynamic phenomenon of the fifties and sixties. It is evident that unemployed Turin workers blamed their plight on the influx of immigrant Southern workers, which several companies, including Fiat, deliberately employed.[17]

In spite of the overall disastrous effects of Fascism on the livelihood of the peasantry, in some rural areas of Italy there was a move, though limited, towards family-based entrepreneurial activities foreshadowing the development of the 'Third Italy' after the Second World War. The phenomenon, which was particularly notable in the area north of Milan and in Tuscany, resulted from a situation in which it was no longer possible to live off the land, yet migration to the cities was no longer an automatic solution. As the research of Anna Cento Bull and Paul Corner demonstrates, the success of this experiment in the former area bears testimony to the resourcefulness of the pluriactive peasant family. Such initiatives were taken by younger men who, having worked in industry in order to supplement the family income but lost their jobs on account of the economic crisis, had gained enough experience in industry to start small independent activities. By contrast, the lesser success of new small firms in Tuscany lay in the fact that the region had seen little factory experience or pluriactivity among the peasantry before the crisis under Fascism.[18]

Consumer power, welfare and housing

As a consequence of both Fascist economic policies and the more general effects of the world depression, the overall standard of living of Italians fell during the inter-war years. This was particularly evident in a decrease in food consumption, notably meat, bread, fresh fruit and coffee, with the result that a large number of Italians, especially those from the poorer classes, were seriously undernourished. The regime attempted to overcome consumption difficulties through an enlargement of the welfare state. In fulfilment of promises made during the First World War, the Liberal government had made state pension and unemployment insurance compulsory in 1919. While during the first years of the Fascist regime many of the Liberal state's welfare functions had been given back to private insurance firms, during the thirties the Fascist state created a system of social insurance and health funds. In order to compensate for a loss in earnings created by the establishment of the 40-hour working week, family allowances were also introduced in 1934, first for industrial workers, then middle-class employees and agricultural workers, with extra allowances for the families of men conscripted for the regime's military campaigns in 1936 and 1940. As part of the regime's demographic campaign (described below) and fight against child mortality, the National Agency for Maternity and Infancy (*Opera Nazionale per la Maternità e l'Infanzia* – ONMI), founded in 1925, supplied educative and health support to children.[19]

The effectiveness of the regime's welfare initiatives is questionable. Moreover, the specifically Fascist value of such initiatives was undermined by the fact that similar measures were being introduced in democratic European countries. As Vannutelli argues:

> On the whole, although social legislation was exceptionally broad during that period, the practical and financial benefits were much more modest. Contrary to the exaggerated claims of those who argued that the regime was ahead of everyone else, its achievements in the field of social insurance were considerably behind those in other countries. . . . But most important, what was missing was the concept (already accepted elsewhere) of establishing a comprehensive system of social insurance.[20]

There were many flaws in what in reality was a partial welfare state. Management of welfare funding was uneven as it was devolved to separate bodies according to occupational categories. It was of little effect outside urban areas and, perhaps most significantly, it was administered by Fascist Party officials, which meant that in practice it was discriminatory. In terms of hospital provision, treatment was readily available to wealthy private patients, while the provision of a decent service for those insured against illness and disease through the Fascist trade unions was far from guaranteed, especially in the South. By 1936 the number of hospital beds per 1,000 inhabitants varied from 6.4 in Liguria to only 0.7 in Calabria. Worse still there was a total absence of hospital structures in 5,000 out of 7,000 municipalities. In terms of maternity provision, Lesley Caldwell notes how, in spite of the institution of ONMI, by 1927 only 20 paediatric and obstetric clinics had been set up in individual municipalities, while a quarter of the villages in the South did not have a qualified midwife. This situation improved little before the Second World War.[21]

Regarding the prevention of disease, some improvement was made in the fight against such social illnesses as tuberculosis (with the institution of compulsory tuberculosis insurance) and malaria. One of Fascism's greatest achievements in the war against malaria was the reclamation project of the Pontine Marshes and the Agro Romano, yet, as Snowden argues: 'The resources administered under the terms of the Mussolini Law [against malaria] were not devoted to the South, where the suffering from malaria was greatest. Attention was focused instead on those zones where the economic rewards and political dividends to be won were highest.'[22] Illnesses such as bronchitis, consumption and typhoid remained common. Poor living and working conditions undoubtedly accounted for many illnesses. Levels of hygiene in habitations remained low in both urban and rural areas. A census of provincial capitals of 1931 estimated that the great majority of Italian homes did not have bathrooms. Yet, there is little to suggest that the demolition of whole working-class urban districts to make way for new monumental city buildings led to better living conditions, in spite of the regime's continual demographically motivated propaganda on questions of health and hygiene. Workers were often rehoused in poorly constructed new apartment blocks on the edge of the cities. Plans for new housing for the working classes were often inhibited or distorted through corruption. De Grazia notes that: 'Not infrequently, subsidized dwellings, embellished with balconies, marble foyers, and other refinements, would end up housing well-off state and party functionaries rather than the "popular classes" for whom they were supposedly destined.'[23]

The much-proclaimed production of mass consumer goods and modernization of the national infrastructures under the Fascists were of limited benefit to most Italians because of serious spending difficulties. Modern household appliances that were introduced on the market during the inter-war years, such as cooking stoves and water-heating systems, were usually unaffordable even to middle-class Italians. New electrical appliances, even when they could be afforded, were expensive to run because of high electricity costs. Cars had yet to become a mass commodity, in spite of the creation in 1932 of the first peoples' car, the Fiat *Balilla*. During the military campaign in Ethiopia (1935– 36) the number in circulation went down because of rising petrol costs. The Fascist period also saw the rapid electrification of the railways and the build- ing of new stations and lines, the most important of which was the *direttissima* between Florence and Bologna, which reduced the journey from five to one- and-a-half hours. Yet, train travel, even on a commuter basis, remained a luxury for the majority of Italians, most of whom reached work on foot or by bicycle.[24]

While Fascist welfare and consumer policies brought limited relief to the poorest classes, it is likely that members of the urban middle classes bene- fited to some extent and that this partly accounted for their consensus for the regime. They also enjoyed the modest consumer benefits (in the form of discounts on household goods and cheap theatre tickets) which membership of 'after-work' organizations (described below) brought. Though they were far from well off, many of them tolerated limited consumer power because they were aware of their privileged position with regard to the lower classes. Moreover, they accepted economic difficulties as inevitable in the aftermath of an international economic crisis and the sacrifices required for imperial expansion, which they welcomed. In this sense, they may have reacted posi- tively to the regime's recommendations of greater frugality, as was evident in company magazines advising their employees to limit meat consumption, to eat less pasta and more rice, of which there was plenty, and persuading them that a good housewife knew how to save on food.

Fascist policies on education and work

Under Fascism the historical imbalance between the number of profession- ally qualified citizens and the demand for labour remained, in spite of early attempts to correct it. Marzio Barbagli argues that the Gentile education reform of 1923, named after the Minister of Public Instruction in the first Mussolini government, beyond paving the way for total subordination in future Italian citizens, 'was *also* a reactionary response to the existing imbal- ance between school and labor market (which was manifested above all in a growing overproduction of intellectual labor) and to the social and polit- ical tensions that this imbalance produced'.[25] Gentile introduced a much more rigorous system of selection, creating two dead-end lower secondary schools, the *scuola complementare* and the *liceo femminile* for girls, and limiting access to university faculties from technical schools. Subsequently, however, the regime abandoned many of Gentile's reforms. This was partly because they excluded large numbers of children from political indoctrination obtained through education and because of pressure from middle-class parents. In 1929 the *scuola complementare*, which had practically been deserted, was abolished. The effects of this change in policy were clearly evident in the dramatic increase between 1930 and 1939 in the number of secondary school pupils (from 325,000 to 860,000) and university students (from 46,262 to 85,555).[26] But extension of the period of education did little to guarantee better chances of good jobs at the end. It rather reflected the need to put off the prospect of unemployment for as long as possible.

Female education and employment was an area in which there was a clash between the regime's need for consent and its desire to relegate women to the domestic sphere so as to safeguard male employment and its demographic requirements.[27] Though the Gentile reform initially attempted to reduce women's possibilities for professionalization, the later abolition of the *liceo femminile* allowed female enrolment in secondary education to increase from 100,000 (1930) to 350,000 (1940). The number of females entering university increased from 13 per cent of the overall student population during the twenties to 21 per cent in 1940, with women receiving nearly a quarter of all higher degrees awarded by that date. However, greater access to education did not generally lead to better professional opportunities for women. From 1923, for example, they could no longer be heads of middle schools or teach history, philosophy or economics in grammar schools or technical schools, demonstrating the regime's cultural bias against them.

The prolongation of female education was strongly motivated by the serious employment difficulties that women faced during the thirties. In 1938, for example, nearly half of Italy's mostly female primary school teachers were without work. Any legislative measures to improve female working conditions masked the regime's intention to prioritize male employment. A law passed in 1934 claiming to protect working mothers, for example, had the intentional effect of discouraging the offer of work to women in general because it introduced maternity benefit, the extension of the maternity leave period and the requirement that factories employing over 50 women should provide breast-feeding rooms. Yet, even when viewed from the point of view of the regime's demographic campaign, there were contradictions in the legislation. Female labour was restricted in some areas of arduous and dangerous work for protection of their reproductive tasks, yet this was ignored in other areas, such as agricultural and domestic work, where women were without legislative protection and often subjected to high levels of exploitation. Moreover, the minimum age at which girls could enter work was actually lowered from 14 to 12. Other legislation directly attacked female employment. From 1933 a 10 per cent ceiling was placed on women's jobs in state administration and this was extended to private firms in 1938.

The influence of Fascist education policies on literacy levels is questionable. Though the regime declared that the problem of illiteracy had been resolved, the census of 1931 (the only census of the Fascist period), while bringing into evidence the continued increase in literacy everywhere, revealed a continued failure to bridge the North–South divide. While, for example, the provinces of the North-West showed minor percentages of illiteracy (3–7 per cent), and the North-East and Centre had clearly made notable gains since the 1911 census (in the Florentine province, for example, illiteracy levels had dropped from 35 per cent to 16 per cent), this compared very unfavourably with Southern provinces like Reggio Calabria which maintained an illiteracy level of 50 per cent (though this had dropped from 71 per cent in 1911). The first census to be carried out after the Second World War (1951) also demonstrated that the North–South divide had not been sufficiently reduced. However, the literacy gap between males and females, which had been removed in the North during the late Liberal period, also disappeared from Central Italy.[28]

Repression and consensus-building: the 'Fascistization' of the Italians

A regime of terror?

If the first part of this chapter mainly focused on the effect of Fascist policies on the quality of life of the Italians, the second part considers the broader psychological effects of a regime intent on not only severely restricting personal liberties but in the long run enforcing Fascism as a concept of life. In terms of the extent of terror (if one can talk of such) that the Fascist regime exercised, it is agreed that levels characteristic of other dictatorships were never reached. Yet, the levels of repression and coercion characterizing Italian Fascism should not be underestimated either. It is widely accepted that, while the Nazi, Francoist and Soviet regimes aimed to root out potential opposition by arresting whole sections and categories of society, the Fascist regime was more concerned to prevent the open manifestation of political dissent and even accepted that it would take time for sections of society to 'come round' to Fascist ideology. A truly totalitarian dictatorship based on Party rule never developed in Italy, making it more difficult to apply a system of terror, since Mussolini relied too heavily on the consent of such conservative institutions as the Church and the monarchy, and groups of 'uncommitted sympathizers', including the industrial and property-owning classes. The police, the army and the judiciary did not undergo significant 'Fascistization' in terms of training or personnel. In spite of this continuity with the Liberal state (which, moreover, had on frequent occasions demonstrated an authoritarian and anti-popular character), powers of repression and coercion were multiplied under Fascism.

In the context of the prohibition of strikes and demonstrations and the abolition of non-Fascist political parties and unions, the police were able to penetrate the lives of individual Italians as never before, with the result that forms of repression characteristic of the Liberal state involving violent confrontation in the streets disappeared to a great extent. The Interior Ministry police were given particular responsibilities in fighting underground anti-Fascist movements and keeping an eye over society in general. This involved a greater concentration on informative forms of policing, with the use of spies and the setting up of myriad secret police organizations, of which the most prominent was OVRA (*Opera Vigilanza e Repressione Antifascismo*). They were assisted by the Fascist Party and Militia. The founding in 1926 of special tribunals (*Tribunali Speciali per la Difesa dello Stato*) composed of Fascist consuls and *squadristi* took judgement of the most serious crimes against the state out of the hands of ordinary judges, while in all trials the right to a proper defence was removed.[29]

Consequently, there was a significant increase in the number of Italians who faced persecution and often brutal treatment at the hands of those running the regime. It is notable that, between 1926 and 1943, 110,000 Italians were registered as subversive, whereas between 1896 and 1926 the figure amounted to a mere 40,000. Similarly, the figures of 160,000 sentences to *ammonizione* or special police surveillance and 17,000 to *confino* (the Fascist term for internal exile) indicated an increase in levels of persecution, if one is to consider that during the politically turbulent 1890s the number of individuals sentenced each year to *ammonizione* and internal exile amounted to a few thousand at most.[30] Anti-Fascist militants were not the only victims of Fascist persecution. A far wider range of citizens was affected, as the definition of anti-Fascist or anti-national practices was broadened to include abortion and homosexuality, for example. The fact that the number of 'crimes against public morality' increased by over a third during the Fascist period is an indication of the far broader interpretation that the regime allowed in defining this kind of crime. Existential forms of dissent not directly linked to political anti-Fascism, such as an open expression of dissatisfaction with Mussolini on account of hunger or wage cuts, could also be punished, though amnesties and acts of clemency on the part of Mussolini were often granted to the benefit of the most 'harmless' of the regime's enemies. Yet, the above statistics are far lower than the two million or so political opponents sent to Nazi concentration camps.

One should not underestimate the psychological effects of the Fascist structures of control and prevention. Individuals started to fear that their own work companions or neighbours might be spies, as the regime blackmailed many of its victims into becoming informers and made use of the collaboration of union, youth and after-work associations, as well as paid informers and ordinary members of the public, to pick up incidents of dissent. Police action against underground anti-Fascist organizations during the late twenties and early thirties resulted in mass arrests, forcing the leadership of the Communists, Socialists and a new Liberal-Socialist group, *Giustizia e Libertà* (Justice and Liberty), to flee the country and set up bases in France, from where they co-ordinated clandestine operations in Italy. Such operations were difficult not only on account of the watchfulness of the Fascist police but also because of the social isolation and consequent Utopian rigidity in which professional anti-Fascist militants lived, enhancing their mistrust of grass-roots opponents of the regime and their lack of understanding of the everyday reality of Fascist society. The distance between the underground Communist Party, for example, and the working class is illustrated by the former's failure to turn the not insignificant number of working-class spontaneous strikes and protests during the early thirties into political forms of organized resistance.[31]

Mass resistance to Fascism was difficult to organize on account of its popularity among the middle classes. According to Corner, beyond the effects of the banning of union organizations and opposition parties, working-class unity itself was undermined as a result of the economic crisis of the thirties, which allowed Fascism to exploit old divisions. Long-existing tensions between established urban workers, commuters from the hinterlands and migrants from other parts of Italy were accentuated in an atmosphere in which there was strong competition for jobs. As a result of this, those workers in employment showed little support to the unemployed, as was evident on the occasion of the massive demonstration by the jobless of Turin in 1930. The Italian working class could not relate to previous experiences upon which to model a potential rebellion against the Fascist oppressors. It looked back over a history of struggles against unequal forces in which there had been more defeats than victories. Even the significant achievements of the *Biennio Rosso* had been short-lived. Consideration also needs to be given to the development, during the Fascist period, of a new generation of workers. While the extent to which they identified with the regime is questionable, they had not personally experienced the political struggles of their fathers.[32]

Nevertheless, recent studies suggest that, after initial successes, the Fascist police became increasingly lax in the repression of anti-Fascism. This was partly a result of a reduction in state funding which limited policing resources to the extent that on several occasions during the early thirties Fascist squads had to be employed to break up illegal public demonstrations. Donald Bell argues that the Italian working class was able to survive on the basis of its cultural traditions, even when its organizations were banned. Referring to his analysis of Sesto San Giovanni, he states that the worker spirit was not completely broken, as was demonstrated by the frequent appearance of clandestine publications and anti-Fascist groups. While clandestine groups of former militants were infiltrated by the police and broken up in 1930–31, more secretive groups followed, formed by younger workers with no past record and not known to the police. Owing to levels of police surveillance inside factories, anti-Fascist networks formed elsewhere. Local bars, *trattorie*, even the soccer club, which edited its underground news sheet and collected funds for *Soccorso Rosso* (a Communist network which provided money, food and clothing for political prisoners and their families), became the main places of contact.[33] The family, which individuals had previously abandoned in order to go into politics, also became the basis of anti-Fascist activities as networks often formed around friendship and kinship relations. According to Giovanni De Luna, the significant role played by women in this clearly responded to practical necessities. They became the main protagonists of *Soccorso Rosso*. While this organization is an illustration of the Communist Party's relegation of women to traditional roles of assistance, such policies were motivated by the reality of Fascist society, in which women continued to be confined to the domestic sphere. Communist women found themselves carrying out their work at home, rather than in the streets and squares, because it functioned as a cover-up for their clandestine activities.[34]

Beyond clandestine militant action, ritualistic forms of action harking back to times of greater political freedom were not infrequent. These included observance of the May Day workers' festival, which the regime had abolished on account of its strong left-wing connotations, and 'Red funerals' in which religious music was refused, coffins were adorned with red carnations and 'subversive' speeches were made. Luisa Passerini, in her study of the Turin working class, examines a wider range of less dangerous anti-Fascist rituals, which included parodies of Fascist expressions and songs, the writing of slogans on street walls and in factory toilets and the symbolic use of the colour red in clothing. Illustrating the limited oppositional engagement of their authors, however, Passerini notes that the ambivalence of such acts lay in the fact that they 'function, at one and the same time, as acts of resistance to Fascism, and as compensations for the fact that people had pragmatically accepted the regime'.[35] Although many of the above activities were frequently disapproved of by militant anti-Fascists, in that they were seen as counter-productive to the underground cause, they were undoubtedly effective in helping to preserve a subversive culture that would be transformed into rebellion during the final years of the dictatorship.

Beyond the repression of anti-Fascism, the police also assisted the regime in taking measures to shut off Italians from information that might bring into doubt the moral and social regeneration Fascism was supposedly bringing to Italy. Under the responsibility of Mussolini's press office, which was expanded into the Ministry of Press and Propaganda in 1935, renamed Ministry of Popular Culture (*Minculpop*) in 1937, this involved the introduction of stricter forms of censorship of newspapers, radio broadcasts, films, theatrical performances and foreign publications. Newspaper editors, for example, were forced to avoid publication not only of anti-Fascist opinion but also of news concerning crimes, suicides and public disasters as well as foreign affairs. According to Edward Tannenbaum, newspapers were mostly concerned with such superficial matters as public ceremonies, the movements of Mussolini and the royal family, and the regime's policies: 'From their own press most Italians must have had the impression of living in a world of day-to-day affairs in which nobody was concerned with power struggles, economic hardship or social grievances.'[36]

Alongside the enforcement of censorship, the Fascist regime also experimented with modern media forms for propaganda purposes, especially radio. As Philip Morgan notes:

> Radio was clearly a more flexible way than a relatively low circulation press to convey the regime's presence and message to rural populations traditionally indifferent to government and its agencies and isolated by illiteracy and distance. Radio quite literally spanned these social and geographical distances, and was capable of delivering a single, uniform message to many different places simultaneously.[37]

Radio broadcasts came under increasing political control from 1927 with the setting up of the EIAR (*Ente Italiano Audizioni Radiofoniche*) agency. This allowed greater ideological penetration of society as radio increasingly came into homes, the after-work (*dopolavoro*) clubs (described below) and the school classroom. Programmes placed emphasis on Fascist values and the most important policies of the regime, such as the campaign for more births, the achievement of economic self-sufficiency and the creation of an Italian empire. Mussolini's speeches, as on the occasion of the announcement of the military campaign in Ethiopia on 2 October 1935, were also broadcast, while such politically and nationally significant events as the signing of the Lateran Pacts with the Vatican in 1929 were widely reported on. During the thirties political programmes included lessons on the History of Fascism and daily political comment on news items. Sports programmes were also popular, allowing the regime to exploit the achievements of professional athletes to build up a strong sense of patriotism. Though the medium of film did not undergo the same extent of 'Fascistization' as the press and radio, the government-controlled film agency, LUCE (*Istituto Nazionale dell'Unione Cinematografica Educativa*), also produced propaganda newsreels and documentaries to be shown during cinema performances.

As the following sections demonstrate, the approach taken in enforcing Fascist ideology varied according to the age group targeted. Indeed, it is difficult to talk of a true process of 'Fascistization' in many cases. Many Party activists hoped that, as a result of the ideological training of the younger generations, a Fascist social and moral order, to which individuals would freely consent, would one day exist. With regard to the adult masses, however, the regime attempted above all to offer, through welfare and the organization of leisure, some relief and distraction from the hardships brought by its own policies and the economic depression, while demonstrating through propaganda and less ideologized forms of political instruction the benefits that Fascism had brought. This approach was motivated by both the limits posed by non-Fascist institutions upon whom the regime depended for survival – indicating how far short of the totalitarian model Italian Fascism fell – and an awareness that certain forms of political indoctrination would be difficult to apply to a generation that had known other political orders. Yet, the ability of the regime to generate genuine support and participation at whatever level must be questioned. As Morgan argues: 'the regime's organizations and initiatives, which aimed at generating support and "consent", operated in the context of a repressive atmosphere that gave a sense of compulsion to any involvement in activities sponsored by the regime'.[38]

The PNF

The major institution entrusted with the 'Fascistization' of Italian society was the Fascist Party, yet within the framework of a dictatorship founded on the subordination of the Party to the state its powers were limited. Reflecting the earlier influences of revolutionary factions, during the twenties the Party retained an élitist character. However, its autonomy from the government was gradually removed, reducing the power of the provincial bosses, who were forced to accept the supreme authority of the prefects. At the end of 1926 the Fascist Grand Council decided that new Party members would only be recruited through the Fascist youth organizations. But reduction in membership during the late twenties and early thirties reflected more a process of bringing the Party under state control than the upholding of élitist principles. Between 1926 and 1931, for example, over 200,000 members were purged under the leadership of August Turati (1926–30), then Giovanni Giuriati (1930–31), mainly for rebelling against the 'normalization' process (the abandonment of radicalism and violence) that Fascism was undergoing. Consequently, membership figures actually went down from 900,000 at the end of 1926 to 800,000 at the end of 1931. However, during the thirties, under the leadership of Achille Starace, the PNF was transformed into a mass organization involving large numbers of Italians in activities sponsored by the regime. By the end of 1939 Party membership exceeded two and a half million, but the figures are much more impressive if one considers the membership of PNF-affiliated organizations. Eight million belonged to youth organizations, 4 million to afterwork clubs and 2 million to women's groups.[39]

There is some debate at present as to the extent to which the PNF represented a truly totalitarian and revolutionary force. This centres particularly around the work of the revisionist historian, Emilio Gentile, who has argued that the Fascist Party represented the first experience for the Italian people of mass political organization conducted through rigid, centralized, totalitarian principles with the aim of forming a collective, national identity. As the capillary Party network reached the remotest villages, a new political élite changed the local balance of power, even in the South, as their organizations took over every aspect of people's daily existence. What is far less certain is the extent to which the PNF organs 'Fascistized' local society. Gentile himself implies this when quoting the words of the Federal Secretary of Nuoro, Sardinia, who argued that the local population was disciplined and patriotic, but saw the PNF as a party of government, not a revolutionary movement. The official went on to argue that: 'They appreciate and love Fascism for what it is doing, but do not have the ardour necessary for removing the obstacles of the old world in order to construct and mould a new life with an ideal sense of restlessness as the Duce [leader] would like'.[40]

In spite of impressive membership figures, Party leaders asked themselves how many true Fascists were among them. While there is little doubt about the totalitarian intentions of some Party exponents, in practice there is more evidence in favour of the argument that through excessive bureaucratization and compulsorization of membership the Party lost all revolutionary character. During the thirties the Party effectively became a major tertiary sector employer through its taking over of many hitherto semi-autonomous groups. While a larger party allowed totalitarian control over more of the population, the voluntary character of membership was eroded by the fact that decrees passed in 1932 and 1933 made possession of the Party card indispensable for appointments and promotions within public employment and the professions. Thompson argues that as a result of this a decisive middle-class conservative stamp was imposed on the PNF:

> From the early 1930s on, personnel from the middle and upper strata of industry, commerce and agriculture, as well as from the lower strata of the urban and rural middle classes, came gradually to dominate the Party and its tutelary organisations in most parts of the country. In effect, this large-scale 'migration' of the old dominant classes under the umbrella of the Fascist State reaffirmed the class nature of Italian society which had been one of its constant features since Unification.[41]

Within Party organizations ideological demonstrations increasingly became merely a necessary formality. Though public employees and workers belonging to the Party had to wear its badge at work and uniforms on Saturday mornings, the imperative of the Roman salute was mostly ignored, as is evidenced in government circulars complaining of this fact, as was Starace's order that each administrative letter had to conclude with the words *Evviva il Duce!* ('Long live the *Duce!*').[42] The above shortfalls are closely linked to the wider problem facing Fascists of how to ensure the loyalties of a non-Fascist state bureaucracy. The regime was increasingly aware of the fact that those sections of society on which it relied most for implementation of its ideological programmes were paradoxically reluctant to undergo a full process of 'Fascistization' themselves. There is little doubt too that the new Fascist institutions risked becoming instruments of local patronage and rivalries. In the South the presence in each town of the local Party section as well as the government-appointed mayor (*podestà*) and the Party Militia made the Liberal-turned-Fascist ruling élite more accountable to the central government. However, such institutions frequently fell into the hands of rival family-based cliques or social groups, underlining the continuing divisions within Fascism. In the village of Bisignano in Calabria, during the mid-thirties, for example, a growing middle class of professionals and school teachers in the Fascist Party came into conflict with the old agrarian élite represented by the *podestà* over control of the local institutions. Illustrating the power of con-servative forces within Fascism, the authorities intervened in defence of the latter.[43]

Education and the organization of youth

If the regime accepted difficulties in bringing over large sectors of the adult population to Fascist ideas, its education policies reflected long-term inten-tions of creating individuals who would consent to Fascism without the need for coercion. While the education reform of Giovanni Gentile of 1923 is seen as putting young Italians in a position of complete subordination to the regime in its reinforcement of the authoritarian and élitist character of the Italian school, closer observation suggests that it did not completely fulfil the ideological requirements of Fascism. Thompson argues that:

> the reform also aimed at instilling in individuals not only a sense of freedom to be themselves but to be their own educator and judge of their own moral and spiritual values – albeit under the aegis of the State's authority, the only true source of lib-erty in Gentile's view. This ideal, in the wrong hands, might prove very dangerous indeed to a regime which sought to present itself as the sole arbiter, the supreme judge, in all things.[44]

As a response to the need for greater control over the minds of the young, ideological penetration of the education system began to take shape in the late twenties. Such policies were stepped up from 1929 in order to offset the effects of the Lateran Pacts signed between Mussolini and the Vatican, allow-ing the Church greater influence in education (with, for example, the intro-duction of religious teaching) and the continuation of Catholic Action youth activities. They were also motivated by the need to perpetuate Fascism, using youth that had not known non-Fascist experience.[45] One of the earliest initiat-ives in the 'Fascistization' of education was the founding under the auspices of the Ministry of Education in 1926 of the *Opera Nazionale Balilla* (ONB), named after the legendary Genoese boy who threw stones at the Austrian oppressors, for the purpose of integrating pre-military training and sports activities into the school curriculum. The emphasis on sport was clearly linked to the need to create a biologically fit race, particularly in view of the fact that the high number of soldiers suffering from exhaustion and illness during the First World War revealed how unfit Italian men were.[46] There was particularly close co-operation between primary schools and the ONB, which also took over the running of rural schools and kindergarten, as indicative of the need to 'Fascistize' children when they were most impressionable. Out of school the Young Fascists organization (*Fasci Giovanili*), founded in 1930 under the auspices of the PNF, provided pre-military training to 18–21 year olds who had not gone on to higher education. The PNF also controlled the Fascist university students' association (GUF – *Gioventù Italiana Universitaria*).

During the thirties the regime also tightened ideological control over school and university teachers, all of whom had to swear an oath of allegiance from 1929 onwards (and as public employees would later be subject to decrees on compulsory PNF membership in order to join the profession). The regime gave particular importance to controlling teachers in the primary sector, introducing a policy of employing those who had received their diplomas after 1923. In 1930 a single Fascist textbook and a variety of reading books were published for primary schools. Reading books were also provided for use in Fascist culture courses at secondary level. Though all books displayed the themes dear to Fascism (the myth of Mussolini, the fatherland, the survival of the Italian race, the myth of ancient Rome – which indicated Fascism as its revival – and the modernizing force of Fascism), the content of the reading books varied in emphasis according to the age of the pupils and the type of school. For primary school pupils in rural schools, for example, greater stress was placed on the symbolic values of nature and the land and the innovation which Fascism had allegedly brought to the countryside.

The regime also made use of modern forms of mass communication for educational purposes. In rural areas the *Ente Radio Rurale* radio board, founded in 1933, brought the voice of Fascism to schools, partly to make up for a lack of books. In all walks of education phrases and mottoes, such as 'You are the hope of the nation. You are tomorrow's army' and 'He who is not prepared to die for a cause is not worthy of professing it', whether written in school books or displayed on the walls of classrooms and youth clubs, aimed to instil in children the values of obedience, patriotism and self-sacrifice. Biblical language and symbolism were also exploited in order to create a sense of myth around the figure of Mussolini and Fascism. This is demonstrated by the introduction of a new Fascist calendar to mark such anniversaries as the founding of the first *Fascio di Combattimento* on 23 March 1919, the March on Rome on 28 October 1922 and the founding of the Italian empire on 9 May 1936 following the invasion of Ethiopia.

In 1937, as part of a general effort to step up the process of 'totalitarianization' of society, Party influence in schools was increased with the founding of the GIL (*Gioventù Italiana del Littorio*), an umbrella organization for youth groups which merged the 'Young Fascists' and the ONB. Employing an increasing number of young instructors, who had been trained in Fascist academies, the GIL controlled the provision of physical education in primary and secondary schools, organized educational trips, ran a variety of pre-military training camps and put on courses in its own schools and colleges. One of the main GIL activities was the obligatory assembly of members in their uniforms for group exercises (and military drill for boys) every Saturday afternoon (known as the '*Sabato fascista*').

Partly linked to the above developments, in 1939 there was a decisive move away from Gentile's basically Liberal concepts of self-fulfilment in education in favour of the corporative ideal. The School Charter (*Carta della Scuola*) of Giuseppe Bottai, Education Minister from 1937, though largely unfulfilled on account of the outbreak of the Second World War, sought to combine manual work, physical fitness and academic study. The introduction of 'productive labour' in primary and secondary school curricula was founded on the philosophy of reconciliation of the social classes, overcoming the division between manual and intellectual labour. In academic study new emphasis was given to science and technology, whereas Gentile's reform had maintained the priority traditionally given to humanities. Beyond the philosophical aim of democratizing education and forging Fascist men and women, however, in practice the system represented an attempt to readapt the education system to the realities of the labour market, bringing once again new limits of access to secondary school and university with the creation of 'dead-end' middle schools for future workers, artisans and peasants.

To what extent were Fascist ideals fulfilled in education? In assessing the compositions of school children, Tracy Koon argues that, while levels of indoctrination were high at primary education level, at secondary school students consciously felt some compulsion to inject elements of Fascism into their themes. She notes: 'It is likely that most of the students had a vague sympathy with the ideas being expressed (if for no other reason than that they had heard them for many years), and that they also realized that such expressions of enthusiasm were sometimes the quickest way to the head of the class.'[47] Koon suggests that a general culture of lip-service to Fascism among adults was felt among older children. In spite of their adoption of Fascist rituals and iconography, schools maintained much of their tradition. The failure of secondary schools to indoctrinate pupils may be partly attributed to the attitudes of the teachers themselves. Though many were convinced Fascists, the rest, even if anti-Fascist in spirit, hid their convictions. Likewise at university, though there were young Fascist teaching recruits, many older professors bowed to political pressure in order to keep their jobs. Yet, some students undoubtedly registered the fact that many teachers were merely conforming to the regime's requirements.

The success of Fascist educational policies depended largely on the extent to which young people were exposed to them. The influence of other cultures and ideologies outside school should not be underestimated. Catholic Action remained a realistic alternative to the ONB, while working-class children may have been exposed to the anti-Fascist beliefs of their parents. The majority of children joined ONB, however. As John Whittam points out:

> Although membership of the ONB only became compulsory in 1937, peer pressure, the aspirations of upwardly mobile families and party propaganda ensured a steady enrolment, especially in the thirties when entry into the PNF via the *leva fascista* (the passage of young Fascists into the party or the militia at the age of twenty-one) became the only sure way of securing employment.[48]

While anti-Fascist parents often objected to their children becoming ONB members, not joining could have been interpreted as a provocation and might have impeded children from receiving welfare benefits, though they were in theory available to all children. In some instances non-membership was punished, as was illustrated by the case of a Turin boy who failed the third-year primary school examination, in spite of good marks throughout the year, because he was the only non-ONB member among the pupils, greatly offending his teacher who was a staunch Fascist.[49]

While those who left school early in order to work, particularly working-class children, were less exposed to Fascist teachings, and may have been equally exposed to the anti-Fascist sentiments of their families, this was partly offset by GIL activities between 1937 and 1941. Yet, Fascist youth initiatives registered high levels of absenteeism and problems of discipline. PNF leaders noticed during the thirties that, if the majority of young Italians enrolled in the youth groups, this was increasingly done out of a sense of conformity in which opportunism or self-interest was greater than real belief, Koon notes. To quote just two of many examples Koon provides, in October 1937 the PNF secretary in Turin claimed: 'The Young Fascists are deserting the meetings. . . . Only the books are full of members, but the truth is that the young no longer go to the groups.' In March 1934 the Reggio Calabria secretary reported: 'It is enough to see these young men march in the streets . . . to realize the indiscipline that reigns in the ranks. You do not see the young proud to wear the blackshirt.'[50] The limited benefits of membership of youth organizations may also account for low attendance levels. Fascism undoubtedly brought a greater opportunity for young people to practise such sports as athletics, cycling, skiing and swimming. Yet, there was a clear bias in favour of boys. *Case del Balilla* (Fascist Youth centres) with sports grounds, gyms, shower facilities, libraries and rooms for listening to the radio were also built. However, sports equipment was often in short supply, especially in the South and rural areas.

The fact that only a minimal number of GUF members went on to join the PNF, when they left university, suggests that many young Italians tolerated the doctrinal aspects of Fascist organizations, in order to be able to make use of the facilities they provided or to participate in their activities. Ironically, it was the regime's encouragement of debate among students, with a view to raising their political and ideological consciousness, as was illustrated by their sponsorship, from 1934, of *Littoriali* competitions in art and culture, that gave youngsters more opportunity to question the regime. The growing disillusionment of GUF members with the regime was undoubtedly also a result of not being able to find a job upon graduating. Barbagli argues that, though the gap between professional aspirations and the reality of the labour market was no wider under Fascism than it was in Liberal Italy, the fact that Fascist propaganda had exalted youth in its role of revitalizing the Fascist ruling class made the disillusionment all the more dramatic. He notes:

> The young person who left after thirteen or seventeen years of school had received a complete fascist training and was therefore in the best condition for accepting without question the foundations for the new regime. But this training could enter into crisis if he found himself facing great difficulties in finding that work for which the school claimed to have prepared him.[51]

On the other hand, as the next chapter illustrates, the support given by a significant number of adolescents to Mussolini during the latter half of the Second World War, even if this meant sure defeat and possible punishment, if not execution, for treason, bears testimony to the partial success of the 'Fascistization' of education. Nor should we dismiss the possible long-term though more subtle effects of Fascist control of education, to the extent that even after the fall of the regime it was difficult for many young Italians to rid themselves entirely of dependence on the state's moral lead and vision, even once they understood the evils of Fascism. Thompson suggests that the mainly conservative political choices Italy made after the war and its refusal of the social and political revolution offered by the anti-Fascist Resistance are an indication of the fact that 'Fascism's particular tutelage of the national consciousness had not failed entirely, even though the new *Homo Fascistus* never materialised. If that was indeed the case then it was perhaps this legacy above all else which represented Fascism's greatest triumph.'[52]

The organization of leisure

While the regime aimed to create a new generation of full-fledged Fascists among the youngest, its policies with regard to the adult masses were ideologically ambiguous, as it found itself divided between the desire to create Fascists and the short-term need to generate consensus, particularly among those unmoved by the political appeal of Fascism. For this purpose a policy of 'going out to the people' (*andare verso il popolo*) combined material assistance to counterpose the negative effects of unemployment and wage cuts on the livelihood of the masses with less ideologically focused strategies of 'socialization' and 'nationalization'. This involved welfare initiatives, as is demonstrated, for example, by the introduction of the family allowance, and the organization of people's free time. The *Opera Nazionale Dopolavoro* (OND) sponsoring company after-work clubs was founded in 1925 under the National Economy Ministry, becoming an auxiliary of the Fascist Party from 1927. The clubs organized sports and amateur cultural activities, theatre visits and excursions for their members and supplied them with such facilities as reading rooms and radio sets. By organizing the leisure activities of Italians after work and at weekends, the regime intended to generate consensus for Fascism, while filling the void left by the banning of Socialist, Catholic and Liberal associations that had previously sponsored them. Yet, indicating the avoidance of a direct ideological approach, Party membership was not required in order to join the clubs.

Dopolavoro activities appealed most to members of the lower middle classes, particularly those employed in the growing bureaucracy, who had more free time and money to spend than workers or peasants. Many of them would play an important role in running the clubs. Fascism was particularly keen to gain the co-operation and consent of this sector of society, since it played a prime role in serving the regime. In 1926, out of a total of 280,000 OND members, 164,000 were salaried employees. During the late twenties the number of blue-collar members grew over that of salaried workers, reaching 1,921,000 (nearly 70 per cent) out of a total membership of 2,755,000 by 1936. Yet, this amounted to only 20 per cent of the industrial labour force and 7 per cent of the peasantry, indicating the difficulties experienced by the OND in adequately replacing the leisure and educational initiatives of the old working-men's clubs.[53] According to De Luna, among the working class the spontaneity of the district or local bar was often preferred to the organized activities of the *dopolavoro*.[54]

While an ideologically restrained approach to after-work activities, as was evident in the OND's sponsoring of popular folklore and festivals, was necessary if participants were not to be driven away, the organization did, however, link its activities to broader concerns of inculcating a greater sense of patriotism and Fascist virtues among its members. Its sponsoring of the *Balilla* radio, for example, at a lower than standard price aimed to exploit the consumer advantages it afforded to its members to bring the voice of Fascism into households. Sports activities were also run by the OND for the purpose of nationalizing the masses and instilling a regime of fitness and unity for the purposes of hard work and, if necessary, for war. These included bowls, tugs-of-war, canoeing, volley ball and *volata*, a hybrid game between soccer and handball. According to Dogliani, by 1933 7,294 OND sections (roughly a third) were devoted to physical activities and engaged in more than 191,773 competitions. The OND encouraged team games, instructing players in team discipline and group solidarity. While games conducive to individual competitive spirit were avoided, 'recreational activities aimed to spread a shared sense of national corporate identity', as was exemplified by teams representing and defending the name of the company.[55] Yet, the extent to which OND activities fostered a greater sense of unity among Italians is dubious. The regime was fearful that too much contact, particularly among members of different social classes, posed a threat to Fascism's survival. In spite of the emphasis placed on the OND as a cross-class association, links between the employee class and the rest of the working population were severed on account of the privileged position of the former within the organization. The fact that clubs were organized at the company level helped to enforce divisions not only between social classes but within social classes.

In the end the OND was only able to offer its members modest advantages. Its activities were often limited for financial reasons. Many clubs could not afford facilities to organize sports activities. Though it brought new opportunities for travel, cost remained an inhibiting factor. Popular trains with a 50 per cent price discount were initially successful, since they allowed a lower-class public which had never taken the train before to go on day-trips, though they were run less frequently once the novelty wore off and, in spite of the lower than standard prices, they were still unaffordable to many. Mass bicycle tours or outings to regional landmarks or monuments evoking the unity and progress of the new Italy, such as the Pontine Marshes, or recalling important national events, such as the First World War battlefields, were more frequent because of the lower costs of such initiatives. The number of radio subscribers remained low in spite of OND sponsorship of cheaper sets. By 1937 around only a third of OND members had access to a radio, purchased by their local section.

As De Grazia's research demonstrates, the success of after-work initiatives also varied according to sex and geographical location. Though women were by no means banned from participation, their traditional social seclusion in many parts of Italy, particularly the South, fostered by the position of the Church and Fascist masculine notions, was a clear inhibiting factor. In the particular case of sports activities, which the *dopolavoro* clubs sponsored, women faced disapproval by the Church for moral reasons, while they were banned from those sports that were risky for their maternal functions. OND initiatives were far less successful in rural areas on account of higher poverty and illiteracy levels. This reflected the overall limited impact of Fascism in the countryside. In the South, where the primitive methods of the *latifondisti* continued, and Fascism failed to remove a strongly clientelistic culture, extreme poverty, limited conceptions of the state, difficult lines of communication beyond the coastlands, high levels of class consciousness and female segregation all played a role in hindering OND initiatives.[56]

Far from creating committed Fascists, much of the after-work activity amounted to an exercise in playing on lower-middle-class desires to participate in more élite forms of Italian culture and to have access to a more privileged consumer market in order to reaffirm their middle-class status as a means of generating consensus. This was achieved by offering opera or theatre ticket discounts, for example, or providing their members with coupons allowing them to buy household goods at lower than market prices. Most OND discounts were on the other hand not high enough to be of benefit to working-class members. Yet, the social advancement that lower-middle-class members aspired to through the material and cultural benefits that the OND offered was only partly fulfilled. The limited availability of discounted theatre tickets, for example, was partly a consequence of theatre managers' reluctance to disturb the traditional public with mass audiences. In any case *dopolavoristi* were strictly segregated from the regular public. As Tannenbaum argues, both the Italian bourgeoisie and Fascist intellectuals looked down on the OND because of its hedonistic and plebeian spirit: 'The adjective *dopolavoristico* became a synonym for vulgar, but this vulgarity was more petit-bourgeois than working-class in its style and taste'.[57]

Culture under Fascism

Many of the activities sponsored by the OND went hand in hand with the regime's attempted creation of a Fascist mass culture. This was directly linked to the idea of spectacle. As Thompson notes:

> What passed for art, in the main, was spectacle, the spectacular, though usually in no more than size or mass or volume; whether it be architecture, sculpture or operatic production its scale was typically such that it dwarfed the individual and emphasised his own insignificance, much as the State did. And so much of public life was spectacle; choreographed parades, rallies, celebrations, costume, *sabato fascista*, ritual response in which again, the voice of the individual was drowned in that of the collective.[58]

The emphasis on such forms of spectacle was also a necessity in a country where levels of literacy were low. The widespread display of simple slogans, such as VINCEREMO! (We will win!) in large block capitals on walls or superimposed on the images of propaganda newsreels was a clear response to this need too. Propaganda films also made use of images to get the regime's message across. In the 1939 documentary, *Believe, Obey, Fight*, a sequence of shots illustrated, for example, how the construction of a dam allowed the electrification of the railways.

Yet, the impact of such exploits as the staging of huge theatrical productions for the expression of the ideals and myths of Fascism on mass audiences is questionable. In the first place they proved to be impracticable. The theatre critic Mario Verdone himself remembers the limited success of the 'theatre of the masses', epitomized by the performance in 1934 of a First World War battle (under the title 18BL) in an open-air location involving a large number of actors and 24,000 spectators, many of whom had been brought in on 'popular trains': 'During the performance, when it had become dark, and military searchlights were being switched on . . . there was a terrible dust storm and, to be honest, one could not see or understand very much, especially if one had been allocated one of the cheaper seats'.[59] In practice the majority of cultural initiatives heralded as 'Fascist', such as the *Dopolavoro* amateur dramatic companies and the travelling theatres (*Carri di Tespi*) were conventional in repertoire. Moreover, as Pietro Cavallo points out, the regime realized that overt 'Fascistization' of the theatre would have the effect of alienating those sections of society on whose support it relied most:

> a theatre of this kind would have implied an overcoming of Fascism itself; or, to be more precise, the superseding of the traditional and reassuring values, which for large strata of the Italian society – especially the petit and middle bourgeoisie in urban centres, who formed the social basis of the régime – represented the main reason for lending their support to Fascism.[60]

With reference to the receptiveness of the working class to Fascist cultural initiatives, Corner notes:

> Fascism had nothing to offer beyond the odd film or theatre production, generally of very low quality, which the workers dismissed immediately as *roba dei fascisti* (more or less 'fascist rubbish'). This dismissal was based often less on ideological grounds than on the fact that the rhetorical material of fascism was, in most cases, boring and laughable. Where it was not, it was not explicitly fascist, and therefore did nothing to reinforce the image of fascism.[61]

'Fascistization' remained incomplete in other artistic spheres. The cinema, for example, though constituting another area of strong propaganda potential, was not fully adapted to totalitarian political requirements before the interruption of the Second World War. Apart from propaganda newsreels, very few overtly Fascist commercial films were produced. This was partly because of the dominance of American films and Italian equivalents of Hollywood melodramas, known as *telefoni bianchi* ('white telephones', referring to the glamorous settings of the films), which did not constitute a political threat to the regime in view of their principally distracting quality. As Carlo Bordoni argues, far more than Fascist propaganda these films constituted 'a cultural model which was imitated and ideally recreated in daily life, especially by the female public'.[62] Film directors maintained a certain artistic freedom, as long as they did not address social or political questions or portray Fascism in a bad light. Political censorship of some foreign films began in the late thirties only. Moreover, the Catholic Church, which by 1938 possessed 546 cinemas, increasingly competed with the regime regarding control over what films the public should be allowed to see, just as it did over the stage, epitomized in a flourishing 'parish theatre' producing numerous Catholic plays during the thirties.[63] The regime similarly exercised limited control over publishing houses, many of which were able to introduce contemporary foreign literature in translation with relative ease. Even in such important areas as the education of the young, the regime increasingly found itself competing with non-Fascist reading material from both Catholic and commercial sources. This was evident in the widespread publication of magazines aimed at adolescents and young adults, particularly girls.

There are several reasons for limits to the 'Fascistization' of culture. According to David Forgacs, like all private industry, the regime depended on the support of the cultural industries, and did not, therefore, intend to make life difficult for them, as long as they ensured a minimum amount of alignment and co-operation.[64] With specific regard to high culture, the regime saw the cultural élite as being too alienated from the masses to influence them seriously. The particular relationship between the regime and the cultural élite also prevented it. The regime avoided suppressing cultural opposition to Fascism led by the Hegelian philosopher Benedetto Croce because his counter-manifesto to Gentile's 1925 'Manifesto of Fascist Intellectuals' was signed by most of the best known Italian cultural figures. Croce's journal, *La Critica*, was able to continue publishing. The majority of artists and intellectuals remained aloof from Fascist cultural policy without publicly condemning it. Moreover, the direct involvement of some in running national cultural organizations like the Royal Academy of Italy allowed them to inhibit the intentions of the most totalitarian-minded Fascists. As De Grand argues: 'In the end, the regime's collaboration with traditional culture enhanced the passive consensus that grew up around Fascism during the early thirties, but it also reinforced the status quo against any effort to push Fascism toward a radical break with the past.'[65] Under Fascism no single ideological or cultural perspective was forced to emerge and consequently the continuity of Italian culture was not disrupted.[66]

Fascist cultural policies clearly aimed at creating a greater sense of national consciousness, but the authoritarian approach to this was probably counterproductive. Behind the façade of boastful propaganda, divisions between regions and between town and countryside remained strong. The regime's attempt, for example, to reduce the use of dialect, as part of the Fascist policy of purifying the Italian language – which also involved the banning of mainly French and English foreign words – rather than bringing Italians closer together, risked cutting off large sections of the population from the cultural mainstream. So did the banning from higher education of minority languages in border areas. In any case, these policies failed. According to Howard Moss, there was 'a weakening of dialect and minority-language use, but at no greater a rate than had been taking place before the Fascist period as the cultures expressed by those languages had begun to give way before the onset of twentieth-century development and its centralizing tendencies'.[67]

Demography, women and the family

The 'Fascistization' of society also involved an attempt at greater control over the form and social practices of the family, and, within the family, women. Fascist policies in this area were directly linked to the regime's demographic campaign, in response to the need for greater military manpower, expressed in Mussolini's demand that the Italian population (which numbered 37 million in 1921) increase to 60 million by 1950. Such a call had no realistic possibility of curtailing a long-term trend of decline in fertility since the 1880s. As De Grazia points out, the demographic campaign was also envisaged as a means of 'moralizing' Italian civil society, thereby guaranteeing public order and consolidating the dictatorship. In order to put its demographic policies into practice, the regime had to deal with the contradiction between Fascist values of male virility and the family. This entailed a policy of sexual 'normalization', which included greater control over prostitution as a means of drawing a clearer line between illicit sex (with loose women or prostitutes) and legitimate sex in marriage for procreation purposes.[68]

Italians were encouraged to marry and have a large number of offspring through the introduction of a combination of penalties and welfare and maternity incentives.[69] An attempt was made to eradicate birth-control practices, as legislation on 'crimes against the health and purity of the race' made contraception illegal and turned abortion into a crime against the state carrying a prison sentence of two to five years. State family planning policy, which also condemned the adoption of *coitus interruptus*, was supported by the Catholic Church as each newly wed couple was presented with a copy of Pope Pius XI's 1930 encyclical, *Casti connubi*, which offered theological support to Fascist policies on birth control. Marriage and procreation were encouraged by a punitive tax on bachelorhood, priority for men with children in public (and some private) employment and in the allocation of cheap housing and the introduction of birth premiums and a family allowance. In 1937, marriage loans were introduced. They were available to couples under the age of 26, when the husband was Italian and had an income of no more than 12,000 lire a year. The repayment of 1 per cent per month was interest free and the debt was successively cancelled as children were born, then finally removed with the birth of a fourth child.

ONMI aimed to place the family and the physical and moral wellbeing of its members under state control. Fascist women's organizations, including the *Fasci Femminili* that worked closely with ONMI, aimed, for example, to help families through charity work. PNF mountain and seaside colonies for children were also a means of checking and inoculating against illness. To assist the regime's demographic policies, propaganda attempted to encourage motherhood by stressing images of women as mothers, while denigrating those of sterile middle-class 'women in crisis'. Fascist demographic policies were directly linked to ruralist propaganda, which exalted the values of peasant fertility against sterile urbanism and attributed the risk of decline of the Italian race to the moral decadence of the cities. Other state propaganda incentives linked to the defence of the Italian race included the institution in 1933 of 'Mother and Child Day' (24 December), during which a national rally was held in Rome for the most prolific women from each of the 90 Italian provinces, while in every town prize-giving ceremonies took place. The Church supported this initiative with celebrations dedicated to the family.

There is little to suggest that Fascist demographic policies were successful. Though the annual rate of population increase almost doubled between 1921 and 1936, this was a result of a fall in the death rate and increased life expectancy, while the birth rate continued to fall. The number of live births per 1,000 inhabitants dropped from 27.7 in 1926 to 23.5 in 1940, while the number of deaths fell from 17.2 to 13.6.[70] During the limited period of time in which the demographic policies were in force little could be done to offset long-term tendencies. As the demographic historian, Massimo Livi-Bacci, notes: 'Italy was in a period of very rapid fertility decline; in many areas of the North and the Centre fertility was already below replacement; in the South and in the Islands the diffusion of birth control had started to produce its first visible effects.'[71] Poor facilities partly impeded Fascist demographic policies. As is mentioned in an earlier section of the chapter, the provision of hospitals and qualified midwives for healthy childbirth was inadequate, particularly in the South. If there was a reduction in infant mortality from an average of 124.8 deaths per 1,000 live births in 1929 to 97.0 in 1939, the rate remained among the highest in Europe. Policies for encouraging and assisting a high birth rate were also limited by the discriminatory and clientelistic character of state welfare services.

But, as Livi-Bacci suggests, more than anything else cultural hostility was the main obstacle to the regime's demographic campaign. During the thirties married women increasingly put off having children and state and ecclesiastical pressure did little to stop birth-control practices, which had become increasingly common since the turn of the century. The attitude of the urban working class was no different here. As Passerini points out, the request that Turin workers should have a large number of children caused much resentment 'because it was taken as an attack on the identity of the real worker who was capable, far-sighted, self-disciplined. Only "Southerners" had a lot of children, being both careless and work-shy. . . . The whole system of bonuses and incentives for large families offended their self-image, cultural identity and moral values.'[72] In the South too notions of family planning spread to the urban lower middle classes, probably as a result of the effects of the international depression, which forced families to recognize the link between large families and poverty, removing the cultural notion that large families indicated wealth.[73]

Inevitably, abolition of information on contraception led to greater acceptance of backstreet abortion, which was practised among both middle- and working-class women, in spite of the health and legal risks this carried. According to Passerini, it is likely that during the twenties and thirties there was a three-fold increase in the overall number of abortions per year to as much as 150,000 as a result of an increase in the number of induced abortions, particularly in the industrial North. Illustrating the tragic side of Fascist demographic policies, Passerini's research on the Turin working class concludes that, since treatment of up to 2,000 lire was often too costly for industrial working-class families on an average of 300 lire a month, abortion was often self-inflicted.[74]

If Fascist policies had little effect on the birth rate, the success of the regime in 'moralizing' Italian society is equally questionable. Data suggesting that in 1933 26 per cent of first-born sons had been conceived out of wedlock bear testimony to the limits of moral control that Fascism and the Catholic Church were able to exercise.[75] It also appears that the contradiction between Fascist values of virility and the family was not fully overcome. Indeed, while eliminating street prostitution, the regime placed greater emphasis than before on the social and educative function of the brothel (destined to survive until 1958), traditionally seen as a means of safeguarding marriage, since it was a better alternative to long-term extra-marital relationships. In a society enforcing strict censorship of manifestations of indecency in films and theatrical performances, the brothel was an accepted outlet for 'healthy Fascist virility', especially since it was agreed that for men married life was oppressed by rigid Catholic codes concerning sexual behaviour.[76]

During the Fascist period women appeared to take on a greater public role than ever before, as was demonstrated by their membership and running of youth groups and charity organizations, their presence at rallies and gymnastics displays and their receiving of prizes at public ceremonies for generating numerous offspring. Yet, the public role of women, as designated by the Fascist policy, was ambiguous and contradictory. It may have acted as an outlet for their emancipatory needs but did not substantially alter their subordinate role in society. Perry Willson argues that women were mobilized through propaganda and mass organizations, which gave them importance and a national profile, but that in doing this the regime drew attention to the role of women in order to emphasize their inferiority and to tie them to domesticity. The *Fasci Femminili* social assistance organizations, for example, gave women no real power: 'Their leaders were excluded from policy making and reduced to simply accepting orders from above.'[77]

The extent to which Fascism influenced women varied according to social class, too. Working-class girls, particularly in rural areas, were much less exposed to Fascist teachings at school and through participation in youth organizations, since they were usually forced to start work at the age of 14. Many of them came from families of anti-Fascist tradition. Middle-class women were far more exposed to Fascist ideology since they had stayed longer at school and were less likely to be influenced by anti-Fascist teachings at home. Independently of class, however, the participation of women in such institutions as the *dopolavoro* or GUF tended to be inhibited as a result of male sexist attitudes. Fascism also had to compete with the Catholic Church over the control of women. Many of them chose to join rival Catholic organizations rather than Fascist ones. The Catholic Church both supported and inhibited Fascist policies on women. Catholic women's groups and magazines may have assisted the regime's aim of restricting women's lives to the home and motherhood, but on occasion actually helped to repress the regime's demographic designs for greater fitness of women, as, for example, in its discouragement of women's sports.

Inevitably, however, the Fascist mobilization of women increased the emancipatory aspirations of a minority of strongly committed Fascist women for a public role equal to that of men. Many even urged that they should be allowed to do compulsory civil service parallel to men's military service. Such aspirations were partly fulfilled by the training of a new generation of female Fascist teachers and GIL youth instructors. During the Ethiopian campaign women were also used for air defence and telephone and telegraphic services as part of the general mobilization of Italian society for war and they were given a prominent role in rallying the nation against the effects of sanctions imposed by the League of Nations. Partial militarization of women took place in 1937–38, with the recruitment of ten thousand Colonial Fascist women. Though the principal aim of this initiative was the extension of Fascist demographic and race policies to the colonies, women underwent military training, during which they were instructed in the handling of firearms for self-defence.[78]

Within Italian society at large some forms of what could broadly be described as female emancipation did emerge during the Fascist period. The younger female generation may have been influenced partly by cosmopolitan mass culture, transmitted through the Hollywood cinema and magazines, which both the Fascists and the Catholics vainly tried to neutralize through their own sponsoring of magazines for the young. This helped to foster an image of women as independent and modern rather than as baby-raisers. However, the extent to which young women were able to put into practice advice given in cosmopolitan literature is questionable. As De Grazia notes: 'Female independence, especially sexual freedom, appeared so risky that marriage was the logical and inevitable culmination of the strategy of the flirt.'[79] The fact that women (like men) began to marry later and put off child-birth was most likely due to economic difficulties. Indeed, apparent female emancipation in urban areas may have been an indirect consequence of the economic burden that Fascism placed on the family. The blurring of gender roles in the domestic sphere among the working class was a consequence of female employment resulting from male worklessness within the family. Similarly, many young lower-middle-class women tended to find jobs as secretarial employees or shop assistants. But while their earnings may have paid for them to enjoy comparatively modern pursuits for women, such as dance halls and the cinema, they did not grant them autonomy from their families. Work remained a temporary activity before marriage, which was still considered the best means of climbing the social ladder.

The limits of 'Fascistization' of Italian society

As the above sections have stressed, the possibilities for creating a Fascist society on a totalitarian scale were limited. This was a result of conflicting ideals within the Fascist élite and the serious compromises upon which the regime was founded in its continued reliance on the support of the monarchy, the army and the Catholic Church, together with the capitalist land-owning and industrial class. No distinct Fascist culture or ideology emerged as it co-existed and was often entangled with other cultures, be they Nationalist, Catholic, Crocean or Gentilean. The creation of the Fascist calendar illustrates how impossible it was to establish a fully independent, new Fascist order, given that it had to compete with generic patriotic and religious values. As Richard Bosworth argues:

> All Souls Day, All Saints Day (1–2 November), Vittorio Veneto Day (4 November, always a somewhat monarchist and nationalist affair rather than a strictly Fascist one) and the King's birthday (11 November), following one another in rapid succession, must have left an ideological blur in most observers' minds, a blur in which both Catholicism and generic patriotism could jostle with Fascism, however defined.[80]

Limited 'Fascistization' was also the result of the persistence of an archaic clientelistic mentality among civil servants denoting a line of continuity with the Liberal state. Many of those entrusted with the task of enforcing Fascist policies were accustomed to a self-guarded passive acceptance of authority but felt little passion for the ideological ideas they were serving. Even the Party began to show this attitude as it became a mass bureaucratic organization during the thirties. The extent to which Fascist policies were sabotaged by this mentality is illustrated by an examination of the role of the police, which involved not only direct repression but surveillance activities for the purpose of guiding the state propaganda machine. Their reports on shifts of public mood were often conditioned by their personal career aspirations or the desire for professional tranquillity. What is most noticeable is the use in reports from year to year of such repeated statements as: 'With unquestioning faith and great affection the masses observe Fascism's gradual fulfilment of all its aims' or 'The police are able to locate the tiniest hint of subversive activity and intervene immediately wherever necessary'. Frequently, such statements were directly copied from previous reports, suggesting that the authors merely wished to pay lip-service to the regime, telling the Fascist leadership what it wanted to be told. Such an attitude clearly accounted for increasing laxness in the repression of anti-Fascism.

Initial promises that Fascism would clean up public life were left largely unfulfilled. The civil service, together with the new para-state economic organizations and the Party bureaucracy, continued to function according to the rules of patronage in the manner in which they administered services and took on employees. For many Italians the Party membership card represented no more than a *meal ticket* for obtaining promotions and welfare benefits, but for those without membership acquaintances in the Fascist bureaucracy could on occasion be turned to in order to obtain those same benefits. Even the repression of anti-Fascism was conditioned by the fact that middle-class activists sometimes had connections in high places. And in Western Sicily, failure to root out the *Mafia* in the late twenties, beyond repressing the lower ranks under the orders of the 'iron prefect', Cesare Mori, was a result of the fact that its leaders were too close to Fascist politicians.[81] Strong family traditions in Italy also prevented the social penetration of Fascism. There was a clear contradiction between greater state interference in the family and the Catholic-inspired Fascist notion of the family as sacrosanct and indivisible. In practice the Fascist family modelled on petit-bourgeois values of individualism, privacy and protection from outside intrusions took from Fascism only the material advantages it offered.[82]

What support was generated for the regime was more focused on the imperialist exploits of Mussolini than on Fascist ideology. The Ethiopian military campaign of 1935, which appeared to fulfil long-standing aspirations for an empire, created some form of mass consensus, which cut across class and political lines. This was also a consequence of the Church's public support of what it considered to be a Christian crusade. The Ethiopian conquest was a propaganda success story in that its promises were clearly understood by most Italians. It was applauded not only as a national exploit, which the League of Nations had failed to prevent (showing Italy's ability to stand up to the world powers, particularly Britain), but also as a means of providing an emigration outlet, solving economic and demographic difficulties. The latter aspirations would quickly be frustrated by the reality of the limited economic benefits of the campaign. Initial enthusiasm for the campaign may have brought Italians closer to Mussolini and their sense of national unity may have been greater than ever before. Yet, there is little to suggest that the popularity of the regime resulting from it was long-lasting or ideologically based. Here a direct comparison may be made with the patriotic enthusiasm generated during the thirties by Italy's professional sporting triumphs, which included international successes at the Los Angeles Olympics of 1932 and

World Cup victories in 1934 and 1938. Fascist propaganda attempted to exploit these victories as a means of heralding future conflict among nations and ideologies but hardly succeeded. The effectiveness of propaganda concerning subsequent war campaigns was limited by the fact that it did not seem to offer the Italians valid solutions to their everyday problems. The ideological justifications for Italian military participation in the Spanish Civil War (1936–39) on the side of the Francisco Franco, in the cause of international Fascism, meant little to many of them, especially since no territorial reward was mentioned and many lives were lost.[83]

The passing, in 1938, of the race discrimination laws, of which the main victims were Italian Jews, was without doubt one of the nastiest episodes of the Fascist period. This marked Italy's closer ideological alignment with Nazi Germany, which was matched at the military level by the signing of the Axis alliance in October 1936 and the Pact of Steel in May 1939 (which committed Italy and Germany to mutual assistance in the case of hostilities). However, it has been argued that the Italian handling of the 'Jewish question' distinguished 'moderate' Italian Fascism from Nazism, since the Mussolinian regime only took discriminatory measures against the 40,000 Italian Jews, who were not interned in concentration camps until 1944 during the Nazi occupation of Northern Italy. Nevertheless, the effects of the laws on the lives of Jewish men, women and children were catastrophic. They were sacked from their jobs and excluded from state education. They could no longer use public facilities and restrictions were placed upon their right to own property. The segregation measures were particularly artificial and brutal in that many Jewish individuals and families had become increasingly assimilated into Italian society as a whole. The measures even cut into families, given that mixed marriages had become common in the preceding decades. They took account neither of whether or not individuals had faithfully served the state or Fascism nor of whether or not they had ceased to identify with the faith or customs of their ancestors.[84]

The race laws, though clearly part of the growing alignment between Fascism and Nazism, were not merely a formal and half-hearted imitation of Hitler's policies, as has often been claimed. To suggest that racism was imported into Italian society from Nazi Germany is short-sighted. Racism was endemic in Fascism, and in large sections of Italian society before the Fascist period. This was demonstrated by the harsh treatment of not only the indigenous peoples of Libya and Ethiopia by the colonial regime, but also ethnic minorities in the North-East. Particularly grave were war crimes committed in Ethiopia. Unknown to Italian public opinion at the time, the military and political occupiers committed atrocities to prevent resistance. This included air raids with mustard gas and the extermination of the Ethiopian intelligentsia.[85] Wanda Newby, a Slovenian girl living near Trieste during the Fascist period, bears testimony to the inferior treatment of minority groups of Slovenes, Germans, Austrians and Jews, in parts of the North-East ceded to Italy after the First World War. She recounts how her father, a school teacher, like all civil servants of Yugoslav origin, was removed from his post and literally deported to another part of Italy because the regime did not trust his loyalty.[86]

Anticipated by a lively press and radio campaign and backed up by a 'Manifesto of racist scientists' and the introduction of racial themes in GIL training manuals and curricula, the race laws responded to Italy's need for an image of racial purity following the Ethiopian conquest and were part and parcel of a policy which aimed from the second half of the thirties, albeit unsuccessfully, to 'Fascistize' the Italians more effectively for the purposes of war. The creation of a new internal enemy, the Jews, would 'regenerate' the energies of the Italian people. However, for most Italians anti-Semitism was mainly of Catholic inspiration and a matter of religion, not race. Within Catholic circles there were reactions both ways. Some felt that the race laws fulfilled their anti-Semitic feelings, others that anti-Semitism should not move beyond religious spheres and certainly not condition civil society (a position voiced officially, though somewhat feebly by the Vatican), while those Catholics closest to Fascism wholeheartedly supported them, and went as far as to argue that even conversion to Christianity should not prevent discrimination against Jews.[87]

Apart from the religious difference, most Italians considered Jews to be Italians like themselves. In their reports to the government many prefects clearly avoided paying lip-service to Fascist anti-Semitism, stating quite openly that the Jewish people living in their provinces did not pose a serious risk to law and order, suggesting a dissociation from the regime's growing radicalism. Yet, while it is true that many individual Italians – including several high-ranking state officials – protected Italian Jews and Jewish refugees fleeing the Nazi persecution in other parts of Europe, this phenomenon has often been interpreted as being the rule, while it was in reality the exception, the rule being 'acquiescence' (which for state employees meant 'enforcement'), though this was without doubt a consequence of fear of adopting a nonconformist attitude. There was a significant minority of individuals, including journalists and intellectuals, who voluntarily took part in the propaganda campaign preceding and accompanying the laws. There is no doubt too that there was consensus for the laws where in a period of economic difficulty there were jobs and property to be gained as a result of them.

The supposedly negative public reaction towards the race laws has been used to suggest that Italian Fascism was nowhere near as evil as Nazism, and that Italians, unlike Germans, were ill-disposed to violence and brutality. This myth of the 'good Italian' (*italiano buono*) would be perpetuated in the wake of the Second World War in which distinction was made between the supposedly humane attitude of Italian soldiers towards occupied peoples and the brutality of German occupying forces. While this comparison is not totally unfounded, it was clearly employed to overcome a sense of guilt concerning Italy's Fascist past – which had involved the violation of human rights and atrocities, though admittedly on a smaller scale – and her alignment with Hitler.

Independent of the sympathies it may have generated on such matters as the creation of an empire, the attitude of Italian citizens towards Fascism was inevitably conditioned by a sense of compulsion typical of dictatorships. Many of those involved in enforcement of the regime's policies felt disgusted at having to act against their consciences, but were equally unable to rebel. With regard to the recollections of Italian journalists and employees of the *Corriere della Sera* national daily, Tannenbaum notes that many 'salved their consciences with indirect little acts of sabotage calculated to erode the dominant mentality and manners of the regime, such as cutting out a line of type, substituting a synonym, omitting a bombastic adjective' and many 'comforted themselves with the knowledge that they were all hypocrites together'.[88] The lip-service which many Italians paid to Fascism in return for material benefits and career advancement may partly be attributed to a broader historical phenomenon of clientelistic behaviour which had existed before Fascism, closely linked to an 'anti-state' attitude, which saw the state as a dealer in resources to be taken advantage of rather than a political entity. While it can be demonstrated that ideological identification with Fascism was often hollow, the motives for this should be sought less in the idea of the 'good Italian' and more in historical factors denoting a particular type of relationship between state and citizen.

Conclusion

From the late thirties onwards there was a clear drop in consensus for Fascism. This was partly a reflection of tiredness at the material sacrifices persistently expected of the Italians as a result of a situation of almost permanent war from 1935 onwards. In many respects too the drop in consensus was a consequence of the accentuation of the differences between the various currents of Fascism at the moment in which the regime attempted to 'totalitarianize' society in line with its war campaigns. As De Grand argues: 'As long as the regime demanded an essentially passive response, fascism benefited from the ability of each person to define the ideology in his or her own way. When the Fascists demanded an active response during the crises leading to World War II, cracks emerged in the consensus.'[89] Many of those dissociating themselves from Fascism belonged to a younger middle-class generation that had grown up under the regime and whose culture had been formed by it. Yet, the influence of the anti-Fascist underground movement over this younger generation is questionable. It was more often the personal experience of incidents or events of wider relevance that was crucial. Some moved away from support of the regime, for example, when a friend of the family or relative fell victim to the race laws.

For an élite of young Fascists, involvement in cultural organizations such as GUF allowed relatively free discussion and cultural experimentation, which if intended to nurture and renew Fascism often bred dissidence, or even anti-Fascism, as a result of a growing sense of disillusionment with the direction in which the regime was moving. Ironically the regime's direct sponsorship of film studies for propaganda purposes allowed the artistic experimentation of a number of young directors and script-writers who in the immediate post-war period backed by anti-Fascist ideology would come to fame through their neo-realist portrayal of society. Similarly many young writers, among them Cesare Pavese, Vasco Pratolini and Elio Vittorini, started a quiet cultural revolt in their literary expression, walking a tight-rope between direct criticism of the regime and conformity, often managing to escape censorship, which in practice was irregular. Many of them worked for independent pub-lishers, including Bompiani, Einaudi and Laterza. Their involvement in the translation of European and North American literary texts provided them with alternative visions to the authoritarian order they had grown up in and moulded their anti-Fascism. Many young Catholics too, though initially sup-portive of the regime and enthusiastic about the founding of the new Italian empire, turned hostile in view of increasing Fascist alignment with Nazism.[90]

A number of anti-Fascist currents were created as a result of the above de-velopments, though they would not be brought together until the military disasters of the Second World War and the Nazi occupation of the Centre and North of the peninsula, as will be revealed in the following chapter. Most crucially, there was no contact between this newer middle class of anti-Fascists and the working class. Working-class culture had survived, if not without difficulty, throughout the Fascist years and had often existed auto-nomously from clandestine organized anti-Fascism. This would play a crucial role in the mass uprisings of the industrial working class in March 1943 in protest against the war. Tobias Abse notes that Allied bombings turned the Italian working class actively against Fascism and its alliance with Nazism, rather than against the British and Americans who were directly responsible, 'a phenomenon that is virtually incomprehensible unless we assume the persistence of the *tradizione sovversiva* amongst significant groups within the working class'.[91]

Notes

1. Whittam, *Fascist Italy*, 60. For an analysis of the Italian economy during the Fascist period, see Zamagni, *The Economic History of Italy*, chapters 8 and 9; Clark, *Modern Italy*, chapter 13.

2. Martin Blinkhorn, *Mussolini and Fascist Italy* (London: Methuen, 1984), 25.
3. Carl Levy, 'From Fascists to Post-Fascists: Italian Roads to Modernity', in Richard Bessel (ed.), *Fascist Italy and Nazi Germany* (Cambridge: Cambridge University Press), 165–96(173–4). See 167–74 for discussion of Fascist economic policy.
4. Gianni Toniolo, *L'economia dell'Italia fascista* (Bari: Laterza, 1980), 273–4.
5. Fabrizio Galimberti and Luca Paolozzi, *Il volo del calabrone. Breve storia dell'economia italiana del Novecento* (Florence: Le Monnier, 1998), 91.
6. Alberto Aquarone, 'Italy: the crisis and the corporative economy', *Journal of Contemporary History*, 4(4), 1969, 37–58(57); Zamagni, *The Economic History of Italy*, 291–2. See also Galimberti and Paolozzi, *Il volo del calabrone*, 188–9, for an analysis of regional economic imbalances in Fascist Italy.
7. Zamagni, *The Economic History of Italy*, 291.
8. For analysis of the Corporate State, see Morgan, *Italian Fascism*, 88–92, 124–7; Aquarone, 'Italy: the crisis and the corporative economy', 37–58.
9. Gaetano Salvemini, *Under the Axe of Fascism* (New York: Fertig, 1969; 1st edn, London: Gollancz, 1936), 59–61.
10. For figures and analyses of the livelihood of workers under Fascism, see Cesare Vannutelli, 'The Living Standard of Italian Workers, 1929–39', in Roland Sarti (ed.), *The Axe Within: Italian Fascism in Action* (New York: New Viewpoints, 1974), 139–60; Paul Corner, 'Italy', in Stephen Salter and John Stevenson (eds), *The Working Class and Politics in Europe and America, 1919–1945* (London: Longman, 1990), 154–71. For an analysis of unemployment in Italy during the thirties, see also Francesca Piva and Gianni Toniolo, 'Sulla disoccupazione in Italia negli anni trenta', *Rivista di Storia Economica*, 4(3), 1987, 345–83.
11. Figures on Brescia from Alice A. Kelikian, *Town and Country under Fascism* (Oxford: Clarendon, 1986), 204; Corner, 'Italy', 159–60.
12. Gian Franco Venè, *Mille lire al mese. Vita quotidiana della famiglia nell'Italia fascista* (Milan: Mondadori, 1988), 114.
13. Paul Corner, 'Fascist agrarian policy and the Italian economy in the inter-war years', in Davis (ed.), *Gramsci and Italy's Passive Revolution*, 239–74(245). See also Andrea Di Michele, 'I diversi volti del ruralismo fascista', *Italian Contemporanea*, 199, 1995, 243–67.
14. Figures from Zamagni, *The Economic History of Italy*, 264.
15. Figures on wheat production and grain consumption from ISTAT, *Sommario di statistiche storiche 1926–1985* (Rome: ISTAT, 1986), tables 9.7 and 8.42. See also Cardoza, *Agrarian Elites*, 440–1; Corner, 'Fascist Agrarian Policy'; Morgan, *Italian Fascism*, 98–103; Mack Smith, *Modern Italy*, 351.
16. Figures from Corner, 'Fascist agrarian policy', 252–3. For analysis of land reclamation projects during the Fascist period, see also Jon S. Cohen, 'Un esame statistico delle opere di bonifica intraprese durante il regime fascista', in Gianni Toniolo, *Lo sviluppo economico italiano 1861–1940* (Bari: Laterza, 1973), 351–71; Zamagni, *The Economic History of Italy*, 260–2.
17. Figures on emigration abroad are taken from ISTAT, *Sommario di statistiche storiche*, table 2.27. For analysis of internal migration during the Fascist period and statistics, see Carl Ipsen, *Dictating Demography: The Problem of Population in Fascist Italy* (Cambridge: Cambridge University Press, 1996), 51–65, 91–144; Anna Treves,

Le migrazioni interne nell'Italia fascista: Politica e realtà demografica (Turin: Einaudi, 1976), 23, 26–7. See also Sori, *L'emigrazione italiana.*

18. Cento Bull and Corner, *From Peasant to Entrepreneur*, 82–9.

19. For statistics and analysis concerning health and welfare provision during the Fascist period, see Levy, 'From Fascists to Post-Fascists', 175–6; Zamagni, *The Economic History of Italy*, 315–16; Venè, *Mille lire al mese.*

20. Vannutelli, 'The Living Standard of Workers', 155.

21. Lesley Caldwell, 'Reproducers of the Nation: Women and the Family in Fascist Policy', in David Forgaçs (ed.), *Rethinking Italian Fascism. Capitalism, Populism and Culture* (London: Lawrence & Wishart, 1986), 110–41(133).

22. Snowden, '"Fields of death"', 46.

23. De Grazia, *How Fascism Ruled Women*, 106.

24. For levels of consumption, and consequent political attitudes, see Venè, *Mille lire al mese*; Zamagni, *The Economic History of Italy*, 308–14.

25. Barbagli, *Educating for Unemployment*, 103. For a detailed analysis of Fascist education policy and the effects on the job market, see 128–209.

26. Statistics on school and university enrolment levels in this section are from ISTAT, *Sommario di statistiche storiche*, tables 4.3, 4.6 and 4.7.

27. For analysis of female education and employment under Fascism, see Barbagli, *Educating for Unemployment*, 159–62; Caldwell, *Italian Family Matters*, 107–9; De Grazia, *How Fascism Ruled Women*, chapters 5–6.

28. Figures and analysis from De Fort, *Scuola e analfabetismo.*

29. For analyses of the particular nature of the Fascist police state, see Jonathan Dunnage, 'Social control in Fascist Italy: the case of the Italian police, 1926–1943', in Pieter Spierenburg, Eric Johnson and Clive Emsley (eds), *Discipline and Control in European Society, 1500–2000*, Vol. 2 (Columbus, OH: Ohio State University Press, 2002) in press; Thompson, *State control in Fascist Italy*, chapter 2; Morgan, *Italian Fascism*, 83, 86–7.

30. Figures from Morgan, *Italian Fascism*, 123; Giovanni De Luna, *Donne in oggetto: l'antifascismo nella società italiana, 1922–39* (Turin: Bollati Boringhieri, 1995), 17, 19. For statistics on sentences to *ammonizione* and *domicilio coatto* during Liberal period, see Jensen, *Liberty and Order*, 302–3.

31. The difficulties involved in organizing the underground resistance are analysed in detail in De Luna, *Donne in oggetto.*

32. Corner, 'Italy', 162, 165–6.

33. Bell, *Sesto San Giovanni*,182–3, 187–90.

34. The attitude of the Communist Party towards female activists is analysed in De Luna, *Donne in oggetto*, 102–6.

35. Luisa Passerini, *Fascism in Popular Memory* (Cambridge: Cambridge University Press, 1987), 126.

36. Edward R. Tannenbaum, *Fascism in Italy. Society and Culture, 1922–1945* (London: Allen Lane, 1972), 262.

37. Morgan, *Italian Fascism*, 116. For Fascist control of radio, see also Carlo Bordoni, *Cultura e propaganda nell'Italia fascista* (Messina–Florence: G. D'Anna, 1974); Philip Cannistraro, *La fabbrica del consenso: Fascismo e mass media* (Bari: Laterza, 1975); David Forgacs, *Italian Culture in the Industrial Era 1880–1980. Cultural Policies, Politics*

and the Public (Manchester: Manchester University Press, 1990, 63–8; Thompson, *State control in Fascist Italy*, 124–6.

38. Morgan, *Italian Fascism*, 87.
39. Emilio Gentile, *La via italiana al totalitarismo. Il partito e lo Stato nel regime fascista* (Rome: La Nuova Italia Scientifica, 1995), 170–1, 195–7.
40. Gentile, *La via italiana al totalitarismo*, 190–1.
41. Thompson, *State control in Fascist Italy*, 80.
42. The reaction of civil servants to Party attempts at 'Fascistization' of working practices is described in Venè, *Mille lire al mese*, 60–1.
43. Jonathan Dunnage, 'Policing and Politics in the Southern Italian Community, 1943–1948,' in Jonathan Dunnage (ed.), *After the War: Violence, Justice, Continuity and Renewal in Italian Society* (Market Harborough: Troubador, 1999), 32–47(36–7).
44. Thompson, *State control in Fascist Italy*, 99–100. See 98–117 for a detailed analysis of the 'Fascistization' of education and youth activities. See also Barbagli, *Educating for Unemployment*, Alexander De Grand, *Italian Fascism. Its Origins and Development* (Lincoln, NE: University of Nebraska Press, 2000), 150–2, 155–6; Tracy Koon, *Believe, Obey, Fight: Political Socialization of Youth in Fascist Italy, 1922–1943* (Chapel Hill, NC: University of North Carolina Press, 1985) and Morgan, *Italian Fascism*, 109–11.
45. Discussed in Michael A. Ledeen, 'Italian Fascism and Youth', *Journal of Contemporary History*, 4(3), July 1969, 137–54(139–42).
46. The organization of sport in the Fascist education system is discussed in Patrizia Dogliani, 'Sport and Fascism', *Journal of Modern Italian Studies*, 5(2), 2000, 326–43.
47. Koon, *Believe, Obey, Fight*, 85.
48. Whittam, *Fascist Italy*, 68–9.
49. Passerini, *Fascism in Popular Memory*, 140. See also Venè, *Mille lire al mese*, 89–90.
50. Koon, *Believe, Obey, Fight*, 113–14.
51. Barbagli, *Educating for Unemployment*, 209.
52. Thompson, *State control in Fascist Italy*, 113–14. The Fascist legacy is analysed in detail in the following chapter.
53. For a detailed analysis of the OND, see Victoria De Grazia, *The culture of consent. Mass organization of leisure in fascist Italy* (Cambridge: Cambridge University Press, 1981). See 55 for figures. See also Thompson, *State control in Fascist Italy*, 81.
54. De Luna, *Donne in oggetto*, 38.
55. Dogliani, 'Fascism and Sport', 340–1.
56. De Grazia, *The culture of consent*, chapter 4, 176–7.
57. Tannenbaum, *Fascism in Italy*, 160. See also De Grazia, *The culture of consent*, 160–2.
58. Thompson, *State control in Fascist Italy*, 120.
59. Mario Verdone, 'Mussolini's "Theatre of the Masses"', in Günter Berghaus (ed.), *Fascism and Theatre. Comparative Studies on the Aesthetics and Politics of Performance in Europe, 1925–1945* (Oxford: Berghahn, 1996), 133–9(138).
60. Pietro Cavallo, 'Theatre Politics of the Mussolini Régime and their Influence on Fascist Drama', in Berghaus (ed.), *Fascism and Theatre*, 113–32(114).
61. Corner, 'Italy', 164.

62. Bordoni, *Cultura e propaganda nell'Italia fascista*, 97.

63. Pivato and Tonelli, *Italia Vagabonda*, 100–8.

64. Forgacs, *Italian Culture in the Industrial Era*, 56–7. See 55–82 for a general discussion of the limited Fascistization of the cultural industries.

65. De Grand, *Italian Fascism*, 145–8 (quotation from 147).

66. For a detailed analysis of the accommodation by Fascist regimes of most aesthetic currents, see John London, 'The Uncertainty of Fascist Aesthetics: Political Ideology and Historical Reality', *Renaissance and Modern Studies*, 42, 1999, 49–63.

67. Howard Moss, 'Language and Italian national identity' in Gino Bedani and Bruce Haddock (eds), *The Politics of Italian National Identity. A Multidisciplinary Perspective* (Cardiff: University of Wales Press, 2000), 98–123(107). See also Arturo Tosi, *Language and society in a changing Italy* (Clevedon: Multilingual Matters, 2001), 7–11.

68. De Grazia, *How Fascism Ruled Women*, 43.

69. Initiatives for encouraging marriage and a large number of offspring are described in detail in Caldwell, 'Women and the Family in Fascist Policy'. See also De Grazia, *How Fascism Ruled Women*; Ipsen, *Dictating Demography*, 65–78, 147–84.

70. Demographic figures in this section are taken from ISTAT, *Sommario di statistiche storiche*, tables 2.12, 2.2 and 2.25.

71. Livi-Bacci, *A History of Italian Fertility During the Last Two Centuries*, 278.

72. Passerini, *Fascism in Popular memory*, 150–5.

73. Peter and Jane Schneider, *Festival of the Poor*, 219–28.

74. Passerini, *Fascism in Popular Memory*, 160–82.

75. Barbagli, *Sotto lo stesso tetto*, 386–7.

76. Discussed in Pivato and Tonelli, *Italia Vagabonda*, 37–43.

77. Perry Willson, 'Women in Fascist Italy', in Bessel (ed.), *Fascist Italy and Nazi Germany*, 78–93 (81).

78. Maria Fraddosio, 'La donna e la guerra. Aspetti della militanza femminile del fascismo: dalla mobilitazione civile alle origini del Saf nella Repubblica Sociale Italiana', *Storia Contemporanea*, 20(6), December 1989, 1105–81(1126–42).

79. De Grazia, *How Fascism Ruled Women*, 117–37 (quotation from 137). Levels of female emancipation are also discussed in De Luna, *Donne in oggetto*, and Willson, 'Women in Fascist Italy'.

80. Bosworth, 'Venice between Fascism and international tourism', 19.

81. This subject is dealt with extensively in Christopher Duggan, *Fascism and the Mafia* (New Haven, CT: Yale University Press, 1989).

82. De Luna, *Donne in oggetto*, 42–3; De Grazia, *How Fascism Ruled Women*, 79–81, 113–14.

83. The link between military campaigns and consensus for Fascism is discussed in Enzo Collotti and Lutz Klinkhammer, *Il fascismo e l'Italia in guerra* (Rome: Ediesse, 1996), chapter 2. See also Dogliani, 'Sport and Fascism', 327, 336–8.

84. Fabio Levi, 'Italian Society and Jews after the Second World War: Between Silence and Reparation', in Dunnage (ed.), *After the War*, 21–31(22–3).

85. Thompson, *State control in Fascist Italy*, 141; Denis Mack Smith, *Mussolini's Roman Empire* (London: Longman, 1976), chapter 5.

86. Wanda Newby, *Peace and War. Growing up in Fascist Italy* (London: Picador, 1991), 57, 63.

87. Thompson, *State control in Fascist Italy*, 143–4; Collotti and Klinkhammer, *Il fascismo e l'Italia in guerra*, 39–40.
88. Tannenbaum, *Fascism in Italy*, 145.
89. De Grand, *Italian Fascism*, 147.
90. The development of anti-Fascism among the younger generations of Italians is discussed in De Grand, *Italian Fascism*, 161–2; Thompson, *State control in Fascist Italy*, 51–5. For the attitude of young Catholics, see Richard J. Wolff, *Between Pope and Duce. Catholic Students in Fascist Italy* (New York: Peter Lang, 1990), 187–95.
91. Tobias Abse, 'Italian workers and Italian Fascism', in Bessel (ed.), *Fascist Italy and Nazi Germany*, 40–60(58).

Chapter 4

War, civil conflict and the defeat of Fascism, 1940–50

Introduction

This chapter examines one of the most traumatic decades in modern Italian history, during which the Italian people faced not only military defeat and occupation but also a civil war, which saw large numbers of Italians fighting each other and concluded with a violent settling of accounts. These events created serious lacerations in Italian society that only began to heal towards the end of the twentieth century. In spite of the victory over Fascism in 1945, which for Mussolini's enemies meant the end of years of oppression, the process of restoring democracy encountered frequent difficulties which often led to disappointment as well as confrontation, whether among different political or social groups or between citizens and representatives of the state. Despite these difficulties, however, with the end of the dictatorship and the war, the majority of Italians were genuinely optimistic about the possibility of creating a better future for themselves, whether in ideological terms or simply – as was more often the case – in their urgent desire to leave behind the traumas and economic hardships of the previous 20 years.

The 'Fascist' war, 1940–43

In June 1940 Italy entered the Second World War, which had broken out in September 1939 when Hitler's troops invaded Poland, on the side of Germany and Japan. Public reaction to this was mixed and ambivalent. The majority of Italians were not enthusiastic about another conflict, after the strain, which the Ethiopian war of 1935–36, the Spanish Civil War of 1936–39 and the Albanian conquest of 1939 had placed on their daily lives. However, radical Fascists saw the war as an opportunity for purifying Fascism, which they believed had lost its revolutionary character. Open enthusiasm was also manifested by the youngest generation, which under the influence of Party organizations and the educational structures saw war as an opportunity for continued fulfilment of Italy's imperial destiny. Conservative forces and the monarchy accepted the war, since they were convinced that imperial expansion could only be achieved with the help of Germany.[1]

Yet, many Italians, much to Mussolini's annoyance, had expressed enthusiasm for their country's position of neutrality when war broke out in

September 1939. If not jubilant at Italy's entry into the conflict, some were at least glad to have a strong ally and, under the illusion that the war would be a short affair, as propaganda claimed, were encouraged by Germany's rapid success in occupying most of Europe, from which they hoped Italy would gain, as long as they themselves were not forced to make significant sacrifices. Many industrialists, for example, had originally been sceptical about the war for fear of losing supplies of raw materials from Britain, but, once war was inevitable, were hopeful of a quick and profitable outcome. Enthusiasm began to wane once it became clear that the war would be a long one and that Italy was not as militarily invincible as propaganda led them to believe.

While Mussolini had originally informed Hitler that Italy would not be ready to join the conflict for several years, he ended her neutrality in 1940 in spite of the discouragement of military leaders and some members of the government, once it seemed possible – in view of Germany's lightning occupation of entire European states – that the war might end before Italy had joined, leaving her with no territorial reward and damaging the image of Fascism. But inadequate planning and provision on the part of Fascist leaders prevented total mobilization, unlike during the First World War. Italy was ill equipped for even a short war (given the huge concentration of arms that this would require). Lack of raw materials – which were supplied in ever-diminishing amounts by Germany – made it difficult for the industrial apparatus to function to full potential, while agricultural production failed to fulfil internal consumption requirements. Such problems were confounded by the incapacity of the state to co-ordinate wartime production.

Where Italy's own territorial interests were concerned, humiliating defeats were suffered, as was evident in the failed invasion of Greece at the end of 1940, from which she had to be bailed out by the Germans, and the loss of her East African empire (Eritrea, Somalia and Ethiopia) to the British in May 1941. Because of Italy's constant need of military help from the Germans, her position within the new Fascist European order was increasingly subordinate to that of her stronger ally, which saw her involved in campaigns that hardly corresponded to Mussolini's goal of Mediterranean hegemony, such as the invasion of the Soviet Union in June 1941 in which thousands of Italians lost their lives. In the occupation of newly conquered territory, Italy's position remained subordinate to Germany and even where she was given political rule, as in Croatia, she was unable to compete with Germany in economically exploiting it.

By 8 September 1943, the day of Italy's surrender to the Anglo-Americans (described below), 200,000 Italian soldiers had been killed and more than that number injured. Between 600,000 and a million had been made prisoners of war.[2] According to Enzo Collotti and Lutz Klinkhammer, letters written by soldiers suggest that within the conscripted army as far as the war was concerned there was mostly neither enthusiasm, nor rebellion, just resignation. Though account should be taken of a certain amount of self-censorship, this is a clear indication of the failure of the regime to create a new order of Fascist men. They rarely participated in the ideological object-ives of the conflict, beyond the Catholic-influenced notion of the Christian crusade against Bolshevism in the war against the Soviet Union. Indicating limited faith in the ability of military leaders, miracles rather than political or military decisions were seen as the only solutions to battle difficulties. There was little expression of hatred for the enemy, while the German ally was both admired for his technical superiority but regarded with horror for his cruel treatment of occupied peoples, particularly Jews and Russians. Such letters contrasted with the naivety of letters received from home which, imbued with Fascist propaganda, insisted upon the inevitability of victory.[3]

Though much blame for military disaster has to be apportioned to the incompetence and superficiality of both the political and the military leader-ships, it is also necessary to look at the role played by those grass-roots institu-tions responsible for the organization of war on the home front in order to appreciate the extent to which Fascist society failed to maintain public support for the war after 1941. While Italy's entry to the Second World War marked the beginning of the end of the Fascist dictatorship, initially the conflict gave a new lease of life to the ideological side of Fascism. This was particularly evident in the Fascist Party, which saw a return to its earlier radicalism, giving power to those who had criticized the mass Party organiza-tion of the 1930s as bureaucratic, middle-class and corrupt. Ettore Muti, who appointed new local leaders often belonging to the old guard of *squadristi*, replaced Starace. In Bologna the new leader took measures to put an end to unaccounted-for spending and petty corruption in the Party. Under the auspices of the state, propaganda committees for the purpose of creating a home front in case of war had been in existence since the early thirties. In 1940 the state passed responsibilities for the committees to the Party, which made use of an intensive network of political activists, particularly primary school teachers, university graduates, doctors and state employees, to en-courage a healthy attitude towards the war and preach Fascist revolutionary ideals. In Bologna, the distribution of leaflets and organization of fund-raising initiatives was accompanied by welfare activities. The *Fasci Femminili* assisted soldiers and their families, through the distribution of welfare subsidies, visits to wounded soldiers in hospital and the provision of food to be handed out to train loads of troops as they passed through the railway station. However, there were complaints of continuing corruption within the Party organizations.[4]

Unpopularity for the war increased because of food shortages. Rationing was introduced relatively late during the conflict, though this was a consequence of naive economic planning founded on the belief that the war would be short. Bread rations were introduced in the autumn of 1941 (200 grams per head per day, reduced to 150 grams in March 1942). Because of administrative inefficiency and petty corruption, food was often unavailable even in its rationed quantity, forcing citizens to rely on the black market, over which the regime had limited control. According to Abse, by January 1943 the ration card of a worker in the Biella wool industry, for example, 'could enable him only to obtain food whose calorific value was of an inadequate 1,000 calories a day'. While poorer sections of the urban working class were particularly deprived, since they had difficult access to the black market, in the country-side food consumption remained more or less at pre-war levels.[5] Personal hardships were compounded by working-class wage freezes and the failure of middle-class salaries to keep up with inflation. Many Italian workers (an estimated 350,000 by February 1942) also suffered as a result of being forced to work in Germany. This, alongside agricultural produce, paid for supplies of coal and iron.[6]

While, since 1941, there had been growing disquiet among Italians in view of the sacrifices forced upon them by the war, from 1942 there was more open opposition to the regime, which the authorities attempted to conceal. A police report claimed that: 'Restrictions, especially in food consumption . . . are accepted with serenity and the full comprehension of the Italian people, who know they are being guided to the inevitable victory as a result of the iron will and genius of he who holds Italy's destiny in his hands.' According to some reports, however, malnutrition among the workers was widespread with incidents of fainting in the factories. Increasing acts of insubordination and dissent were partly encouraged by the infiltration of the Fascist unions by the older generation of anti-Fascist workers, while the younger generation became increasingly restless and disaffected with the regime. This attitude was intensified by the return home of soldiers who were either injured or ill with tuberculosis, so breaking the isolation between Italian society and the reality of the military fronts.

In the provision of air protection the Italians quickly realized that assurances by Fascist propaganda about the invincibility of their air force were false. Worse still, the authorities had not provided proper air raid shelters, arguing that bombings would in any case be prevented by ground artillery. According to Clark:

> Northern Italy was one of the few places where mass aerial bombing proved effective in the Second World War. It disrupted production, it shattered morale, and it forced thousands of people to flee from the cities. In Turin, 25,000 dwellings had been wrecked by the end of 1942; and 500,000 people had left Milan.[7]

The intensification of Allied bombings and the defeat of the Axis forces in North Africa in the autumn of 1942 shattered any illusions that Italians still held on to. Many, though disillusioned with the general corruption and incompetence of Fascist leaders and administrators, had until that moment retained a certain faith in Mussolini. When in a speech to the nation in December 1942 he advised them to evacuate the cities to escape the bombings, many realized that they had held on too naively to the myth of the all-powerful and all-caring *Duce*.

The Party initially reacted to increasing public disquiet with violent language and actions (as is demonstrated by the ritual of slapping individuals who publicly voiced their opposition to the war). But within the Fascist organizations themselves there was growing disillusionment. Many of the younger supporters of the regime were angered by the fact that too many high-ranking Fascists fit for war had been exempted from fighting. There was growing criticism of the inefficiency and corruption of the home front and consequently a dramatic fall in Party and Militia membership numbers. Notably, in Bologna at the celebrations of the twentieth anniversary of the March on Rome in October 1942 only 800 out of 4,600 *squadristi* and old-guard Fascists invited were present.[8]

With the Fascist organizations increasingly taking only half-hearted steps to maintain discipline, the home front began to collapse and social order with it. The Church, which had assisted the war effort, urging respect of the regime's calls for discipline and obedience in the face of increasing hardships, also began to lose influence as individuals found themselves having to solve such problems as essential food provision on their own initiative (by resorting to the black market, for example), while other sources of socialization such as school education and organized leisure activities were interrupted. As Enzo Collotti states: 'If on the military front soldiers no longer had to respect the lives of their fellow men, but were indeed forced to kill without facing any penalties, on the home front, even though there was no authorization to kill, many models of behaviour were abandoned'.[9] In particular, this affected the role of women. They were once expected to contain transgression within their families. Now they found themselves ignoring moral principles in the desperate search for food.

In March 1943 for the first time in nearly 20 years mass industrial strikes against the war and its economic repercussions took place in Turin and Milan. In the face of ever-increasing opposition to the war, the Party and police were less prepared to act as they had in the past. This allowed a gradual return to better-organized forms of political agitation, as the anti-Fascist movements were able to emerge from 17 years of underground activity. Nevertheless, the role of political militants in the strikes is questionable, with worker spontaneity playing a key role. According to Tim Mason, this is illustrated by the fact that several weeks later in Turin the Communist Party failed to mobilize the workers to carry out strikes and protest demonstrations on May Day.[10] The strikes quickened the process of dissociation from Fascism of conservative sections of society, including the Church, the monarchy and the industrialists. Though they had originally supported the war initiative, they feared that military defeat would result not only in mass destruction but also in social anarchy or a Communist take-over and had since the end of 1942 contemplated firing Mussolini without abandoning authoritarian rule. Mussolini himself reacted only moderately to the strikes for fear that violent repression would be counter-productive.

For many young Italians the reality of military defeat led to a personal crisis as the credibility of a regime that had formed the basis of their daily existence was lost. Some of them moved with old-guard *squadristi* towards the fanatical Fascism of the Italian Social Republic created in the autumn of 1943 under the auspices of the occupying Nazi forces. Many others became anti-Fascists, taking part in the partisan war against the Social Republic and the Nazi occupiers. Widespread opposition to Mussolini on the home front brings to the fore the inability of the regime to create genuine consensus for what had originally been intended as a new concept of life, which would condition individuals' thoughts and actions. At the same time, however, there was much ambivalence in this mass opposition to Fascism. Many Italians had previously 'tolerated' the regime. Others had materially benefited from it. Most had identified to some extent with its national exploits. This is particularly true with regard to the middle classes, whose growing dissatisfaction with the regime was very much a result of economic difficulty. Those on fixed incomes quickly became disaffected from Fascism once inflation, as a result of the regime's need for capital in pursuing the war effort, increasingly depressed the value of their earnings.

The opposition of the working class is equally ambivalent. According to Tobias Abse, the widespread support of the strikes cannot be attributed to food shortages, bombing and military defeats alone: 'The causes lay not just in the material conditions of 1943 but in the failure of Italian Fascism over two decades to win the lasting allegiance of a stubbornly recalcitrant working class, despite deploying a combination of repression, propaganda and mass organizations of a type that no previous Italian regime had had at its disposal'.[11] The question remains, however, whether the working class would have manifested such levels of protest, if the economic and military situation had not deteriorated so suddenly. It is most likely that the gravity of the situation shook many Italians out of a state of apathy (partly nurtured by propaganda) into more determined opposition to Fascism. The deterioration of their livelihood during the previous 20 years had been much slower and therefore experienced less dramatically. According to Thompson:

> The fear that many had lived with for long periods during the *ventennio*, the possible loss of livelihood (which had also been a factor in particularly the acquiescence of the industrial proletariat) was now realised for very many more. In these circumstances of disorientation and dire necessity, the usual mechanisms of daily compromise with the regime no longer served . . .[12]

The vote against Mussolini at the meeting of the Fascist Grand Council of 25 July 1943, which led to his dismissal from government and arrest, was prompted by both the impending military defeat of Italy following the Allied invasion of Sicily on 9 July and the state of national rebelliousness against the Fascist regime.[13] Those Fascists who remained loyal to Mussolini failed to organize resistance to army units, which moved in to control the capital, and many went into hiding. After the fall of Mussolini, a new government was set up under Field Marshal Pietro Badoglio, who until 1941 had been commander in chief of the Italian military forces in Mussolini's government. Thousands of Italians manifested their jubilation at Mussolini's downfall in the streets, as statues of the dictator were pulled down and Fascist mottoes scrubbed off walls. Most Italians believed that the end of the conflict and oppression was imminent, little realizing that for many of them far worse was to come.

The Armistice and the founding of the Italian Social Republic

Immediately after Mussolini's ousting, Badoglio announced that Italy was to continue the war as an ally of Germany. During the summer of 1943, however, he secretly negotiated a surrender with the Anglo-American forces, which in the meantime had reached the mainland in Calabria and started to advance northwards. On 8 September 1943, Badoglio announced the Armistice on the radio, ordering the Italian army to react to attacks from all quarters. However, when in response to the Armistice Hitler's troops occupied the Centre and North of the peninsula, Badoglio and the King fled to the South to avoid capture by the Germans, setting up a government in Brindisi. Subsequently, most Italian army commanders dissolved their units, leaving their men to make for home. More than half a million of them were made prisoners and deported to Germany. Although anti-German resistance was limited, Paul Ginsborg refers to 'innumerable testimonies to a new spirit being born among certain, as yet very restricted, minorities of the Italian population'. Six hundred members of the army and the civilian population died trying in vain to prevent the Germans from taking Rome. On the Greek island of Cefalonia the Italian occupying garrison of 10,000 troops refused to surrender to the Germans. Nearly all of them were killed.[14]

Mussolini, who in the meantime had been rescued from his mountain prison at Gran Sasso (Abruzzo), created a new state, the Italian Social Republic (*Repubblica Sociale Italiana* – RSI, also known as the Republic of Salò), though its autonomy from the Nazi occupiers was limited. Alongside the imperative of continuing the war on the side of Germany and preventing the Anglo-American advance, the RSI claimed to be founded upon the need to move away from the conservative Fascism of the previous regime, which had become unpopular on account of high levels of corruption, and a return to the revolutionary and syndicalist Fascism of the 'first hour'. Point 9 of the Republic's founding Manifesto of Verona of November 1943 stated that its basis and primary objective was manual, technical and intellectual labour. This represented a clear attempt to put the ideals of the 1927 Labour Charter and the Corporate State into practice. RSI policies claimed to place more emphasis on the needs of the people with a programme which envisaged the partial running of companies by workers, the nationalization of some industries, the expropriation of uncultivated land, limits on profits and a more efficient system of welfare.[15]

Prominent among adherents to the RSI were those individuals who had been most supportive of the previous regime, particularly primary school teachers, municipal Party secretaries and *podestà*. Many of them were young-sters who had been educated to believe in the myths of Mussolini and the Fatherland. The overthrow of their leader and the disbanding of the Fascist Party and the Militia were a traumatic experience, since they were suddenly left with no points of reference. Moreover, they had been brought up to see war as a life purpose and refused to accept the Armistice, which they saw as a shameful betrayal of their German ally. Their support of Salò was motiv-ated by the need to put right Italy's lost honour and the injustice suffered by the *Duce*.[16] The RSI also provided an outlet for those young women who under the previous regime had sought a more significant political role. Maria Fraddosio argues that the militant and uniformed Women's Auxiliary Service (*Servizio Ausiliario Femminile* – SAF), which played a key role in mustering male support for the revival of Fascism and the continuation of the war on the side of the Germans, represented a move away from previous Fascist policies towards women. Traditional issues of motherhood and family more or less disappeared from propaganda intent upon emphasizing the support of women outside the home. This is illustrated by a propaganda postcard of June 1944 in which an old woman says to a young SAF member: 'I have done my bit by having a child and you are doing your duty, so that Italy can live on!' The fact that most female Salò supporters volunteered to join the SAF rather than traditional women's organizations, and that many even hoped that they might be able to fight for their country alongside men reflects a strong emancipatory spirit that had also existed among an élite of women Fascists during the *ventennio*.[17]

From the outset, however, there was limited support for the RSI, if only because most Italians were tired of continuing the war alongside Germany and eagerly awaited the arrival of the Anglo-Americans. Membership of the newly constituted Republican Fascist Party (*Partito Fascista Repubblicano* – PFR) was notably low. While the PNF had 2,600,000 members by 1939, in March 1944 the PFR had only 487,000 members, though allowance has to be made for the fact that RSI territory was limited and that, as part of the drive to restore Fascist purity, membership of state employees was no longer compulsory.[18]

In spite of widespread indifference, if not hostility, towards the RSI, most Italians did not actively oppose it. They had to deal with it as part of their day-to-day survival tactics and this automatically implied establishing relationships with the Nazi occupiers too. Industrialists, for example, were forced to establish economic relations with their German counterparts. Civil servants were inevitably involved in acts of a political nature such as the drafting of workers to serve in the German factories, the deportation of Jews, and the capture and frequent execution of partisan forces fighting an armed Resistance against the RSI and the Nazi occupiers (described in the following section). For them the only alternatives to collaboration with the Nazi-Fascists were the exercise of internal sabotage, resignation from their posts or desertion.

The ambiguous position of many Italians regarding the RSI is illustrated by the constitution of the Republican armed forces. Statistics suggest serious recruitment difficulties and high desertion levels. Yet, this cannot be attributed to dissent alone. The fact that over 50 per cent (88,329) of young men born in 1923, 1924 and 1925 responded positively to a military call-up in April 1944 might indicate the deep loyalties of Italian youth to Fascism, especially since the probability of victory against the advancing Allied forces was very low. Yet, it is also true that the RSI was the only point of institutional reference and, for many, joining its armed forces might not have been directly conceived as a political gesture. Hunger almost certainly played a role in encouraging military conscription too. And there was clearly a strong element of coercion behind the call-up, since failure to present oneself at the local military headquarters was punishable by death, though an amnesty did allow a further 45,000 draft dodgers and deserters to come forward.[19] Many members of the armed forces were encouraged to desert once they realized that the operations for which they had been trained were mainly directed against Italian partisans rather than the advancing Anglo-American forces. Desertion was also encouraged by Nazi plans from the summer of 1944 onwards to dismantle the Italian armed forces (considered incapable and untrustworthy) and employ their personnel in German factories and military units, as well as the growing inevitability of defeat. Allowing oneself to be disarmed by partisan units without offering resistance, as the RSI police chief complained to the prefects in June 1944, was not, therefore, an automatic measure of ideological support for the Resistance. While desertion rates were high, the majority of members of armed forces stayed in their jobs.[20]

The RSI has been the subject of recent historiographical debate centred on a desire to rehabilitate its supporters who after the Second World War were socially and politically ostracized on the grounds of their treasonable collaboration with the Nazi occupiers and the numerous atrocities they committed against partisans and civilians. Many of the protagonists themselves have argued that Mussolini founded the RSI upon the ideals of patriotism, social solidarity and independence from Germany. Their motives for support for the RSI lay above all, they claim, in the need to defend Italy from foreign dominion, be it Anglo-American, Soviet or German. Such claims to patriotism were indirectly backed up by the assertion of revisionist historians that the Armistice of 8 September 1943 marked the death of the Italian nation.[21] RSI veterans also insist that atrocities were committed as a result of a state of exasperation in the face of constant partisan attacks (which they claim were equally ruthless) or were the work of a minority of delinquents who had managed to infiltrate their organizations. Nor, they claim, had the RSI played an active role in the Jewish deportations.

The reality of the RSI is rather different. Mussolini's attempt to create an independent state founded on the principles of socialization was prevented by the Nazi occupiers, who wanted to control and exploit the Republic's economic resources for their own purposes and who accordingly dismantled many industrial plants, which were transported, along with large numbers of Italian workers, to Germany. Furthermore, the development of the RSI was negatively affected by serious ideological divisions, which saw the emergence of two main factions. The moderate one, represented in particular by the armed forces, advocated the creation of a new Italy founded on national reconciliation, which was to be achieved through dialogue and concession, rather than force. Many journalists and several intellectuals (the most prominent among them being the Hegelian philosopher and cultural ideologue of the previous regime, Giovanni Gentile) lent their support to propaganda urging social justice in a move against the corruption of the pre-1943 regime, which was seen as the cause of Fascism's loss of consent. Such language was increasingly contrasted by that of the other faction, made up of revolutionary and often violent elements, many of which were 'Fascists of the first hour' who had been isolated under the previous regime. Represented by the leader of the PFR, Alessandro Pavolini, this faction was more closely aligned to the Nazis. Believing that one could not be an Italian without being a Fascist, it violently criticized non-supporters, who were considered traitors to the Fascist cause, while praising the German allies to the point of emphasizing the inferiority of Italians.[22]

Those belonging to the extremist faction of the RSI represented by the PFR Militia (Black Brigades) and other armed organizations, many of which dissolved into criminal gangs over which the authorities had no control, committed the worst kinds of atrocities against partisans and civilians as a result of a growing sense of frustration as mass support for the Republic and the continuation of the war alongside Germany failed to materialize. According to the Resistance historian, Claudio Pavone, claims to the humane motivations behind the creation of the RSI ignore the cultural basis of Republican Fascism, which was strongly linked to the cult of violence. This is demonstrated by its use of symbols of death and such names as *Battaglione Della Morte* ('Death Battalion'). These nihilistic concepts were intensified as defeat became increasingly imminent. Nor did the Fascism of Salò merely represent a return to 'Fascism of the first hour'. Although the earlier Fascism was characterized by high levels of violence, it was part of a future-looking strategy. By contrast, in a situation of no possibility of success the forces of Salò became increasingly irrational and self-destructive in their actions.[23]

Claims by ex-Saloists that the impact of Nazi occupation on the civilian population would have been far more brutal without the protective shield of the RSI are equally questionable. Though there were cases of individual Fascists and civil servants protecting civilians against the effects of Nazi economic exploitation, political repression and racial persecution, this was the exception, not the rule. The Salò government and the state apparatus as a whole may have fought for certain concessions from the Nazis (including, for example, better treatment of Italian prisoners of war), but it did not prevent the forced drafting of large numbers of workers to serve in German factories. And it was the Interior Minister who began to place Jews in internment camps before the Nazis started their deportation programme, so rendering the job of the latter all the easier (though he would later claim that this was to prevent the Jews from suffering a worse fate under the Nazis). The RSI collaborated with the Nazis not only in order to obtain concessions from them but also as part of a strategy for the re-establishment of the regime and the survival of Fascism. There is no doubt that the Nazis had strong powers of interference in the affairs of the RSI, such that the success of many of its policies was jeopardized. To argue, however, that such policies would have met with mass approval, had the Nazis not prevented them, is an over-statement. The Nazis opposed RSI socialization policies for fear of the negative effects they would have on war production. Yet, the industrialists and workers were equally sceptical.

The partisan Resistance

The gradual Allied occupation of Central and Northern Italy (leading to the final liberation of the whole of the peninsula in April 1945) was anticipated by the military liberation of whole areas by partisan groups that had formed in enemy territory from the end of 1943. Many partisans were soldiers whose military units had been disbanded after the Armistice of 8 September 1943. While some of them managed to cross enemy lines into Allied occupied territory, others took to the hills. They were joined by other young men, who had left their homes to avoid deportation to Germany for work or conscription into the Salò armed forces, and by women and escaped prisoners of war. The bands were either 'political' – usually led by Party activists – or 'apolitical' – made up of ex-soldiers and led by army officers, though strongly pro-monarchy, and known as 'autonomous'. The Communist Party was the most prominent among the political bands, making up 50,000 Resistance fighters, followed by those of the recently formed Action Party, the Christian

Democrats and the Socialists (allied to the Communists). In the long run the political bands outnumbered the autonomous ones, though in practice their membership was often heterogeneous since individuals would join the first group they came upon irrespective of political colour when they took to the hills and mountains. The partisan groups were co-ordinated by clandestine Committees of National Liberation (*Comitati di Liberazione Nazionale* – CLN) set up all over German-occupied territory, of which the supreme organ of Resistance, the National Committee for the Liberation of Upper Italy (*Comitati di Liberazione Nazionale per l'Alta Italia*), was based in Milan.[24]

In urban areas the partisans attempted to organize mass opposition to German occupation. In the towns and cities the factories were a strong base of clandestine support for the Resistance, helped by the release of 3,000 political prisoners in July 1943, which gave the Communist Party an efficient army of partisan recruiters. Factory workers were encouraged to carry out acts of sabotage and mass strikes. In March 1944 industrial strikes took place in Turin, Milan, Florence, Venice and other urban centres. In Bologna peasant demonstrations occurred in conjunction with worker ones, while in Florence one of the Fascist headquarters was burned down. The strike was particularly effective in Milan, where all production came to a standstill for a week. Yet, the risks in participating in such activities were not light. Up to 2,000 workers were arrested by the German and Fascist police and deported to concentration camps in Germany as a result. Indeed, support was not easy to gather everywhere. Delzell notes that 'in such cities as Trieste, Genoa, Biella [the strike] was a failure, partly because of wage boosts, fear, and hastily called "preventive holidays" ascribed to alleged "electric power shortages" '.[25] In rural areas partisans encouraged support from the peasantry by getting them to consign their produce to their bands rather than to the occupation forces. On occasion they supported their economic battles in return.

Recent historiographical debate has centred on the question of whether the Resistance provided a sound basis for post-war national unity and democratic renewal. While this had never been denied by traditional anti-Fascist historiography, revisionist historians questioned this assumption during the nineties, arguing that the majority of Italians were not involved, while the partisans themselves had been politically divided. Moreover, the democratic and patriotic credentials of the political group making up the largest number of partisans, the Communists, were dubious.[26] There is no doubt that the Resistance was experienced by many Italians as a moment of national unity, whatever their political outlook. The signing of the Armistice placed them in a situation in which for the first time since the founding of the dictatorship they faced a political choice: whether to collaborate with the Social Republic and Germans or to oppose them. While for a minority of Italians continuation of the war against the Anglo-Americans on the side of Germany was seen as the only way forward, for many others the Resistance was experienced as liberation from a shameful state of blind obedience to the dictatorship. Their concept of patriotism moved away from support of the imperialist exploits of Fascism towards more specifically human values of social equality, personal responsibility and solidarity. Taking up the values of the *Risorgimento* (which, however, were also adopted by the Social Republic to justify continuation of the Fascist war), they saw the Resistance as representing the moral rejuvenation of Italy based on national dignity rather than national aggression. This would also allow her to regain an international standing after the disrepute into which Fascism had brought her.[27]

After 1945 the concept of the Resistance as a war of national liberation was mythicized, however, to the point of ignoring many internal disagreements over the purpose of the conflict. Pavone has recently situated the partisan Resistance in three parallel and often confused wars:

> If the German enemy was considered the prime element, it took on the character of a patriotic conflict. If, alternatively, attention was drawn to the Fascist enemy it looked more like a civil war. If from Fascism as a political enemy the line was traced back to the bosses and masters (the capitalists and the landowners) as the social enemy that had created and nurtured Fascism (according to the Marxist, and more generally left-wing, interpretation of Fascism), it took on the distinct characteristics of a class conflict.[28]

Politically moderate partisan bands, including Liberals and Catholics, supported by the leadership of the anti-Fascist government in liberated territory, insisted on the patriotic character of the Resistance and were concerned that it should not be transformed into a Left-dominated civil war. They wanted to spare the civilian population from involvement where possible so as to protect it from the risks of Nazi–Fascist reprisals. In contrast many grassroots left-wing partisans saw themselves as being in the thick of a bloody civil conflict, which at the community level often took on strong class-war connotations. In urban areas their guerrilla warfare groups (GAP – *Gruppi di Azione Patriottica*) were formed for the purpose of carrying out assaults on prominent members of the Nazi–Fascist authorities and acts of sabotage against the enemy armed forces. Violence was employed as a pedagogic revolutionary strategy for encouraging mass insurrection, consequently exposing civilians to reprisals. This position clashed, however, with the strategy of the Communist leader, Palmiro Togliatti, who discouraged civil conflict and believed that any serious attempt at insurrection would be crushed by the Anglo-American forces. Having joined the Badoglian government in March 1944 following his return from exile in the Soviet Union and desiring to present his party as a force of national unity, he argued that any social changes were to be put off until after the Liberation.

In practice, however, there was usually peaceful co-existence among the different partisan groups, as was illustrated by the temporary setting up of republics in areas where they had gained complete control during the summer of 1944. In these republics the CLN allowed a return to formal democratic principles after more than twenty years and attempted to enforce social and economic policies. Councils were elected to administer the distribution of food, fix prices, levy taxes and even run hospitals and schools. Even within the Communist camp revolutionary aims were normally put aside in favour of the leadership policy of national unity in the albeit mistaken belief that revolution was merely being put off until the end of the war. According to Ginsborg, the Communists avoided the implementation of 'revolutionary' policies, such as the progressive taxation of the rich, precisely out of a desire to preserve national unity.[29]

Levels of ideological participation characterizing the Resistance varied. For older militant partisans, the Resistance represented a return to active political life after years of clandestine activity. Yet, for many there was undoubtedly a less mature level of ideological participation. Among them were a younger generation of Italians who had been brought up and educated under the dictatorship. It is claimed that initially existentialist decisions, as in the case of those young men joining to avoid being deported to Germany or drafted into the Salò military forces, often formed the basis of future political commitment. However, as Philip Cooke argues: 'Although the bands themselves nominally had some political allegiance, many of the men and women who fought had little, if any, knowledge of political theory. They were much more interested in defeating the enemy than in gaining an understanding of, say, communism or socialism'.[30] At the individual level there existed myriad factors at play in the manner in which political events were perceived. For many women who joined the partisans, there was undoubtedly a desire to become equal to men.

How widespread was participation in and support for the Resistance? The 220,000 Italians officially recognized as partisan soldiers clearly represented only a minority of the population at large.[31] Moreover, as Roger Absalom points out, the social composition of the partisans, of which 40 per cent were factory workers and artisans, 20 per cent peasants and rural workers and 25 per cent middle-class intellectuals, was remote from the general pattern of society.[32] Equally significantly Southern Italy was geographically excluded from the experience of the Resistance. Though conscripted by the Badoglian government in the South to take part alongside the Allied armies in the liberation of RSI territory, many Southerners showed little enthusiasm for a return to war, which did not involve them directly, and many of them reacted by demonstrating violently or deserting.

Historians are divided over the extent to which the population at large gave support to the partisans in enemy-occupied territory. The revisionists, as part of a thesis claiming that the majority of Italians were caught between and indifferent towards a bloody civil war between partisans and Fascists, argue that during the period of the Nazi occupation there existed a widespread attitude of *attendismo* ('wait and see'). While much of the civilian population did not support the Fascists and Germans, they were not ready to support the Resistance either, since they felt that doing so would increase the risk of reprisals. Nazi atrocities such as the shooting of 335 prisoners at the Ardeatine caves in March 1944 in reprisal after Roman partisans blew up 32 German military police are seen as having been inflicted upon innocent citizens caught up in a war which did not belong to them because of the negligent behaviour of left-wing partisans who escaped back into hiding after terrorist attacks, leaving the local population defenceless. Acts of solidarity (such as the sheltering of Jews and escaped prisoners of war), the revisionists argued, were often the consequence of a civil war situation in which they could not avoid being involved, but are not to be considered true and proper acts of resistance.

A less negative view of the Resistance sees more committed participation by the civilian population. The partisans enjoyed greater freedom of movement than the Fascists, as a result of more widespread support, which manifested itself in a civil resistance in which women, for example, played an important role. According to Jane Slaughter, through such networks as the *Gruppi di Difesa della Donna* (Women's Defence Groups), they encouraged spontaneous rebellions against the Nazi–Fascist authorities over such matters as food rations, recruited new members, encouraged women to provide shelter and clothing for partisans and created an information network that linked the civilian population to the partisans: 'Their social placement gave women "natural" disguises, information about their neighbors, and a tradition of collective activity that enabled them to tap community resources for recruits, demonstrators, money, and hiding and meeting places and to spread the word that Italy was to be liberated and all citizens should join the cause.'[33]

Yet, the ambiguities surrounding the question of civilian support of the Resistance remain. In the cities it is likely that much of the support for the Resistance lay in economic motives. The partisans were able to take advantage of the fact that working-class daily wages dropped dramatically (from 13.91 lire in 1943 to 5.16 lire in 1944 at constant 1938 prices) to encourage strikes.[34] According to Absalom, the great mass of the Italian peasantry never went beyond passive resistance to the Social Republic and the Nazis, partly because their own sons were often members of its armed forces. Their resistance consisted above all in withholding food supplies from enforced collections, a phenomenon also happening in the liberated South. He notes:

> Although few peasants were strongly influenced by the official ideologies of either Fascism or anti-fascism, their 'common sense' provided models of interpretation and response which reflected a long history of exploitation and more or less successful passive resistance to it, while they possessed a traditional technique of survival through concealment and displacement, and a framework of values tending to legitimate such behaviour.[35]

Levels of peasant support for the Resistance varied, however, according to economic, social, geographical and cultural factors. Thus, in rural areas where the farming system was socially more inward-looking peasant attitudes towards the civil war and German occupation were based more on the individualistic fight for survival. Philip Cooke argues that there was only limited peasant solidarity in Piedmont during the Resistance. Belonging to an ancient isolated world, the peasantry viewed partisans as profiteers and felt threatened by their frequent requisitioning of their produce. Their support of the partisans was often passive, with the same kind of compliance shown towards the Nazis and the Fascists, or opportunistic, as was evident in their running of a flourishing black market. Support was lacking where there was a risk of reprisals.[36] However, in regions like Emilia, peasant attitudes were more collective in line with the *braccianti* tradition of solidarity. Their support of the Resistance was directly linked to the idea of a class war to be declared against the landowning élite at the moment of Liberation.[37]

Final liberation occurred as territory was invaded by the Anglo-American armies, often with the assistance of the partisan groups. On many occasions the partisans organized full-scale popular insurrections to liberate whole cities in advance of the Allied arrival. The toll of casualties resulting from the war of Liberation is considerable. Overall approximately 35,000 partisans were killed and 21,000 injured throughout the period of the Resistance, while nearly 10,000 civilians were killed in Nazi–Fascist reprisals. 10,000 Italian soldiers died fighting alongside the Anglo-American forces and another 30,000 were killed abroad fighting in other liberation movements. Around 8,000 Italian political deportees died in Nazi concentration camps, too.[38] The 800,000 Italian soldiers captured by the Germans after the Armistice are often forgotten by historians. They were interned without the internationally recognized status of prisoners of war, which left them without the right to care by the international Red Cross or the guarantee of protection by neutral powers as established by international conventions. Seventy-five per cent of them refused to join the Wehrmacht and Salò forces, even though they were aware of the fact that they would be subjected to forced labour, alongside all kinds of humiliation and maltreatment, as a result of their 'betrayal' of their ex-ally. 33,000 never returned to their homeland.[39]

Violence and conflict in the post-war community

Liberation by no means brought immediate peace to Italy, characterized as it was by widespread violence and general lawlessness. Many Fascists, together with individuals accused of collaborating with them and the Nazis, were killed in a settling of accounts – of which the most emblematic episode was the shooting of Mussolini and his mistress, Claretta Petacci, as they tried to reach the Swiss border on 27 April 1945. Figures on the number of killings vary according to different sources. While right-wing sources suggest the fictitious number of 300,000, an Interior Ministry report calculated a more accurate total of 9,911 individuals who disappeared or were killed for being 'politically compromised'. The killings were a result of summary executions, the death sentences of CLN political courts put into function before the arrival of the Allies in the immediate aftermath of the Liberation, mob violence, and a prolonged phenomenon of partisan murders.[40]

The post-Liberation killings have only recently been the object of historical analysis, having been ignored for decades. It is important, however, to examine them in the context of the nature of the war of Liberation and preceding 20 years. At the level of the community, whether in the rural village or town district, known individuals were seen as responsible for the rise to power of Fascism and for the oppression of the *ventennio* and the Salò period, and personal grudges for ills suffered were translated into particularly violent reactions. Moreover, the final phase of Fascism preceding the Liberation had seen worse atrocities committed by the other side. It is no coincidence that the provinces registering the highest number of killings (including Turin, Bologna, Milan and Genoa) were those that had borne the brunt of Nazi–Fascist violence. At the moment of liberation of communities summary executions by partisans and public lynching were frequent, as was the head shaving of female collaborators. Later, as it became clear that the legal system was failing to bring Fascists to justice (described in the following section), partisans supported by communities often took the law into their own hands. Emblematic in this sense was the killing of 51 arrested Fascists in Schio (Vicenza) in July 1945, a reaction to the news of their imminent release from prison coinciding with the return to the town of refugees from Mauthausen concentration camp.[41]

Partisan killings continued well after the Liberation, representing the prolongation of class and civil conflict. Many at first glance appeared remote from the moment of Liberation, however. In Bologna in the summer of 1945, for example, sharecroppers killed several agricultural employers because of their refusal to alter employment contracts dating back to the Fascist period. Several priests were also murdered. According to Mirco Dondi, it is likely that the high incidence of murders of agricultural employers in Emilia–Romagna lay in the fact that they had enjoyed the protection of the Fascist regime and the RSI. It is noticeable that there were fewer such killings in Tuscany, where landowner support of the RSI had been weaker. Regarding the murder of priests, the victims had on occasion been supportive of the RSI, while on others the killings were due to the need to eliminate from the community the presence of a conservative figure of mediation between the peasantry and the landowners.[42]

Demonstrating the blurring of partisan and collective violence, the murder of three Fascist landowning brothers, the Counts Manzoni from the village of Lavezzola in Romagna, in July 1945 has the connotations of a peasant anti-feudal revolt. Communist partisans attacked their villa, killing the counts, as well as their elderly mother, the maid and their dog. This was followed by the invasion of the property by the whole community, which proceeded to share out the spoils. Crainz interprets this episode of violence, alongside others, as characteristic of a closed peasant culture, which refused to recognize official state justice (especially once that system appeared to be absolving Fascist crimes) in favour of its own justice system and codes of behaviour. Consequently, the whole community was prepared to keep silent about the perpetrators of atrocities.[43]

The immediate post-war period also saw the development of neo-Fascist terrorist groups. They were made up of ex-Fascists, together with collaborationists of the RSI, who felt threatened by the possibility of being brought to trial, if not killed by partisans. According to Clark, by the end of 1945 five groups were active in Rome and even more were based in the North. Moreover, they would benefit from the support of conservative forces against the growing 'Red threat' resulting from the restoration of political freedom, being recruited to fight Republican groups in the referendum on the monarchy of June 1946 and more generally to disrupt left-wing meetings and break strikes.[44] This failure on the part of the post-war government to deal sufficiently with the Fascist legacy (described below) was also evident in the creation in 1946 by the defeated Fascists of a political party, which, if not calling itself Fascist, clearly indicated itself as the successor to the RSI by calling itself the Italian Social Movement (*Movimento Sociale Italiano* – MSI).

The state of violence and conflict was further exacerbated by a dramatic increase in 'ordinary' crime levels. The number of armed robberies, for example, rose from 1,254 in 1940 to over 18,000 in 1946.[45] Economic desperation was clearly a prominent factor in explaining this. The fact that during the war individuals had increasingly been abandoned by state organizations in the provision of food and other life essentials had led to a general downgrading of moral codes of behaviour, as they were forced to rely on their own resources. Lawlessness had been encouraged by the tendency of the authorities to maintain a low profile at the moment of the change in regime. The authorities also lacked the resources necessary for maintaining law and order. This resulted in both collective action such as the raiding of military food stores or bakeries and, more seriously, the development of organized crime (helped by the wide availability of arms). Moreover, in the South the Allied occupation allowed the resurrection of *Mafia* organizations, which had been temporarily subdued by Fascist repression, as a result of the nomination of bosses as mayors in Sicily, Calabria and Campania in return for their services to the invading forces. In Campania the Allied occupation allowed the criminal activities of the *Camorra* to flourish. Their help to the occupying forces was indispensable, since they controlled economic resources in the region.[46]

According to John Foot, post-war violence was to some extent a consequence of the taste that individuals had acquired for warfare during the recent conflict, creating a culture in which the use of force and arms seemed the best way to achieve ends. Criminality resulted partly from the development during the period of the RSI of a state of 'anarchy within dictatorship', as numerous semi-criminal Fascist and Nazi police corps and militia came into being, over which the central authorities had limited control. Often the line between political crime and ordinary acts of delinquency was blurred. The famous bandit Ezio Barbieri, who terrorized Milan in the immediate post-war years, formerly had close links with the semi-criminal Muti Legion of the RSI, notorious for its violence and use of torture. A number of partisans also became involved in post-war organized crime. As Foot argues with reference to Milan, the criminal groups 'would not have existed without the war experience (the vast majority were ex-members of either Fascist militias or Resistance groups) and many did use political arguments to justify their actions'.[47]

Even the more democratic initiatives of the post-war period on occasion dissolved into lawlessness. After 20 years of dictatorship the concept that many Italians had of democracy was distorted, and this led to the adoption of violent solutions, whether on the part of those governing or the governed. Newly proclaimed democracy heralded the long-awaited fulfilment of social aspirations, such as the granting of land to the peasantry to end centuries of poverty and exploitation, particularly in the South. But – indicating high levels of resistance to democratic renewal within the Italian state (as discussed in the following section) – these were difficult to reconcile with existing laws, which were slow to be removed or changed. The impatience and frustration resulting from this often led to the law being overlooked (since it was seen as no longer relevant), as was evident in illegal land occupations, which were frequently put down with police bullets.

Harsh government measures were a consequence of both a genuine state of disorder and its fear of revolutionary initiatives by the Left, which succeeded, for example, in organizing peasant occupations of the Southern *latifondi*, one of the few moments of peasant solidarity to be achieved in the South. The worst incidents of state repression occurred in Palermo in September 1944 when the army killed over 90 civilians in a demonstration provoked by the failure of the council to pay its employees and in Ragusa, Sicily, in January 1945, when 19 civilians and 18 soldiers and *carabinieri* were killed during demonstrations in protest at military conscription.[48] The late forties also saw the return of *Mafia* dominance as it employed violence in support of the landowners against the growing peasant movement. The worst massacre occurred at Portella delle Ginestre near Palermo, where, in the aftermath of the left-wing victory in the Sicilian regional elections of April 1947, the *Mafia* fired against a crowd of 1,500 people, who had gathered to celebrate 1 May, killing 11 of them.[49]

134

The legacy of Fascism, institutional continuity and democratic renewal

The violent 'settling of accounts' of the immediate aftermath of the Liberation brought to the fore the urgent necessity for the new administrators to deal with the Fascist legacy, if only as a means of preventing further uncontrolled violence. What was to happen to those people who had played a prominent role in enforcing the 20-year dictatorship? And what about those responsible for crimes associated with Fascism, among whom were military commanders accused of atrocities in Ethiopia and the Balkans? The question also arose as to whether individuals compromised with Fascism could maintain their positions in the state administration, in the education sector and even in private companies, given the potential threat they posed to the new democratic order, even if they had not committed crimes. An even more pressing problem was how to deal with institutional and political collaborationism underlying the Social Republic. Its creation had effectively constituted an act of treason against the government that had legally overthrown Mussolini, and had resulted in serious atrocities. But could one ignore the fact that there was a certain element of compulsion behind the decision of thousands of state employees and civil servants to keep their jobs in the autumn of 1943? And could the younger generation of Italians who remained loyal to Mussolini on account of the extent of their exposure to Fascist propaganda be punished for treason where no actual crimes had been committed?

Although most of the anti-Fascist governing parties agreed that only those guilty of the worst crimes associated with Fascism or seriously compromised in other ways should be punished or purged, the majority of those concerned got off with light sentences or kept their jobs and this partly explains prolonged partisan violence. The main reason for this failure lay in the very nature of Mussolini's downfall. The fact that Mussolini was removed by members of his own government, supported by the monarchy, the army and the industrial leadership, is fundamental, because it ensured an institutional continuity that prevented mass ferment against Fascism from turning into a full-scale uprising, with possible revolutionary consequences. Such continuity would in the long run inhibit the post-war democratic process. The appointment of Badoglio as prime minister saw the dissolution of the Militia, the PNF, the Grand Council, the Special Tribunal and the Chamber of Fasces and Corporations (which had replaced what remained of the Chamber of Deputies in 1939). But much of Badoglio's entourage had played an important role in the previous government and this accounted for his failure to put effectively into practice measures to purge the state administration of Fascists and to have individuals responsible for crimes arrested. Badoglio himself was accused of war atrocities in Ethiopia.

By restoring a minimum amount of political freedom, reducing censorship and allowing the recreation of workers' factory commissions, Badoglio was able to present both the Allied occupiers, with whom he secretly negotiated an Italian surrender during the summer of 1943, and the Italian people with an image of dissociation from Fascism. In reality, Badoglio was reluctant to allow anything more than formal democracy. He prohibited public demonstrations and was slow to free anti-Fascist prisoners from the penal colonies. Only Allied intervention quickened the process of releases. Badoglio's troops frequently resorted to violent repression to maintain control, a situation that would continue under his successors, in spite of the increasing influence in political affairs of the anti-Fascist parties, which had in the meantime come out of hiding. According to Mirco Dondi, 'More than a revived liberal monarchy or a Fascism without Mussolini, the new regime (including Prime Minister, Field Marshal Pietro Badoglio himself) embodied the authoritarian current in Italian history, anxious to rule directly and impatient of obstacles.'[50]

The appointment of the old anti-Fascist Liberal, Ivanoe Bonomi, in Badoglio's place after the liberation of Rome in June 1944 did not constitute a significant victory for the parties of the CLN. The new prime minister resurrected the central bureaucracy without purging it of Fascist personnel so that the main features of the new Italian state were established before the North was liberated and the Resistance could seriously influence the choices of central government. Moreover, Bonomi did not recognize the CLNAI as the government of the North, delegating to it instead the task of representing his government in the enemy zones. This effectively meant that the achievements of the CLNs were reversed as power passed to the Italian authorities almost immediately after the liberation of territory. Although one of the major Resistance leaders, Ferruccio Parri, was prime minister of an anti-Fascist coalition government between June and November 1945, he himself was reluctant to push for radical social reforms. In analysing the failure of the anti-Fascist sanctions, therefore, it is important to consider the broader context of a 'conservative restoration' of power, which would effectively slow down the overall process of democratization in Italy. Accordingly, the majority of Fascist laws were not removed until the late fifties and some remain in force even today. In particular, the police code of 1931 continued to be used as a means of limiting political freedom, even after the founding in 1948 of a democratic Constitution.

In view of the above political developments, it comes as no surprise that few individuals were purged or seriously punished. While the Allied occupiers were reasonably rigorous in their sacking of high-ranking civil servants and in their arrest of individuals accused of Fascist crimes, once they had passed their administrative powers back to the Italian government there was a noticeable drop in the number of individuals purged or put on trial. There was also a deliberate concentration on the more serious crimes surrounding Salò collaborationism in order to minimize the crimes of the *ventennio*. The Allies took the matter of anti-Fascist sanctions seriously because they felt that this would contain partisan demands. In several cases they arrested individuals, and in doing so saved them from the risk of mob violence, summary execution or an overtly politicized trial, but once those individuals were handed over to the Italian authorities they were often released.[51]

While partisans and anti-Fascists were appointed to government posts, as heads of purge commissions and supervisors of special courts, and as provincial prefects and police chiefs, the administrative ground work was often in the hands of state personnel who, in their reluctance to put into motion a machine to which they themselves might fall victim, sabotaged the democratic process by protecting individuals or simply ignoring orders from above. Roy Domenico notes that, according to Allied statistics on the progress of purges by January 1945, of 10,063 names submitted by the Italian government to the purge commissions, 'about one third had been judged serious enough for formal judgment'. This resulted in only 587 dismissals, while 1,461 received minor sanctions and 1,530 were acquitted.[52] As an example of a kind of corporate self-protection within the Italian state underlying the 'de-Fascistization' process, it is noticeable that, while the law courts sentenced many individuals, such as members of the Black Brigades of the RSI, to prison for such crimes as murder, they were far more lenient towards high-ranking state officials accused of crimes of collaborationism.[53]

The increasingly lenient attitude towards ex-Fascists was also encouraged by a widespread feeling that forgiveness was preferable to harsh punishments dictated by feelings of vendetta, particularly after it was revealed that many of them were suffering in overcrowded and unhygienic prisons. This was not helped by the fact that court sentences were frequently uneven and therefore seen as unjust. Anti-Fascist sanctions became more and more difficult to impose on account of their being interpreted by the centre and right-wing parties of the governing coalition as a springboard for Communist revolution. Many Fascists accused of serious crimes benefited from the leniency of judges because of their connections in high places. Others were able to go into hiding, especially in the South where they were fed, housed and even employed by right-wing sympathizers.

While generally lenient towards the Fascists, the judiciary began to concentrate their attention on partisan 'crimes' very quickly after the Liberation. Whereas special legislation dealing with collaborationism and crimes associated with Fascism took account of the particular circumstances in which they were committed and in this way allowed many individuals to forgo harsh punishments, in the absence of legislation concerning activities connected with the Resistance, judges were able to use Fascist laws to prosecute partisans for common crimes. Hence, for example, the shooting of spies was prosecuted as murder. Though many partisans were arrested for acts of violence committed after the Liberation, many others found themselves criminalized for acts committed during the war, which should, therefore, have been considered legitimate. Though an amnesty was passed in June 1946 to deal with crimes committed in both the Fascist and partisan camps, in practice appeal court judges were given wide discretionary powers, which allowed them to apply the amnesty liberally with regard to Fascist criminals and sparingly with regard to partisans. The Cassation Courts scandalously annulled many prison sentences for the worst kinds of atrocities committed by members of the Black Brigades. Domenico notes that as a result of this situation at the start of 1947 Emilia's political prison inmates were overwhelmingly left-wing: 'In Bologna, for example, 3 lonely Fascists languished alongside 321 Communists, 84 "communist sympathizers", 116 "aparatchiks", and 18 Socialists'.[54] The judicial persecution of the partisan movement became even more intense from 1948 under the newly elected Centre government.

The great mass of Italian citizens who had in some way or other been involved in Fascism but were not seriously compromised did not face sanctions. As was illustrated in the last chapter, their support of Fascism in an atmosphere of compulsion and overwhelming propaganda was not necessarily an expression of ideological faith, or unfettered free will. In many cases it was dictated by the need to survive. Yet, there is no doubt that Italians had grown accustomed to non-democratic procedures or absorbed anti-democratic ideas. However, if individuals who were in any way involved with Fascism (if only by having been a member of the PNF or the Fascist unions, for example) were to be removed from their posts, hundreds of thousands of Italians would face the sack and the practical consequences (in terms of the running of the country) would be disastrous, as the purge commissions quickly realized. The reluctance of the state apparatus to carry out a far-reaching purge was also linked to the desire of the anti-Fascist parties to recreate national unity. Evident in this sense is the Communist Party's long-term policy of opening its doors to ex-Fascists, including Saloists, particularly of the younger generation, with its emphasis on their having been 'deceived' by Fascism.[55]

The effects of Fascist propaganda were not countered by any far-reaching or systematic process of examination of consciences or re-education. Many Italians conveniently chose to forget what had happened between 1922 and 1945. Indeed, until the sixties the themes of Fascism and the Resistance were notably absent from the school classroom, run by teachers who had often made their careers during the dictatorship. The general indifference towards the plight of Italian Jews under Fascism is a prime example of failure to accept responsibility for the past. Fabio Levi argues that there was little attempt on the part of Italian society to appreciate the suffering of Italian Jews as a result of the 1938 race laws and the later deportations of the Salò period. Any remedies for such suffering came in the form of impersonal legislation restoring Jews' civil and political rights, reinstating them in their jobs and returning their property to them. Yet, it is evident that in practice many Jews were unable to return to the professions from which they had been expelled in 1938, while Jewish company owners found themselves facing bills for running costs incurred by the state, after it had confiscated them.[56]

The more subtle effects of Fascism on the minds of Italians should not be underestimated. According to Dondi, many individuals held on to a kind of 'involuntary Fascism', which manifested itself in conformity, and assessment of events through slogans once provided by Fascist propaganda, which created a negative attitude towards democracy. The blind faith and belief in absolute truths instilled by Fascism were often applied to new political parties, hence – paradoxically – many found sanctuary in Communism. As Dondi argues, 'a fall off in "consent" did not mean a wiping out of the more deeply rooted aspects of a Fascist political consciousness'.[57]

Between tradition and renewal: the effects of war and the Resistance on Italian society

The war of Liberation undoubtedly marked an important turning point in Italian history. Yet, the somewhat ambiguous mass dissociation from Fascism and the limited long-term innovative effects of the Resistance were partly reflected in lingering conservative attitudes that would inhibit democratic renewal. On 2 June 1946 elections were held in which women were allowed to vote for the first time in Italian history. The Italians were asked to choose between the continuation of the monarchy and a republic and they voted for the latter, though only by a small margin. Indeed, in the South the Monarchist vote prevailed. They also elected their representatives to a Constituent Assembly, which would have the responsibility of drafting a new constitution to form the basis of the Republic. The most powerful political parties emerging were the Christian Democrats (*Democrazia Cristiana* – DC), who, under the leadership of Alcide De Gasperi, gained 35 per cent of the vote, followed by the Socialists with 20 per cent and the Communists with 19 per cent.[58] Though the 1948 Constitution allowed for the creation of a democratic parliamentary system, the institutions of the state that had survived the 'de-Fascistization' process, together with Fascist laws that had not been repealed, would stand in the way of the enactment of many of the principles it voiced.

The resounding victory of the Christian Democrats at the general election of 18 April 1948, with an even larger vote than that of 1946, has often been interpreted as an indication of the essentially conservative mentality of the Italian people and their apparent dissociation from the Resistance (or at least its more radical aims). The Christian Democrats achieved an impressive majority of 48.5 per cent, obtaining 305 out of 574 seats in the Chamber of

139

Deputies, and absorbing right-wing extremism that was particularly strong in the South by taking most of the votes of the Monarchists, the neo-Fascists (MSI) and the short-lived pseudo-Fascist 'Common Man's Front' (*Fronte dell'Uomo Qualunque*), which had gained over a million votes in 1946. However, the Popular Front of Communists and Socialists also gained a considerable portion of the vote, taking 31 per cent, though this marked a notable drop from 39.7 per cent polled at the 1946 election. The final section of this chapter analyses the political choices of the Italian electorate against the broader background of social transformation during the immediate aftermath of the world conflict.

The main reason for the Christian Democratic victory lay in the Party's ability to make tangible promises for future economic wealth. Most Italians had suffered some form of material hardship from the mid-thirties onwards and this had intensified during the war. After the conflict Italy had to deal with the effects of war damage and an economy that remained backward by comparison with other Western powers. The potential for economic renewal in Italy was good on account of limited war damage. The main problem the country faced was a lack of raw materials and poor lines of communication on account of the bombing of roads and railways. But though 85 per cent of Northern plant capacity had survived (with losses varying from 25 per cent in the metallurgical industry at 1938 value, to only 5 per cent in the wool and cotton textile sectors), industrial output stood at 29 per cent of pre-war levels in 1945 and agriculture at 63.3 per cent.[59]

Italy remained a largely backward country in which precarious standards of living had been compounded by war. By 1945 Italians consumed a third less proteins, fats and carbohydrates than they had before the conflict. This is all the more significant, if we are to consider that by the late thirties consumption levels were already low on account of Fascist policies. A parliamentary inquiry of 1951–52 into poverty revealed that 11.8 per cent of families lived below the subsistence level, and classified 11.6 per cent of families as poor. The traditional wealth gap between the North and the South had not been closed. Poor housing, much of which had been destroyed or damaged, and low standards of hygiene also constituted a serious problem. Only 50 per cent of houses had an inside toilet and just over 10 per cent contained a bathroom, while less than 50 per cent had running water. Few new houses were built during the late forties. Of 66,000 planned in 1946, for example, only 34,000 were completed.[60] Large numbers of Italians faced unemployment and poor working conditions. Although the presence of the Communists and Socialists in the coalition government allowed the introduction of wage-indexing (*scala mobile*) to safeguard workers' income against the effects of inflation, the unions lost ground to the employers over mass sackings in 1946 and the achievement of national-level wage agreements, which reduced union influence at the shop-floor level.

Much of the material basis for the Christian Democrats' electoral victory was provided by the nature of economic measures undertaken by the Italian government in the months leading up to the election. The Liberal Budget Minister, Giulio Einaudi, appointed to De Gasperi's government in June 1947, brought inflation and a foreign exchange crisis under control. In many respects the results of this were devastating for ordinary Italians. As Ginsborg notes, credit restrictions hit small and medium-sized firms, leading to an overall decline in investment and production and further mass redundancies. Unemployment was at a monthly average of over two million by 1948. Nevertheless, there was a general feeling that the economy was being brought under control, while the urban middle classes dependent on fixed incomes greatly benefited. Tactics such as Confindustria's granting of a substantial pay rise to white-collar workers just before the election also helped to isolate support for the Left.[61]

In the context of the onset of the Cold War and indicating the possibilities for exploiting two decades of Fascist propaganda, the success of the Christian Democrats was also the result of a strong anti-Communist campaign, which saw the mobilization of the Catholic Church and the United States in their support. While Pope Pius XII warned that it was a mortal sin not to vote, or to vote for lists and candidates not respecting Christian rights, the United States government (which had already pressurized De Gasperi into ousting the Communists and Socialists from his government in May 1947) in as ceremonious a way as possible designated huge sums of money and aid to Italy, assuring the Italian people that it would continue in the case of a Christian Democrat victory, but would immediately cease in the event of a Communist majority. This was accompanied by a private campaign by the Italian-American community. As David Ellwood points out, ten million letters and cables were sent from individual Italian-Americans to friends and relatives in Italy urging them to vote against the Communists. Famous stars including Frank Sinatra and Gary Cooper recorded radio programmes, while a 'Friendship Train' distributed piles of gifts gathered in America.[62]

The hard-line attitude of the Christian Democrat Interior Minister, Mario Scelba, towards strikes and demonstrations assured many voters that law and order would be maintained under Christian Democrat rule, while electoral posters warned of the hunger, Soviet revolution and anarchy that would follow a left-wing victory. The popularity of the Left was not helped by the Soviet-supported Communist seizure of power in Czechoslovakia two months earlier. During the election campaign the Christian Democrats benefited from the support of Catholic Action which organized local civic committees with the task of convincing Catholics to vote en masse and instructing the illiterate and aged how to vote. Prefects and police chiefs aided the Christian Democrat campaign by using their powers to make life difficult for the Left, banning electoral demonstrations where possible on the grounds of a threat of public order.

In many respects, however, the Christian Democrats were successful because they were closer to the social reality of post-war Italy than the Left, which had mistakenly interpreted mass support for the Resistance as ideologically based. As Absalom notes: 'The Communists and Socialists had assumed that "Resistance values", with their stress on "national" solidarity for liberation and reconstruction, would easily overcome the deep-rooted traditions at every level of the population of "looking after the family" and distrusting "authority", even the leadership to which one had given one's vote.' Even within the trade union organizations the Communists and Socialists failed to attract substantial support because they tended to call strikes and demonstrations for non-economic purposes, such as protests against American aid, while failing to win improvements in pay and conditions.[63]

Rather than the victory of democracy against left-wing totalitarianism, the losers interpreted the Christian Democrat rise to power as constituting further denigration of the values of the Resistance and blocking the democratic process. This was partly confirmed by events of the summer of 1948: Many left-wing supporters saw the attempt on Togliatti's life by a deranged individual on 18 July as the culmination of a period of repression which had seen consistent violation of workers' rights and failure to purge or punish Fascists. There followed a number of violent demonstrations in parts of the North and Centre, which, though discouraged by the Communist Party leadership, effectively gave the government a pretext for heightening its repression. Between November 1948 and February 1949 as many as 95,000 former partisans and party activists were arrested. Most of the arrests and detentions were for intimidation purposes, resulting as they did in only 19,000 prosecutions of which 7,000 returned guilty verdicts.[64] The removal of partisans from among the prefects and the police and their replacement by individuals purged immediately after the Liberation, a process that had begun in 1946, was also intensified. The way was left open for high levels of state repression of working-class manifestations and left-wing political activities during the following decades, confirming the historical divide between large sections of the population and the ruling classes and the wide gap between democratic ideals enshrined in the new Constitution and institutional practices.

Undoubtedly, the basically conservative political choice of the majority of Italians in 1948, besides being partly attributable to the subtle but longer-lasting effects of Fascist propaganda, was also an indication of the strength within Italian society of tradition, which, if not always standing in the way of innovation, tended to absorb it and neutralize its most radical aspects. How were the transformations brought about by such dramatic events as the war registered at the social level? The question is best answered by looking at rural Italy. As the research of Catia Sonetti on Tuscany demonstrates, during the war country folk were strongly influenced by the experience of meeting urban refugees with a different culture and way of life. As a result of developing acquaintances and friendships new professions were learnt and stronger links with urban areas established. The traditional family hierarchy was partly broken by the fact that during the war women were given positions of public responsibility for the first time, as was illustrated by the assistance they gave to the partisans. Women were thereby entrusted with levels of freedom in ways that before the war no father or elder brother would ever have permitted. Men returning from the Front were equally changed in the manner in which they saw life and its values. Sharecroppers no longer felt bound by the rituals of religion and traditional deference towards the agrarian élite and this clearly prompted demands for land reform.[65]

Yet, the subsequent development of Italian society, discussed in the following chapter, shows that in the long run it was the very survival of family tradition that represented a fundamental vehicle for social transformation that would characterize Italy in the fifties and sixties. As had happened during the early process of industrialization at the end of the nineteenth century, 'familist' strategies played a key role in protecting individuals from the alienating effects of change from an agricultural to an industrial economy. The Italian family represented a kind of mediating body between old and new. But at the same time this allowed the survival of less forward-looking characteristics and inhibited some of the advances made during the Resistance. It is evident that patriarchal values survived too. There is little doubt, for example, that most Italian men, whatever their politics, remained suspicious of female emancipation. According to Slaughter: 'Italian society during the years of the war and Resistance was destabilized enough to open doors to some women, but when the conflict was over, return to a patriarchal order occurred quite quickly.'[66]

The post-war institutions clearly played a role in reinforcing patriarchal values, as Caldwell illustrates. The Fascist civil and penal codes remained in force and so weakened the effectiveness of Article 3 of the constitution, which stated that all citizens were equal before the law. Other articles in the constitution itself reinforced the subordinate position of women, reflecting the controversial inclusion of the 1929 Lateran agreements. While the patriarchal family remained a strong component of the Catholic political subculture, even the Left was cautious about pushing too far in the direction of emancipation. Though more committed to women's struggles than other political parties, the Communists continued to insist on traditional images of motherhood and femininity and saw female emancipation only in terms of strengthening and supporting the family (through a shorter working day or the provision of consumer goods), so that women would not lose their individual personalities. This attitude stemmed not only from the realization of the existence of a widespread patriarchal culture in Italy and the initial desire not to antagonize conservative partners in the governing coalition, but also from the conservative attitude of many Party militants towards women. Some new left-wing women's groups linked to the *Unione Donne Italiane* (Union of Italian Women), which had its roots in the *Gruppi di Difesa della Donna* of the Resistance, were partly modelled on traditional women's associations with strong Catholic roots.[67]

Conclusion

The events of the late forties left a strong sense of disappointment in the minds of many of those Italians who had fought in the Resistance believing that their sacrifices would create a fairer, more democratic society for their children. In the artistic sphere, the short-lived neo-realist movement bore testimony to their initial hopes and eventual disappointments. Emblematic in this sense is Roberto Rossellini's 1944 film, *Rome Open City*. Set in the Nazi-occupied capital, it depicts the resilience of ordinary people against oppression and heralds a better future for their children. Only a few years later that sense of hope had all but disappeared from neo-realist works. Vittorio De Sica's film, *Bicycle Thieves*, produced in 1948, in its depiction of the eternal struggles of the underprivileged, focuses on a young worker's search for a stolen bicycle in the streets of a post-war Rome that seems indifferent to his plight.[68] The film director's distance from the mood of the nation is illustrated by the general unpopularity of neo-realist films among the cinema-going public. The values of solidarity and democracy idealized by people like Rossellini and De Sica would be held back over the next decade by both state repression and the dominance of consumer values accompanying the economic boom, to which the following chapter is dedicated. However, the overriding desire of Italians for peace-of-mind and a higher standard of living after years of war and economic hardship – and perhaps even for a rest from serious ideological engagement after two decades of continuous subjection to aggressive political propaganda – is comprehensible, especially in view of the limited ideological impact of the Resistance on a large number of them.

Notes

1. Italy's role in the Second World War and the attitude of the Italian people to this are discussed in Morgan, *Italian Fascism*, 173–82; Thompson, *State control in Fascist Italy*, chapter 5; Collotti and Klinkhammer, *Il fascismo e l'Italia in guerra*, chapters 3 and 4; Aurelio Lepre, *Le illusioni, la paura, la rabbia. Il fronte interno italiano (1940–1943)* (Rome: Edizioni Scientifiche Italiane, 1989).
2. Enzo Collotti, 'Guerra mondiale, seconda', in Bongiovanni and Tranfaglia (eds), *Dizionario storico dell'Italia unita*, 423–34(433).
3. Collotti and Klinkhammer, *Il fascismo e l'Italia in guerra*, 75–82.

4. For Fascist home front and public response, see also essays in Brunella Dalla Casa and Alberto Preti (eds), *Bologna in guerra, 1940–1945* (Milan: Franco Angeli, 1995), esp. Dalla Casa, 'Il Pnf e la mobilitazione bellica', 65–101.
5. Tobias Abse, 'Italian workers and Italian Fascism', 58.
6. Morgan, *Italian Fascism*, 177.
7. Clark, *Modern Italy*, 289. The shameful lack of provision of air shelters is described in detail in Lepre, *Le illusioni, la paura, la rabbia*.
8. Dalla Casa, 'Il Pnf e la mobilitazione bellica', 99–100.
9. Collotti and Klinkhammer, *Il fascismo e l'Italia in guerra*, 85.
10. Tim Mason, 'Arbeiter ohne Gewerkschaften: Antifascistische Widerstand in Deutschland und Italien', *Journal für Geschichte*, 6, 1983, 28–36(34).
11. Abse, 'Italian workers and Italian Fascism', 60.
12. Thompson, *State control in Fascist Italy*, 149.
13. For a detailed account of the events of the summer and autumn of 1943, see Richard Lamb, *War in Italy, 1943–1945. A Brutal Story* (Harmondsworth: Penguin, 1993), 11–33.
14. Paul Ginsborg, *A History of Contemporary Italy: Society and Politics, 1943–1988* (London: Penguin, 1990), 13–14.
15. The RSI is analysed in detail in Collotti and Klinkhammer, *Il fascismo e l'Italia in guerra*, chapters 6 and 7; Frederick W. Deakin, *The Brutal Friendship. Mussolini, Hitler and the Fall of Italian Fascism* (London: Weidenfeld & Nicolson, 1962), Vol. 2, Part 3; Luigi Ganapini, *La repubblica delle camicie nere* (Milan: Garzanti, 1999); Morgan, *Italian Fascism*, 183–8; Lamb, *War in Italy*; Luisa Quartermaine, *Mussolini's Last Republic: Propaganda and Politics in the Italian Social Republic (R.S.I.) 1943–45* (Exeter: Elm Bank Publications, 2000).
16. See Carlo Mazzantini, *A Glorious Death* (Manchester: Carcanet Press, 1992) and *I balilla andarono a Salò* (Venice: Marsilio, 1995) for a personal account of the period by a veteran of the RSI.
17. Maria Fraddosio, 'The Fallen Hero. The Myth of Mussolini and Fascist Women in the Italian Social Republic (1943–5)', *Journal of Contemporary History*, 31(1), 1996, 99–124.
18. Brunello Mantelli, 'Repubblica sociale italiana', in Bongiovanni and Tranfaglia (eds), *Dizionario storico dell'Italia unita*, 756–69(765).
19. For the military call-up of April 1944, see Nicola Cospito and Hans Werner Neulen, *Salò-Berlino: l'alleanza difficile* (Milan: Mursia, 1992), 79.
20. The desertion of Interior Ministry policemen and *carabinieri* is analysed in Jonathan Dunnage, 'Inhibiting Democracy in Post-war Italy: The Police Forces, 1943–48', *Italian Studies*, 51, 1996, 167–80(171–3).
21. This is the main argument of Ernesto Galli della Loggia in *La morte della patria* (Bari: Laterza, 1996). See also Renzo De Felice, *Mussolini l'alleato, II: La guerra civile, 1943–1945* (Turin: Einaudi, 1997).
22. Jonathan Dunnage, 'Making better Italians: issues of national identity in the Italian Social Republic and the Resistance', in Bedani and Haddock (eds), *The Politics of Italian National Identity*, 191–213(193–9).
23. Claudio Pavone, *Una guerra civile. Saggio storico sulla moralità nella Resistenza* (Turin: Bollati Boringhieri, 1991), 231–4, 427–37.

24. For detailed reading on the Resistance, see Roberto Battaglia, *The Story of the Italian Resistance* (London: Odhams Press, 1957); Philip Cooke (ed.), *The Italian Resistance. An Anthology* (Manchester: Manchester University Press, 1997); Charles F. Delzell, *Mussolini's Enemies: The Italian Anti-Fascist Resistance* (Princeton, NJ: Princeton University Press, 1961); David Ellwood, *Italy, 1943–1945* (Leicester: Leicester University Press, 1985, particularly helpful for the relationship between the partisans and the Allies); Ginsborg, *A History of Contemporary Italy*, chapter 2; Lamb, *War in Italy*, chapters 11 and 12; Stuart J. Woolf (ed.), *The Rebirth of Italy 1943–1950* (London: Longman, 1972).
25. Delzell, *Mussolini's Enemies*, 372. See 371–2 for full details of the industrial strikes.
26. The main revisionist analyses of the Resistance are to be found in De Felice, *Mussolini l'alleato, II*; Galli della Loggia, *La morte della patria*; Gian Enrico Rusconi, *Resistenza e postfascismo* (Bologna: Il Mulino, 1995). For an assessment of revisionist treatment of the Resistance, see R.J.B. Bosworth, *The Italian Dictatorship. Problems and Perspectives in the Interpretation of Mussolini and Fascism* (London: Arnold, 1998), chapter 8.
27. Dunnage, 'Making better Italians', 203–6.
28. Claudio Pavone, 'The General Problem of the Continuity of the State and the Legacy of Fascism', in Dunnage (ed.), *After the War*, 5–20(10).
29. Ginsborg, *A History of Contemporary Italy*, 55.
30. Cooke, *The Italian Resistance*, 4.
31. Pavone, 'The General Problem of the Continuity of the State', 12.
32. Absalom, *Italy since 1800*, 172.
33. Jane Slaughter, *Women and the Italian Resistance, 1943–1945* (Denver, CO: Arden Press, 1997), 70.
34. Clark, *Modern Italy*, 312.
35. Absalom, *Italy since 1800*, 172–3. For a more detailed analysis, see Roger Absalom, 'A resistance to the Resistance? The Italian Peasant in History, 1943–1948', in Judith Bryce and Doug Thompson (eds), *Moving in Measure. Essays in honour of Brian Moloney* (Hull: Hull University Press, 1989), 169–79.
36. Philip Cooke, 'Il partigiano Johnny. Resistenza e mondo contadino nelle Langhe', *Italia Contemporanea*, 198, 1995, 63–76. See also Philip Cooke, *Fenoglio's Binoculars. Johnny's Eyes. History, Language and Narrative Technique in Fenoglio's 'Il partigiano Johnny'* (New York: Peter Lang, 2000), 121–6.
37. Crainz, *Padania*, 218–19.
38. Delzell, *Mussolini's Enemies*, 548.
39. Mantelli, 'Repubblica sociale italiana', 760–2.
40. Statistical details are to be found in Mirco Dondi, *La lunga liberazione* (Rome: Editori Riuniti, 1999), 91–101. For an English analysis of post-war partisan violence, see Luca Alessandrini, 'The Option of Violence – Partisan Activity in the Bologna Area', in Dunnage (ed.), *After the War*, 59–74.
41. The Schio massacre is discussed in detail in Sarah Morgan, 'The Schio killings: a case study of partisan violence in post-war Italy', *Modern Italy*, 5(2), 2000, 147–60.
42. Dondi, *La lunga liberazione*, 150–9.
43. Crainz, *Padania*, 228–30. Also referred to in Alessandrini, 'The Option of Violence', 65–6; Dondi, *La lunga liberazione*, 156–7.

44. Martin Clark, 'Italian Squadrismo and Contemporary Vigilantism', *European History Quarterly*, 18(1), 1988, 33–49(42–5).
45. Figures from ISTAT, *Sommario di statistiche storiche*, table 6.15.
46. Discussed in Norman Lewis, *Naples '44* (2nd edn, London: Eland, 1983) and *The Honoured Society. The Mafia Conspiracy Observed* (Harmondsworth: Penguin, 1967).
47. John Foot, 'The tale of San Vittore: prisons, politics, crime and Fascism in Milan, 1943–1946', *Modern Italy*, 3(1) (1998), 25–48(33).
48. Domenico Tarantini, *La maniera forte. Elogio della polizia. Storia del potere politico in Italia: 1860–1975* (Verona: Bertani Editore, 1975), 302–4.
49. Described in Ginsborg, *A History of Contemporary Italy*, 111–12.
50. Mirco Dondi, 'The Fascist Mentality after Fascism', in R.J.B. Bosworth and Patrizia Dogliani, *Italian Fascism. History, Memory and Representation* (Basingstoke: Macmillan, 1999), 141–60(142).
51. The role of the Allied occupying forces in the 'de-Fascistization' process is analysed in Hans Woller, *Die Abrechnung mit dem Faschismus in Italiane 1943 bis 1948* (Munich: Oldenbourg, 1996).
52. For a detailed analysis of the post-war trials and purges of Fascists, see Roy Palmer Domenico, *Italian Fascists on Trial, 1943–48* (Chapel Hill, NC: North Carolina Press, 1991). For figures quoted, see 253.
53. The question of judicial treatment of the RSI and the Resistance is analysed in Guido Neppi Modona, 'Post-war Trials against Fascist Collaborationists and partisans: the Piedmontese Experience', in Dunnage (ed.), *After the War*, 48–58.
54. Domenico, *Italian Fascists on Trial*, 219.
55. This is the subject of Paolo Buchignani's book, *Fascist rossi. Da Salò al PCI, la storia sconosciuta di una migrazione politica 1943–53* (Milan: Mondadori, 1998).
56. Levi, 'Italian Society and Jews after the Second World War', 24–30.
57. Dondi, 'The Fascist Mentality after Fascism', 146.
58. For detailed analysis of the political events of 1946–48, see Ginsborg, *A History of Contemporary Italy*, 98–119; Absalom, *Italy Since 1800*, 190–203.
59. John L. Harper, *America and the Reconstruction of Italy, 1945–1948* (Cambridge: Cambridge University Press, 1986), 1.
60. Figures from ISTAT, *Sommario di statistiche storiche*, tables 8.42, 8.43 and 11.2; Zamagni, *The Economic History of Italy*, 323–4.
61. Ginsborg, *A History of Contemporary Italy*, 112–13, 117.
62. David Ellwood, *Rebuilding Europe: Western Europe, America and Postwar Reconstruction* (London: Longman, 1992), 116.
63. Absalom, *Italy since 1800*, 201.
64. Alessandrini, 'The Option of Violence', 64.
65. Catia Sonetti, 'The Family in Tuscany between Fascism and the Cold War', in Dunnage (ed.), *After the War*, 75–88(81–5).
66. Slaughter, *Women and the Italian Resistance*, 127–8.
67. Post-war institutional and political attitudes towards women are discussed in Caldwell, *Italian Family Matters*. For PCI attitudes, see chapter 2.
68. For a detailed analysis of these two films, see Millicent Marcus, *Italian Film in the Light of Neorealism* (Princeton, NJ: Princeton University Press, 1986), chapters 1 and 2.

Chapter 5

Social, cultural and economic transformation in post-war Italy (1950–80)

Introduction

This chapter examines how the post-war economic boom affected the lives of Italians in terms of not only the greater wealth it offered them but also the overall changes it brought to their lifestyles in such areas as work, education, health, the family and social relations, leisure and civic participation. As the chapter illustrates, though the boom enabled Italy to become a major industrial power, many areas of the economy were left out and several regions, particularly those of the South, although transformed, did not undergo healthy processes of economic development. Many walks of Italian society and culture remained backward, as indicated by the growth once again of *Mafia* power and a failure to modernize public services. Desire for social, political and cultural emancipation, which the economic miracle inevitably encouraged, was partly frustrated by the conservative attitude of Italy's rulers. In the scenario of the Cold War, Fascist legislation governing social norms and limiting personal freedoms was slow to be removed as the ruling classes, backed by the Catholic Church, attempted to repress all manifestations seen as threatening the status quo. The wave of mass protest that spread through many parts of the country during the sixties and seventies – analysed in the second part of the chapter – was partly a result of the failure of the institutions to adjust adequately to the pace of change brought by the miracle.

Italian society and the economic boom

Post-war economic development

As indicated in the last chapter, the potential for economic growth in post-war Italy was good on account of limited war damage. Only 10 per cent of industrial plants had been destroyed. The main problem the country faced was a lack of raw materials, weak transport structures and inadequate housing. Aid from the United States in the form of food, fuel, low-interest loans and capital (including 1.3 billion dollars from the Marshall Plan for European recovery which operated between 1948 and 1951) proved invaluable in reviving the Italian economy so that by the end of the decade most sectors of the economy had returned to pre-war levels of production. The economic miracle of the fifties and sixties was a result of several factors. Anti-inflationary policies, the devaluation of the lira against the dollar and government-enforced price stability alleviated balance of payments difficulties and allowed the purchase of raw materials and food and the modernization of industrial plants. Industrial growth was particularly dynamic in the engineering, metal, energy and chemical sectors. After the economic isolation of the Fascist years, Italy's growing presence on the international market was a key to successful internal growth, as is demonstrated by a notable increase in exports (particularly cars, chemicals, oil products, electrical goods, furniture, plastics and artificial fibres). The creation in 1957 of the European Common Market, of which Italy was one of the founder members, stimulated further investment. However, indicating the human costs of the boom (described in detail below), industrial growth was also facilitated by low salaries, making it possible for companies to increase investment, and the introduction in the factories of advanced management techniques and mass assembly lines requiring unskilled or semi-skilled labourers.[1]

Taken at face value statistics concerning economic development in Italy during the fifties and sixties are impressive. Italy's growth was exceptional, since, matched only by West Germany, it saw a tripling of its GNP (compared with a doubling of the GNP in other industrialized countries). Between 1951 and 1964 industrial production grew from 4 per cent to 12 per cent of the GNP. To quote just a few examples of the dynamism of the period, annual steel production increased from 3 to nearly 10 million tonnes. Chemical fibre production more than doubled (from 137,000 to 320,000 tonnes). The annual production of petrol increased from 1,358,685 tonnes in 1951 to 8,511,734 tonnes in 1964, while that of electricity grew from 29,223 million to 76,739 million kilowatts. In 1950 Italy produced just under 100,000 cars. By 1963 it was producing over a million a year, with Fiat becoming one of the major European producers in the sector. As an example of development in the electrical and mechanical goods industries, the number of typewriters produced increased from 150,000 in 1951 to over 750,000 in 1964. The most dynamic years were those following the founding of the Common Market (1958–63), which saw an annual growth rate of 6.4 per cent in income, 7.4 per cent in family consumption, 15 per cent in plant investment and 14.2 per cent in exports.[2]

However impressive, these statistics hide strong regional and sectorial contrasts. The industrial triangle was the initial beneficiary of the boom. By 1963 parts of the Po Valley had also been industrialized as a result of the development of oil refining and petrochemical industries along the Northern Adriatic coast and the exploitation of recently discovered methane reserves. For Northern Lombardy, Veneto, Emilia–Romagna, the Marches, Tuscany and

Umbria, the boom came at the end of the sixties and during the seventies. In contrast to the industrial development characterizing the North-West, and demonstrating the significant relationship between tradition and innovation, the creation of what has become known as the 'Third Italy', was centred on the growth of small family firms of peasant origin specializing in crafts, light manufacturing and the provision of services. As Anna Cento Bull and Paul Corner note, the success of post-war family enterprise depended on the extent of previous industrial experience. The greatest success came in areas like Northern Lombardy and Veneto where there had been a long transition period from agriculture to industry. In Como, for example, the fifties and sixties saw the installation of ten thousand silk looms in the homes of families previously employed by silk factories, such that between 1951 and 1982 the number of self-employed households almost doubled, while wage-earning ones increased by only a sixth and declined in relative terms.[3]

The small family-based firms of the 'Third Italy' were often clustered together in industrial districts forming integrated territorial systems with varying degrees of sectorial specialization. Though traditional areas of industry, such as textiles, clothing, shoes and furniture, were dominant, they also represented modern sectors, particularly the machine tools industry. As Carlo Trigilia points out, the particular dynamism of the districts during the seventies and early eighties was indicated by a high rate of growth of value added, investments, productivity and employment. Industrial districts predominated and grew fastest in areas where there was a lack of concentration of large firms. They were also linked to the existence of subcultural traditions in their areas of development – Communist and Socialist in Central Italy and Catholic in the North-East – which in their defence of the local territory cut across class boundaries in an attempt to render the transformation from an agricultural to an industrial society as smooth and untraumatic as possible.[4]

Economic development in Northern and Central Italy was not matched by significant growth in the South. Southern production nearly doubled between 1951 and 1976 but failed to catch up with that of the rest of the country with its contribution to the Gross National Product actually decreasing from 24.1 per cent to 23.7 per cent.[5] Attempts to modernize agriculture and stimulate industrial development largely failed. Under the government of the Christian Democrats, the agrarian reforms of 1950 aimed at the creation of a conservative class of small landowners. This was envisaged as a means of preventing the development of a rural proletariat that would fall under the influence of the Left and offsetting the political effects of an increasingly large urban working class in the North produced by economic growth. The reforms amounted to a series of linked laws passed in 1950, which allowed the expropriation, reclamation, transformation and assignment of land to peasants in parts of Southern Italy, as well as Tuscany and the Po Delta. This saw the creation of 8 reform zones totalling 8.5 million hectares, covering 30 per cent of the national territory over 36 provinces and mainly divided into large estates under absentee ownership. 700,000 hectares of land were expropriated (70 per cent of which was in the South), but nearly all of it lacked housing, irrigation or roads, indicating the government's fear of alienating the support of the agrarian class by taking away from them anything more than the most isolated and unfertile land. Consequently, with the exception of the Po Valley, Italian agriculture remained largely backward, uncompetitive and unable to satisfy increased demand resulting from greater prosperity brought by the boom. Though 108,000 Southern peasant families were assigned land, with the consequent break-up of the *latifundia*, the success of the reforms was negatively conditioned by the insufficient number of hectares which each family received, lack of technical competence, capital and entrepreneurial spirit and, most importantly, the contemporary economic boom in the North, which enticed the more enterprising members of the work force away from their places of origin.[6]

Despite the huge amount of money invested via the funds of the Common Market and the *Cassa per il Mezzogiorno* (Fund for the South) set up in 1950, and in spite of an urban growth rate equal to that of Northern Italy, industrial development in the South was just as poor as in agriculture. Geographically, the most important developments were confined to Southern Latium, the Naples–Caserta–Salerno area, the Bari–Brindisi–Taranto triangle and the Catania–Siracusa axis, reflected also in the distrubution of *Cassa per il Mezzogiorno* funds, with very little spending in Calabria, Basilicata and Molise. Most of the well-publicized Southern industrial developments, including the construction of large petrochemical plants and steelworks in Naples, Sicily and Apulia undertaken by the state and Northern private concerns, ran at great losses.[7] These shortcomings may also be attributed to a limited local response to what was effectively colonial industrial investment, bad management resulting from clientelistic practices and the presence in certain areas of the *Mafia* (discussed below). In the South the 'third way' of development of small and medium family enterprises, successful in parts of Northern and Central Italy, was difficult to achieve in view of the completely different agricultural structure and the total dependence of the peasant on the land, giving him rare opportunities to expand into non-agricultural activities. Where the move into entrepreneurial activity was possible, the type of production concerned, for example the canning of tomatoes and the packing of fruit, imparted few skills.[8]

How did the boom affect the composition of the Italian work force and the nature of the working environment? During the fifties and sixties the number of agricultural employees fell to below 25 per cent of the work force while industrial employees (including construction workers) exceeded 40 per cent and tertiary and state employees grew to 35 per cent. However, though the period saw a steady increase in the number of industrial workers, which grew from 3,410,000 in 1951 to 4,800,000 in 1971, manufacturing employment did not grow spectacularly, the increase in such jobs accounting for only part of the outflow from agriculture, with many more people going into employment in construction and public administration. The majority of new manufacturing jobs were limited to the engineering, chemicals, clothing and metal-working sectors. Moreover, the boom only further emphasized the traditional polarization between a few large companies and myriad tiny workshops. In 1971 88.8 per cent of manufacturing plants still employed fewer than 10 people, accounting for 23.3 per cent of the overall workforce. Indeed, the number of artisans remained steady, since any decline in traditional workshops was compensated by new trades such as car mechanics and electricians. In line with developments in all advanced countries, the number of white-collar workers (including technicians) increased from 1,970,000 (9.8 per cent of the work force) in 1951 to 3,330,000 (17.1 per cent) in 1971. Of these about half worked in the public sector.[9]

The success of the economic boom has to be measured against the sacrifices faced by Italian workers, many of whom endured low pay and forwent basic rights to job security. Only at the height of the boom was there a significant drop in the number of jobless Italians, which was almost halved from 7 per cent in 1959 to 3.9 per cent in 1963, though the unemployment level in the South (4.9 per cent) was twice that of the North-West (2.4 per cent). From the mid-sixties unemployment increased again as a result of slower growth, reaching 5.4 per cent in 1970 (8.3 per cent in the South and 3.2 per cent in the North-West).[10] With specific regard to the South, between 1951 and 1976 the number of industrial employees increased from 20 per cent to 32 per cent of the work force and tertiary employees from 23 per cent to 40.5 per cent, while those employed in agriculture declined from 57 per cent to 27.5 per cent. However, new jobs failed to absorb the 2.1 million Southerners who left agriculture. According to Clark, the total number of jobs actually went down by over half a million so that in the mid-seventies unemployment was three times the Northern rate. Only 150,000 new jobs in modern industries had been created by the early seventies, while the construction industry and public works provided a further 350,000 jobs in 1975 compared with 1951. As King notes, new industrial jobs were concentrated in a limited number of industrial sectors, mainly chemical, mechanical and metallurgical, mostly large capital-intensive units, with a more limited development of small to medium-sized labour-intensive units in traditional sectors, such as textiles and foodstuffs. Managerial and technical jobs associated with industrial developments were initially taken by Northerners, reflecting lack of local expertise. Local employment was boosted when large numbers of workers were hired for the construction of plants, but on completion most of them were laid off: 'In this way the type of industrialisation pursued by the Cassa has had a destabilising effect on local labour markets, dislodging rural workers from their farming backgrounds but not giving them satisfactory permanent jobs.'[11]

As a consequence of the failed agrarian reforms and limited industrial growth in the South, three million of its inhabitants migrated to Northern cities in search of work. However, the boom period saw a migratory movement throughout Italy from the mountains to the coastal areas and towards internal lines of communication – including the Rome–Florence axis and the Via Emilia between the Adriatic coast and Milan. Within regions people moved from villages to towns, while many began to commute daily to work in the largest cities. Between 1951 and 1961 70 per cent of municipalities were seriously emptied as a result of migration, while the largest cities continued to grow in population. Notably, that of Milan increased by nearly half a million to 1,724,000 inhabitants between 1950 and 1970, while that of Turin grew even more dramatically from 700,000 to 1,200,000. The number of Italians emigrating abroad each year, initially to the Americas, but increasingly to Germany and Switzerland, grew from 200,000 in 1950 to a peak of 387,000 in 1961.[12]

Economic development, patronage and anti-Communism

The unsuccessful economic modernization of the South is just one example of the negative consequences of unhealthy state intervention throughout the Italian economy, characterized by the exploitation of patron–client relations for political ends. This was linked to the Cold War scenario in which it was imperative to keep the Communists out of power and created a system whereby private wealth was generated at the cost of sacrificing efficient long-term investment in the economy and public services. From 1954, under the new leadership of Amintore Fanfani, the Christian Democrats heralded a process of political 'patronization' of the state economy in an attempt to create a catch-all party independent of the Vatican and the powerful economic forces of Confindustria. This became all the more imperative after a failed attempt to monopolize control over parliament through the passing of a law – referred to by the Left as *legge truffa* ('swindle law') – granting two-thirds of the seats of the Chamber of Deputies to the alliance of parties polling over 50 per cent of the vote. Indeed, the Christian Democrats lost 8 per cent in the 1953 general election in comparison with the 1948 result, while the Communists and Socialists between them increased the left-wing vote by over 4 per cent (polling 22.6 per cent and 12.7 per cent respectively) and the Monarchists and the MSI also made significant gains.

The process of 'patronization' of the state economy saw the appointment of Christian Democrats to key positions in the growing number of organizations entrusted with industrial and commercial development. These included state banks, welfare agencies, holding companies – including IRI and the state oil and chemical agency, ENI (*Ente Nazionale Idrocarboni*) – and economic reform agencies (such as the National Federation of Farmers (*Coldiretti*) and the *Cassa per il Mezzogiorno*). The system tied economic development to electoral engineering, since the concession of land, financial assistance, permits for setting up private enterprise, works contracts, jobs and pensions was dependent on votes and clientele membership. Thus state power continued to function to the benefit of particular rather than national interests. The South provided the main territory for the Christian Democrats' pursuit of their patronage politics as a means of counterposing the presence in the Northern industrial cities of strong left-wing groups and more democratically minded public opinion. This involved a transformation of patron–client relationships. According to the cultural anthropologist, Carlo Tullio-Altan, given the demise of the agrarian élite, the traditional patron figure, represented by the *latifondista*, was replaced by the state apparatus itself, which provided vast financial resources, by means, for example, of the *Cassa per il Mezzogiorno*, through the mediation of local politicians (who in certain areas of the South were linked to *Mafia* organizations).[13]

The patronage system allowed the Christian Democrats to speculate on the failed agrarian reforms of the South, where urban unemployment resulting from the immigration en masse to the cities was not absorbed by economic development but by the employment of individuals in the growing state administration. Naples, for example, saw an increase in municipal employees by 400 per cent over 15 years, totalling 15,000 by 1968.[14] Many of these positions served no particular function within the local economy. The system of patronage appointments naturally stifled initiatives in the direction of proper professional development, with individuals more concerned about maintaining a safe job than becoming better qualified. It also nurtured a cynical attitude towards politics. On the basis of his field work on Naples, Percy Allum notes: 'Neapolitan youths know that the achievement of their aspirations and ambitions depends upon membership of the government parties or, more specifically, the dominant government party, the DC.'[15] The vicious circle of the patronage system is demonstrated by the fact that many of the state bodies set up not only generated votes as a result of the jobs they created, but were responsible for welfare payments to the poor, the unemployed and the disabled, according to the rules of patronage, with the result that a widespread system of *assistenzialismo* further inhibited healthy economic development in the South and put money into private pockets rather than public services. As part of the 'jobs for votes' system the state bureaucracy as a whole was 'Southernized'.

It should come as little surprise that as a result of the political patronization of the state administration many projects of economic development were never completed, while those brought to completion often proved to be unprofitable. Not rarely did tragedies occur as a result of technical incompetence. This is illustrated by the recent collapse of apartment blocks in Foggia (1998) and Rome (1999) constructed during a period of uncontrolled building speculation. Nor was the situation improved with the formation of a Centre-Left government in 1963 (described below). The Socialist Party demanded a share in the profits of the patronage system. Nowhere were the negative consequences of patronage-based economic development more accentuated than in *Mafia*-controlled areas. In post-war Italy the *Mafia* grew once again from the ancient stems, which the Fascist regime had failed to uproot. During the late forties, once it became clear that the Christian Democrats were the new dominant political force, *'mafiosi'* formed links with local Party representatives, allowing them subsequently to lay their hands on the funds of the *Cassa per il Mezzogiorno*. Many took up positions within the Christian Democratic Party and the public offices it controlled.

The *Mafia* followed and exploited the trend towards urbanization, changing from an agricultural phenomenon centred around the *latifondi* to an organization which drew its strength from the urban building programme and state financial resources. In the city of Palermo, for example, under the authority of two Christian Democrats close to the *Mafia*, the mayor, Salvo Lima, and the councillor in charge of public works, Vito Ciancimino, during the fifties and sixties, the great majority of building permits were awarded, in return for votes, to *Mafia* entrepreneurs for the construction of bridges, roads, apartment blocks to house new inhabitants, and for land reclamation projects. The *Mafia* also controlled the hiring of labour, acting as a kind of mediator between employers and workers in the absence of trade unions. This model was later imitated by the Neapolitan *Camorra*, which capitalized on the reconstruction programme after a devastating earthquake hit Campania in 1980. There is little wonder that thousands of people are still living in prefabricated houses that were intended for temporary use only.[16]

Where the Christian Democrats were unable to use the patronage system to obtain support, particularly in Northern urban areas, repression was employed to limit the extent of political opposition. This was particularly evident in their harassment of the working-class movement. In spite of the end to a ban on free trade unions after the fall of Fascism, the government continued to restrict their activities, which, in their defence of workers' rights and opposition to the employment of cheap labour, were seen as standing in the way of economic progress. In 1948 the all-party union confederation was weakened after it split over ideological divergences into three separate organizations: the left-wing General Confederation of Italian Labour (*Confederazione Generale Italiana del Lavoro* – CGIL), the *Unione Italiana dei Lavoratori* (UIL), representing the Social Democrats and Republicans, and the Catholic union confederation, CISL (*Confederazione Italiana dei Sindacati Liberi*). A strong union presence was more or less removed from the shop-floor level as national contracts were negotiated at government level – from which the CGIL was frequently excluded. This precluded the possibilities of collective bargaining at the local level. Moreover, employers attempted to root out CGIL influence in the factories, often through dismissals. In the Fiat union elections of 1955 workers were intimidated into deserting the ranks of the left-wing organization, which suffered a historic drop from 63 per cent to 36 per cent of the vote, while CISL gained 41 per cent. The growth in popularity of CISL was also due to the fact that its strategies focused on individual worker categories, whereas CGIL maintained a more abstract and less effective strategy of increasing the well-being of the working class as a whole. But there was an overall decline in support for the workers' movement during the fifties and CISL gained little from CGIL's defeats.[17] The left-wing co-operative movement also fell foul of the government because of its collectivist credentials. In spite of provisions favouring co-operation in the Constitution, and in a similar atmosphere of internal ideological divisions to that of the union organizations, during the mid-fifties co-operatives faced the harassment and persecution of the government, which subjected them to stringent tax inspections, put them under government-appointed commissioners, withdrew their licences or forced them into liquidation.[18]

Strikes and demonstrations continued to be confrontational affairs as they had during the late forties, partly owing to a failure to substantially democratize the police after the fall of the dictatorship. Indeed, legislation passed in 1948 gave the police more latitude in the use of firearms and in the arrest of protestors than had been enjoyed during the Fascist period. Though not as dramatic as during the immediate post-war period, the number of workers killed by the police remained high. And farmworkers continued to be killed by landowners or their agents during agricultural strikes, indicating a general state of impunity enjoyed by employers. During the fifties limited union power led to greater violation of contracts and ignoring of safety regulations. In many of the smaller companies, there was no control over the number of hours employees were forced to work and there were frequent accidents as a result of poor safety precautions. Moreover, until 1961 Fascist legislation banning internal migration allowed a conspicuous number of immigrants to be treated as clandestine and thereby exploited.

Wherever possible the bosses employed workers without a history of union activity. Catia Sonetti notes that in Tuscany, for example, the landowners took up extreme positions as a consequence of demand for land reform by the sharecroppers, assigning land to less rebellious peasants from the South. As the peasant Albano Querci remembers:

> There were no more sharecroppers, there were small landowners. They all came from the South, though. It was a political arrangement. No land was given to the residents. And the sharecroppers who previously worked here, they all went to work in the factories, some in Livorno, some in Piombino. . . . Now it is easy to talk about it, but it wasn't so easy, at the time, to sustain this kind of lifestyle, to have an ill mother. Nobody looked at you, everybody tried to avoid you. Nobody wanted to give you a job, nobody wanted to give you a farm. . . . There was a certain B., who

acted as a contact and looked for those peasants from the South in order to send us away. . . . Many of those peasants and their families were tied to the DC and were very Catholic.[19]

Illustrating the link between the politics of patronage and anti-Communism, this pattern of importation of less militant workers was commonplace in many traditionally 'red' provinces.

The above practices formed part of a broader anti-Left strategy affecting the rights and livelihood of whole sectors of the population within the exercise of an 'informal dictatorship'.[20] This was in part a consequence of Italy's strategic position as a member country of the North Atlantic Treaty Organization (NATO) bordering along the Soviet bloc. Moreover, the Italian government faced continued pressure from the Americans over its internal politics, given the presence of prominent Communist and Socialist parties which were opposed to what they saw as the aggressive nuclear military power of the United States and supportive of Soviet politics. In spite of the new 'democratic' climate of the post-war period, from a strictly legal point of view the state had the same powers at its disposal that it had enjoyed under Fascism, indicating the failure of the post-war governing coalitions, of which the Left had formed a prominent part, to remove Fascist legislation in line with the new political climate. In this sense, even the Constitution was largely ineffective, since the democratic rights it endorsed were easily inhibited by Fascist criminal and police codes created in support of anti-democratic principles. Socialists and Communists continued to be placed in the police register of subversives created during the Liberal period and enlarged during Fascism, and left-wing school teachers were the object of constant investigations. Conversely, the anti-democratic tendencies of neo-Fascists and 'mafiosi' were ignored and even public denunciation of extreme poverty and the power of the *Mafia* by figures like the social reformer, Danilo Dolci, resulted in harassment by the law.

Indicating a desire for the continuation of a strong centralized state, post-war governments ignored the provisions of the Constitution for regional devolution for fear of granting power to the Communists in such 'red' areas as Emilia–Romagna and Tuscany. Only five 'special' regions were created immediately after the Second World War in areas threatened by separatism – Sardinia and Sicily – and areas with substantial ethnic groups – French-speaking Valle d'Aosta, Friuli–Venezia–Giulia with its Slovene minority and German-speaking South Tyrol. Governments were also unwilling to dispense with the provincial prefects, traditionally associated with undemocratic state control. During the fifties and sixties the majority of prefects in office had, alongside the provincial police chiefs (*questori*), made their careers during the Fascist period. According to Robert Fried, the prefects maintained most of the powers granted to them under Fascism, which they used to suppress strikes and demonstrations and harass left-wing local government. Between

1946 and mid-1958 they suspended 81 left-wing mayors and dissolved 38 left-wing councils. They also maintained their traditional role as electoral engineers for the governing parties. This involved the negotiation of agreements with local notables, the creation of alliances for election campaigns and the last-minute distribution of relief aid (and the threat of deprivation of state funding in the case of a left-wing victory) as a means of influencing the decisions of voters. Though the outcome of prefectoral electoral interference was slight, in view of new heavily populated constituencies, highly organized political parties and proportional representation, it was more significant in the South, where there were fewer politically relevant organizations outside the state bureaucracy.[21]

The Catholic Church also played a significant role in limiting the influence of the Left in Italian society in return for the state's support of its moral positions. In 1949 the Vatican excommunicated all those espousing Communist doctrine. The church worked in league with the government and employers in discriminating against Communists in job allocations, because employers often required references from the local parish priest when taking on personnel. As a result many non-believers felt obliged to turn up at mass on Sundays in order to gain or maintain jobs, and even then often remained in an insecure position, as the words of a young Neapolitan Communist whom Percy Allum quotes illustrate: 'I always go to mass and the priest sees me, but they [his neighbours] told him that I am a communist and so he is not very friendly with me. For the record, two or three times he has got me a job, but always temporary jobs.'[22]

Quality of life, the family and civil society in the light of the boom

In spite of the above limitations, the quality of life of most Italians improved remarkably during the post-war years. There was more living space as the number of occupied houses increased by 50 per cent between 1951 and 1971. At the start of the fifties less than 8 per cent of houses contained electricity, running water and washing facilities. The figure had nearly quadrupled to 30 per cent a decade later. Many Italians were able to buy such household appliances as washing machines and fridges (owned by 50 per cent of families by 1965). Indicating that personal transport had become an affordable mass commodity, made possible by the design of vehicles of a smaller dimension, such as the Fiat 600 and 500, there were 5.5 million cars on the road by that year.[23] There is no doubt that the arrival of modern goods reflected the ability of many Italians to live comfortably for the first time. The initial beneficiaries were the middle classes, however, while many working-class families put off domestic modernization until the sixties. Interesting in this sense is a comparative analysis of the speed with which new systems of personal hygiene were adopted according to class. According to Maria Chiara Liguori, if the working classes were slower than the middle classes, this was not only due to cost factors but also a result of ignorance about the require-ments of basic hygiene and a class-based belief that certain commodities, such as private bathrooms and water-closets, were a luxury of the 'signori'.[24]

Most Italians were now better fed than ever before. If the average Italian consumed 5.3 kg of beef a year during 1941–50, this had increased to pre-war levels by 1951–60 (9.7 kg), growing dramatically to 14 kg in 1961 and 25.2 kg in 1971. Milk consumption almost doubled over the same period, while that of sugar nearly quadrupled. The state of health of the Italians dramatically improved too. Life expectancy increased from 64 years for men and 67 years for women in 1951–53 to 69 and 75 respectively in 1970–71, reaching 71 and 78 by 1981. The infant mortality level also dropped from 86.8 per 1,000 live births (within the first year of life) in 1946 to 40.7 in 1961, reaching 21.2 in 1975, though Italy still remained behind other West-ern European countries. There was a dramatic fall in the number of cases of most major diseases. Most importantly, malaria was more or less eradicated with the help of spraying with DDT, firstly in Latium in 1944–45, Sardinia in 1946–47 and the rest of the South in 1947–50, so that by 1955 the disease had been vanquished completely.[25]

As a sign of greater well-being, the number of marriages per 1,000 inhabit-ants which had dropped after a temporary peak during the late forties, began to rise again during the early sixties. There was a baby boom during that period, which saw a population increase from 50 million in 1961 to 54 million a decade later though in the long term the birth rate continued to decline (from 17.9 live births per 1,000 inhabitants during the forties to 14 in 1976). Indicating a general modernization trend, the average size of the Italian family declined from 4 members in 1951 to 3.3 in 1971, though there were strong regional variations. The smallest families were registered in Liguria and Valle d'Aosta (2.8) and the largest in Campania and Sardinia (3.9).[26] As a result of agricultural decline in the Centre and North of Italy there was a natural process of nuclearization of the family, though the strong link between agriculture and industry in many areas allowed the survival of multiple households. While increased wealth may have allowed individual family members to buy or rent their own property, such that the multiple family broke up, family solidarity often remained as each member pooled his resources for the success of the family firm.[27]

The great exodus from the countryside to the Italian cities represented a radical change in the lifestyle of hundreds of thousands of Italians. Many immigrants experienced a sense of alienation as they abandoned their home communities and were forced to live in far from ideal conditions. According to Clark:

Dreary housing estates arose all round city outskirts, most of them put up without benefit of planning permission and often without roads, schools, lighting or even sewage. Parks and open spaces were destroyed. The hapless immigrants were often put into huge blocks of flats, with densities of 500 people per hectare in some parts of Rome. Even worse were the hideous shanty-towns, providing shelter but little else for thousands of newcomers.[28]

Southern immigrants encountered a high level of prejudice and discrimination in the Northern cities. As John Foot notes:

> Southerners were accused of various 'crimes' which were linked to classic stereotypes – jealousy, excessive noise, violence, lack of respect for others. On public housing estates such as Comasina in Milan the divisions were often along immigrant/non-immigrant lines, which often coincided with social fissures. Often, bars and public spaces (like playgrounds) became known and frequented by Southerners or Northerners.[29]

While factory work formed a basis for the gradual integration of the immigrants, family solidarity also played an important role in easing the transition from an agricultural to an industrial society. In this sense the migration of the fifties and sixties did not weaken the family structure. An individual from the South or from rural areas of the North was most likely to emigrate to a city where a member of the family or relative already lived, obtaining accommodation and work, and financial assistance through the family contact.

Within the family women continued to maintain a subordinate position, facing legal and cultural pressure not to work in order to prioritize their role as mothers. While the law of 1950 on working mothers offering long periods of maternity leave with 80 per cent pay was hailed as one of the most protective in Europe, in practice it acted as a disincentive to employ married women, given the costly maternity benefits it granted, and in this sense was little more effective than protective legislation passed during the Fascist period. It is likely that the law encouraged employers to dismiss women from their jobs on the publication of their marriage bans, driving them back into the home. During the fifties most female employment remained home or family-based (since it was unaffected by the legislation). The Church also played a key role in encouraging women not to go to work, on the grounds that this would mean sacrificing the family, while greater contact with the outside world would make them turn to 'sinister' pleasures.[30]

To some extent the above restrictions on the lives of women continued to be eroded by the spread of mass education. As one would expect during a period of economic development, there was a continued growth in the number of Italians attending school and university. Those over six years of age unable to read or write decreased from 12.9 per cent in 1951 to 5.2 per cent in 1971, though levels for the South, even if greatly improved, remained twice as high (15.3 per cent). The number of Italians with middle-school diplomas increased from 5.9 per cent in 1951 to 14.7 per cent in 1971, while those completing secondary school education increased from 3.3 per cent to 6.9 per cent. Those holding university degrees increased from 1 per cent of the population in 1951 to 1.8 per cent in 1971.[31] Nevertheless, the system maintained a strong bias in favour of middle-class children. Before 1961 compulsory education was not increased beyond primary level and, in partial enforcement of Bottai's School Charter of the late Fascist period, the Christian Democrats attempted to limit access to upper secondary and higher education among working-class children by means of dead-end middle schools.[32]

When analysed according to region, the figures for 1971 demonstrate that the number of Southern Italians with high school or university qualifications was not lower than elsewhere. Calabria and Sicily, for example, equalled Piedmont in the percentage of high school diplomas (6.5 per cent), while a higher percentage of Sicilians (1.9 per cent) held university degrees than Lombards (1.8 per cent). On a less optimistic note, the fact that there was actually a higher number of Southern youngsters in secondary and higher education than their contemporaries in the North and Centre, is interpreted by Marzio Barbagli as a reflection of the historically inverse relationship between economic development and education. The strongest pressure for access to education was, he argues, in those areas where levels of youth unemployment were the highest. Though there was increased investment in the education of Southerners at upper-secondary and higher education levels, the qualified personnel created usually emigrated to industrial and commercial jobs in the North or administrative employment in Latium, such that resources originally destined for the economic modernization of the South effectively flowed back northwards.[33]

Nevertheless, increased literacy and schooling is proof of the arrival of 'modernizing' influences in post-war Southern Italian society, even if there were strong inhibiting factors. According to Jane and Peter Schneider, though land reform failed economically, it played an important social role, shaking loose the political power of the landed class, which had previously claimed a quasi-feudal hold over local social relations. This notably marked a conjuncture at which peasant fertility declined as many in that class adopted birth-control methods during the fifties and sixties. This has to be considered alongside the effects of the economic miracle, which created the structures for economic reform and saw the adoption of welfare measures allowing fewer lives to be taken by disease and malnutrition. The increase in public sector posts in the South stimulated a greater number of individuals to compete for the jobs by acquiring an education. On the basis of their oral research of a Sicilian community, the Schneiders reveal that the arrival of public works projects for the first time guaranteed the Sicilian peasant class good, regularly paid salaries and humane treatment at the workplace. 'Family wages' were high enough to allow a man to liberate his wife from serving other families, and the employer no longer made a claim on the labour of his wife

161

or daughters, though ironically such liberation meant that women were more confined to the home than in the past, devoting their energies to their own family, not others. Better working and living conditions (as gas or electric stoves and fridges became accessible to them, for example) encouraged Sicilian working-class families to decrease rather than increase in size in spite of added costs: 'The majority in this class began to contracept after 1950 in order to have a decent life and because decency had become a target worth pursuing'.[34]

As shown by the nature of post-war economic development, the end of quasi-feudal forms of land ownership and the arrival of modernizing influences in the South did little, however, to inhibit traditional 'familistic' practices and patron–client relationships and encourage higher levels of horizontal solidarity. In an environment in which there was lack of trust between citizen and state, where public life was influenced by power rivalry rather than ideology and where there was no traditional solidarity of unions, the system of jobs in return for votes, for example, was not seriously contested, even when there was no guarantee of a quid pro quo at elections. Given that poverty levels, while improved, remained high, 'the mere promise of a job or loan was enough to create a patron–client bond', as Christopher Duggan argues: 'This promise did not have to be fulfilled: the important thing was to ensure that the supplicant was kept in "hope".'[35]

Nevertheless, care has to be taken not to overstress the negative effects of the persistence of traditional social practices, nor to over-emphasize differences between the South and the rest of Italy. While strong patron–client ties governed most economic relations in the South, forms of horizontal solidarity were not completely absent, though they were not always manifested in associative forms. In his study of a Calabrian community in the late sixties, the Norwegian sociologist, Jan Brögger, argues, for example, that, while there was a lack of voluntary associations and co-operation, kinship ties were established so that families could help each other out in the form of work parties for those periods of the farming cycle, particularly the grape harvest, in which family manpower was inadequate.[36]

Elsewhere familism and patronage remained as a means of obtaining economic resources. If it is, indeed, possible to make a clear distinction between the South and the rest of Italy, it lies in the fact that patronage practices were more likely to be contained in Northern and Central Italy as state agencies and political parties limited the benefits of individual patrons. Sydel Silverman's research on practices in the small town of Montecastello di Vibio in Umbria reveals, for example, that patronage functions did not disappear but were dispersed among a variety of persons and agencies, now that the state was the most important source of services to the community. Although the pattern of personal, informal patronage persisted, 'the range of functions carried out in such relationships is limited by the economic and political power of the patron, and by the narrowed social difference between patron and client'.[37]

The above contrast is also illustrated by an examination of the Catholic and Communist subcultures dominating Northern and Central Italy during the post-war period. Although ideologically opposed, there were striking similarities in their functions, such that it might be more appropriate to make a distinction between the civic practices of Northern and Central Italy on the one hand and those of the South on the other. Certainly, as a result of competition between the Catholic and Communist subcultures, two different ways of life often existed side by side. This is eloquently revealed in David Kertzer's research on a district of the 'red' stronghold of Bologna, where the municipal council unscrewed the silver crosses from the top of their hearses for Communist funerals and screwed them back on again for religious burials.[38] The two subcultures have also traditionally been seen as encompassing different levels of civicness. The power of the Church and the continued influence of religion in many walks of Italian life are seen as having encouraged Italians to put their families before the wider community. The most damaging aspect of Catholic influence was, undoubtedly, a separatist view of the relationship between Church and state, which, resulting from a historical mistrust of the latter, encouraged a restricted view of the duties of the Catholic citizen to the state and justified such offences as tax evasion.[39] Ideological discrimination and patronage were clearly behind the workings of Catholic organizations providing work and assistance, many of which were responsible for rallying support for the Christian Democrat Party. The Communist Party with its strong power base in Central Italy was traditionally distinguished from its Catholic rivals in its encouragement of collective rather than individualistic solutions to problems and its emphasis on horizontal as opposed to vertical solidarity in the defence of the working class.

In spite of the supposed differences, in practice the two subcultures showed a surprising number of similarities. In the North and Centre of Italy, both encouraged modern civic attitudes, as was evident in welfare initiatives, after-work organizations, youth groups and festivals, even if, as a result of ideological restrictions, they did not fully encompass the community. In terms of patronage, too, it is not always easy to distinguish the Communists from the Catholics. It is widely accepted that, like the Christian Democrats, the Communists handed out municipal appointments to their supporters. Nevertheless, Trigilia argues that both the Catholic and Socialist (later Communist) subcultures developing from the end of the nineteenth century and forming the basis of the post-war 'white' and 'red' subcultures in the 'Third Italy' 'brought about an emancipation of the political system from civil society', so that 'politics became more autonomous from individual or family interests and more bound to the defence of collective interests, even though with a strong localist connotation'.[40] In contrast to Northern and

163

Central Italy, in the South the firmly established and personalized patronage system rendered the existence of either subculture difficult, so that despite the popularity of the Christian Democrat Party even organizations like Catholic Action had a low following. At the local level the parish priest, a key figure in the system of patronage, was often forced to negotiate with the *Mafia* in those areas where it was well organized. Even left-wing politicians, where they held positions of power, were not always immune to similar involvement.

The extent to which the *Mafia* formed an integral part of Southern Italian society is more questionable, however, than ever before in the post-war scenario. Following restructuring during the fifties and sixties in line with the post-war economic transformation, the *Mafia* maintained far less moral influence over society than previously, since it had become a large-scale criminal organization – founded first on urban development and from the seventies onwards the trafficking of drugs – of which personal profit was the central element. Though there is no doubt as to the extent of territorial control exercised by the *Mafia*, the threat of violence played a fundamental role in obtaining compliance more often than consensus. The fact that the post-war *Mafia* spread throughout Sicily, Campania, Apulia and Calabria (whereas previously limited to certain areas of those regions and absent from Apulia) is further proof of the limited anthropological basis of the phenomenon. If the post-war *Mafia* played a social role, it was a result of its ability to capitalize on problems of social and economic alienation, where state intervention was inadequate, and this inhibited the long-term chances of survival of civic movements.[41]

Leisure and cultural consumption during the fifties

In post-war Italy a higher number of Italians than ever before were able to enjoy a greater variety of pastimes. Figures suggest that spending per Italian inhabitant on various forms of cultural entertainment (including theatrical and cinema performances, concerts and spectator sports) nearly doubled during the fifties.[42] The development of modern forms of cultural consumption in Italy was not, however, strictly a product of the boom, David Forgacs argues. It can be traced back to the immediate post-war period, when American troops occupied Italian territory and their government promised economic aid in a strongly propagandized form. American influences had also been felt in Fascist urban society, as was evident in cinema films and young women's magazines. Just a few years after the end of the Second World War signs of cultural modernization began to be detected in rural areas too. This was clearly matched by government initiatives to cut illiteracy, but not necessarily accompanied by relief from high levels of poverty, particularly in the South. Hence, during the fifties Calabria despite being one of the poorest and most culturally deprived regions in the country saw one of the fastest rates of growth in expenditure on cinema, sport and radio, reflecting the new consumer interests of its younger generation. According to Forgacs, this demonstrates that 'despite the relatively low wages and consumer spending compared with the 1960s, changes in cultural consumption were visible all over the country'.[43]

An important protagonist in the new consumer era helping to shape the moods and aspirations of the period was the cinema. While mainly a lower-middle-class urban phenomenon during the Fascist years, immediately after the Second World War the cinema spread to rural areas through the creation by the Catholic Church of over 5,000 parish cinemas. The annual number of cinema tickets sold grew from 525 million in 1947 to a historic peak of 819 million in 1955. Italian cinema was strongly dominated by Hollywood imports for much of its history. Between the thirties and sixties the Hollywood stars filled the pages of film fan magazines, becoming role models for many young Italian men and women. Nevertheless, from the fifties onwards the number of Italian films greatly increased so that by the late sixties 300 were being produced per year. With emphasis placed on the entertainment value of cinema, the majority of Italian productions were comedies, featuring such actors as the Neapolitan Totò (Antonio De Curtis) and Alberto Sordi. They also engaged a number of Italian *dive*, such as Gina Lollobrigida and Sofia Loren, with whom audiences strongly identified, because of their humble social origins. Though not of the high quality of the world-famous art cinema of such Italian directors as Fellini, Antonioni, Pasolini and Bertolucci, this was the popular cinema of the day. [44]

To some extent the arrival of modern forms of cultural consumption was untimely in that it coincided with, and somewhat inhibited, the spread of literacy brought by mass education. Robert Lumley notes that between 1915 and 1980 the readership of the daily press remained constant at around 5 million, so that Italy remained well behind Great Britain, France, Germany and the United States. In 1956 a survey found that 64.5 per cent of Italians never read anything at all. Unlike the British press, Italian newspapers were predominantly regional and pluri-regional rather than national and they were strongly influenced by outside business interests, with the result that they were not properly autonomous. More significantly, however, whereas in nineteenth-century Britain the spread of literacy gave way to the development of a popular press, in Italy the growth of literacy coincided with an end of the monopoly on information held by the newspaper to the advantage of radio (the number of licences of which doubled during the fifties), and more crucially, television, which saw its first broadcasts in 1954 and the purchase of nearly three million licences in the space of the first four years. Weekly magazines, such as *Epoca*, *Gente* and *Oggi*, boomed during the fifties, since unlike the newspapers they were linguistically accessible to large sectors of the population. With their numerous photographs, brilliant graphics and strong Hollywood star content they gave readers a sense of their new and forward-looking social status.[45]

The arrival of modern forms of cultural consumption also brought into evidence serious tensions within Italian society between tradition and innovation, revealing a ruling class and ecclesiastical hierarchy that, while supportive of economic progress, was fearful of the emancipating effects of social and cultural transformation accompanying the boom. Indicating both the constraints brought by Cold War and fear of the moral breakdown of society, during the fifties Fascist legislation continued to be used to censor cinema films, theatrical productions and newspaper publications. The state also attempted to enforce rigid moral standards by prohibiting kissing in public and waging war on the bikini. Likewise, the Christian Democrats saw the new medium of television as a means of enforcing traditional mores and anti-Communism, as the RAI (*Radio Audizioni Italia*) state broadcasting company was regulated with a powerful system of internal censorship.

The Catholic Church backed the government in its cultural policy, capitalizing on television for the purpose of transmitting religious programmes, though this was not without serious contradictions. According to Ginsborg, it quickly came up against the reality of consumerism which television promoted, as was evident also in the half-hour evening transmission of *Carosello*. Representing an attempt at avoiding a direct American-style approach to advertising, *Carosello* consisted of spots, which combined product advertising and little stories, cartoons and fairy tales. Ginsborg notes: 'As such, "Carosello" exercised a great appeal for children, who were introduced in this familial, homely and seemingly innocuous way to the delights of consumerism.'[46] The Church was equally fearful of the 'liberating' effects of greater mobility that the boom brought, as a result of which holidays became a mass phenomenon, so reducing the social control of the parish. It denounced the dangers posed by holidays and invited young people to avoid the lure of dance-halls, which had became very popular since the war and, promoting the collective and dynamic enjoyment provided by American-imported 'boogie-woogie' and 'rock 'n' roll', marked the end of forms of sociality characterized by sexual segregation associated with rural societies.[47]

The above policies demonstrated the threat posed to an institution that claimed the right to determine how people lived and behaved. Religious education remained a compulsory subject at school, as a result of the inclusion of the Lateran pacts in the Constitution. Society was permeated by a spirit of Christian celebration and Marian devotion, the main purpose of which was to counteract the influence of Communist ideology. As well as excommunicating Communists, the Church stigmatized those who dared to marry outside the Church, as was evident in the denunciation in August 1956 by the Bishop of Prato of a recently wed couple as 'public concubines and sinners', which he had read from the pulpit of their parish.[48]

The Communists were equally suspicious of many of the changes brought to Italian society by the boom and were also afraid of the limitations they would place on their ability to control individuals. Illustrating the inevitable lure of consumerism among some Party comrades, Ginsborg describes how in a Tuscan village the installation of a television set at the local Christian Democrat headquarters split the Communists. Half of them went along to watch in spite of strict prohibitions.[49]

The new instruments of mass media were also employed to contain the aspirations of women. According to Liguori, under the control of the Christian Democrats television reinforced an image of the subordinate role of women within the family while emphasizing their status as consumers. Television publicity intended to suggest that less domestic work achieved through the purchase of household appliances would leave women more time for dedication to the family. It may in some cases have achieved the opposite effect, resulting in more free time for women outside the household and greater desire for emancipation, as was evident in fashion influences which saw the introduction of jeans, alongside a demand for equal access to education, work and mobility (by obtaining a driving licence, for example). In general terms, however, for many housewives consumerism was experienced as a form of greater confinement to the home (since, for example, there was less need to do daily shopping if one owned a fridge). This point needs to be considered within a broader context of a general decrease in the sociality of women brought about by urbanization, which broke up family and friendship networks.[50]

Protest and violence, 1960–85

Protest, 1960–70

Following the repression of the fifties, from the early sixties there was greater institutional tolerance of civil rights and modern social and cultural mores. This may be attributed to several factors. On the one hand there was modernizing reform from within the Catholic Church which, following the death of the ultra-conservative Pope Pius XII, moved in the direction of ending its interference in people's electoral preferences, publicly rejected the free play of market forces in society and called for greater social justice. Promoted by Pope John XXIII, this policy represented the Church's desire for greater contact with the people – demonstrated by the celebration for the first time of mass in Italian instead of Latin – and an end to a policy of discrimination against non-Catholics which had dominated the fifties as well as its attempt at achieving international reconciliation in the wake of the Cold War, the basis of the papal encyclical of 1963, *Pacem in Terris*. Another important factor was the move endorsed by John XXIII towards the formation that year

167

of a Centre–Left government accommodating the Socialist Party. This paved the way, at least theoretically, for the introduction of social reforms and institutional adaptation to the reality of a rapidly changing society, on the basis of a programme for creating a firmly democratic state founded on the Constitution. This envisaged, among other things, the introduction of a national social insurance and health system, regional devolution and greater state economic planning in order to overcome the North–South divide.[51]

Yet, this climate of change at the institutional level was also a response to pressure from below reflecting a growing sense of public intolerance towards corrupt government and repression. Greater awareness of the ills of government had since the late fifties been spurred on by a break away from traditional conservatism by the press. This also entailed investigations by such papers as *Il Giorno* and magazines like *L'Espresso* into political corruption and the negative social phenomena produced by the boom.[52] The success of a growing movement for change, which would culminate in the mass civil rights and union action towards the end of the decade, lay in the fact that it brought together different categories of citizens all wishing to end social, political and cultural repression. The starting point of such mass protest was Fernando Tambroni's formation in the spring of 1960 of a Christian Democrat government with the support of the neo-Fascist Italian Social Movement (MSI) and the Monarchists. The following July violent demonstrations took place against the decision to hold the MSI annual congress in the anti-Fascist stronghold of Genoa and the particularly provocative invitation to the congress of the ex-RSI prefect of Genoa, Emanuele Basile, responsible for the deportations of large numbers of workers and anti-Fascists. Pitched battles between demonstrators and the police forced the government to postpone the congress. If the police bore the brunt of the conflict in Genoa, being literally forced to retreat, in Sicily and Reggio Emilia they opened fire on crowds of demonstrators, killing several. The public outrage this provoked forced Tambroni to resign.

Among the tens of thousands of demonstrators of July 1960 were not only those of the older generation defending the memory of the Resistance but also a large number of youngsters. Their new mood of protest stemmed directly from the experience of the boom. On the one hand it allowed the formation of a youth culture epitomized in the arrival of rock music and motor scooters from America and the establishment of the local bar – equipped with billiard table and juke box – as a venue for young people. This strongly shaped the nature of their pastimes and made class distinctions between them less obvious, allowing the development of a proper youth culture, in turn making the collective strategies of protest possible. At the same time, however, their rebelliousness stemmed from a sense of disorientation as a result of the rapid transformation of society that the boom was creating. Representing a break with the older generation, they increasingly refused to be moulded by a consumerist society, which they saw as hypocritical, unjust and oppressive.[53]

Young Italians were becoming increasingly politicized. They were aware of a link between what they saw as the *malgoverno* of the day and the oppression that their fathers had fought 15 years earlier. Until the sixties, the subjects of Fascism and the Resistance had been largely absent from public life, including the school curriculum. According to Stephen Gundle, 'only in "red" areas was there an active pedagogy of the Resistance that recurred in songs, stories, education of children and young people and active, political commemoration'. Avoidance of the theme of the Resistance by the ruling Christian Democrats was not the only reason for its absence from official memory in other parts of Italy. The boom years had transformed Italy to the extent that the mainly rural society with which it was associated had been fully displaced.[54] Youngsters now demanded to know more about recent Italian history, which schools and television began to address. In the former case this was helped by the arrival of a new cohort of younger teachers who gradually replaced an older generation that had qualified during the Fascist period. [55]

Representing a move away from the attitude of submission of the fifties, from the early sixties onwards there was a notable growth in union membership and an increase in the number of strikes and demonstrations. 1963 saw a dramatic peak in the number of strikes, of which 2,782 involving 2,441,000 participants took place in the industrial sector alone. The protests represented on the one hand a reaction against the failure of the industrialists to invest their boom profits in higher worker salaries and on the other the refusal of workers to continue to accept sacrifices and maintain a submissive attitude towards management. The strikes were important in that they saw the development of greater solidarity from both within and outside the worker environment. In this sense those at Fiat of 1962 saw the coming together of Northern and Southern and different categories of workers. Also particularly significant was the participation in strikes of a younger generation of Catholic workers of CISL – that had previously avoided any form of confrontation with the bosses. Moreover, the strikers had the support of university students, who identified their cause with their own struggle against a state of subordination within a conservative education system and, on a broader international scale, with that of Communist Cuba as it faced a naval blockade by the United States. Another motive for the workers' success in obtaining concessions lay in the fact that the bosses no longer enjoyed the full support of the government. Greater union freedom was matched in the cultural sphere by a relaxation of previous television and cinema censorship in 1962 and a move away from direct political control of television by the Christian Democrats.[56] There were also new developments in education. In 1961 students from technical schools were granted access to university. The establishment

169

the following year of a single middle school (*scuola media unica*) allowing access to upper-secondary education and the raising of the compulsory schooling from age eleven to fourteen marked an end to previous class-based discrimination.[57]

In spite of the move towards greater political and social emancipation during the early sixties, tension remained. The institutions were unable to follow the pace of economic development and social transformation to which much of Italian society aspired. Most significantly, the Centre–Left governing coalition failed to implement most of the reforms it had set out to achieve. This was partly a result of the attitude of the PSI. In government it failed to stand up to the Christian Democrats and began to imitate the clientelistic strategies of its main coalition partner. The submissive attitude of the PSI was also a consequence of memories of the rise of Fascism to reverse the gains of the working-class movement during the *Biennio Rosso*, and fears that something similar might happen. In many respects such fears were not unfounded in the Cold War scenario, as is demonstrated by the revelation in *l'Espresso* in 1967 that in the summer of 1964 the Italian secret services – subordinate to US and Nato intelligence – had planned a military coup, referred to as the *Piano Solo* ('Solo Plan'), that would have seen left-wing 'suspects' imprisoned in concentration camps in Sardinia. Entrusted to the *Carabinieri* high command, it was never brought to completion. Yet, it was clearly indicative of the presence of secret forces linked to both extremist political groups and the Italian state that would condition Italian life well into the eighties.[58]

With regard to the Catholic Church too it is significant that change, though definitely there, was slow to take place. As Caldwell notes, there was some willingness to recognize the need for more permissiveness and equality within the sphere of conjugal relationships during the sixties. The Church had by then given up opposing female employment and, though continuing to see sex as having a fundamentally procreative function, accepted that it could be enjoyed between husband and wife. Yet, in broader terms there was a huge gap during the fifties and sixties between the legal definition of the family (still based on the civil code of 1942, which reiterated inequality) and social reality, characterized as it was by a not insignificant percentage of single mothers, separations, extra-marital unions and illegitimate children, often caused by migration, that was partly addressed by the introduction of divorce in 1970 and the new family law of 1975.[59] In spite of the church's attempt to modernize itself, it increasingly lost its hold over society. Mass attendance fell from 69 per cent of adults in 1956 to 53 per cent in 1961, 48 per cent in 1968 and 35.5 per cent in 1972. Catholic Action membership dramatically dropped from 2.6 million in 1966 to 1.3 million in 1970, mostly as a result of youth defections, while the number of young men applying to join the priesthood also decreased.[60] Partly as a consequence of this process of secularization, from the early sixties a more open attitude towards questions of morality and sexuality developed, as was evident in newspaper and magazine publications.

The explosion of rebelliousness characterizing the late sixties may be explained, therefore, by the creation of an atmosphere of greater freedom and permissiveness within Italian society from the early sixties onwards, coinciding with the formation of the Centre–Left government, in turn creating serious expectations which were not adequately fulfilled. While the Socialists achieved little in government in the way of reforms, their presence created the conditions for mobilization for change from outside the institutions, since it was more difficult to resort to police repression than before. Apart from the large number of strikes and demonstrations characterizing the period, the fact that a high percentage of the protests were outside the sphere of the institutions, accounts for the extent to which the left-wing political parties and unions had lost contact with grass-roots supporters. The protagonists involved were strongly influenced by ferment among left-wing intellectuals who, in groupings known as the New Left or extra-parliamentary Left, were highly critical of the institutionalized state of the working-class organizations and theorized a new revolutionary strategy of 'autonomy' by which workers refused to define their needs and demands 'according to capital's need for labour power subordinate to the rhythms of the production process' and saw themselves as independent from unions and parties considered 'subservient to capital'.[61] Paradoxically, however, the growing gap between the Old Left and grass-roots supporters was also a consequence of the long-term process of 'embourgeoisement' of Italian society brought by the boom. Rather than being focused on the ascendancy of the working class, the protest movement demanded emancipation on a whole range of issues.

The student protests

Roughly coinciding with similar developments in other European countries and the USA, the mobilization of Italian students, which began in 1967, may be traced back to the inadequacy of reform of the school and university system during the early sixties. Above all the reform had failed to create social equality. Indeed, one of the cult texts of the student movement was a book published in 1967 by a dissident priest, Don Milani, entitled *Letter to a Teacher*. In the book eight young working-class boys from a mountain village near Florence denounced, by means of carefully documented research, the middle-class bias of the education system, as perfectly expressed in the first lines of the book:

Dear Miss
You won't remember me or my name. You have failed so many of us.
    On the other hand I have often had thoughts about you, and the other teachers, and about that institution which you call 'school' and about the boys that you fail. You fail us right out into the fields and factories and there you forget us.[62]

171

Although access to upper secondary and higher education had been facilitated as a result of the reforms, working-class students remained disadvantaged. Given limited financial assistance, many poor students were forced to work rather than attend university classes. These factors resulted in a high drop-out rate. Moreover, the universities failed to move away from their traditional élitism and were not re-structured in order to cope with higher numbers in terms of staff and teaching space. According to Robert Meade, in 1965–66 almost 40 per cent of the student population fell into the category of *fuori corso* (those failing to complete examinations within the normal time but who remained enrolled). 'Ultimately, only about one out of four students ever triumphed over the obstacles and emerged from the chaos with a diploma in his hand.'[63]

Secondary school students influenced by a general climate of cultural rebellion also demanded greater democracy through, for example, the elimination of forms of selection, the right to education of all and the freedom to hold meetings. They also disputed the inability of the education system to prepare them for the outside world and to engage them in discussions of contemporary issues. But there were other reasons behind the protests. While it is true that the numbers attending secondary school almost doubled between 1959 and 1969 as a result of changes during the early sixties, when the boom ended in 1963 the number of unemployed school graduates dramatically increased, as there was a drop in demand for qualified work in the industrial sector. According to Barbagli, therefore, the student protest 'arose from a plurality of factors . . . But it was also the effect of the growing imbalance between school and labour market'.[64]

Another important factor in the protests was a change in the nature of student–police relations during demonstrations. For the first time ever the students were no longer prepared to be driven off the streets by the authorities. Emblematic in this sense was the 'Battle of Valle Giulia' of 20 March 1968 centred around the Architecture Faculty of Rome University when students ignored a ban on demonstrations and defied tear-gas and truncheon charges and drove the police off the streets. As Alessandro Portelli's oral research demonstrates, although the experience of Valle Giulia was seen as a kind of collective initiation in conflict with the state, at the individual level the symbolic value of the event varied. More experienced 'actors' emphasized their victory over the police who were forced to allow the student occupation of the Faculty. For others the experience of battling with the police for the first time was traumatic in that it brought home the realization that in a situation of conflict, contrary to what they had been educated to believe, rules and fair play no longer counted.[65]

The determination of students was undoubtedly a consequence of police brutality. During the sixties protest policing in general had been less repressive than previously with not one single demonstrator killed between 1963 and 1967. The toll of deaths and injuries from police charges, bullets and tear-gas during student demonstrations, industrial strikes and land occupations escalated from the end of 1968. The killing by the police of two workers during a strike in Avola, Sicily, in December 1968, and another two the following April in Battipaglia, near Naples, only encouraged further strikes and protest demonstrations, many of which were promoted by the students. Yet, the behaviour of the police, which on many occasion was brutal, involving beatings both on the scene of demonstrations and in police stations, was also a reflection of poor professional training and bad working conditions, also revealed by a number of illegal police strikes. Many policemen anonymously complained to both police journals and the Communist Party daily, *L'Unità*, of their maltreatment by superiors, their exhaustion as a result of overtime and cancelled holidays and their being more or less ordered to behave violently towards protesters.[66] At the end of 1969 further impulse was given to the protests by an event that signalled the beginning of over a decade of terrorism. On 12 December a bomb exploded in a bank in Piazza Fontana in Milan killing 16 people and injuring 90. While the attack was initially blamed on anarchists, attention was increasingly focused on right-wing groups and the state itself, especially following the mysterious death of an arrested anarchist, Giuseppe Pinelli, after he 'fell' out of a fourth-floor window of the Milan police headquarters.

The student action not only represented a protest against the education system. Influenced by the cultural climate of the Chinese and Cuban revolutions, many young Italians expressed disaffection with the Western society of their parents, which they saw as socially repressive and imperialistic. This also accounted for student support of union protests and their campaign for greater equality within society at large. Universities also became the main focus of the peace movement founded in Italy in 1967 in protest against the Vietnam war. The students' desire for an alternative lifestyle was partly put into practice as occupied universities were turned into revolutionary communes. The student movement also challenged the national press over the manner in which it represented worldwide events by means of 'counter-information' in the form of graffiti, leaflets, slogans and such weekly newspapers of the extra-parliamentary Left as *Lotta Continua* (founded in 1969) and *Il Manifesto*. Counter-information sought to reveal the truth about terrorist attacks and neo-Fascism, and this in turn encouraged the more radical journalists working within the commercial press to follow suit. Similarly, radical artists and intellectuals including the playwright, Dario Fo, and the writer and film director, Pier Paolo Pasolini, sought to re-create a popular culture autonomous from official middle-class culture in which denunciation of a repressive state was not missing, as in Fo's play, *Accidental Death of an Anarchist*, inspired by the Pinelli affair. The student action should be considered, therefore, within the context of the coming together of broader cultural forces

173

of opposition to the status quo that would strongly influence the following decade. As Lumley notes:

> In every Italian city (and perhaps more so in Milan than elsewhere) bookshops, cultural centres, political centres, bars and eating places testified to the existence of a world separate from and in conflict with the dominant urban institutions. Its boundaries were often marked out by graffiti. But the cultural revolution also penetrated the practices of those working within the dominant institutions, especially the professions.[67]

The latter point is demonstrated by the fact that individuals who could have remained aloof from the protests became involved. Doctors began to campaign for health and safety at the workplace, while university lecturers and school headmasters supported occupations.

This attitude was also evident in the Church. It was no coincidence that the first epicentres of student protest and the peace movements were the Catholic universities of Milan and Trento. While many Catholic Action members deserted to the youth movements, several dissident Catholic organizations denounced the Church as the ally of the rich and privileged. Anti-conformist priests began to run communities, mainly in the South and Centre of Italy, often in the most socially deprived urban outskirts, in an attempt to reinterpret their roles as Christians. This often led them to support workers in labour disputes and to participate openly in peace protests.[68] Once again the obvious plurality of ideological and social backgrounds of the protagonists involved indicates the distance between the protest movements and the working-class orthodoxy of the Italian Communist Party.

The workers
The industrial action of 1968 and 1969 was marked not so much by the number of strikes, which was in fact lower than during the previous period of serious agitations, the early sixties, but by an increase in the number of participants (3.2 million in 1968 and nearly 5 million the following year compared with the previous peak of under 2.5 million in 1963) and the number of working hours lost (233 million in 1969 compared with 127 million in 1962).[69] The scale and success of the industrial strikes, which started as a series of unconnected agitations in the spring of 1968 and culminated in the mass industrial action of the 'Hot Autumn' (*Autunno Caldo*) of 1969, may be attributed to several factors. Although in the early sixties the unions had regained ground after more than a decade of submission, working conditions in the factories actually worsened during the following years. According to John Low-Beer, the unions' gains in the 1963 national pay contract led to a substantial increase in labour costs in manufacturing, which employers reacted against by increasing labour productivity. This was achieved through rationalization of production, placing greater pressure on their

employees, so that in 1968 the cost of labour actually went down 4 per cent. However, an upturn in the economy in 1969 put the workers in a strong position to struggle successfully against management.[70]

Another factor determining the increase in worker militancy was the availability of cheap labour supplies, which dried up in the mid-sixties with full employment, giving the working classes greater leverage than before in their confrontation with the bosses. As Ginsborg notes, this was partly a result of the increase in educational opportunities during the decade, which took growing numbers of workers out of the factory. At the same time greater educational opportunities meant that those who went into the factories were more literate and aware than previous generations: 'The hidebound text books of the Italian schools in the 1960s were hardly manuals for militants, but the connection between increased literacy and the agitations of the "hot autumn" is evident.'[71] From a broader perspective the protests were a result of the negative social effects of urbanization and mass migration and the failure of the Left to address them effectively. There was a growing sense of division among workers, as migrants moved in from outside, working-class strongholds were undermined as they became inhabited by the middle classes and the generation gap between the younger and older workers widened. As a result of such developments, the control of union organizations over workers – and the assistance that they were able to bring them in such areas as housing and cost-of-living difficulties – diminished.

The mass of new workers had little experience of union action. However, if the impetus for revolt initially came from highly politicized skilled workers, it quickly spread to unskilled non-union sectors of labour and this also accounted for limited union control. White-collar workers and technicians, who again were traditionally non-unionized, also played a major role in the strikes, as the diffidence between them and the blue-collar sector was gradually overcome. According to Low-Beer, their militancy was in part explained by their increasing recruitment from blue-collar or peasant backgrounds. Moreover, as technicians' qualifications were increasingly devalued, there was greater willingness to participate in collective strategies as they identified less with the middle class and more as belonging to a large central working class 'within which there is a range of inequality, but with no sharp boundaries'.[72]

The protests went far beyond demands for better pay. Emphasis was placed on greater democracy within the factory, the organization of work and the reduction of health hazards. The motives for agitation in turn moved out of the factory owing to concern for workers' social conditions. As such the struggle was linked up to that of the students and the extra-parliamentary Left in its quest for the achievement of democracy and social justice. As Joanne Barkan argues: 'Students and New Leftists leafleted at factories, marched on picket lines, and attended labor rallies. The nonworker activists often played a positive role in the labor mobilization by encouraging political discussion and new forms of struggle. The relationship was usually strongest in large, highly visible workplaces and in those where the unions were weak.'[73]

The protests quickly brought into evidence the isolation of union leaders from the factory shop-floor. In many plants committees of activist workers and students pushed for action rather than negotiation, as was demonstrated by the adoption of new strike tactics designed to disrupt the production cycle and give workers direct control over the forms that the struggles were to take. *Autoriduzione* (literally 'self-reduction'), for example, involved the co-ordinated slowing down of factory output. Other tactics involved skipping pieces on the factory line and the temporary shutting down of factory sections, one after the other. While the focal point of the agitations was the industrial triangle, there were some isolated cases outside it. Although protest did not spread to the South, Lumley suggests that traditional Southern rebelliousness influenced the forms of struggle. At Fiat, for example, migrant workers rejected socialization into work discipline and adapted their own traditions and culture of resistance to the Turin situation, though this often led to acts of sabotage. This type of action, while condemned by union officials, was admired by the intellectuals of the extra-parliamentary Left for its spontaneous revolutionary character.[74]

While the unions were taken by surprise at the strength of the workers' action, they were able to regain control of the situation by co-ordinating and unifying the struggles, in order to lead the mass revolts of the autumn of 1969. In the renewal of national contracts the unions included many new rank and file demands. Regarding the overall phenomenon of student and worker contestation, Tarrow advocates the idea of a cycle of protest, during which action developed its own momentum, independent of the control of the union and political institutions. The starting point was 1967, the year in which there was an increase in the number of working-class protests, despite the previous year of contract renewal negotiations, and a decrease in the participation of known organizations in all forms of protest. The internal dynamic of protest intensified in 1968 before, from 1969, it started to be institutionalized through the introduction of reforms. By 1971 the cycle was nearly complete, though not without having left a profound mark on forms of protest and levels of participation. In fact the events of the late sixties set in motion a process by which during the following decade protest spread to groups and geographical areas previously excluded.[75]

The legacy of the student protests and the 'Hot Autumn'

What did the student and worker protests achieve and what were their long-term effects on Italian society? Starting with the education system, the results are questionable. Though accessibility to upper-secondary school and university increased as a result of the protests of the student movement, social inequalities survived. Secondary school exams became easier, so facilitating access to university, but the percentage of new working-class students remained low. Authoritarian and restrictive educational practices were partly overcome, with the institution of 'open' degree curricula and the possibility of taking and repeating examinations on a monthly basis, though the effect of this on academic standards must be questioned. The student movement was also allowed greater political influence inside schools and universities. Yet, structural problems arising from overcrowding and lack of investment persisted, while university barons continued to hold excessive power.

By comparison the workers achieved far more. There is little doubt that life in the factories was made much easier as a result of the industrial action of the late sixties and early seventies. Barkan remarks that:

> Remembering for a moment the repressive conditions in many Italian factories – exile departments, blacklisting, political surveillance, workers summarily dismissed for talking on the assembly line or glancing at a newspaper during lunch hour – the breadth of the 1969 victory becomes clear. In addition to improvements in wages and work conditions and some protection against arbitrary authority, the workers had reasserted the right to organize themselves as a collective body.[76]

Such achievements were safeguarded by new laws. National contracts no longer precluded local collective bargaining and most importantly, for the first time in over 20 years, legislation ratified article 39 of the Constitution which guaranteed workers the right to form trade unions and enter into collective labour contracts, as the Workers' Rights Statute (*Statuto dei Lavoratori*) of 1970 secured union presence at company level and allowed unions to take employers to court. Workers also benefited from the introduction of the *cassa integrazione* (short-term wage guarantee scheme), whereby some laid-off categories received unemployment compensation at 80 per cent of full wages, and from the strengthening of the *scala mobile* in 1975.

During the early seventies the union battles spread beyond the initial sectors of conflict. They involved an increasing number of Catholic workers as their union, CISL, began to accept the new confrontational model of industrial relations. There was also a consistent growth in public-sector membership. Teachers in the CGIL, for example, increased from 4,000 in 1968 to 90,000 in 1975.[77] The increase in middle-class union membership marked the dramatic growth in the number of tertiary employees in Italy, increasing from 40 per cent to 50 per cent of the work force between 1971 and 1981.[78] But on many occasions middle-class protests, while inspired by the example of the industrial workers, were a result less of solidarity than of competition. Many public-sector strikes aimed at keeping pace with the gains of workers in industry. The increase in middle-class participation in union activity created the basis for a gradual process of de-ideologization of the labour movement which stemmed from the growing hegemony of the more specifically libertarian and socially more encompassing values of the protest movement over traditional solidaristic working-class politics.

The 'Hot Autumn' did not benefit all workers. The smaller factories and companies were largely unaffected and their employees were not covered by the *Statuto*, as were large numbers of women home-workers. Moreover, all working-class wages were eroded by severe inflation set off by the international oil crisis of 1974. Partly as a result of this, the protest movements began to concentrate on broader social concerns. The direct action strategies of the factories were now applied in the community at large. These included the organization of squatting to overcome housing problems, and new forms of *autoriduzione*, to overcome rising prices, such as the non-payment of bus tickets and electricity bills. These protests were also a result of the failure of the government to adequately carry through social reforms in the wake of the 'Hot Autumn'. Medical care, for example, did improve during the seventies and a proper national health system was introduced in 1978. But it was difficult to overcome high levels of inefficiency and political patronage within the health service as well as serious imbalances between the North and South in the provision of hospital beds and in the modernization of social services.[79]

Though in the South the left-wing parties and trade unions were of limited influence, towards the mid-seventies the social movements organized various campaigns. In Palermo, for example, a housing movement of several hundred families was organized by students to the left of the PCI in order to overcome problems resulting from extreme overcrowding and inadequate sanitary facilities. According to Judith Chubb, this took the form of occupations of empty units of council housing and unrented private apartments and mass demonstrations along the major streets of the city and in front of public offices. Housing occupations also took place in Naples, which was additionally the scene of the movement of an army of 'organized' unemployed people against the political hiring of workers. In both cities the campaigns allowed the official Left to gain political influence, at which point, however, the dynamism of the movements began to fade. In the case of Palermo the formation in January 1976 of a Centre–Left city government with Communist support encouraged people to return to a position of passivity, awaiting resolution of the housing problem from above. In Naples the newly elected Communist majority found itself having to absorb unemployment by the traditional means of 'assistance', because of a serious lack of alternative resources, leading to accusations of clientelism.[80] The ephemeral nature of the social movements in the South is also demonstrated by the enrolment at the end of the seventies of the 'organized unemployed' in a new *Camorra* army – which claimed to redistribute wealth to the advantage of the poorest strata of the population – and in the Neapolitan columns of the left-wing terrorist Red Brigades (described below).[81]

Throughout Italy the initiatives of the social movements were gradually absorbed by the official Left and taken up at higher levels of union representation, as part of the overall strategy of institutionalization of protest. Consequently, union and party officials often appeared as allies of local institutions and the government rather than representatives of workers. The economic crisis of the seventies encouraged even greater union aloofness, as the confederations looked towards long-term political and economic policies and moved away from the shop-floor in favour of consultation with the institutions. During the years of 'national solidarity' (1976 to 1979), in which the 'historic compromise' produced an explicit form of co-operation between the Communist opposition and the Christian Democratic government, the union confederations supported a policy of wage restraint and fiscal austerity, in respect of the generally misguided belief of the Communist Party leader, Enrico Berlinguer, that in return for its sacrifices the working class would achieve hegemony in Italian society and serious transformations would take place in the country's economic, social and state structures. Though the unions gained institutional status as a result of this, the grass roots clearly lost out as a result of the government's failure to prevent redundancies and control inflation.[82]

The social movements were only partially successful in speeding up reforms that the Centre–Left government had planned in other areas. Regional devolution, for example, had forever been put off by post-war governments and, once implemented, proved disappointing. In 1970 some autonomy was granted to those Italian regions that had not been awarded full autonomy immediately after the Second World War. But only in 1977 was there a moderate transfer of powers to the regions, which were granted autonomy in such areas as housing, health, and education, though the central government maintained control over regional funding and could veto regional legislation. As Putnam demonstrates, regional performance levels varied. Results were best in the North and Centre, with particular success in Emilia–Romagna, Umbria, Tuscany and Lombardy, but poor in the South. Though the advent of regional government was hailed as enhancing democracy, the clientelistic practices of the central state administration were far from absent, particularly in the South. This clearly affected the quality of personnel. Putnam argues that: 'Clientelism and party affiliation, rather than expertise and experience, were the main criteria for recruitment where the decisions were left to the regional authorities. . . . In many regions parties saw the new governments as a lucrative new source of money and jobs.'[83]

Pressure for reform was applied and partially achieved in areas of cultural policy too. In the media, for example, the boom years had seen a process of nationalization of mass culture, particularly with the advent of state-controlled national television. In the climate of the seventies the state monopoly over the media and the creation of a national culture at the expense of regional and local cultures were brought into question, as part of a more general challenging of a centralized political system, which had ignored the Constitution's provision for regional reform. There was undoubtedly an anti-authoritarian shift allowing greater freedom of expression. This is aptly illustrated by the fact that newspaper journalists were less constrained in what they could write, while, as Lumley points out, political cartoonists were able for the first time to work for national newspapers – such activities having in the past been restricted to newspapers run by political parties.[84] Yet, in other areas the reforms were often disappointing. In television, for example, which had witnessed an increase in the number of licences from under 3 million in 1961 to over 10 million a decade later,[85] 'partitocratic' concerns prevailed in spite of the passing in 1975 of a new regulatory law, which reduced government control over the RAI. Christian Democrat influence was not totally removed but shared out with first the Socialists, who were given control over the second state channel (RAI 2), and then the Communists, who were granted control over RAI 3 when it was introduced in 1979. As Elena Dagrada notes: 'This was not a truly pluralistic television committed to debate and mutual progress. Rather, *lottizzazione* [the allocation of positions of influence according to party affiliation] was an effect of the continued organization of television in a centralized and hierarchical manner, as an instrument needing to be regulated in order to control public opinion.'[86] The cultural implications of the arrival during the mid-seventies of private television following deregulation were far from positive as poor-quality commercially based channels began to compete with the RAI.

If television deregulation had originally been motivated by the need to favour community-based transmissions, the national dimension prevailed. In spite of such tendencies, new expression was also given to local and regional cultures. Many anthropologists and historians, themselves protagonists of the protests, began to take an interest in direct forms of folkloristic expression in the environment of the movements. Songs, tales and sayings were recorded on tape and reproduced as long-playing records. This type of study was clearly the result of a feeling of nostalgia for the associative life of rural Italy caused by the industrialization and urbanization process. There was, for example, an initiative to rehabilitate regional popular music, as in Naples, and the revival of local dances, fairs and village festivals in the 'Third Italy'. Regional reform also led to new political initiatives to protect regional heritage and promote cultural activities, though there were serious imbalances in cultural provision and expenditure between the regions, which, moreover, suffered a lack of decentralized funding from the government.[87]

The social movements also played a significant role in promoting alternative forms of culture which challenged the cultural and political strategies of both the government and the parliamentary Left. Particularly emblematic in this sense was the *1977* (*Settantasette*) youth movement that developed in reaction against the government's proposal to restrict accessibility to university once again. The protest confirmed the ideological gap between large sections of Italian youth linked to the extra-parliamentary Left and the Communist Party, which led to violent demonstrations, particularly in Rome and Communist-run Bologna. According to Ginsborg, socio-economic as well as political factors were at play here. There was increasing unemployment in manual and intellectual sections of the labour market, with the gap between these sectors contracting for the young as more and more people went to universities but found themselves without work after graduation. 'Disaffected from traditional politics' and 'unable or unwilling to find more than marginal or occasional work', many youngsters desired, above all, to 'be together' and 'enjoy themselves'. They practised *autoriduzione* on the price of pop-concert tickets and in Milan occupied buildings which were converted into social centres for such activities as concerts, films, yoga classes, discussion groups and counselling for drug addicts (the latter activity indicating the dire effects on an underemployed and disillusioned generation of the arrival of hard drugs in the Italian cities).[88]

The urban social movements, whether catering for problems associated with youth, community action, feminism and gay activism (the latter two discussed in the following section), saw culture and politics as inextricably linked and challenged the traditional distinction between 'high' and 'low' cultural forms. During the late seventies and early eighties many left-wing councils run by a new generation of politicians took account of this, offering open-air festivals to increase the opportunities for participation in public life for people of different ages, sexes, social classes and lifestyles. Moreover, a return to the use of the town square for cultural manifestations was seen as a means of counteracting the trend towards increased home-based cultural consumption caused by such factors as television, terrorism (discussed below) and economic difficulties resulting from the oil crisis.[89]

The effect of the social movements on the family and gender relations

By the end of the sixties the Italian institutions had made little progress in coming to terms with the reality of sexual and family practices and it was women who were the main victims of this. The failed attempt of the Christian Democrats and Catholic Church to abrogate divorce by means of a referendum in 1974 demonstrated the extent to which they were out of touch with society. Lack of information about contraception and sex led to an inevitably high rate of abortion practised by a thriving back-street business, abortion effectively functioning as an illegal form of birth control. Though women had participated in the demonstrations of 1968 and 1969 their action had rarely focused specifically on women's rights. Since the end of the Second World War the only political party that had concerned itself with the question was the Communist Party and even then it had tended to fight for women's gains within the context of the emancipation of the working class.[90]

The need for women to act autonomously derived from the failure of the first protest movements to take up women's specific grievances and aspirations. The experience of new ideas of freedom and equality of 1968 and 1969 increased their sense of injustice. Feminists angrily criticized male activists for oppressing them at home, referring to them in one of their slogans as *Compagni in piazza, fascisti nella vita* ('Comrades in the square, Fascists in life'). The policies of a number of feminist groups founded between 1969 and 1972 encompassed a wide range of issues. *Rivolta Femminile*, founded in Milan in 1970, campaigned for a radical social segregation of women from men; the *Movimento di Liberazione della Donna*, founded in 1969 and linked to the Radical Party, which was to become the principal pressure group for civil rights reform in the seventies, mainly focused on the right to abortion and contraception; *Lotta Femminista* campaigned for a housewives' salary, while *Gruppo Demistificazione Autoritarismo* attempted to remove familistic values from the female psyche.[91] The creation of a voice for Italian women was also achieved through writing, whether collections of testimonies of women by Giuliana Morandini and Armanda Guiducci (following in the footsteps of neo-realist efforts to create space for the marginalized and forgotten in society), or the fiction (often in documentary or autobiographical form) of such authors as Dacia Maraini and Francesca Durante.[92]

The mobilization of women during the seventies helped pressurize the state into passing long-awaited legislation, which took account of the reality of social practices. Their action, which interwove with the mass social movements and coincided with parliamentary-level struggles, promoted debate about women, challenging previous traditional Catholic hegemony on issues of sexuality, motherhood and the family. Particularly important was the mass mobilization between 1974 and 1976 for legalization of abortion, the biggest since the demonstrations of 1968, characterized by the public confession of women who had previously undergone illegal treatment. As a result of their campaign, legislation was passed in 1978 allowing free abortion for women up to 90 days pregnant (and more in cases where the health of the mother was threatened), though parental consent was required for girls under the age of eighteen. However, the law contained a conscientious objection clause for doctors, which made its application, particularly in the South, difficult.

Alongside the legalization of abortion, which was confirmed by a referendum in 1981, another important achievement was the passing of a new Family Law of 1975, which achieved equality for women, as the principle of paternal authority within the family was replaced by that of parental authority. According to Caldwell, the community of property between spouses was introduced and full property rights were granted to the surviving spouse on succession. New laws were also passed in favour of female employment. Among them Law 1204 of 1971, an updated version of the law on working mothers of 1950, brought job protection to home workers and increased the equality of treatment in different sectors. There were further limits on women being assigned to dangerous or heavy work during pregnancy and up to seven months after giving birth. The length of maternity leave was also increased. Yet, as Caldwell points out, in practice the survival of a traditionalist mentality limited the possibilities for abortion and in other areas resulted in court settlements that were disadvantageous to women. So feminism played a role not only in achieving new legislation, but in campaigning for its correct enforcement and possible amendments to it.[93]

Linked to the feminist movements, the seventies also saw the founding of the first gay and lesbian movements. It needs to be emphasized that, while homosexuality had never been illegal in Italy (in so far as it was not specifically mentioned in any criminal code), given that homosexuals could still be prosecuted for 'obscene acts' and 'immoral behaviour', they had been forced to lead double lives. Tolerance on the part of both the state and the Catholic Church had in the past depended on the willingness of homosexuals not to make public their sexuality, the idea being that open discussion might have a 'corrupting' effect on society. For that very reason attempts during the sixties, mainly by the MSI, to illegalize homosexuality had failed. The Italian gay movement was, therefore, founded above all on the need to make public, by means of action groups, publications, conferences, demonstrations and the 'coming out' of many prominent figures, a part of society that until that moment had existed only clandestinely.[94]

To what extent was family life changed as a result of the above developments? Figures on divorce, for example, can be misleading. Though initially high, a fall in average after 1974 to under 12,000 per year until 1982 meant that divorces were far fewer than in most other European countries and the United States. Remembering that divorce, once legally introduced, was only granted five years after separation, a more realistic comparison of Italian rates of separation with divorce rates in other countries reveals less striking differences. Yet, as Barbagli argues, it is clear that it took time to overcome traditional social mores. The influence of religion, though diminishing, kept many people from divorcing at the rate of other countries. Although during the seventies and eighties a higher number of Italians were able to separate or divorce because of fewer economic constraints, a less traditionalist outlook and more familiarity with lawyers, the lower classes continued to lag behind. While there was a sudden drop in the number of marriages in Italy from 1974, this trend took place at a later stage than in many other Western nations, as did the pattern of living together, which was more a consequence of the five-year waiting period between separation and divorce than of a change in social practices.[95]

The extent to which new legislation made women equal to men is also questionable. At the workplace women's wages remained on average 12 per cent lower than those of men. 67 per cent of women as opposed to 23 per cent of men were in the lowest grades. Although between 1973 and 1985 90 per cent of new jobs created in Italy were filled by women and there was an increased presence of women in the professions, it is equally true that female unemployment rose during that period. Sexual segregation remained strong with most women concentrated in less than 15 per cent of occupations. Women also remained highly under-represented in the unions.[96] In the South the majority of female employment continued to take place within domestic walls and, even where women worked outside the home, they did not become involved in union activism. Victoria Goddard's analysis of negative attitudes towards this among Neapolitan women during the late seventies and early eighties – even in sectors where they constituted the vast majority of workers – provides a clear explanation:

> There was a problem of confidence and of engaging in a language that most of these women did not know and did not feel comfortable with. There was the problem of the pressures of running a household and having to rush off after work to do shopping and cook and take care of the family. There was also the problem of parents or husbands who opposed their staying behind for a meeting. Finally, the women themselves frequently felt alienated from the issues at stake. This was largely because, for many, working in a factory was seen as a temporary step. Few had visions of a career or of a life-long dedication to their work. For most the hope was that this was a stop-gap and that at marriage they would give up factory work.[97]

Nevertheless, there is firm evidence that women often played an important public role in the urban environment of the South where issues regarding the wellbeing of the family were at stake. With regard to the illegal occupation of housing in the old centre of Palermo in 1975, Chubb argues that 'it was the women of the *quartieri popolari* [working-class districts] who made up the real backbone of the movement, demonstrating a degree of aggressiveness and combativity that shocked party leaders and city administrators accustomed to a much more passive and submissive female constituency'.[98] In questioning the extent to which traditional Southern cultural mores were challenged by the development of feminism, it is significant that abortion figures for the South were not drastically lower than in the rest of the country. Indeed, Apulia was above the national average, with higher levels than several Central and Northern regions.[99]

It is clear that, while the levels of female freedom remained geographically uneven, emancipation was experienced almost everywhere. Alessandro Portelli speaks of an 'extraordinary combination of women's oppression and women's emancipation' in a trade of 'picture brides' during the seventies. In rural areas of Northern and Central Italy local girls, as they demanded greater freedom, were no longer prepared to marry local men, who expected women to maintain their traditional roles. This resulted in the arrangement – via the exchange of photographs – of marriages with rural girls of the South: 'The emancipated Northern girls who refuse to marry rural men are replaced by Southern women who may still be traditional enough to adapt to farm life. . . . For these Southern women, the North may appear as a step on their way out of their environment and families, towards personal emancipation.'[100]

Terrorism

Parallel, and in some respects linked, to the protest of the late sixties and the seventies, Italian terrorism left deep scars on the lives of many Italians as well as assisting a process of social atomization, as people were literally frightened off the streets. Terrorism was a phenomenon of both the Right and the Left. The former represented a violent reaction against the protest movements and the growing influence in government of the Left. Left-wing terrorist violence was employed in opposition to the reforms, seen as a deliberate means of neutralizing the protest movement and maintaining traditional power by the ruling and social élite. Both extremisms clearly fought and fed off each other. Moreover, Italian terrorism, particularly that of the Right, was inextricably bound up with the criminal activities and destabilization policies of secret societies, the *Mafia*, and individual representatives of the state, that exploited terrorism as a means of conditioning the manner in which Italian society was governed. Beyond the specific political motivations for terrorist activities, Tullio-Altan emphasizes longer-standing psychological motives which were common to both Left and Right. The prolonged frustration of the younger generation at their social alienation led to aggressive and regressive tendencies, particularly among young Southern Italian worker immigrants who had been uprooted from their traditional cultural environment and the young Northern lower middle classes in desperate need of social advancement. Such alienation, he argues, resulted from the persistence alongside the reforms of backward social structures and a system of patronage.[101]

Right-wing extremism manifested itself in two forms. In reaction against the student mobilizations of the late sixties and early seventies, many moderate and right-wing students took to the streets in protest against university occupations, attacking left-wing students, as well as newspaper and political headquarters. In this they often enjoyed the protection of the police, who were not unhappy about this counter-reaction, given the extent to which the student demonstrations were draining their resources and forcing them into overtime. At another level, however, many extreme right-wing groups gained from the moral if not material support of those conservative elements of society who stood to lose from the gains of the social movements. With the encouragement of the military secret services they pursued a 'strategy of tension' which aimed to seminate terror through indiscriminate bomb attacks, which could be blamed on the extreme Left and justify authoritarian forms of government that would redress the 'imbalance' caused by recent democratic reforms. In the immediate aftermath of the student and worker protests, which the state seemed unwilling to repress with the same vigour with which it had previously acted, many members of the ruling élite were willing to give their support to such forms of terrorism.

A key role was played in the 'strategy of tension' by the P2 (Propaganda 2) masonic lodge of businessmen, financiers, leaders of the secret services and armed forces, magistrates and politicians, who also helped to place obstacles in the way of those investigating terrorist crimes. While the Piazza Fontana bombing of December 1969 is usually considered to be the starting point of the 'strategy', it should be placed within the broader historical context of underground anti-Communist plots, the roots of which may be traced back to the planned military coup of 1964 (*Piano Solo*) and even further back to the creation during the fifties, under the auspices of NATO, of paramilitary groups that were to establish territorial control in the event of a Soviet invasion or a Communist electoral victory (*Operazione Gladio*).

From an ideological point of view, extreme right-wing terrorism was founded on vague notions of order, tradition, élitism and racial superiority, which, however, bore little relation to social reality. With reference to the *Ordine Nuovo* group (ON), founded in 1954, Franco Ferraresi argues that:

> Whatever representation was used, these were abstract, mythical communities/ collectivities, devoid of any link with existing social groups or entities that the ON may claim to defend or represent. . . . The negative referents, on the other hand, comprised practically everything else in contemporary society. The modern world, where traditional values are cast away, where matter triumphs over spirit, and where merchants are honored over heroes, was for the ON one single great historical perversion.[102]

According to Ferraresi, the level of engagement of right-wing groups in terrorist activities varied. While ON with its particularly strong bases in Sicily, Latium and Veneto and upper- and middle-class membership was mainly culturally and ideologically orientated, *Avanguardia Nazionale* (AN), composed of middle-class students and based in Rome, concentrated on more practical activities, as was demonstrated by its institution of paramilitary training camps.

Between 1969 and 1980 extreme right-wing groups were responsible for the majority of deaths and injuries caused by terrorist attacks. Though AN and ON were brought to trial in 1972, many of their militants formed new groups to take their place. These included *Ordine Nero* and the *Nuclei Armati Rivoluzionari*, the latter being responsible for some of the worst atrocities committed during the late seventies and early eighties. Besides the Piazza

Fontana massacre of December 1969, the right-wing terrorist campaign included numerous train bombings, the most serious of which happened in 1974 and 1984 on the Bologna–Florence railway line, and the bombing in August 1980 of Bologna station which caused the death of 85 people. The MSI, though officially maintaining democratic respectability, was also strongly suspected of involvement, and, furthermore, put forward individuals suspected of involvement in right-wing terrorism for election to the Chamber of Deputies so that they could enjoy parliamentary immunity from prosecution.

Apart from the large number of victims of neo-Fascist terrorism, it is important to understand the threat that such attacks posed to the democratic system as a whole. The decision of the Communists not to attempt to form a government on their own, even though at the general election of 1976 they obtained a historic 34 per cent of the vote – less than 5 per cent below the number polled by the Christian Democrats – was in part due to the climate of terrorism. Reminded by the military coup of 1973 against the left-wing Chilean government of Salvador Allende, the Italian Communists felt the threat of a return to authoritarian rule as had happened in 1922, especially since the state was believed to have a hand in the 'strategy of tension' and was conspicuously unsuccessful in bringing right-wing terrorists to justice. Moreover, Barkan notes that this was often hinted at by business leaders and conservative officials as a possible reaction to working-class mobilization. Though probably only amounting to fear-mongering, it 'threw the unions on the defensive and stimulated popular sentiment against the labor movement.'[103]

Much of the debate surrounding the left-wing terrorist groups (Red Brigades – *Brigate Rosse*) is centred on their links with the protest movements. Though representing only a minority of protest activists, the founder members of the Red Brigades had played an important role in the mobilizations of 1968 and 1969. Their future vocation as terrorists was shaped by the birth in 1969 of several extreme-Left extra-parliamentary groups strongly emphasizing the leading role of the working class in the revolutionary process and rejecting the 'reformist' strategies of the Communist Party. Such groups, which were directly involved in the labour agitation in the autumn of 1969, included *Avanguardia Operaia, Potere Operaio* and *Lotta Continua*. Athough they were not terrorist groups themselves, they played a critical role in creating the climate in which terrorism was to grow. As Meade notes: 'These groups stoked the fires of rebellion, spread the revolutionary ideology and myths, and served as way-stations on the line to terrorism, and "Lotta Continua" and "Workers' Power" for a time lent rhetorical support to the activities of the *Brigate Rosse*.'[104] Many of the founder protagonists of the Red Brigades had also been strongly influenced by the more general revival of the myth of the Resistance characterizing the sixties. According to Luigi Manconi, in the face of a

new 'Fascist threat', which the protest movement interpreted in the authoritarian trends of the Christian Democrats, the criminal activities of the Right
and factory-management policy, Red Brigade members sought to appropriate the moral content of the partisan struggle, whose slogans, iconography,
literature and mythology had been brought back to life by the movement,
thinking of themselves not as terrorists, but as the 'new Resistance' carrying
out 'partisan operations'.[105]

Nevertheless, Lumley argues against overstressing the continuity between
left-wing terrorism and the protest movements: 'What remained contradictory and complex in the social movements was drastically transformed and
simplified by the Red Brigades.'[106] In this sense, the idea of a nascent revolution put forward by the movements was *literally* interpreted by the terrorists,
as were the negative conceptions of democracy common to thousands of
activists. In line with structural changes within the social movements the
terrorist groups developed within the context of an intensification of
violence among a minority of actors only. Donatella della Porta notes that
after 1971 there was a general decline in the number of protests and
violent events, though the decline was far less sharp for the latter, as 'the
more spontaneous violence of the beginning of the cycle tended to be
substituted by semimilitary forms of violence'.[107] The fundamentally open-
minded and pluralistic nature of the protest movements was replaced by an
anti-democratic and totalitarian vision of how to solve problems.

Initially Red Brigade activities were limited to industrial areas of Northern
Italy, revealing a desire to maintain links with the interests of a broader
political and trade-union movement.[108] Justifying their action by the need to
defend the working class against the threat of an authoritarian reaction, the
Red Brigades inflicted beatings or kidnapped managers and factory foremen,
as well as attacking the extreme Right. During the mid-seventies they moved
beyond the factories and the industrial triangle, targeting members of the
Christian Democratic Party, judges, policemen and *carabinieri*. As such the
Brigades set up their own counter-system of law, justice, interrogation and
imprisonment to which their victims were subjected for 'crimes against the
people'. Notable, for example, was their kidnapping and placing on 'trial' of
the judge, Mario Sossi, seen as a fanatical persecutor of the working class and
student movement.

For the first time too the Red Brigades started to kill their targets, according to a logic by which their victims were *absolute* enemies of the working
class, whose physical elimination became a humanitarian act for the proletariat. In June 1976 the Brigades killed the general public prosecutor of Genoa,
Francesco Coco, and two of his bodyguards, in order to prevent the trial of
the founders of the organization, who had been arrested. The intensification
of violence coincided with declining levels of protest within society at large,
which enhanced a loss of faith in legal forms of collective behaviour and in

the ability of the Communist Party, trade unions and even the New Left to bring about change. This in turn created younger and highly militant re-cruits for the Brigades (replacing the first-generation members as they were caught by the police and imprisoned). Among them were socially alienated individuals belonging to the *1977* youth movement.

Towards the end of the decade the terrorist organization reached its most violent phase in line with a new concept of the 'enemy'. If at the beginning of their history the Brigades had seen themselves as the vanguard of the workers' movement, they now believed that, in the context of the 'historic compromise', the 'bourgeois' state had assigned the task of controlling the working class to the trade unions. Trade-union leaders and promoters of the 'historic compromise' strategy within both the Communist and Christian Democrat Parties became their main targets. This was the logic behind the kidnapping in March 1978 and execution the following May of the secretary of the Christian Democrat Party, Aldo Moro, one of the strongest advocates of the 'historic compromise'. Yet, failure to obtain concessions from the government in return for Moro's freeing, followed by the decision to kill Moro, produced strong controversy among both militants of other clandes-tine groups and the kidnappers themselves.

The Moro murder is shrouded with mystery. It has been argued that the failure of the Italian state to rescue Moro lay in the very logic of opposition to the 'historic compromise' which many ultra-conservative elements, par-ticularly the secret services, shared with the terrorists. Moreover, conspiracy theories have claimed that after the arrest of the historic members of the Red Brigades during the mid-seventies the organization was infiltrated by ele-ments who either had links with or were manipulated by the secret services, themselves driven by the American secret services, according to a logic that refused to accept a Communist Party in government. While such theories are difficult to demonstrate in practice, and are vehemently denied by the Red Brigades themselves, it remains a fact that many of the secret service leaders entrusted with the task of co-ordinating Moro's rescue operation were members of P2, which has been associated with the overall terrorist 'strategy of tension' characterizing the seventies and eighties.[109]

How much popular support did the Red Brigades enjoy, particularly among the workers on whose behalf they claimed to be acting? Here a certain distinc-tion needs to be made according to the type of strategy employed. There is little doubt that, during the early years of left-wing terrorism, many workers were not sorry about the Red Brigades' targeting of factory bosses and foremen. It was often felt that, they deserved ill-treatment after the hardships they had inflicted upon their employees. The increasing violence characterizing Red Brigade actions from the mid-seventies onwards and their decision to go underground isolated the terrorists from working-class members, though the attitude of the latter towards terrorism remained ambivalent. Barkan argues that, even though the number of terrorists and sympathizers among Italian workers was small (just as the number was small in the population as a whole), many more workers may have known something about terrorist activity or had suspicions but were generally reluctant to speak out: they were justifiably afraid of reprisals, did not like the idea of spying, saw the role of the management and the state in the fight against terrorism as ambivalent and even felt that, while the terrorists might be completely wrong, the bosses and government were just as bad. Indeed, when in 1977 the Red Brigades shot the vice-director of the Fiat-owned newspaper, *La Stampa*, the workers ignored a protest strike called by the unions, arguing that 'no one made a comparable fuss when a worker was killed on the job', while the older employees recognized the victim's previous role in anti-worker and anti-union repression.[110]

The final years of the Red Brigades (1979–82) amounted to little more than a private war for survival against the forces of the state as they became increasingly isolated from the rest of society. Their difficulties were compounded by the fact that many ex-*brigatisti* started to repent and collaborate with the judiciary, aided by a law, passed in 1981, which allowed a reduction in prison sentences for terrorists who collaborated with the state and special treatment for those who publicly dissociated themselves from the armed struggle. While the protest movement, whatever its limitations, helped to create a climate of greater freedom, terrorism restricted the possibilities for enjoying it. Apart from the fact that people were frightened into staying at home in the evenings, a controversial series of laws passed between 1976 and 1978 gave the police powers to impose greater restrictions on personal liberties in an attempt to reduce the number of attacks. In the long run, however, even the police moved towards their own internal reform, which would result in their demilitarization and long-awaited achievement of the right to form unions in 1981. As they became the targets of the terrorist and *Mafia* attacks, which the state often seemed unwilling to prevent, they increasingly identified the search for democracy within their own institution with that which the protest movements demanded for society as a whole. In this they had the increasing support of citizens, as the polarization of society between Left and Right of the late sixties and early seventies gradually weakened.

Conclusion

As the above section demonstrates, the struggles for reform in Italy were more painful and drawn out in comparison with other Western countries experiencing mass protest. The extent to which Italy was transformed as a result of such struggles is questionable. The achievements of the protesters were disappointing in many areas, as indicated by an overall failure to improve public services and investment in the South and to remove administrative corruption, though in other areas, such as relations between the sexes, norms governing the family and workers' rights, the movements were more successful in bringing about change. Ginsborg argues, however, that the 'revolutionary' aims of the protest movement failed, as the core values of the protagonists – anti-capitalist, collectivist and egalitarian – were rejected by society as a whole. He suggests that above all the movement could not halt the long-term social and cultural trends created by the economic miracle, which saw an accentuation of atomization, individualism and a strengthening of the family unit: 'Italy's modernization, as so many others, was not based on collective responsibility or collective action, but on the opportunities it afforded individual families to transform their lives'.[111]

Whatever the disappointments, there is no doubt that for the protagonists involved the experience of the protest years had a lasting impact on their social, political and moral attitudes. According to Silvio Lanaro, though the majority returned to a 'normal' way of life after the protest cycle, there was a sense of having been part of an important democratic, anti-authoritarian and modernizing movement, an experience that would influence their future behaviour, and that, above all, they would apply to their professions. Their lives had been permeated by a sense of energy and optimism about being able to achieve a better society: 'It is possible to play a social role, to be fraternally happy, to disobey rationally, to achieve something collectively without submitting to others or to the rules of individual competitiveness.'[112] If examined over the post-war period as a whole, it is clear that by the end of the seventies Italy had made notable inroads, having established herself as a major industrial power and having begun to tackle serious obstacles to democratic development and healthy social and cultural modernization, a process that would continue – not without considerable difficulties – over subsequent decades, to which the next chapter is dedicated.

Notes

1. Post-war economic development is discussed in detail in Zamagni, *The Economic History of Italy*, 325–78; Russell King, *The Industrial Geography of Italy* (Beckenham: Croom Helm, 1985); Galimberti and Paolozzi, *Il volo del calabrone*, chapter 3; Balcet, *L'economia italiana*, chapter 3; Clark, *Modern Italy*, 348–60.
2. Statistics from ISTAT, *Sommario di statistiche storiche*, tables 7.1, 7.4, 8.13, 8.18, 8.33, 10.5–10.11, 13.1, 13.2, 13.10; Galimberti and Paolozzi, *Il volo del calabrone*, 130–1.
3. Cento Bull and Corner, *From Peasant to Entrepreneur*, 116. For a detailed discussion of the development of entrepreneurial households, see chapters 5 and 6.
4. Carlo Trigilia, 'Work and politics in the Third Italy's industrial districts', in Frank Pyke, Giacomo Becattini and Werner Sengenberger (eds), *Industrial Districts and Inter-firm Co-operation in Italy* (Geneva: International Institute for Labour Studies, 1990), 160–84.
5. Tullio-Altan, *La nostra Italia*, 146.

6. Tullio-Altan, *La nostra Italia*, 149–50; Zamagni, *The Economic History of Italy*, 333–4.

7. The problems of Southern industrial development are discussed in detail in King, *The Industrial Geography of Italy*, chapter 11; Guido Crainz, *Storia del miracolo italiano. Culture, identità, trasformazioni fra anni cinquanta e sessanta* (Rome: Donzelli, 1998), 120–4.

8. Cento Bull and Corner, *From Peasant to Entrepreneur*, 163.

9. For figures and more detailed analysis, see Ginsborg, *A History of Contemporary Italy*, 237–9; King, *The Industrial Geography of Italy*, 70–5.

10. ISTAT, *Sommario di statistiche storiche*, table 7.1; Galimberti and Paolozzi, *Il volo del calabrone*, 217.

11. King, *The Industrial Geography of Italy*, 288–9. For figures, see also Clark, *Modern Italy*, 359–60; Tullio-Altan, *La nostra Italia*, 145–6.

12. Facts and figures on migration in this section are from Crainz, *Storia del miracolo italiano*, chapter 4; ISTAT, *Sommario di statistiche storiche*, tables 2.27 and 2.28. For city population figures, see Mitchell, *European Historical Statistics*, table A4.

13. Tullio-Altan, *La nostra Italia*, 158–63.

14. Duggan, *A Concise History of Italy*, 261.

15. Percy A. Allum, *Politics and Society in Post-war Naples* (Cambridge: Cambridge University Press, 1973), 160–1. For analysis of the personnel of Italian public administration, see Paul Furlong, *Modern Italy. Representation and Reform* (London: Routledge, 1994), 89–96; David Hine, *Governing Italy. The Politics of Bargained Pluralism* (Oxford: Clarendon Press, 1993), 236–41.

16. James Walston, *The Mafia and Clientelism. Roads to Rome in post-war Calabria* (London: Routledge, 1988), 85–6; Luciano Violante, *Il patto scellerato. Potere e politica di un regime Mafioso. La relazione alla Commissione parlamentare antimafia* (Rome: Crescenzi Allendorf Editori, 1993).

17. Gino Bedani, *Politics and Ideology in the Italian Workers' Movement. Union Development and the Changing Side of the Catholic and Communist Subcultures in Post-war Italy* (Oxford: Berg, 1995), 66–7.

18. Earle, *The Italian Co-operative Movement*, 30–2.

19. Sonetti, 'The Family in Tuscany between Fascism and the Cold War', 84.

20. The effects of state anti-Communist policies are discussed in detail in Crainz, *Storia del miracolo italiano*, chapters 1 and 2.

21. Fried, *The Italian Prefects*, chapter 5.

22. Allum, *Politics and Society in Post-war Naples*, 105.

23. Figures from ISTAT, *Sommario di Statistiche*, table 14.4; Crainz, *Storia del miracolo italiano*, 83–4.

24. Maria Chiara Liguori, 'Donne e consumi nell'Italia degli anni cinquanta', *Italia Contemporanea*, 205, 1996, 665–89(677–8).

25. Figures on nutrition, health and life expectancy are from ISTAT, *Le regioni in cifre* (Rome: Istituto Nazionale di Statistica, 1990), tables 2.12, 17.4 and 17.16; Stafano Baldi and Raimondo Cagiano de Azevedo, *La popolazione italiana. Storia demografica dal dopoguerra ad oggi* (Bologna: Il Mulino, 2000), 46, 159. For the eradication of malaria, see Snowden, '"Fields of death"', 48–50.

26. Figures on the family are from ISTAT, *Sommario di statistiche storiche*, tables 2.2, 2.7, 2.8, 2.12.
27. Cento Bull and Corner, *From Peasant to Entrepreneur*, 118.
28. Clark, *Modern Italy*, 361.
29. John Foot, 'Immigration and the city: Milan and mass immigration, 1958–98', *Modern Italy*, 4(2) 1999, 159–72(169).
30. Caldwell, *Italian Family Matters*, 22, 113–15.
31. Figures from ISTAT, *Sommario di statistiche storiche*, table 2.5. Illiteracy decreased further to 3.1 per cent by 1981.
32. Barbagli, *Educating for Unemployment*, 296–7.
33. Barbagli, *Educating for Unemployment*, 248–9, 252–3, 323–7.
34. Jane and Peter Schneider, *Festival of the Poor*, 258. For general discussion see, 250–9.
35. Duggan, *A Concise History of Italy*, 260. For a more detailed account of social and political practices in post-war Southern Italy, see Walston, *The Mafia and Clientelism*.
36. Jan Brögger, *Montevarese: A study of peasant society and culture in Southern Italy* (Oslo: Universitetsforlaget, 1971), 122–3.
37. Sydel Silverman, *Three Bells of Civilization. The Life of an Italian Hill Town* (New York: Columbia University Press, 1975), 102–3.
38. David I. Kertzer, *Comrades and Christians. Religion and Political Struggle in Communist Italy* (Cambridge: Cambridge University Press, 1980), 133.
39. This is discussed in Paul Ginsborg, 'Italian Political Culture in Historical Perspective', *Modern Italy*, 1(1), 1995, 7–8. For more detailed discussion of post-war subcultures, see also Paul Ginsborg, *L'Italia del tempo presente. Famiglia, società civile, Stato, 1980–1996* (Turin: Einaudi, 1998), 199.
40. Trigilia, 'Work and politics', 179.
41. Salvatore Lupo, 'The Mafia', in Patrick McCarthy (ed.), *Italy since 1945* (Oxford: Oxford University Press, 2000), 153–70; Lupo, *Storia della mafia*, 11–12; Walston, *The Mafia and Clientelism*, 33.
42. Unless otherwise indicated, figures in this section on cultural consumption are from ISTAT, *Sommario di statistiche storiche*, table 5.3.
43. David Forgacs, 'Cultural consumption, 1940s to 1990s', in David Forgacs and Robert Lumley (eds), *Italian Cultural Studies. An Introduction* (Oxford: Oxford University Press, 1996), (273–90)278.
44. For analysis of the post-war Italian cinema, see Christopher Wagstaff, 'Cinema', in Forgacs and Lumley (eds), *Italian Cultural Studies*, 216–32; and Stephen Gundle, 'Fame, Fashion, and Style: the Italian Star System', in Forgacs and Lumley (eds), *Italian Cultural Studies*, 309–26.
45. Robert Lumley, *Italian Journalism. A Critical Anthology* (Manchester: Manchester University Press, 1996), 1–8; Robert Lumley, 'Peculiarities of the Italian Newspaper', in Forgacs and Lumley (eds), *Italian Cultural Studies*, 199–215(202–6). See also Paolo Murialdi, 'Dalla Liberazione al centrosinistra', in Valerio Castronovo and Nicola Tranfaglia (eds), *La stampa italiana dalla Resistenza agli anni sessanta* (Bari: Laterza, 1980), 232–301.
46. Ginsborg, *A History of Contemporary Italy*, 241.

47. Crainz, *Storia del miracolo italiano*, 138; Pivato and Tonelli, *Italia Vagabonda*, 83–4.
48. Much of the letter of denunciation read out in church is reproduced in Kertzer, *Comrades and Christians*, 131. See also Clark, *Modern Italy*, 370–1.
49. Ginsborg, *A History of Contemporary Italy*, 241.
50. Liguori ,'Donne e consumi', 665–89.
51. For analysis of the foundations of the Italian Centre–Left government and changes within the Church, see Ginsborg, *A History of Contemporary Italy*, 258–67.
52. The climate of change leading to the creation of the Centre–Left government is well documented by Crainz in *Storia del miracolo italiano*, 142–73.
53. Crainz, *Storia del miracolo italiano*, 70–8; Marcello Flores and Alberto De Bernardi, *Il Sessantotto* (Bologna: Il Mulino, 1998), 165–8.
54. Stephen Gundle, 'The "civic religion" of the Resistance in post-war Italy', *Modern Italy*, 5(2), 2000, 113–32(126–7).
55. Adriano Ballone, 'La Resistenza', in Isnenghi (ed.), *I luoghi della memoria*, 422–30.
56. ISTAT, *Sommario di statistiche storiche*, table 7.11; Crainz, *Storia del miraiolo italiano*, chapter 5.
57. The process leading to changes in the Italian education system is discussed in Barbagli, *Educating for Unemployment*, 257–315.
58. Philip Willan, *Puppetmasters. The Political Use of Terrorism in Italy* (London: Constable, 1991), 35–40.
59. Caldwell, *Italian Family Matters*, 25–7; 'The Family in the Fifties: A Notion in Conflict with a Reality', in Christopher Duggan and Christopher Wagstaff (eds), *Italy in the Cold War. Politics, Culture and Society, 1948–1958* (Oxford: Berg, 1995), 149–58(152–5). See also Ginsborg, *A History of Contemporary Italy*, 243–4.
60. Clark, *Modern Italy*, 371.
61. Robert Lumley, *States of Emergency: Cultures of Revolt in Italy from 1968 to 1978* (London: Verso, 1990), 34–41. Lumley's work provides a highly comprehensive account of the protests. See also Sidney Tarrow, *Democracy and Disorder: Protest and Politics in Italy, 1965–1975* (Oxford: Clarendon Press, 1989).
62. School of Barbiana, *Letter to a Teacher* (Harmondsworth: Penguin, 1973), 17.
63. Robert C. Meade, *Red Brigades: The Story of Italian Terrorism* (London: Macmillan, 1990), 19–21.
64. Barbagli, *Educating for Unemployment*, 316.
65. Alessandro Portelli, *The Battle of Valle Giulia: Oral History and the Art of Dialogue* (Madison, WI: University of Wisconsin Press, 1997), 193–8.
66. The relationship between the police and the protesters is analysed in detail in Donatella della Porta, *Social movements, political violence, and the state: A comparative analysis of Italy and Germany* (Cambridge: Cambridge University Press, 1995).
67. Lumley, *States of Emergency*, 120. See 119–39 for an analysis of the cultural revolution taking place. See also Flores and De Bernardi, *Il Sessantotto*, 165–82.
68. The role of Catholics in the protests is discussed in Flores and De Bernardi, *Il Sessantotto*, 178–80.
69. ISTAT, *Sommario di statistiche storiche*, table 7.11.
70. John R. Low-Beer, *Protest and Participation. The new working class in Italy* (Cambridge: Cambridge University Press, 1978), 33–4.

71. Ginsborg, *A History of Contemporary Italy*, 310.
72. Low-Beer, *Protest and Participation*, 225.
73. Joanne Barkan, *Visions of Emancipation: The Italian Workers' Movement since 1945* (New York: Praeger, 1984), 73. See 68–91 for a general analysis.
74. Lumley, *States of Emergency*, 211–13.
75. Tarrow, *Democracy and Disorder*, 63–7.
76. Barkan, *Visions of Emancipation*, 77.
77. Bedani, *Politics and Ideology*, 168–9.
78. ISTAT, *Rapporto sull'Italia: Edizione 1999* (Bologna: Il Mulino, 1999), 183. The number of industrial workers declined from 40 per cent to 37 per cent and those employed in agriculture from 20 per cent to 13 per cent of the work force between 1971 and 1981.
79. Lumley, *States of Emergency*, 252, 262–7; Ginsborg, *A History of Contemporary Italy*, 322–5, 391–3.
80. Judith Chubb, *Patronage, power and poverty in southern Italy. A tale of two cities* (Cambridge: Cambridge University Press, 1982), 180–202, 223–30.
81. Percy and Felia Allum, 'The resistible rise of the new Neapolitan Camorra', in Stephen Parker and Stephen Gundle (eds), *The New Italian Republic: from the Fall of the Berlin Wall to Berlusconi* (London: Routledge, 1996), 234–46(238–9).
82. For the 'historic compromise', austerity politics and the role of the unions, see Bedani, *Politics and Ideology*, 197–248; Frederic Spotts and Theodor Wieser, *Italy: A Difficult Democracy* (Cambridge: Cambridge University Press, 1986), 207–8; Lumley, *States of Emergency*, 257–67; Miriam Golden, *Labour Divided. Austerity and Working Class Politics in Contemporary Italy* (Ithaca, NY: Cornell University Press, 1988).
83. Putnam, *Making Democracy Work*, 50. Putnam's volume gives a detailed assessment of the success of regional reform.
84. Lumley 'Peculiarities of the Italian Newspaper', 210–11, and 'The Political Cartoon', in Forgacs and Lumley (eds), *Italian Cultural Studies*, 266–70.
85. ISTAT, *Sommario di statistiche storiche*, table 5.3.
86. Elena Dagrada 'Television and its Critics: A Parallel History', in Forgacs and Lumley (eds), *Italian Cultural Studies*, 233–47 (241). See also Christopher Wagstaff, 'The Media', in Baranski and West (eds), *The Cambridge Companion to Modern Italian Culture*, 293–309.
87. Cultural reform and the role of the protest movements is discussed in Portelli, *The Battle of Valle Giulia*, 186, 246–7; Peppino Ortoleva, 'A Geography of the Media since 1945', in Forgacs and Lumley (eds), *Italian Cultural Studies*, 185–98; Franco Bianchini and others, 'Cultural Policy', in Forgacs and Lumley (eds), *Italian Cultural Studies*, 291–308(294–9).
88. Ginsborg, *A History of Contemporary Italy*, 381–2.
89. Bianchini and others, 'Cultural Policy', 295–6.
90. The women's social movements and their achievements are analysed in detail in Lumley, *States of Emergency*, chapter 21; Caldwell, *Italian Family Matters*. The latter volume also provides detailed information on legislation passed in favour of women.
91. Silvio Lanaro, *Storia dell'Italia repubblicana. L'economia, la politica, la cultura, la società dal dopoguerra agli anni '90* (Venice: Marsilio, 1992), 361–3.

92. Ann Hallamore-Caesar, 'Post-War Italian Narrative: An Alternative Account', in Forgacs and Lumley (eds), *Italian Cultural Studies*, 248–60(256–9).

93. Caldwell, *Italian Family Matters*, 85–6, 101.

94. Giovanni Dall'Orto, 'La "tolleranza repressiva" dell'omosessualità', *Quaderni di Critica Omosessuale*, 3, 1987, 37–57; Luisa Passerini, 'Gender Relations', in Forgacs and Lumley (eds), *Italian Cultural Studies*, 144–59(153–5).

95. For figures and analysis, see Marzio Barbagli, *Provando e riprovando. Matrimonio, famiglia e divorzio in Italia e in altri paesi occidentali* (Bologna: Il Mulino, 1990).

96. Figures taken from Lumley, *States of Emergency*, 326; Caldwell, *Italian Family Matters*, 116.

97. Victoria A. Goddard, *Gender, Family and Work in Naples* (Oxford: Berg, 1996), 179.

98. Chubb, *Patronage, power and poverty*, 182.

99. In 1980 Apulia registered 383.3 abortions per 1,000 live births in comparison with 342.0 in Italy as a whole, 368.9 in Latium and 272.5 in Veneto (ISTAT, *Sommario di statistiche storiche*, table 2.19).

100. Portelli, *The Battle of Valle Giulia*, 238.

101. Tullio-Altan, *La nostra Italia*, 189–92.

102. Franco Ferraresi, *Threats to Democracy. The Radical Right in Italy after the War* (Princeton, NJ: Princeton University Press, 1996), 55–6. See Spotts and Wieser, *Italy: A Difficult Democracy*, 175–8, for a brief but useful analysis of right-wing terrorism in Italy. See also Meade, *Red Brigades*, 34–7.

103. Barkan, *Visions of Emancipation*, 108.

104. Meade, *Red Brigades*, 30.

105. Luigi Manconi, 'The political ideology of the Red Brigades', in Raimondo Catanzaro (ed.), *The Red Brigades and Left-Wing Terrorism in Italy* (London: Pinter, 1991), 115–43(122–3).

106. Lumley, *States of Emergency*, 290. For general discussion, see 286–90.

107. Della Porta, *Social movements, political violence, and the state*, 29.

108. The various phases of Red Brigade development described in this section are analysed in detail in Gian Carlo Caselli and Donatella della Porta, 'The history of the Red Brigades: organizational structures and strategies of action (1970–1982)', in Catanzaro (ed.), *The Red Brigades*, 70–114. See also Manconi, 'The Political Ideology of the Red Brigades', and Meade, *Red Brigades*.

109. This is discussed in detail in Richard Drake, *The Aldo Moro Murder Case* (Cambridge, MA: Harvard University Press, 1995).

110. Barkan, *Visions of Emancipation*, 111–12. Worker and union attitudes towards left-wing terrorism are also discussed in David Moss, *The Politics of Left-Wing Violence in Italy, 1969–85* (London: Macmillan, 1989), 81–115.

111. Ginsborg, *A History of Contemporary Italy*, 342. See 340–7 for general discussion.

112. Lanaro, *Storia dell'Italia repubblicana*, 353.

Chapter 6

Affluence and moral crisis: Italian society in the eighties and nineties

Introduction

This final chapter examines the processes by which Italy became a leading world economic power. During the eighties and nineties many Italians enjoyed levels of affluence that not even traditionally more prosperous nations like Great Britain had witnessed. Yet, as is demonstrated in the first part of the chapter, when analysed in the broader context of continued structural weaknesses in the economy and institutions, regional imbalances and the survival of highly damaging elements of backwardness, such wealth generation becomes more qualified. The second part of the chapter examines the effect on Italian society of the crisis of the early nineties provoked by several shocking *Mafia* murders and the chain of corruption scandals rocking the Italian economy and political system.

The Italian quality of life on the eve of the twenty-first century

The Italian economy

An analysis of Italy's economic performance during the last two decades of the twentieth century reveals both areas of dynamic growth and serious weaknesses. Initially the economy was disadvantaged by problems of inflation, carried over from the previous decade, which reached a peak in 1980 as a result of a second international oil crisis and uncontrollable price and wage growth. Nevertheless, rigorous government anti-inflation policies combined with a drop in labour costs were behind a second economic boom, largely founded on the success of small and medium-sized businesses and the growth of the tertiary sector. Consequent to growth in manufacturing productivity and investment, the notable increase in Italy's GDP together with an improved export performance enabled her to become the fifth world economic power in 1987, overtaking Great Britain.[1] However, weaknesses in the Italian economy remained, as is demonstrated by a brief recession during the early nineties. Up to that period Italy continued to suffer a balance of trade deficit as imports increased while exports did not catch up. Only in 1993, following devaluation of the lira after it left the European Monetary System, did the trade balance swing into surplus, with exports growing by 18.4 per cent between 1993 and 1994 (compared with 7.9 per cent for imports).[2] Economic stability was also threatened by an acute financial crisis in the public sector, partly caused by the close link between government spending and the system of political patronage. The situation began to be corrected from 1992 onwards – parallel to the demise of the political system in the wake of widespread corruption scandals – through greater austerity in government spending and a privatization programme.

The success of the Italian private sector economy may partly be attributed to dramatic restructuring in the industrial sector during the eighties. Large companies were forced to scale down or diversify production in the face of the government's anti-inflationary policies and refusal to devalue the lira. The restructuring of large private industry was achieved by means of increased automation and investment in high technology, a massive reduction in the number of workers, the introduction in 1984 of legislation controlling the inflationary effects of the *scala mobile* (confirmed by a referendum the following year), the construction of plants abroad where labour was cheaper and the subcontracting of the most labour-intensive work to smaller companies as part of a programme of decentralization. Nevertheless, while large companies like Fiat were able to overcome the recession, regaining high levels of productivity, their position on foreign markets became increasingly defensive during the nineties, especially in view of increasing competition from producers in Far Eastern countries.

Italy's share of international trade grew dramatically during the eighties and nineties, allowing her to become the sixth largest exporter. Yet, the overall drop in productivity of the large Italian company is demonstrated by the diminishing success of the car, electrical and chemical industries on the world market. Between 1985 and 1998, for example, Italy dropped from eighth to tenth position among top world car exporters, as did its share of the world car exporting market (from 4.5 per cent in 1980 to 3.6 per cent in 1998). In contrast there was a notable export boom in products more associated with smaller companies. The Italian share of world exports of textiles increased, for example, from 7.4 per cent in 1980 to 8.6 per cent in 1998, occupying third position throughout the two decades.[3] It was the smaller companies, therefore, particularly those functioning within the industrial districts, that were among the main protagonists of the second economic boom. After a period of crisis, there was a notable growth in industrial districts as they adapted to the need to overcome competition on the world market from the Far East and Third World by pooling resources together more effectively, finding new market outlets and producing higher quality products. By 1997 the industrial districts produced 57 per cent of the total of Italian exports.[4]

The production of silk in Como, studied by Cento Bull and Corner, is an example of the success of the industrial district during this period. Making up most of the national silk industry and accounting for one tenth of Italy's textile clothing sector, Como exported between 50 per cent and 70 per cent of silk production during the eighties. While the core manufacturing activity within the district was the production of silk fabrics, a whole series of subsidiary activities gravitated around it, including fashion design, the wholesaling and retailing of clothes and the provision of services to the industry, such as marketing and consultancy, credit, financing, fashion shows and export and research centres. These companies were linked together in such a way as to ensure high levels of investment and technical and design innovation throughout the district, which functioned like a large family, the members of which pooled together their skills and resources.[5]

The success of the Italian economy during the eighties and nineties was also a result of the increasing dominance of the tertiary sector, which by 1996 accounted for 71.4 per cent of companies. By 1998 Italy held fifth position among top tertiary exporters making up 5.1 per cent of the world total, compared with 7.6 per cent for Great Britain and 6.4 per cent for France. Notably, Italy increased its world share of travel services exports (from 6.2 per cent in 1990 to 7 per cent in 1998).[6] According to Paul Ginsborg, however, the key areas of tertiary production developed distortedly in comparison with other leading economies. In particular he notes the poor structures of the banking and insurance sectors, a dynamic television industry, which was nevertheless over-monopolized by the private sector, a historically weak public administration and an inefficient tourist industry incapable of exploiting Italy's immense cultural heritage. On a more positive note, Ginsborg draws attention to a flourishing sector of shopkeepers, restaurant and bar owners, equal in number to private-sector employees, which had not been undermined by the development of supermarkets, and which, therefore, helped to preserve the livelihood of town districts. Often networks of private retailers were closely linked to industrial districts, selling their products directly to the consumers.[7]

The economic disparity between the South and the rest of Italy widened during the last decades of the twentieth century, with the Southern contribution per capita to the GDP decreasing from 61 per cent of the North–Centre contribution in 1980 to 55.6 per cent in 1997. The effects of the economic crisis of the early eighties were not redressed by a restructuring phase comparable to the rest of the country. Many of the large industries that had been set up during the fifties and sixties by means of state and external private investment closed. The colonial manner in which they had developed prevented the formation of local industrial roots, that would have allowed the creation of a self-propelling Southern economy, also made difficult by the emigration of the most dynamic and well-qualified individuals to the North. The proportion of unemployed in the South increased in comparison with the North, while public services and welfare state provisions fell behind the rest of the country. State finance created private wealth by means of the clientelistic channels of *assistenzialismo*, allowing families to survive, but it was not sufficiently invested in public services and did little to create real economic wealth, much of which was based on the activities of organized crime of the *Mafia*, which limited levels of profitability, plagued small companies and discouraged investment from outside.

In view of the huge pressure it placed on the state coffers and its questionable impact on the economy, public investment in the South decreased from the nineties onwards, as was evident in a reduction of pension and invalidity payments. Long-term special economic intervention in the South ceased as the *Cassa per il Mezzogiorno* was dismantled. It is plausible that the removal of state funding and its replacement with tax benefits and cost-of-work reductions encouraged investment and produced new entrepreneurial energies in the South, as suggested by a higher growth in exports than in the rest of Italy during the late nineties. In particular, the South-Eastern regions showed higher growth levels in comparison with Calabria and Sicily, such that it became less easy to talk of the South as a homogeneous economy. This was marked by a process of industrialization of the Southern Adriatic coastline, influenced by the 'Third Italy' model, as is demonstrated by the development of several industrial districts.[8]

The agricultural sector continued to show notable levels of backwardness. The dominant farming system remained the smallholding (accounting for 95 per cent of farms), in spite of a dramatic drop in number and the virtual disappearance of sharecropping.[9] Consequently, though Italy still had the highest number of agricultural employees and farms in the European Union, productivity levels were low as it continued to import more food than it exported, reflecting the lack of a modern entrepreneurial mentality among farmers. This was particularly true of the South, which had a higher quantity of agricultural workers than the rest of the country but witnessed a notable stagnation. Its value added per employee dropped from 70.4 per cent of that of the North and Centre to 55.6 per cent in 1990. While the Southern agricultural system remained backward, other parts of Italy witnessed the development of several highly productive and specialized agricultural zones, modelled on the industrial districts. In Emilia–Romagna, for example, they specialized in the production of Parmesan cheese, pork products and fruit. There was also a notable growth in Italy in the number of multi-national food industries, which were attracted by the success of Italian food and the large number of small farms that could be bought at low cost. The negative side of such developments lay in the limited consideration they took of the need to preserve the rural landscape.[10]

During the final decades of the twentieth century, state industry, which had played an important role in economic development during the fifties and sixties, became more and more unsustainable in view of low levels of productivity and huge financial losses. An attempt was made during the second half of the eighties to retain the two state-holding giants, ENI and IRI, by selling off some of their loss-making companies to the private sector. For example, the Alfa Romeo car company was sold off to Fiat in 1986. While this may have temporarily arrested the decline of public-sector industry, from 1990 onwards there was a more determined move in the direction of privatization, so that by 1996 the state electricity, oil, gas and telephone companies had been privatized, as well as many banks, finance and insurance companies and several industries.

The privatization programme was part of the drastic measures of economic austerity first undertaken in 1992 by the Socialist prime minister, Giuliano Amato, in order to increase economic efficiency and competitiveness and meet the criteria for greater European integration stipulated by the Maastricht agreement of February that year. Such measures represented a reaction to a dramatic crisis during the early nineties in the state of the economy, which overshadowed the success of private enterprise. Though partly regulated by Italy's entry to the European Monetary System in 1979 and greater control over wage-indexing (*scala mobile*), inflation remained higher than that of the other European partners. The Italian economy suffered as the result of a public deficit of over 10 per cent of the GDP and a foreign deficit reaching 11 per cent of the GDP by 1992, demonstrating that the country was con-suming far more resources than it produced. In particular, the public coffers were overburdened by uncontrolled spending on welfare payments and loss-making state industries which were not compensated by tax revenue as a result of high levels of evasion. During the early nineties the Italian public finances were no longer sustainable as a result of a spiralling public debt inherited from the 1970s (reaching 125.5 per cent of the GDP in 1994). The debt crisis was exacerbated by the manner in which the state attempted to deal with it, namely by the use of a system of treasury bonds which carried high interest rates and were tax-free, but which consequently had the effect of reinforcing it.

In September 1992, as a result of the effect of a rise in German interest rates, the lira was forced to exit from the European Monetary System. Only then was the Italian public deficit acted upon vigorously as a result of Amato's programme of increased income tax, salary freezes and cuts in welfare ex-penditure, a programme almost uninterruptedly carried forward by succes-sive governments so that in 1995, for the first time since 1980, the public debt percentage of the GDP began to fall. That same year the lira exchange rate stabilized, allowing the possibility of re-entering the European Monetary System, achieved in November 1996 under the government of Romano Prodi. In 1997 Prodi introduced a programme of further financial recovery which succeeded in reducing the public deficit to less than 3 per cent of the GDP and inflation to below 3 per cent, in conformity with criteria necessary for

joining the single European currency (euro), which came into force in January 2002, seen as essential for Italy's economic future.[11]

The changing face of the Italian work force

As a result of the above transformations, the period concerned saw a change
in the composition of the work force according to area of production.
Between 1981 and 1998 the number of agricultural workers halved (from
13.3 per cent to 6.6 per cent of the work force), while that of industrial workers
decreased from 37.2 per cent to 32 per cent.[12] Between 1980 and 1996, for
example, the number of car workers dropped from nearly 300,000 to 173,000.
In some sectors of industry, such as textiles and clothing, the number of
employed workers declined, while that of self-employed workers increased,
indicating the success of small companies. As would be expected there was
an increase in the number employed in the service industry (from 49.5 per
cent in 1981 to 61.4 per cent in 1998). Those working in the commercial
sector, for example, increased by nearly 25 per cent between 1980 and 1996
(from 7,504,400 to 9,959,200).

Parallel to changes in the composition of the work force was a significant
process of vertical social mobility with 62 per cent of citizens in the mid-
nineties belonging to a different class from that of their parents and 48 per
cent of workers' children now part of the middle class. As Giulio Sapelli argues,
in reality, however, class differences rather than being erased were only more
complex and invisible. The growth of economic wealth during the eighties
and nineties, though allowing a rise in family income for the majority of
Italians and the growth of a new high-income middle class, was achieved at
the cost of economic restructuring which destroyed working-class strongholds
of employment.[13] The number of unemployed Italians in fact grew from
8.4 per cent in 1981 to an almost constant figure of 12 per cent during the
nineties, though there were strong regional disparities. Unemployment levels
were extremely low in Veneto and Emilia–Romagna as a result of the success
of small-to-medium sized companies. They were higher in the Turin area as
a result of a crisis in the car sector.

The South was most disadvantaged with unemployment levels reaching
23.6 per cent in 1998, compared with 6 per cent in the North and 9.7 per cent
in the Centre. This can be explained by several factors: export-orientated
firms typical of the North that were able to resist falls in domestic demand
were scarce. In the South there was a higher proportion of state workers who
felt the consequences of contraction of the public sector. The South was still
dependent on agriculture in spite of the continued downward trend in
employment in that sector. Nevertheless, there was a disparity between Apulia,
Basilicata and Sardinia where unemployment levels were not as high as those
in Sicily, Calabria and Campania, the latter particularly affected by a crisis in
the construction industry. It has, however, been argued on a more positive

note that the unemployment in the South of the nineties cannot be compared with that of the fifties and sixties which had caused en masse migration. Immigrant workers from the Third World were increasingly employed in manual work in this part of Italy, while excess local labour was mainly intellectual.[14]

Women and young people were the main victims of job shortages. Women were far more likely to be unemployed than men, with levels reaching 30 per cent in the South during the nineties. Among those unemployed, the largest component was of people looking for their first job. Partly indicating the inability of the education system to provide the young with adequate vocational skills, youth unemployment levels reached well over 30 per cent during the nineties, the highest in the European Union. If women and young Italians found work during this period, it was more often in fixed-term and part-time posts (particularly in the South) that increased as a result of the introduction of greater flexibility in employment from the mid-nineties onwards. Also indicating a decline in secure employment was the increasing number of irregular, often unregulated, jobs that reached over three-and-a-half million in 1997. They were mostly in agriculture (accounting for nearly 30 per cent of workers in the sector), though also prevalent in the building trade and some areas of the tertiary sector.

As the above-mentioned data indicate, while there was an apparent increase in career opportunities and status for Italian women, they remained strongly disadvantaged. The number of working women grew as a result of the development of the tertiary sector. They also began to occupy more managerial and professional positions. Yet, according to Ginsborg, such gains were modest in comparison with other countries. As an indication of continuing discrimination in the workplace, they occupied the lower ranks of the tertiary and industrial sectors, doing work which rarely reflected their qualifications, while even those women occupying the most prestigious jobs often found themselves relegated to lower-status positions within the company or institutions they worked for.[15]

From the late eighties onwards the Italian work force was also characterized by a significant presence of foreign immigrant workers. Although Italy converted from a country of net emigration to one of net immigration during the early seventies, the most dramatic growth took place during the eighties and nineties. The number of foreigners in Italy increased from 147,000 in 1970 to 781,200 in 1989 to 1,240,721 in 1997. The proportion of those from Third World and Eastern European countries grew from a quarter in 1975 to four-fifths in 1997, with the highest figures for Moroccans, Albanians, Filipinos, Tunisians and members of the ex-Yugoslavian states. The employment of migrant labour responded to the growing need for workers in low-level jobs which many Italians were no longer prepared to accept. Most immigrant women, for example, were employed as domestic workers. Men's work was more diversified, ranging from agriculture in Southern areas to low-level tasks in the Northern industrial, construction and services sectors. In 1997 the highest regional concentrations of immigrant workers were in Lombardy, Latium, Veneto, Tuscany and Emilia–Romagna. The proportion of migrant workers in the North of Italy increased during the nineties and this reflected their search for more stable and better paid work. Those who settled in the South were likely to be employed in the underpaid black-market sector – particularly in agriculture – that was often run by criminal organizations.[16]

Strongly connected to the decline in job security, from the eighties onwards the trade unions were increasingly unable to muster support for and successfully carry out industrial action. In part this represented management regaining control over the shop-floor after high levels of industrial conflict during the seventies. A notable event at Fiat in the autumn of 1980, for example, was the unsuccessful strike against massive temporary lay-offs, which concluded with the organization by foremen and supervisors of a march of 40,000 people (including blue-collar workers) against the unions. Partly as a result of this defeat, Confindustria was able to reverse several of the advantages gained by workers during the previous decade. This included measures to limit the *scala mobile*, which was finally abolished in 1993. Gino Bedani notes that the decline of trade-union power was also due to the fact that the industrial working class in the traditional sense no longer held a position in society which enabled it to exercise its previous role of leadership. Dependent labour as a whole was in continual expansion, but this increasingly included sectors which had not been encouraged to join unions in the past, among them technicians, highly skilled workers in new technologies, part-time, casual and unqualified workers, but also those employed in the growing tertiary sector. Unionization levels were particularly low among women and young adults. According to Mimmo Carrieri, the crisis of the social representation of the trade-union confederations was also symbolized by the birth of confrontational unions. These were particularly strong in the service sector, for example among school teachers and railway workers. They frequently outflanked the traditional unions with militant action, which, though carried out by a minority of workers, paralysed public services. As a result of this, a law was passed in 1990 regulating public-service strikes. Nevertheless, when compared with other European countries, it is clear that the Italian union confederations still played a prominent social and political role, such that many employers continued to prefer a collaborative approach to labour relations to one of confrontation.[17]

Marriage and fertility trends, gender relations and the family

The final decades of the twentieth century witnessed quite dramatic changes in marriage and fertility patterns reflecting a modernization trend bringing Italy closer in line with other industrial powers. From the seventies onwards there was a notable drop in the number of marriages (from 7.5 per 1,000 inhabitants in 1971 to 5.6 in 1981 and 4.8 in 1998). Indicating the extent of decline of religious influence, there was also a significant increase in the number of civil weddings (from a mere 3.9 per cent in 1971 to 12.7 per cent in 1981 and 20.3 per cent in 1996). Young people increasingly delayed marriage, with the result that the average marriage age increased (from 24 in 1981 to 27 in 1996 for women and from 27 to 30 for men). The number of separations and divorces more than doubled during this period. Between 1986 and 1997 alone the number of separations increased from 35,205 to 60,281 and the number of divorces from 16,857 to 33,342. There was also a notable growth in the number of couples living together (340,000 by 1998).[18]

In considering the above data according to regional divisions, the South was slower to adapt to the pace of modernization. At the end of the nineties there was a higher percentage of marriages there than in the rest of the country, though it is equally true that the number had decreased over ten years from 6.2 to 5.3 per thousand inhabitants, while figures for the Centre and North remained more or less stationary. Similarly the number of separations and divorces remained higher for the regions of the North, as did the percentage of couples living together (60.7 per cent). Though Italy as a whole continued to show lower levels of marriage instability than most other European countries, at the end of the nineties the increase in separations and divorces seemed set to continue. However, the rate of increase in natural unions remained lower than the rate of decrease in marriage in Italy. Indeed, most natural unions later proceeded to marriage. Often they were a result of young couples experimenting with unions before marriage or separated individuals not being able to re-marry until they obtained a divorce, a process which often took many years, in spite of a law of 1987 which reduced from five to three years the waiting period between legal separation and divorce.[19]

It appears that the above changes did not seriously affect the cohesion of Italian families. Ginsborg argues that they continued to be safeguarded by high levels of intergenerational solidarity, as grandparents, parents and children often lived close together, if not under the same roof, so that in spite of the process of social and economic modernization in Italy it was more realistic to talk about the prevalence of 'modified extended families' than isolated nuclear families. The closely knit family also helped to protect its younger members against the effects of growing youth unemployment.[20] Indeed, young adults increasingly stayed in the parental home well beyond their teens. Between 1990 and 1998 the number of people aged between 18 and 34 living with their parents grew from 51.8 per cent to 58.8 per cent. This phenomenon, which distinguished Italy from other European countries, was in part a result of employment difficulties, particularly but not only in the South. In the North and Centre the majority of young people living with their parents were actually employed. The results of an inquiry that took place during the eighties suggested that most young people were happy to enjoy the comforts of the parental home as long as they could successfully negotiate for areas of autonomy within the family.[21] There is little doubt that this had a negative effect on the ability of young people to become independent from their families and more responsible within society. Moreover, the figures suggest that the phenomenon was more common among young men than women, which may be attributed to the persistence of particularly strong psychological ties between mother and son characterizing Mediterranean peoples.[22]

In terms of gender roles within the family, it is clear that, while obtaining greater autonomy and equality, Italian women continued to remain less emancipated than those of other Western countries. Figures for the nineties indicate an increase in the number of young women refusing the traditional roles of wife, housewife and mother and taking up higher education or entering the job market. Yet most Italian women maintained responsibility for running the household and looking after children, while men failed to do their fair share of domestic chores, even if their wives or partners were in full-time employment. It is equally likely that in some cases women were slow to give up their traditional domestic role because of the influence and relative autonomy that such a role, while subordinating them to patriarchal values, awarded them. In Southern Italy this attitude was directly linked to continued familistic strategies as a means for survival. Victoria Goddard notes with reference to research conducted on Naples that:

> The family was important for many individuals because it could provide the framework for many petty entrepreneurial activities and, more generally, it still operates as a pooling device and as a means of redistributing income among a number of people. . . . The costs of this are mainly shouldered by women, who are the principal agents in the creation and reproduction of kinship networks and who sustain the daily, routine actions which make for the perpetuation of the household. State interventions which have favoured subsidies rather than services have reinforced the importance of the family and have strengthened the position and increased the responsiblity of women within it.[23]

In spite of the relatively limited emancipation of Italian women within their families, during the nineties Italy witnessed a dramatic decline in fertility levels. With a birth rate of 1.19 children per woman registered in 1998 (compared with 1.89 for Great Britain, and 1.6 for Germany), Italy had one of the lowest fertility rates in the world, with the average family size having declined from 3.01 members in 1981 to 2.7. There were notable regional variations behind these statistics, however, with even lower birth rates for the North and Centre (between 1.03 and 1.06) and higher rates for the South (1.4), with the exception of Sardinia. Northern couples desiring a family generally planned to have one child only, as opposed to the South where two children were usually envisaged. The anticipated long-term effects of this demographic trend are hardly encouraging. In 1993 births were overtaken by deaths for the first time in Italian history. It has been estimated that by 2050 the Italian population, which numbered 57.3 million in 1995, will fall back to the figure of 47 million registered in 1951, and that the number of Italians over 65 (15.3 per cent in 1991) will increase to 32 per cent of the overall population.[24]

Clearly the decline of marriage stability in Italy is an insufficient explanation for this phenomenon, since it was often happily married couples who decided not to have children or to limit their offspring. Similarly, while the legalization of abortion in 1978 may initially have influenced fertility levels, it is equally true that the number of voluntary pregnancy interruptions notably declined from a peak of 16.7 per 1,000 women (aged 15–49) registered in 1982 to 9.3 in 1997. According to Ginsborg, it was 'incomplete female emancipation' that – paradoxically – was partly responsible for the decline in births in Italy. On the one hand women married later as a result of greater education and employment opportunities. This, together with the wider diffusion of contraceptive methods and the legalization of abortion, inevitably limited the number of births. On the other hand, those women who desired to have children were often unable to because of the heavy demands of both their jobs and their homes and families, for which they still carried far more responsibilities than their husbands. Ginsborg also considers other factors contributing to the dramatic decline in the number of births in Italy. The continued influence of Catholic culture dissuaded couples living together from having children. And once again paradoxically, family responsibilities particular to Italy encouraged a reduction in the number of components. Where offspring increasingly stayed in the family home until well into their thirties, and where it was not unusual to have an elderly parent within the household, many couples took a conscious decision to limit the number of children. Added to this was insufficient state provision of support in the form of child-benefit allowances and modern maternity clinics. Inadequate nursery provision too was a product of 50 years of rule by the Christian Democrats, who were influenced by the Catholic social doctrine of encouraging small children to stay at home with their mothers, or at most attend church-run institutions.[25]

Education, leisure and cultural consumption

In terms of education the final decades of the twentieth century saw continued progress, though this was partly hindered by social and regional disparities. Between 1981 and 1991 the number of illiterate Italians dropped from 3.1 per cent to 2.1 per cent of the population aged over six.[26] In particular the number of children going into upper-secondary education increased dramatically. Whereas in 1987–88 82.4 per cent of 14-year-olds decided to stay at school, the figure rose to 94.2 per cent 10 years later. Regional differences remained, however, with a notable drop-out rate in the South. Between 1988 and 1998 the school diploma pass rate improved (from 96.9 per cent to 98.9 per cent for the middle school and from 92.8 per cent to 94.6 per cent for the upper secondary school). However, when compared with other European Union countries, the overall number of young people in possession of upper-secondary school diplomas (79 per cent) in 1998 was lower than all countries except Spain (73 per cent). The quality of secondary education was conditioned by failure to put into practice long-awaited reforms, not least regarding the compulsory leaving age, which remained at 14. A positive response to the need for more emphasis on the teaching of mathematics, foreign languages and information technology and greater curricular flexibility in order to address both local employment requisites and Europeanization was continually inhibited by political forces.

The number of university students also increased (from 1,025,000 in 1981–82 to 1,773,686 in 1996–97). In 1996–97 49.8 per cent of 19-year-olds decided to go into higher education. However, there remained notable differences in the percentages of school leavers going into university according to the professional status of their parents, with the highest among the children of managers, entrepreneurs and self-employed professionals and lowest among children of the non-employed, blue-collar workers and self-employed workers. Yet, in some parts of Italy, like the North-East, better employment prospects lowered the likelihood of going to university. The overall number of students going into higher education was much larger than for other European countries, reflecting both the absence of any form of selection – beyond possession of the upper-secondary school diploma in itself – in most university faculties and the limited vocational value of Italian school qualifications (including those of technical and professional institutes), which induced youngsters to continue studying. Yet, a large proportion (66 per cent) of Italian students continued to drop out of university, so that in the end the system produced the same number of graduates as in Great Britain (12 per cent out of the corresponding age group) in spite of higher levels of selection in the latter country. In contrast to most other European countries, Italian university degrees allowed only a minority of graduates to enter employment within a short period of time.

In line with increased literacy levels, the number of people reading newspapers increased during the eighties. According to Robert Lumley, by 1990 6.5 million Italians were buying a daily paper, though the figures were lower for the South, where the ratio of one newspaper per 16 inhabitants compared unfavourably with 7.4 in the Centre and 6.6 in the North.[27] Italians participated in a greater variety of cultural activities than ever before, as is demonstrated by an increase in the number of theatre and concert ticket sales. However, television – reinforced by the growth of the private sector –

continued to strongly influence and undermine the positive effects of better education in Italy by contributing to the trend towards home-based leisure developing during the seventies. Cinema audiences continued dropping, as films were increasingly shown on television or video-recorders, until the nineties, when the Italian cinema industry achieved a partial turn-around, though hardly in terms of quality, by focusing on the production of comic films that would guarantee large audiences and could be sold on video.[28]

While television dominance was partly offset by new developments in information and communication technology, including personal computers (registered in 14 million homes in 1996), video games and the Internet, it remained the main source of culture for certain sections of society, particularly the elderly, the less well-off, women and Southerners. As David Forgacs remarks with reference to Italy of the mid-nineties:

> for a Milanese middle-manager television is just one cultural consumption among many in a repertoire which is likely to include opera, cinema, meals in restaurants, and novel-reading; whereas for an unemployed worker, a busy housewife, or an African immigrant worker in Bari television is probably the only one of these 'free-time' activities on the social agenda'.[29]

Italian television provided poor-quality programmes that failed to take account of the social and political transformations the country was undergoing. Those of the private channels were highly consumeristic (dominated by frequent advertising breaks) and entertainment-based, with a large proportion of serials and soap operas. While the RAI, following the demise of the post-war political parties in the early nineties (described below), initially moved in the direction of better-quality television with less emphasis on entertainment and more on the diffusion of objective information, it soon returned to its old ways. Rather than attempting to distinguish itself from the private sector, state television tried to match its low-quality programmes for fear of losing viewers.[30]

The eighties saw a notable increase in the number of Italians practising sports, according to Stefano Pirato: over 22 per cent, compared with only 6 per cent during the mid-seventies and as little as 2–3 per cent during the fifties. Italians also began to practise a greater variety of sports, including skiing, tennis, basketball, volleyball, free-climbing and windsurfing. Yet the last two decades of the twentieth century also saw the development of an unhealthy overlap between sport, politics and business deals, exemplified in excessive overspending for the Football World Cup hosted in Italy in 1990 and epitomized in the figure of the media magnate, Silvio Berlusconi, who was president of the AC Milan football club and leader of a Centre–Right political alliance (described below) from 1994. Television coverage turned sport into a highly lucrative commercial product and this partly accounted for a drop in ground attendance at football matches.[31]

Health, poverty and the state

As the above analysis demonstrates, a large number of Italians grew wealthier than ever before during the eighties and nineties. The number of owned households, cars and holidays abroad increased dramatically. There was a boom in the consumption of designer clothes and such commodities as mobile phones. Between 1984 and 1985 alone the amount of money that the Italians spent on sports and leisure activities increased by 10 per cent. As Anna Tonelli argues, 'well-being meant spending time at the gym to shape one's body according to aesthetic criteria, at the cinema, which offered various role models, at parties at various venues in order to celebrate oneself, and at holiday resorts (sea in the summer and mountains in the winter) which amplified the symbols and rituals of this new hedonism'.[32] While overall consumption levels were lower for the South in comparison with the North and Centre, they were not far behind the national average. However, greater consumer power in the South than previously enjoyed was not invested in a wider variety of cultural or leisure activities.

The above figures give a relatively superficial vision of the overall quality of life of the Italians at the end of the twentieth century. Typical of the Western world as a whole, behind the image of mass wealth produced in the eighties and nineties lurked serious inequalities. In 1999 2.6 million families (7.5 million Italians) were categorized as living below the poverty line. Sixty-six per cent were concentrated in the South, characterized by high levels of youth unemployment and the presence of large families with only one source of income.[33] The Italian welfare state continued to be of limited assistance to poorer sections of society, despite taking up a very large proportion of public spending (56 per cent of the government budget during the early nineties). In comparison with other European Union countries, it did not pay out unemployment benefit to those who had never worked before or who had not paid welfare contributions when previously working. This was because the welfare state was closely linked to the deep-rooted system of political patronage, which aimed to benefit the population as a whole, rather than focusing on those seriously in need. This left it open to abuse and, contemporaneously, the general dissatisfaction of the Italian public. For example, a comparatively advantageous pensions system with one of the lowest minimum retirement ages in the world – 55 for women and 60 for men until 1992 – and one of the most generous calculation formulas was inadequate for those on the lowest salaries, while ceilings were imposed on those at the top of the scale.[34]

Subsequent correction in 1992 of the minimum retirement age for both the private and public sectors to 65 for men and 60 for women alongside a reduction in benefits, which from 1995 onwards were calculated according to social security contributions rather than earnings, in order to overcome a mounting public deficit, worsened the retirement prospects for the active Italian population. To some extent, however, such reforms aimed to correct a system, which had allowed unrealistically high lifestyles (particularly for public employees, who had been able to receive retirement pensions after as little as 15 or 20 years' service) and from which many had unfairly benefited. From the mid-nineties onwards moves were also taken in the direction of reducing the huge number of invalidity pensions (5.5 million certified in 1992 – almost one in ten Italian citizens!), the majority of whose beneficiaries (mainly in the South) were fit to work.[35] While this system may have helped to overcome unemployment difficulties in the short term, the overall cultural and economic effects were devastating.

Italians continued to become healthier during the final decades of the twentieth century, though once again there were geographic disparities. During the eighties and nineties life expectancy continued to rise, increasing from 71.1 years in 1980 to 74.8 years in 1996 for men and from 77.8 years in 1980 to 81.2 years in 1996 for women. Southern men were more likely to live longer than their counterparts in the rest of Italy, whereas Southern women were likely to live less long. The rate of infant mortality continued to drop (from 12.3 deaths per 1,000 live births within the first year of life in 1981–85 to 7.0 in 1991–96), with again less positive figures registered for the South.[36] The greater longevity was accompanied by a general health improvement. However, at the end of the nineties there were serious regional differences in the quality of health provision. For example, Veneto offered as many as 7.3 hospital beds per thousand inhabitants, but Campania only 4.9, when the national requirement was of 5.5. Southern Italians continued to take trips northwards for specialists visits and tests. Moreover, the news headlines often denounced the disastrous state of the Southern health sector, with tragic cases of citizens dying because they could not find hospitals able to treat them in time. By the eighties the health service as a whole was plagued by serious functional and financial difficulties, necessitating slimming down in line with health rationalization measures occurring in other European countries.[37]

Citizens were still plagued by the poor quality of other public services in Italy, affected as they were by high levels of inefficiency and poor-quality personnel, in spite of the large amount of state resources invested in them. During the second half of the nineties, however, this was partly resolved by the start of a programme of privatization. Additionally, a serious effort was made to improve the relationship between citizens and the service sector in general by making offices more accessible in terms of both more flexible open hours (previously restricted to a few hours in the morning), and simplification of bureaucratic procedures, partly achieved through the introduction of information technology in public offices. Yet, this did little to increase the faith of the Italian public in the state bureaucracy, which in 1999 remained lower than in any other European Union member state.[38]

The quality of Italian life was also negatively affected by environmental problems, especially in urban areas. High levels of air and water pollution, particularly in the industrial triangle, the illegal dumping of toxic substances, an inadequate refuse collection system and widespread unregulated building were a result of limited environmental consciousness, bureaucratic inefficiency and laws that were easy to breach. Only after the disaster at the Soviet nuclear plant at Chernobyl in 1986 did a popular environmental movement develop which in November 1987 succeeded through a number of referenda in forcing the government to modify plans for constructing new nuclear plants and restricting the scope of nuclear planning and research. Nevertheless, laws on the environment remained inadequately enforced, indicating that there was limited political support over environmental issues given their obvious link to job losses, in turn generating fear that votes would be lost. On several occasions, for example, citizens who had constructed illegally benefited from amnesties.[39] The dangers of environmental neglect and abuse were tragically illustrated by the death in May 1998 of 200 inhabitants of two towns in the Campania region, Sarno and Quindici, as they were engulfed by a mud-flow following heavy rainfall.[40]

Fear of crime constituted another obstacle to the sense of wellbeing of Italian citizens at the end of the millennium, though such fears were not always confirmed by crime statistics. There was an increase in crime levels at the start of the nineties, with a drop in most crimes, including murders, muggings and car thefts between 1993 and 1997. Certain crimes (including bank raids, extortion, fraud and drugs-related crimes) continued to rise, however. A very high proportion of them were committed in the main cities. Moreover, many citizens felt inadequately protected against crime by the state. In 1997–98 42 per cent of a statistical sample claimed they had limited access to police stations, particularly in the South. Though the police underwent notable reforms at the beginning of the eighties (see previous chapter), it was difficult to dissociate them from their previous function as an instrument at the service of the state rather than citizens. Indeed, in the above-mentioned survey 42 per cent declared that they had little faith in the ability or willingness of the forces of law and order to protect them.[41]

There was also a notable increase in the number of crimes committed by foreign immigrants, particularly in the Centre and North. Such crimes were often linked to drug and prostitution rackets, which had sprung up as a result of widespread clandestine immigration. In fact, 80 per cent of immigrants charged for crimes in 1996 were without stay permits. This created the misleading impression among a significant number of Italians that the majority of crimes were being perpetrated by immigrants, which helped to fuel the anti-immigration policies of several political parties and led to a number of racist attacks. In reality, in 1996 immigrants committed 22 per cent of thefts and 30 per cent of drugs-related crimes. Though such figures were far from insignificant, given the relatively low number of immigrants in Italy, they have to be considered in the light of the particularly desperate

conditions in which large numbers of foreigners living in Italy found themselves, as discussed in a later section of this chapter.[42]

The public morality crisis and the collapse of
the 'First Republic'

The Mafia and Tangentopoli, 1980–93

In Southern Italy crime levels were directly linked to the activities of the
Mafia. During the early eighties it became clear that this part of the country
remained poor and undeveloped as a result. Northern industrialists avoided
investing there, since they knew they would have to pay out protection money
to local bosses, who also siphoned away subsidy money from the Italian
government or the European Union with the complicity of politicians.
Throughout the decade *Mafia* violence increased. This was a result of infighting over control of resources and a response to the determination of
several judges and policemen to fight organized crime. Many of them paid
for such determination with their lives, as demonstrated by the murder of
the *Carabinieri* general, Alberto Dalla Chiesa, in 1982, shortly after he was
appointed prefect of Palermo. During this period the Sicilian *Cosa Nostra*
gained greater control over other organizations, including the Neapolitan
Camorra. The strength of the *Mafia* lay in high levels of complicity on the
part of representatives of the state and political parties. However, the rise to
supremacy within *Cosa Nostra* of the particularly violent Corleonesi clan at
the end of the eighties and failure to prevent over 400 *mafiosi* being brought
to trial – assisted by the revelations of supergrasses – began to threaten the
previously existing truce between the *Mafia* and the state. In 1992 that truce
ended as Salvo Lima, the chief vote-collector in Sicily of the Christian Democrat prime minister Giulio Andreotti, was murdered after failing to use his
political contacts to have those condemned at the trial released on appeal,
and two judges at the centre of the judicial investigations into *Mafia* activities, Giovanni Falcone and Paolo Borsellino, were killed, along with their
bodyguards, in car-bombings.[43]

Public anger against the political class on account of its links with organized crime had been brewing since the late eighties. Television in particular
had played a role in sensitizing the public on this issue. The drama serial,
La Piovra, brought the *Mafia* to the attention of vast sectors of the Italian
population for the first time. Heated television debates on political corruption also took place on the third RAI channel which, under the control of
left-wing political forces, fought the establishment over censorship and the
public's right to information.[44] The brutality of the murders of Falcone and
Borsellino set off a public revolt against the *Mafia* and perhaps even more
the politicians. During the state funeral in Palermo of Falcone, his wife and

213

bodyguards, those political representatives who came to pay their last respects met chants of 'murderers' by a furious crowd awaiting them.

Such public outrage was part and parcel of a general rebellion against political corruption, particularly among the Christian Democrats and Socialists, which had recently seen the beginnings of judicial investigations at the other end of the country into the system of *tangenti* (bribes), whereby successful economic transactions, such as the assigning of public works projects to private contractors, had depended on the willingness of the latter to pay the politicians running public companies. The Milan-based 'Operation Clean Hands' under the command of judge Antonio Di Pietro started in February 1992 when detectives arrested Mario Chiesa, the Socialist manager of a charitable institution (Pio Albergo Trivulzio–PAT), for taking a bribe of 7 million lire from the owner of a cleaning company. As Mark Gilbert notes:

> The PAT owned more than a thousand flats in the centre of Milan, as well as shops and offices, so Chiesa had plenty of contracts – for maintenance, cleaning, and funerals (the beneficiaries of the PAT's charity are mostly impecunious old people) – to hand out. He soon won a reputation as 'Mr 10 Percent'. As Chiesa himself would later admit, he took a slice of every contract he awarded (including a fixed tariff of 100,000 lire per corpse levied on the undertakers) and used it to finance his political ambitions.[45]

Chiesa's arrest set off a chain of investigations reaching the heart of the Milan Socialist Party, fiefdom of the Party secretary, Bettino Craxi. Di Pietro's investigations quickly spread beyond Milan, once the 'moral' capital of Italy and now named 'Bribesville' (*Tangentopoli*), to the rest of Italy, reaching the Christian Democrat Party and other smaller parties. Even within the recently reformed Communist Party, the Democratic Party of the Left (see below), a number of individuals were suspected of corruption in spite of the party's reputation for clean politics and civic virtues. By September 1993 2,600 individuals were under investigation, including 325 parliamentarians.[46]

It was revealed that the whole interface between the public- and private-sector economy had functioned on the basis of kickbacks, with politicians and their clienteles getting rich at the expense of the ordinary tax-payer. At the same time the government had built up a huge public deficit in order to buy votes through such activities as the granting of false invalidity pensions and subsidizing the *Mafia*. Signalling the apparent end of what has become known as the 'First Republic', the huge number of judicial investigations led to the demise of the Socialist and Christian Democrat parties, as well as many of the smaller Centre parties which had played a minor role in previous governing coalitions. Such parties were publicly branded as criminal, especially after Craxi fled to Tunisia in order to avoid being put on trial and Andreotti was accused (though later acquitted) of complicity with the *Mafia*. In January 1993 Totò Riina, head of *Cosa Nostra*, who was accused of issuing Falcone and Borsellino's execution warrants, was arrested. In spite of recent set-backs, the determination of the *Mafia* to take advantage of the political instability caused by *Tangentopoli* was evident in bomb attacks during the summer of 1993 in Florence, Rome and Milan, which claimed ten lives and damaged several historic monuments.

Independent of political considerations, one of the reasons why it was so difficult to eradicate political corruption and organized crime lay in the extent to which they were deep-rooted in Italian society. For members of the political and economic élite, involvement in shady dealings had become almost respectable. Those affected by judicial investigations defended themselves on the grounds that they were acting according to established (if unofficial) norms. Indeed, several of them committed suicide because they could no longer face public humiliation or the prospect of prison. Even though at the height of the *Tangentopoli* investigations it became quite usual for once-respected politicians to be the object of public derision and contempt, whether in the press or on the streets, large numbers of 'ordinary' citizens from all parts of Italy had accepted or benefited from the system that had been erected. There is little doubt that, for many Italians, receiving a false invalidity pension or making use of 'the right people' to pass a state competition was not perceived as immoral, especially since this was seen as part of a natural system of survival. Moreover, everyone else seemed to be acting in the same way and this was, after all, the standard set by state institutions and political parties, which the judiciary and the media were apparently unwilling to tackle, partly on account of their own involvement in the spoils system.

This brings into question the success of both the state and politicians in nurturing a sense of civic consciousness in Italian society towards the end of the twentieth century. The Italian state's failure to create a broadly felt sense of community and citizenship was heightened by its inability to provide efficient social services, which became a symbol of national disintegration. There was consequently a widespread perception among citizens that the tax system was unfair because they were getting little in return for their contributions and that consequently tax evasion was not a serious moral issue. This made it difficult to create a sense of national solidarity. Even the Catholic and Communist subcultures, while clearly encouraging collective solidarity, community spirit and economic well-being, had prevented the full development of national solidarity from the moment that they fostered strong ideological, social and territorial divisions.[47] Moreover, if education and modern media forms, such as television, had succeeded in creating a greater sense of national identity and a language common to nearly everyone, a strong regional identity persisted – with statistics of the early nineties suggesting, for example, that over a third of Italians continued to speak dialect in some measure alongside standard Italian – to which there corresponded a weaker identity with state and nation.[48]

Problems of civic consciousness were linked to a more general process of de-ideologization taking place in Italian society. On the one hand political conflict and terrorist activities declined. Though there was considerable protest during the eighties over peace issues, prompted by the deployment of cruise missiles throughout Western Europe by NATO, and over environmental matters and opposition to the *Mafia*, the level of confrontation with the state was much lower.[49] However, as Della Porta argues, as a result of de-ideologization, political parties were effectively transformed from ideological centres into businesses, which in turn increased corrupt practices. As a result of this, the party leadership of the PCI, DC and PSI was strengthened at the expense of the rank-and-file membership. The subcultural roots of the DC and PCI were weakened as they transformed themselves into ideologically diluted catch-all parties with a reduced role for the rank and file. While PSI sections were not shut down, they mainly functioned in order to maximize gains from the spoils system. Ordinary citizens were integrated into the system of political corruption through the encouragement of votes in exchange for favours, leading to the creation of a value system based on the fulfilment of individual objects.[50] The co-operation of citizens in this was also a consequence of an increased demand for patronage protection as a result of growing unemployment, particularly in the South, and diminishing union support and emigration outlets to overcome it.[51]

There was a notable drop in political activism within the Communist Party from the late seventies onwards. Not only was there a downward trend in party membership, in line with a decrease in votes, but those who remained in the party increasingly stopped participating in local social and political initiatives. Although the PCI had stood for the creation of a modern society founded on strong civic values and had often been alone in its fight against the *Mafia*, partly as a result of the experience of power-sharing during the mid to late seventies, individual Party members had been caught up in the system of *lottizzazione*, sharing in the division of illicit spoils with the DC and PSI. This naturally coincided with the party's gradual dissociation from its previous pro-worker militancy and its embracing of broader social and political issues.[52]

Even the most positive aspects of the economic boom of the eighties and nineties were to some extent bound up with problems of civic consciousness. The growth in dominance of small firms, for example, was partly a result of the huge savings they made on labour costs and the common practice of tax evasion. According to Mario Mignone, Italian law companies employing under 15 people did not have to be unionized or pay standard wages and social benefits. Nor did companies with low incomes have to make their accounts available for checks by the Customs and Excise police. From 1984 onwards astonishingly 95 per cent of Italian firms declared turnovers of under the minimum figure necessary for such checks.[53] Employment irregularities in this sector on occasion led to tragedy. In 1987 in the port of Ravenna 13 underpaid casual workers died after being overcome by fumes while cleaning a ship's hold for a small company, which had failed to apply the necessary safety regulations. This revealed, in the words of Paul Ginsborg, 'both the seamier side of the Third Italy's "economic miracle" and the stratum of families that was excluded from its benefits'.[54]

Changes to the Italian party system during the nineties

The *Mafia* crisis and the *Tangentopoli* corruption scandals prompted an attempt to speed up processes of institutional and political reform that had been called for since the eighties in the hope of ending political instability, as a result of which few governments had lasted over a year, reducing corruption and making politicians more accountable to the electorate. During the early nineties the Italian people were given the opportunity to sanction proposed changes to the political system in two major referenda. In June 1991 they voted in favour of a proposal to reduce the number of preference votes that each elector could use to support an individual candidate by name, a proposal described by Denis Mack Smith as, 'a major attack against clientelism, against boss rule and machine politics, and against *mafiosi* who by intimidating electors had used preference votes to manipulate elections on behalf of friendly politicians'.[55] In April 1993 the positive outcome of a referendum on reform of Senate elections paved the way for a change in voting from proportional representation to a system whereby 75 per cent of the parliamentary seats were awarded according to the results of the uninominal vote of single-member constituencies and the remaining 25 per cent were awarded in proportion to the votes gained nationally. The very high popular vote in favour of this change was undoubtedly a result of a belief that electoral reform would create governments with more secure parliamentary majorities, make the elected more accountable to electors and weaken the grip of party barons, though in practice there was much confusion and little consensus about the way this could be achieved.[56]

The new electoral system appeared to pave the way for a reduction in the number of political parties and the development of a bi-polar system of alternation of governments. The first general election since *Tangentopoli*, held in March 1994, saw the creation of two large alliances, one of the Left and one of the Centre–Right. By far the largest party making up the left-wing 'Progressive' alliance was the recently formed Democratic Party of the Left (*Partito Democratico della Sinistra* – PDS). Founded in 1991 in place of the PCI in the aftermath of the fall of the Soviet block, and representing the culmination of a painful process of de-ideologization, it claimed to have severed all links with Marxist and Leninist theory in favour of the creation of a modern democratic movement.[57] There were other smaller parties within the left-wing alliance, including the Sicilian anti-*Mafia* movement, *La Rete*, founded

217

by Leoluca Orlando, ex-Christian Democrat mayor of Palermo, the Green Party and the Communist Refoundation Party (*Rifondazione Comunista* – made up of those Communists who opposed the creation of the PDS). Led by the PDS secretary, Achille Ochetto, who had been the main promoter of reform of the PCI, the 'Progressives' based their campaign on the need to reform the state, reduce the public deficit and fight unemployment.

The Centre–Right 'Freedom Pole' alliance (*Polo della Libertà*) included two parties that until then had been very much on the fringe of Italian politics, and a new political body that would make history with lightning speed. The alliance was brought together by the media tycoon, Silvio Berlusconi, who, claiming to represent the new face of Italian politics, in January 1994 founded a highly personalized political organization, *Forza Italia* ('Let's Go Italy!'), which was more a commercial company than a political party. Taking advantage of his influence over much of the media, his programme of free-market liberalism called for a reduction of the role of the state in the economy, greater privatization and lower taxes and promised the electorate a million new jobs. Among the other parties making up Berlusconi's alliance were the federalist Northern League (*Lega Nord*) of Umberto Bossi, and the National Alliance (*Alleanza Nazionale* – AN), which consisted of the MSI and small groups of right-wing conservatives. *Alleanza Nazionale* was founded by the MSI leader, Gianfranco Fini, who aimed to capitalize on the void left by the demise of the DC and was eager, therefore, to break any previous links with Fascism. A third, much smaller Centrist alliance, of which the Popular Party (*Partito Popolare Italiano* – PPI) was the most significant protagonist, was made up of ex-DC members, who claimed to represent the resurrection of a clean Catholic party.[58]

In reality, however, as Diego Gambetta and Steven Warner argue, the alliances existed only to field candidates in the first-past-the-post constituencies and they were certainly not political parties. For the election of the remaining 25 per cent of parliamentary seats they put forward their own separate lists of candidates. Most crucially, the 'Freedom Pole' was in reality made up of two distinct alliances:

> In the Northern constituencies, candidates were fielded in the name of an alliance between the Lega Nord and Forza Italia under the label of the Polo della Libertà; there is no sense that these candidates might be associated with the ex-Fascists of Alleanza nazionale. Conversely, in the Southern constituencies, candidates were fielded in the name of Forza Italia and the Alleanza nazionale, here under the label of the Polo del buon Governo, again with no indication that these candidates might have anything to do with the Northern successionists of the Lega, who would deny the South its extensive economic assistance.[59]

As a result of *Forza Italia*'s ability to form an alliance with both the *Lega* and *Alleanza Nazionale* and at the same time the presentation of two separate bipartite alliances, the 'Freedom Pole' came to power under the prime ministership of Silvio Berlusconi, with a parliamentary majority of 266 seats, over the 202 won by the Left and the 46 gained by the Centrist alliance. Berlusconi's government turned out to be short-lived in view of the inevitable weakness of a coalition, which had been formed less on the basis of a common programme and more as part of the tactical device employed, which had effectively allowed two alliances to form a government. Infighting between the coalition parties forced Berlusconi to resign in December 1994.

In Berlusconi's place, Lamberto Dini, the finance minister in his government, led a caretaker cabinet of technocrats until the general election of April 1996 saw the victory of a Centre–Left alliance known as the 'Olive Tree' (*Ulivo* – winning 246 parliamentary seats). Though dominated by the PDS, the prime ministerial candidate, Romano Prodi, was a member of the ex-Christian Democrat PPI. The Centre–Right, which gained only 169 seats, was clearly disadvantaged by the decision of the Northern League to fight the election separately and the passing of a decree (*par conditio*) limiting the use that Berlusconi could make of his media powers for electoral ends. The following 28 months of relatively smooth government appeared to herald greater political stability. There was also more willingness than before on the part of the new political class to implement institutional reform and enforce those policies required to restore the state economy to health and allow Italy to join the European single currency. In 1997 a bicameral commission was created to address such issues as strengthening the executive, revising the electoral law, the granting of greater federal autonomy to the regions, redesigning parliament and judicial reform.

However, increasing fragmentation within the governing coalition showed that the bipolar system remained fragile. Nor was government stability helped by the continued presence in parliament of numerous small parties. A crisis in the Centre–Left government grew as a result of the difficult relationship between the Communist Refoundation Party and the governing majority, the former a necessary part of the 'Olive Tree' coalition but only an external supporter of the government, which it did not join. The party's withdrawal of support in October 1998 led to a change in political alliances within the Centre–Left in order to hold on to a parliamentary majority and the formation of a new government, led by the ex-Communist Massimo D'Alema. It also saw the creation of two more small parties, the Italian Communists (*Comunisti Italiani*) resulting from a schism in the Communist Refoundation Party and another offshoot of the former DC, the Democratic Republic Union (*Unione Democratica della Repubblica*, led by former President Francesco Cossiga).[60] Reminiscent of the practices of the 'First Republic', the above manoeuvres prompted bitter accusations from the Centre–Right opposition that the government no longer represented the electorate. Carlo Tullio-Altan interprets such manoeuvres as emblematic of a political system still strongly conditioned by clientelistic practices, which, following the end of the Cold War and in the aftermath of *Tangentopoli*, was characterized by the proliferation, alongside renewed or new parties, of movements, locally based groups and the initiatives of individual personalities, which made the process of formation of sufficiently homogeneous governing majorities all the more difficult.[61] Alongside Cossiga, another prominent personality to form his own political movement during the late nineties (following retirement from the judiciary) was Antonio Di Pietro. It is no coincidence that proposals for institutional change put forward by the bicameral commission reached a state of deadlock when discussed in parliament as a result of strong political divisions.

Separatism, racism, post-Fascism and neo-Liberalism

The Centre–Right victory in 1994 came as a shock to many Italians, to whom it had seemed that the Left – which had emerged from the corruption scandals relatively unscathed and had been the chief winner in the local elections of June 1993 – was most likely to win. Even more shocking to them was the fact that Berlusconi had gone into politics for the first time on the eve of the election campaign, becoming prime minister in his first ever political contest. The election to power of a governing coalition containing a party threatening an already undermined national identity, and even more significantly, an ex-Fascist party, one of whose parliamentary representatives was the granddaughter of Benito Mussolini, prompted several political commentators to ask themselves whether an already weakened Italian democracy was seriously under threat. The following paragraphs analyse the performance of parties of the Centre–Right against the background of broader social attitudes prevalent in Italy during the nineties.

First, the federalist movements of Northern Italy played a crucial part in the victory of the 'Freedom Pole'. The most prominent of these were the Lombardy League (*Lega Lombarda*) and the Veneto League (*Liga Veneta*). Attacking the corruption of the central state, they called for greater regional autonomy and the safeguarding of regional interests, demanding that native inhabitants should be given priority over Southerners and foreign immigrants in the allocation of jobs and housing. While making limited political inroads during the early to mid-eighties, their fortunes began to rise towards the end of the decade when in the general election of 1987 the *Lega Lombarda* under the leadership of Umberto Bossi won 3 per cent of the vote for the Chamber of Deputies and 2.5 per cent for the Senate, gaining a seat in each house. During the European elections in 1989 it took 6.5 per cent of the popular vote in Lombardy but in 1990 its share of the vote rose to 16.4 per cent at the regional elections. In December 1990 the *Lega Lombarda*, the *Liga Veneta* and similar organizations of Piedmont, Emilia–Romagna, Tuscany and Liguria joined together to form a federal organization, the Northern League (*Lega Nord*), under the leadership of Bossi. In the general election of 1992 it gained 8.7 per cent of the national vote in the Chamber of Deputies, winning 55 seats. It was most successful in Lombardy, winning 34.9 per cent of the vote for the city council of Mantua in September 1992 and becoming the largest party in the Milan city council the following June.[62]

As is demonstrated by the above electoral fortunes, its ascendancy to government as a coalition partner in the 'Freedom Pole' alliance in March 1994 and its even higher vote in 1996 (increasing from 8.4 to 10.1 per cent), the League phenomenon cannot merely be written off as a vulgar protest movement simply capitalizing on misgovernment, as many journalists and politicians claimed. In referring specifically to the earlier manifesto of the Lombard League, Mark Gilbert argues that the views it expressed were shared by millions of Northern Italians, representing 'a plausible critique of the state of the Italian nation': the North was supporting the South by its labours; it was carrying an undue share of the national tax burden; the dominant political parties were leading Italy into bankruptcy as a result of their corrupt practices; and there was even some justice in the claim that Southerners were taking Northern Italian public-sector jobs, representing as they did a disproportionate portion of employees there.[63] The League could also be considered an important democratic movement, if only in so far as it spontaneously mobilized large sections of the population against misgovernment. Indeed, the willingness of individual judges to investigate political corruption during the early nineties, making a democratic revolution a real possibility, was largely determined by its protest campaigns.

The League was initially written off as vulgar in so far as many of its exponents, starting from Bossi himself, did not maintain any form of aloofness from grass-roots society, which they claimed was more typical of the politicians of 'corrupt' parties. Their use of everyday language, particularly dialect, in contrast to formal political language was undoubtedly attractive to many voters who desired to be represented by people who were close to them. On occasion such language was sexist and phallocratic.[64] The unpleasant side of the League was evident in its occasional lack of respect for democratic rules and the law (which it justified on the grounds that the establishment was corrupt). When during the mid-nineties the League temporarily changed its programme from federalism to secession, its organization in the summer of 1996 of a mass gathering in Venice to declare a 'Northern Republic' was compared by some political commentators to the Fascist March on Rome of 1922. Though Bossi was often portrayed as a Mussolini-like figure and his party seen as representing a revival of Fascism, or the Italian face of a developing anti-immigrant extreme Right in other European countries, in reality the League kept a distance from the Italian Fascist tradition.[65] Certainly, the League pandered to racist sentiments, particularly after the increase in immigration from countries outside the European Community from the late eighties onwards. During the nineties, League opposition to immigration heightened, independent of the fact that many politicians and industrialists recognized the need for immigrant labour. This included the organization of citizens' patrols allegedly against immigrant crime and a protest march in October 2000 against the construction of a mosque for the benefit of the Muslim population of the town of Lodi near Milan.

In an essay published in 1996, Anna Cento Bull carefully examines the racist origins of the Northern League, concluding that its ideology was founded on both cultural criteria (applied to Southern immigrants) and skin colour (applied to foreign immigrants). Yet it was different from an organization like the French National Front, which was characterized by the articulations of both racism and Fascism and racism and nationalism. The former was totally lacking in the League and the latter was 'reshaped as an articulation between racism and ethnoregionalism'. League racism can be attributed to the myth it created of Lombard ethnicity founded on such cultural characteristics as a strong work ethic, entrepreneurship, a spirit of sacrifice and a high propensity to saving. Yet, Cento Bull argues, such a myth was not merely founded on the idea that Northerners were productive and efficient while Southerners were parasitic and inefficient. The cultural characteristics upon which the myth was erected were identified by economists and sociologists as belonging to a specific type of economy and society. Much of Northern Italy had not undergone total industrialization, thereby maintaining high levels of continuity with the old rural economy and society. It was strongly influenced by Catholic and Socialist territorial subcultures, which limited integration into the national body politic. The predominance of small family-based companies in the provinces operating within closely knit communities often speaking local dialect brought out a strong sense of community-based trust and solidarity, creating a 'communitarian differentialist' type of racism, politically exploited and 'ethnicized' by the Northern League, founded on the idea of 'Us against the Other'. However, geographical outsiders, such as Southerners and immigrants, could be considered 'insiders' if useful to the local economy of small manufacturing. Conversely, public administration occupations within the community were considered foreign. This attitude was intensified as a result of industrial recession and tertiarization from the end of the eighties onwards. The League was particularly successful in Christian Democrat strongholds in Lombardy and Veneto as the latter party was seen as having betrayed its traditional role of defender of small-scale industrialization.[66]

The League was not the only political party representing racist feeling among not insignificant numbers of Italians. Demonstrating Italy's difficult transition to a multi-cultural nation, throughout the country immigrant workers risked not only to exploitation at the work place but also discrimination when it came to obtaining housing and other services. On occasion, for example, posters were fixed to the doors of bars stating 'North Africans not allowed here'. While Italian citizens were increasingly exasperated by the effects of the involvement of illegal immigrants in drug and prostitution rackets, which the state appeared to be unable to prevent, they increasingly perceived crime as being automatically linked to all immigrants. This was reinforced by the attitude of not only the Northern League but also *Alleanza Nazionale* and *Forza Italia*, which were partly behind community-level initiatives in 'policing' immigrant crime and regaining control of territory which had allegedly been 'taken away' from local residents, initiatives which sometimes resulted in conflict and violence.[67]

Areas with strong left-wing traditions were not necessarily less hostile towards immigrants. Though there was more willingness on the part of left-wing councils to provide assistance and solidarity, it was often done in an authoritarian manner betraying an underlying sense of racial superiority. With reference to the provision of shelter and food for Rom refugees by Bologna City Council, Davide Però states that, 'despite its self-proclaimed sensitivity to and defence of cultural diversity, the Left appears to be involved in oppressive, culturally imperialist processes of top–down, external, essentialist, stereotypical and prejudice-driven definition and attribution of difference and identity'.[68] While it is true that most of the voluntary assistance to immigrants came from Church organizations, pronouncements by some members of the ecclesiastical hierarchy on the risks to Christian society and the family posed by the increased presence in Italy of Muslim immigrants helped to legitimize right-wing opposition to immigration.

Racist sentiment in Italy during the nineties was by no means a new phenomenon. As Jacqueline Andell noted in 1990, 'Current attitudes towards black immigrants may derive partially from Italy's colonial experience in Ethiopia. The fascist regime was emphatic about the inferiority of the indigenous Ethiopian population.'[69] *Alleanza Nazionale*'s own pronouncements on immigration were emblematic of a party which was trying to replace its extremist past with an image of respect for democratic principles. While opposed to the evolution of a multi-cultural society, it attempted to avoid accusations of racism by arguing that immigration was just as bad for immigrants as it was for Italians. If the Party leadership claimed respect for ethnic minorities, rejecting racism and anti-Semitism, skinheads at the grass roots of the organization were often responsible for violent attacks against them. Likewise, *Alleanza Nazionale*'s relationship to its Fascist past remained ambivalent. In spite of Fini's official consignment of Fascism to history and his use of the term 'post-Fascist' to describe his party, many extreme elements from the MSI (dissolved in January 1995 as AN was proclaimed a democratic right-wing conservative party) continued to support him. McCarthy notes that, at the 1994 general election, *Alleanza Nazionale* performed well, gaining 13.5 per cent of the vote with peaks of 27.5 per cent in Apulia and 27 per cent in Rome. In Molise and Abruzzo it emerged as the largest party. The particular success of the party in the South and Latium was partly to be expected in view of the limited anti-Fascist tradition and the significant inroads of post-war neo-Fascism in those regions. But even in 'Red' regions it did well, gaining 9 per cent of the vote in Emilia–Romagna and 11 per cent in Tuscany. Demonstrating the long-term popularity of the new Right, *Alleanza Nazionale* gained an extra 2.2 per cent of the vote in the 1996 general election, and was far more successful than previously in Northern constituencies.[70]

Does the success of *Alleanza Nazionale* bring into doubt the democratic credentials of those who voted for it? According to Simon Parker:

> It is also not difficult to see in the massive rise in support for the neo-Fascist MSI/Alleanza Nazionale in the 1994 parliamentary elections (especially, but not only, in the South and Rome), the political articulation of a petty bourgeois nostalgia for order and authority that had been rather overshadowed in the First Republic by the DC's obsession with political consensus-building and the art of non-decision making.[71]

The vote for AN also revealed, however, that a significant number of Italians did not identify with the anti-Fascist tradition on which the Republic had been founded. The entry to government of *Alleanza Nazionale*, indeed, saw an attempt to redress the political balance in view of the fact that the democratic system of anti-Fascist inspiration had previously excluded the participation of the political Right, given the MSI's links with Fascism. This led to several controversial initiatives and pronouncements on Italian national identity, Italy's Fascist past and anti-Fascism, which, though condemned by many commentators as an attack on democracy, struck a chord in the minds of large numbers of Italians.

A heated debate between the Left and the Right was sparked in April 1994 by the showing on state television of the original gruesome footage of a crowd spitting at and kicking Mussolini's corpse and that of his mistress Clara Petacci in Piazza Loreto in Milan, following their execution in April 1945. The document was seized upon by many neo-Fascists as proof of the hypocritical anti-Fascism of the majority of Italians who had allegedly supported Mussolini until 1943. A second television instalment showing the desperation of relatives of the victims of the Ardeatine caves massacre after their remains had been discovered exacerbated political tensions, prompting the Left – fearful of the political consequences of the rise to power of *Alleanza Nazionale* – to organize a rally for 'national reconciliation and against Fascism' in Milan on the occasion of Liberation Day (25 April), for which 200,000 people turned out. Though both Gianfranco Fini and Berlusconi did not take part in the rally, they avoided provocation by claiming that the anniversary was an occasion for national reconciliation between Fascists and anti-Fascists. Yet, Fini's attitude towards Fascism remained ambiguous. He claimed that his party was no longer Fascist, but – in order not to alienate hard-liners – insisted that Mussolini was not to be demonized.[72]

From the late eighties onwards the often provocative statements of revisionist historians, the most prominent among them being Renzo De Felice, gave some credence to the claims of nostalgic neo-Fascists. They argued that the history of twentieth-century Italy had been hegemonized by left-wingers and that consequently Fascism and the Resistance had been misrepresented. Fascism, they claimed, had enjoyed genuine mass consensus until 1943 and had helped to generate a greater sense of national identity among Italians. Anti-Fascism on the other hand had formed the basis of 50 years of imperfect democracy founded on *partitocrazia* (party rule) and only partially representative of the Italian people. In particular the Italian Communist Party – the most prominent political player in the Resistance – had falsely claimed a leading role in the process of national unity upon which the Resistance had allegedly been founded, while in reality it had been a servant of the Soviet Union. If the Fascists had behaved brutally during the war of Liberation, the Communists had also committed atrocities. Moreover, Communist terroristic tactics had often provoked unnecessary reprisals against innocent civilians on the part of the Fascists and the Nazi occupiers.[73]

The claims of the revisionists were bitterly contested by the anti-Fascist camp as politically motivated. However, several left-wing historians and politicians, while questioning the historical accuracy of such claims, admitted the need for new research into the recent past that was to be free of the ideological constraints of the Cold War period. They also called for reconciliation between the two factions that had fought each other so bitterly between 1943 and 1945, which 50 years later still left society divided between anti-Fascists and anti-Communists, in order to strengthen national unity which had been shaken by the crisis of *Tangentopoli* and was at that moment threatened by the rise of the Northern League. This more positive response to the provocations of the revisionists was also evident in the publication during the mid-nineties of interviews with ex-members of the Italian Social Republic in left-wing newspapers and journals.

There is little doubt that the Right took advantage of revisionist pronouncements – no matter how scientifically questionable they were – more to bolster their anti-Left politics than to encourage national reconciliation. Richard Bosworth argues that, rather than praising Mussolini and Fascism, the revisionists espoused an 'anti-Anti-Fascism' which helped to legitimize the creation of a proper right-wing party, while at the same time encouraging the execration of the Left. Their pronouncements clearly appealed to anti-Communist sentiment and to those Italians who did not strongly identify with the Resistance (or at least the more radical aspects of it espoused by the Left). As Bosworth notes, however, such a stance was of even greater significance in the light of *Tangentopoli* and a strongly felt desire among many Italians to get over it: 'If anti-Fascism and its past were the canker at the heart of Italy, then the responsibility of Craxian Italy for paving the way to *Tangentopoli*

225

could be denied. If the Republic had been flawed in its first creation, then there was no need to ponder its most recent past.'[74]

Neither *Alleanza Nazionale* nor the Northern League could have come to power in 1994 without the votes that went to Silvio Berlusconi's *Forza Italia* movement. Taking 21 per cent nationally, *Forza Italia* reached over 25 per cent of the vote in the North-West, surpassed the PPI in Veneto and through-out the North took away many of the votes that had previously gone to the Northern League. In the Centre it came second to the PDS, while in Sicily it gained 30 per cent of the vote to the great disadvantage of Orlando's *La Rete* anti-*Mafia* movement. *Forza Italia* gained the most votes from professionals, employees in small industries and housewives. It obtained a large amount of support from young people (winning just under 40 per cent of voters under the age of 25) and even managed to win some working-class con-stituencies, such as that of Lingotto–Mirafiori in Turin, where many Fiat workers lived.[75]

As Joseph Farrell illustrates, the success of *Forza Italia* partly lay in its ability to create an image of its leader as a highly charismatic personality able to take Italy out of the political and economic turmoil created by the *Tangentopoli* investigations. *Forza Italia*'s election campaign to a certain extent represented a successful exercise in marketing a product. Demonstrating the susceptibility of a significant part of the electorate to media manipulation, Berlusconi's three national commercial television channels, together with the newspapers and magazines he controlled, played an essential part in this exercise. According to Farrell, the appeal of *Forza Italia* was founded on the carefully cultivated myth of Berlusconi himself, national sentiment and anti-Com-munism. Berlusconi's involvement in political corruption associated with the previous regime was concealed in order to present him as a new, clean face in politics, a man of the people who had become rich through hard work as opposed to privilege. In terms of national sentiment, the language used painstakingly avoided association with overtly right-wing nationalist sentiment. Instead Berlusconi chose the subdued, apparently innocent nationalism of football – he owned the very successful AC Milan football team – to present himself as the saviour of Italy. Sporting metaphors were used to describe both his own entry into politics (*Scendere in campo* – 'Come on to the pitch') and the make-up of *Forza Italia*, itself a popular football chant, and later his own government, referred to as his 'team'. On the eve of the election, Berlusconi's private television newsreaders and show hosts urged their viewers to vote for him.[76]

Independent of the cosmetic skills of his media empire, which have often been overstressed, Berlusconi was above all an expression of the demise of traditional political ideologies and their substitution by the new dominant neo-Liberal ideals of personal wealth creation and success (epitomized in Berlusconi's claim that he would turn Italy into a large company and that the wealth he had created for himself would be created for all). While *Forza Italia* claimed to represent a revolutionary force in politics, Farrell argues that in reality the *Forza Italia* vote was the expression of a 'middle Italy' which had lost its political referent with the collapse of the political parties of the 'First Republic' and that was unsure of the direction of the country after *Tangentopoli*. It indicated that, far from revolution, that section of the population that identified itself with Berlusconi merely wanted to get 'back to normal'.

A 'return to normal' was suggested by Berlusconi's amnesty on illegal constructions that had ruined several beauty spots and hundreds of miles of coastline. Even more significant was his attempt to 'normalize' the judiciary. In the summer of 1994 his government issued a decree, which made it illegal to arrest politicians and businessmen suspected of corruption. Fierce opposition from the magistracy, supported by the public, prevented its implementation. It is widely believed that this move was prompted by the intentions of the *Tangentopoli* investigating magistrates to prosecute collaborators within the prime minister's own company, Fininvest, who were accused of paying bribes to the Customs and Excise police. Though claiming to be a new face in Italian politics with no involvement in the corruption scandals, Berlusconi owed much of the success of his private enterprise to the support of Bettino Craxi. He also faced accusations of involvement with the *Mafia* on the part of Sicilian campaigners of *Forza Italia* and *Alleanza Nazionale* during the election. It is likely that this prompted his public criticism of the Palermo magistracy. The chief magistrate, Gian Carlo Caselli, feared that Berlusconi's attacks would damage the anti-*Mafia* campaign, drawing attention to parallels between his language and the imprecations of Totò Riina.[77]

After his fall from power at the end of 1994, the war between Berlusconi and the investigating magistrates continued. In the face of new charges of corruption against him, Berlusconi accused them of acting on behalf of the Left in order to ruin him politically. He also seized upon the fact that *Tangentopoli* magistrates had often used preventive detention beyond the limits of the law in order to charge politicians and businessmen with corruption, as proof of the conspiratorial nature of the investigations. It was admittedly difficult for the magistracy to claim political immunity from the very moment that the judicial system of the Republic had always been subject to political interference and patronage, which had also affected the process of selection and promotion of judges. For the obvious reason that the ruling parties of the 'First Republic' had often made their life difficult, particularly in the war against the *Mafia*, it was easy to appreciate how some judges were sympathetic towards the Left and continued to be so after Berlusconi had attempted to reduce their powers of investigation during the summer of 1994. In reality, the great majority of judges had not supported the more determined efforts of a minority of colleagues to fight against political corruption and collusion with the *Mafia*. While highly politicized, the judiciary was

227

divided ideologically to the point that its investigations could still have negative consequences for the individuals and interests identified with the Left. This is demonstrated by a new phase of corruption investigations from the autumn of 1996, which implicated a number of left-wing figures.[78]

Moreover, David Nelken argues that, while *Tangentopoli* itself may have been seen positively by large numbers of Italians, the public also saw the judiciary's many failings in television and newspaper reports: large numbers of prisoners awaiting trial, often in shameful conditions, and the incredible delays involved in reaching the final verdict when trials did take place.[79] Popular support for the magistracy, particularly Antonio Di Pietro, which in 1993 had never been stronger, waned from the late-nineties onwards, and Berlusconi's attacks – bolstered by his private media powers – were undoubtedly partly behind this. Public opinion was also negatively conditioned during this period by conflict within the magistracy, which started with a judicial investigation of Di Pietro by the magistrates of Brescia. As Ginsborg notes:

> A sinister atmosphere was created in which no public figure seemed any longer to be what he claimed to be, and in which the judiciary as a whole seemed an unstable and politically divided institution. It was difficult to understand whether this was a spontaneous process or a carefully organized attempt to stir up trouble.[80]

Once the initial euphoria of *Tangentopoli* had passed, many Italians returned to feeling that the judiciary could not be trusted. Yet, whatever in the judiciary could be criticized, the suspicion remains that the leader of the political opposition acted not to achieve judicial independence but in order to protect himself from prosecution.[81]

In similar fashion Berlusconi played on public ill-feeling towards the RAI state television company, attacking it for its crimes of *lottizzazione* and its monopolization by 'Communists', most probably in order to safeguard his own media powers. In the wake of *Tangentopoli*, the RAI was struggling to achieve reforms to break the past practice of political domination. This entailed the formation of a new RAI board of managers not aligned to political parties to ensure that television and particularly news programmes observed high standards of objectivity. On coming to power in 1994, Berlusconi argued that the RAI had become pro-left-wing, showing antipathy to his government, but he did little to solve any alleged political bias when he replaced the reformist managers and news and network directors with individuals who were far less autonomous. Many were members of the prime minister's Fininvest media empire.[82]

The fact that Berlusconi polled the same percentage of votes in the 1996 general election as in 1994 was indicative of his continued popularity with the electorate in spite of his facing serious corruption charges. The particularly violent language of the leader of *Forza Italia*'s electoral campaign (particularly against the state) did not prevent people from voting for him and the victory of the Centre–Left was only due to the outmanoeuvring of Berlusconi in coalition building. Similarly, an attempt to restrict Berlusconi's grip on television and advertising by means of a referendum, held in June 1995, failed.[83] The popularity of the Centre–Right as a whole was confirmed once again in the general election of May 2001 in which a new alliance of *Forza Italia, Alleanza Nazionale* and the Northern League under Berlusconi's leadership won a significant parliamentary majority (though only gaining 600,000 more votes than the Centre–Left).

Conclusion

Several political commentators have argued that the recent successes of the Centre–Right represent the failure of a civic revolution that many believed would follow the crisis of the early nineties. It must be stressed, however, that automatically associating 'uncivic' attitudes with Centre–Right politicians or voters fails to take into account the complexity of political cultures. Many Italians voted for the Centre–Right coalition in 1994 (and continued to do so in 1996 and 2001) because it appeared – rightly or wrongly – to present a new form of politics at a time when the party system was discredited. In this sense the PDS, although the heir of the PCI's historic struggle for democracy and civic values, was at a disadvantage. According to Martin Bull, it was difficult to present the PDS as the chief movement of political reform since its identity remained ambivalent. The party's break with its Communist past in 1991 was unconvincing to many voters. Moreover, its image as the party of honesty and integrity was weakened by the exposure of corruption in its ranks and revelations of the PCI's previous illicit dealings with the Soviet government.[84]

The survey conducted in early 1994 by Anna Cento Bull on the Lombard towns of Sesto San Giovanni and Erba, the former Communist and the latter Catholic and increasingly 'Leghist', tells us much about civic attitudes within different political subcultures. According to the results of the survey, League voters were distinguished for their individualist and localist attitudes. They identified with their locality as opposed to the nation state, as was exemplified by their tendency to read only the local press, and were disillusioned with the socio-political system. In their opposition to immigration and the creation of a multi-ethnic society, they rejected the values of solidarity expressed by PDS and Catholic subcultures. PDS voters were generally less receptive to the idea of localism, and showed a strong feeling of belonging to the nation state, while DC/PPI voters identified with both. DC/PPI and PDS voters mainly expressed feelings of solidarity, with that of the latter orientated along class lines. However, it is significant that a 'substantial minority of PDS voters', especially in Sesto, felt that immigration caused social problems and therefore 'did not feel bound to extend their class-based solidarity to extra-EU immigrants'. Cento Bull's study also shows that there was a difference in attitude between the two towns on some issues among voters of the same party. The DC/PPI and PDS voters of Sesto alone, for example, were supportive of the idea of paying higher taxes in exchange for better public services, suggesting the predominance of a culture of class solidarity in that town as opposed to the existence of a 'market-orientated, small-business culture' in Erba, which encouraged greater support for neo-liberal policies in general.[85]

It is not always possible, therefore, to make a clear distinction between political subcultures in terms of civic attitudes. If the sense of community espoused by the Right is often based on the exclusionary idea of 'Us against the Other', as is demonstrated by the example of the League, the Left no longer constitutes a focal point for solidarity within the community. The traditional Communist subculture is destined to disappear in the face of the reduction in the size of the traditional working class, the growth of greater wealth among the working and lower-middle classes, and the PDS's move towards the centre of the political spectrum in order to attract more middle-class voters. In this sense, it is no coincidence that the PDS dropped the PCI's earlier demand that treasury bonds, from which the middle classes benefit at the expense of the public debt, should be taxed. The fact that the Left no longer constitutes a constant and stable point of reference in the community means that weaker elements in society, particularly those in irregular work and with low levels of education, are more easily marginalized.[86]

Notes

1. For economic development, see Richard M. Locke, *Remaking the Italian Economy* (Ithaca, NY: Cornell University Press, 1995); Galimberti and Paolozzi, *Il volo del calabrone*, chapter 5; Zamagni, *The Economic History of Italy*, 337–78.
2. H.M. Scobie, S. Mortali, S. Persuad and P. Docile, *The Italian Economy in the 1990s* (London: Routledge, 1996), 12–15.
3. Figures from World Trade Organization, *International Trade Statistics*, Annual Reports, 1985–98.
4. Galimberti and Paolozzi, *Il volo del calabrone*, 280–3. See also Balcet, *L'economia italiana*, 125.
5. Cento Bull and Corner, *From Peasant to Entrepreneur*, 133–8.
6. Figures from World Trade Organization, *International Trade Statistics*, Annual Report, 1998.
7. Ginsborg, *L'Italia del tempo presente*, 9, 18–26.
8. For an analysis of the Southern economy, see Zamagni, *The Economic History of Italy*, 369–75; Galimberti and Paolozzi, *Il volo del calabrone*, 267–8; Balcet, *L'economia italiana*, 102, 105–6. For a detailed analysis of state investment in the South, see Fiorella Padoa Schioppa Kostoris, *Italy. The Sheltered Economy. Structural Problems in the Italian Economy* (Oxford: Clarendon Press, 1993), chapters 7 and 8.

9. ISTAT, *Rapporto sull'Italia: Edizione 1999*, 49–51.
10. For figures and a discussion of the evolution of Italian agriculture during the eighties and nineties, see Ginsborg, *L'Italia del tempo presente*, 41–6.
11. For the crisis in Italian public finance (and relevant figures), see Balcet, *L'economia italiana*, chapter 5; Galimberti and Paolozzi, *Il volo del calabrone*, chapter 5. For a shorter but highly acute analysis in English, see Simon Parker, 'The end of Italian exceptionalism? Assessing the transition to the Second Republic', *The Italianist*, 19(1999), 251–83(265–70).
12. The figures used for this section, unless otherwise indicated, are from ISTAT, *Rapporto sull'Italia: Edizione 1999*, 24–33, 64–6, 183–6; ISTAT, *Contabilità nazionale. Tomo 1: Conti economic nazionali. Anni 1970–1996* (Rome: ISTAT, 1998).
13. Discussed in Giulio Sapelli, 'The Italian Crises and Capitalism', *Modern Italy*, 1(1), 1995, 82–96(83–4). See 84 for figures.
14. Regional differences in employment levels are discussed in Parker, 'The end of Italian exceptionalism?', 272–3; Scobie, Mortali, Persuad and Docile, *The Italian Economy in the 1990s*, 42–3; Salvatore Lupo, 'The Changing Mezzogiorno. Between Representations and Reality', in Gundle and Parker (eds), *The New Italian Republic*, 247–60(255–6).
15. Ginsborg, *L'Italia del tempo presente*, 70–6.
16. For information and statistics concerning immigration to Italy, see Russell King and Jacqueline Andall, 'The geography and economic sociology of recent immigration to Italy', *Modern Italy*, 4(2), 1999, 135–58.
17. Bedani, *Politics and Ideology*, chapters 19–22; Mimmo Carrieri, 'Industrial relations and the labour market', in Gundle and Parker (eds), *The New Italian Republic*, 294–307. For Fiat strike, see Locke, *Remaking the Italian Economy*, 108–9.
18. Figures and analyses in this section, unless otherwise indicated, are from ISTAT, *Rapporto sull'Italia: Edizione 1999*; ISTAT, *Le regioni in cifre* (Rome: ISTAT, 1990), table 17.4; Baldi and Cagiano de Azevedo, *La popolazione italiana*, 151–6.
19. Barbagli, *Provando e riprovando*, chapters 1 and 2.
20. Ginsborg, 'Italian Political Culture in Historical Perspective', 5; Ginsborg, *L'Italia del tempo presente*, 144–6.
21. Alessandro Cavalli and Antonio de Lillo, *Giovani anni 80. Secondo rapporto Iard sulla condizione giovanile in Italia* (Bologna: Il Mulino, 1988), 110.
22. Motherhood and mother–son relationships in Mediterranean countries are discussed in Goddard, *Gender, Family and Work in Naples*, chapter 9.
23. Goddard, *Gender, Family and Work in Naples*, 174–5.
24. Figures concerning long-term demographic trends are from Vittorio Mapelli, *Il sistema sanitario nazionale* (Bologna: Il Mulino, 1999), 33.
25. Ginsborg, *L'Italia del tempo presente*, 137–41.
26. Data and analytical considerations in this section are from ISTAT, *Profile of Italy* (Rome: ISTAT, 1997), chapter 6; ISTAT, *Rapporto sull'Italia: Edizione 1999*, 67–83; ISTAT, *Le regioni in cifre*, tables 2.4, 4.1–4.5.
27. Lumley, 'Peculiarities of the Italian Newspaper', 202–4.
28. For an analysis of cultural consumption in Italy during the eighties and nineties, see Pivato and Tonelli, *Italia Vagabonda*, chapter 5.
29. Forgacs, 'Cultural Consumption', 286. See 284–7 for a general discussion.

30. Stephen Gundle and Noëllenne O'Sullivan, 'The Media and the Political Crisis', in Gundle and Parker (eds), *The New Italian Republic*, 206–20(213–15).

31. Stefano Pivato, 'Sport', in McCarthy (ed.), *Italy since 1945*, 171–82(179–82).

32. Pivato and Tonelli, *Italia Vagabonda*, 168.

33. Figures from Baldi and Cagiano de Azevedo, *La popolazione italiana*, 86.

34. Discussed in Fiorella Padoa Schioppa Kostoris, 'Excess and limits of the public sector in the Italian economy. The changing reform', in Gundle and Parker (eds), *The New Italian Republic*, 273–93(279–81). See also Parker, 'The end of Italian exceptionalism?', 274–5, 277.

35. Mario B. Mignone, *Italy Today. A Country in Transition* (New York: Peter Lang, 1995), 130. For recent reforms in the Italian welfare system, see Martin Rhodes (ed.), *Southern European Welfare States. Between Crisis and Reform* (London: Frank Cass, 1997); ISTAT, *Profile of Italy*, 150–1.

36. Data from ISTAT: *Rapporto sull'Italia: Edizione 1999*, 180, 188; ISTAT, *Le regioni in cifre*, tables 2.10–2.12, 3.4.

37. Mapelli, *Il sistema sanitario nazionale*, 66, 70. According to the author, the average number of hospital beds available in Italy was higher than in Great Britain and the United States but lower than in France and Germany.

38. Parker, 'The end of Italian exceptionalism?', 263–4.

39. Discussed in detail in David Alexander, 'Pollution, policies and politics: the Italian environment', in Filippo Sabetti and Raimondo Catanzaro (eds), *Italian Politics. A Review*, Vol. 5 (London: Pinter, 1991), 90–111; Paolo Ieri, 'The nuclear power issue: a new political cleavage within Italian society', in Raffaella Y. Nanetti, Robert Leonardi and Piergiorgio Corbetta (eds), *Italian Politics: A Review*, Vol. 2 (London: Pinter, 1988), 71–89.

40. Simonetta Tunesi, 'Italian environmental policies in the post-war period', in McCarthy (ed.), *Italy since 1945*, 118–32(122–6).

41. Figures and analysis from ISTAT: *Rapporto sull'Italia: Edizione 1999*; 161–6.

42. Figures from Marzio Barbagli, *Immigrazione e criminalità in Italia* (Bologna: Il Mulino, 1998), 50, 108.

43. For a detailed account of the events leading to the murders of 1992, see Absalom, *Italy since 1800*, 283–5; Mack Smith, *Modern Italy*, 467–82. See also Alexander Stille, *Excellent cadavers. The Mafia and the death of the first Italian Republic* (London: Jonathan Cape,1995).

44. Gundle and O'Sullivan, 'The Media and the Political Crisis', 207–8, 210–11.

45. Mark Gilbert, *The Italian Revolution. The End of Politics, Italian Style?* (Boulder, CO: Westview Press, 1995), 126. For a general discussion, see 126–51.

46. For the involvement of individual parties in *Tangentopoli*, see Sondra Z. Koff and Stephen P. Koff, *Italy. From the First to the Second Republic* (London: Routledge, 2000), 32–42; Patrick McCarthy, *The Crisis of the Italian State. From the Origins of the Cold War to the Fall of Berlusconi and Beyond* (Basingstoke: Macmillan, 1997), 140; Gilbert, *The Italian Revolution*, 171–2.

47. Discussed in Absalom, *Italy since 1800*, 296–7; Roberto Cartocci, *Fra Lega e Chiesa* (Bologna: Il Mulino, 1994), chapters 2 and 3.

48. Anna Laura and Giulio Lepschy and Voghera, 'Linguistic Variety in Italy', 74–5; Moss, 'Language and Italian national identity', 109–10.

49. The evolution of the protest movements during the eighties is discussed in Della Porta, *Social movements, political violence, and the state*.
50. Donatella della Porta, 'Political Parties and Corruption: Reflections on the Italian Case', *Modern Italy*, 1(1), 1995, 97–114.
51. Moss, 'Patronage revisited', 79–80.
52. This is discussed in Stephen Hellman, 'Italian Communism in the First Republic', in Gundle and Parker (eds), *The New Italian Republic*, 72–84(80–1). See also 'The Italian Communist Party between Berlinguer and the Seventeenth Congress', in Leonardi and Nanetti (eds) *Italian Politics*, 47–68.
53. Mignone, *Italy Today*, 125.
54. Ginsborg, *A History of Contemporary Italy*, 416.
55. Mack Smith, *Modern Italy*, 477. See 467–91 for political reforms.
56. For further details, see Richard S. Katz, 'The 1993 Parliamentary Electoral Reform', in Carol Mershon and Gianfranco Pasquino (eds), *Italian Politics. Ending the First Republic* (Boulder, CO: Westview Press, 1995), 93–112.
57. For the transformation from the PCI to the PDS, see Gilbert, *The Italian Revolution*, 67–82.
58. For detailed accounts of the change in the party system, institutional reforms and the 1994 and 1996 elections, see Koff, *Italy*; McCarthy, *The Crisis of the Italian State*, 157–65, 167.
59. Diego Gambetta and Steven Warner, 'The rhetoric of reform revealed (or: If you bite the ballot it may bite back)', *Journal of Modern Italian Studies*, 1(3), 1996, 357–76(368).
60. Parker, 'The end of Italian exceptionalism?', 258–9.
61. Carlo Tullio-Altan, *Gli italiani in Europa. Profilo storico comparato delle identità nazionali europee* (Bologna: Il Mulino, 1999), 210–11.
62. For the evolution of the Northern League, see Joseph Farrell and Carl Levy, 'The Northern League: Conservative Revolution?', in Levy (ed.), *Italian Regionalism*, 131–50(134–9); Gilbert, *The Italian Revolution*, chapter 4.
63. Gilbert, *The Italian Revolution*, 50.
64. Percy A. Allum and Ilvo Diamanti, 'The Autonomous Leagues in the Veneto', in Levy (ed.), *Italian Regionalism*, 151–69(155).
65. Farrell and Levy, 'The Northern League', 138.
66. Anna Cento Bull, 'Ethnicity, Racism and the Northern League', in Levy (ed.), *Italian Regionalism*, 171–87.
67. The life of immigrant workers in Italy is vividly described in essays published in the special issue of *Modern Italy*, *The Italian experience of immigration*, 4(2), 1999.
68. Davide Però, 'Next to the dog pound: institutional discourses and practices about Rom refugees in left-wing Bologna', *Modern Italy*, 4(2), 1999, 207–24. For an account of the treatment of immigrants in left-wing areas, see in the same issue Faïçal Daly, 'Tunisian migrants and their experience of racism in Modena', 173–89.
69. Jacqueline Andall, 'New migrants, old conflicts: the recent immigration into Italy', *The Italianist*, 10, 1990, 151–74(161).
70. Figures taken from McCarthy, *The Crisis of the Italian State*, 162, 224. For the ambivalent position of AN regarding its Fascist past and ethnic minorities, see 160–2, and Koff, *Italy*, 47–8.

71. Simon Parker, 'Political Identities', in Forgacs and Lumley (eds), *Italian Cultural Studies*,107–28(118–19).
72. The 1994 political row surrounding Mussolini's execution and the Ardeatine caves massacre is discussed in detail in Matt Frei, *Italy. The Unfinished Revolution* (London: Arrow, 1998), 197–201.
73. Discussed in detail in Chapter 4.
74. Bosworth, *The Italian Dictatorship*, 237.
75. McCarthy, *The Crisis of the Italian State*, 167; Gilbert, *The Italian Revolution*, 174–5.
76. Joseph Farrell, 'Berlusconi and Forza Italia: New Force for Old?', *Modern Italy*, 1(1), 1995, 40–52.
77. McCarthy, *The Crisis of the Italian State*, 151–2, 170–80.
78. The question of the political independence of the Italian judiciary is discussed in Carlo Guarnieri, 'The Judiciary in the Italian Political Crisis', in Martin Bull and Martin Rhodes (eds), *Crisis and Transition in Italian Politics* (London: Frank Cass, 1997), 157–75.
79. David Nelken, 'A legal revolution? The judges and Tangentopoli', in Gundle and Parker (eds), *The New Italian Republic*, 191–205(202).
80. Ginsborg, *L'Italia del tempo presente*, 558, note 188.
81. In October 2001 Berlusconi was acquitted of personal involvement in Fininvest's bribery payments.
82. Stephen Gundle and Noëlleane O'Sullivan, 'The Crisis of 1992–1994 and the Reform of Italian Public Broadcasting', *Modern Italy*, 1(1), 1995, 70–81.
83. For the election of 1996, see McCarthy, *The Crisis of the Italian State*, 224–5. For the referendum of June 1995, see Gundle and O'Sullivan, 'The Media and the Political Crisis', 220, note 9.
84. Martin Bull, 'The PDS, the Progressive Alliance and the Crisis', *Modern Italy*, 1(1), 1995, 30–9.
85. Cento Bull, *Social Identities and Political Cultures in Italy*, 203–16.
86. The question of the PDS's policy on the taxation of treasury bonds and role in the community is discussed in Paul Ginsborg *et al.*, 'Italy in the present tense: a roundtable discussion', *Modern Italy*, 5(2), 2000, 175–91.

Italian society at the dawn of the twenty-first century

In examining the lives of the Italian people over the twentieth century, we have seen how Italy has become a modern economic power providing many of its citizens with an enviable quality of life. Yet, as the previous chapter has demonstrated, many social, economic and cultural disparities remain. They are linked to historical factors, frequently referred to in this volume, of regional wealth imbalances, particularly between the North and South and the persistence of inhibiting elements of backwardness. Closely related to such factors, the process of democratic development in Italy has been difficult and even today the relationship between state and citizen remains problematic. As shown in the previous chapter, problems surrounding levels of civic consciousness and national identity have become all the more pressing for Italians in the aftermath of the moral crisis of the mid-nineties centred round *Mafia* atrocities and *Tangentopoli*.

The Italian institutions and political class played a key role in determining the direction in which Italian society was to move after 1993. The most optimistic Italians hailed the demise of the DC and PSI as ushering in a fresh political start for Italy, making way for a 'Second Republic' founded on a more transparent democracy and new civic values. Yet, as demonstrated by the type of change the party system underwent and the frequent stalling of urgent constitutional reform, there were strong lines of continuity with the 'First Republic' and this partly accounted for continuing illicit political activities. Although the main parties indicted for corruption and *Mafia* connections more or less disappeared from the political spectrum after 1993, members of the old political nomenklatura were strongly present in the new political groupings or joined those parties that had survived *Tangentopoli*.

As a result of this, there was little political support for the imposition of harsh sanctions on corrupt politicians and businessmen. In spite of the far-reaching investigations of the magistracy, few were punished, let alone imprisoned, for their crimes. As David Nelken points out, no legislation or administrative re-organization was implemented to deal with the causes of corruption so that: 'Although its immediate deterrent effect, particularly on the public administration, was considerable, few of the collusive practices which bind administrators and worlds of business or finance together have been dismantled.'[1] Illicit practices involving politicians, businessmen and

235

state administrators continue to take place. And 'ordinary' citizens are involved too. To cite just one of many examples of this, the summer of 2000 was dominated by newspaper headlines revealing corruption behind the management of state competitions for lawyers and primary school teachers. Considerable numbers of candidates had offered state officials large sums of money, and even the use of their holiday homes, in return for guarantees that they would get through the selection process successfully.

After 1993 there was an end to the *Mafia* killings of representatives of the state that had characterized the eighties and early nineties, indicating both the force of public opinion and the newly gained strength of the state itself. The large numbers of arrests of *mafiosi* taking place during the mid to late nineties were a reflection of greater determination on the part of judges and policemen, who in turn had more positive backing from the government. Yet, though there has been greater willingness on the part of the state to protect and compensate businesses falling victim to extortion, it is notable that at the end of the nineties four-fifths of Palermo's shopkeepers were still paying *Cosa Nostra* protection money. Today *Mafia* murders continue as a result of clan rivalry, while instances of state inefficiency and complicity remain an obstacle to the eradication of organized crime. Occasional terrorist killings and small-scale bombings since the late nineties have attempted to upset an already vulnerable political and institutional stability, too.

Much of the blame for continued corruption and *Mafia* power in Italy has been attributed to the negative attitude towards the judiciary of the forces of the Centre–Right, which have recently been returned to power. Berlusconi's continued attacks against the judiciary and the media have divided the country, with political debate focusing on whether the media magnate is justifiably defending himself against the 'intrusions' of institutions allegedly manipulated by the Left, or quite simply trying to create excessively wide and undemocratic powers for himself and re-legitimize the shady dealings of the 'First Republic'. The popularity of the Centre–Right, founded on a mixture of neo-liberalism, racism and anti-statism, has been interpreted by some political commentators as indicative of a failed civic and democratic revolution that many Italians had hoped for in the immediate aftermath of *Tangentopoli*. However, as indicated in the previous chapter, it is not always easy to make distinctions in civic attitudes according to political outlook.

Since the mid-nineties there have, indeed, been positive signs of growth in civic consciousness in Italy. In spite of the decline in traditional forms of political activity, public participation in associative activities continues to increase. Alongside the development of numerous anti-*Mafia* support groups, voluntary health, welfare and environmental organizations, many Italians have involved themselves in support campaigns for the victims of war in the Balkans. Although most voluntary organizations are concentrated in Northern areas, the traditional image of a socially apathetic South has recently been challenged by the solidarity shown by the citizens of Apulia and Calabria towards thousands of refugees from Eastern Europe and Asia landing on their shores. In the North-East, Catholic voluntary associations flourish, confirming the persistence – in spite of the high League vote – of a solidaristic Catholic tradition in that part of Italy.

What is notable, however, is that voluntary associations are increasingly detached from the political sphere. According to Parker, 'in recent years the ideological motive has been replaced by a desire to contribute to the life of the community outside the confines of "formal politics" and working life'. Parker continues:

> Contrary to what one might imagine, the 'volunteeers' tend to be reasonably high-earning males in early middle age. Not only does this confirm the idea that the new *dopolavoro* is a therapeutic antidote to the stresses and contortions of modern Italian life, it also suggests that Italy is witnessing the steady abandonment of 'strong' or party-based political activity in favour of a much weaker, more varied and dynamic form of social self-realization.[2]

The de-ideologization of associationism as a whole is particularly evident in the attitude of young Italians. A survey carried out in 1996 concluded that, while they were increasingly involved in associative activities, they belonged less and less to political and union organizations. There was, for example, a notable increase in youth involvement in religious and social activities organized by Catholic associations – suggesting that the demise of the DC had actually strengthened rather than weakened levels of religiousness and Catholic associationism – but a huge drop in consensus for Catholic political parties. More significant, however, is the fact that the 1996 survey revealed a notable swing to the Right among young Italians. *Alleanza Nazionale* was the most popular of all parties among young people, while at the opposite end of the political spectrum, there was increased support for the Refoundation Communist Party. This is seen as indicative of a sense of disorientation and consequent fascination for 'extremist' points of view rather than active political engagement.[3]

Closely connected to questions of civic consciousness, there is at present much debate on levels of national identity among Italians. This was partly reflected in an attempt during the nineties to overcome the Fascist/anti-Fascist schism dominating the post-war Republic. In many respects the cultural and social diversity making identification with an Italian nation problematic is no longer so marked, as John Dickie argues: 'Broadly speaking, following great internal migration, and the spread of the mass media after the Second World War, this problem has largely been overcome.'[4] But, Dickie continues, the other obstacle to nation building, namely an unhealthy political and institutional culture and the difficult relationship between the citizen and the state, persists – as has been indicated above. It is significant that Italian

237

support for European integration remains stronger than in any other member state. This partly reflects an awareness of the extent to which Italy's economic future depends on European integration but also indicates a tendency to trust supranational more than national government, in turn a consequence of a limited sense of identity with the Italian state in a country where local cultures and dialects remain strong. As Fabrizio Galimberti and Luca Paolazzi argue: 'In no other Community state would it have been possible, as happened in Italy in 1997, to call the extra financial contribution asked of its citizens a "tax on Europe" and to enforce it without too much dissent.'[5]

It is also true to say that, in spite of the development of separatist movements, at a cultural level most Italians, particularly the younger generation, identify with both the locality in which they live and Italy as a whole. Patriotic feeling is not only manifested during international sports events, as epitomized in the widespread celebrations that took place following Italy's victory at the 1982 football World Cup. Most Italians are proud of their country's natural beauty and cultural heritage and would agree that, despite the malfunctioning of their administrative and political system, the Italian way of life – founded on family values and the simple pleasures of friendship and the table – is healthier and more rewarding than that of historically more advanced countries. Yet, as Ilvo Diamanti points out with regard to the attitude of the younger generation during the nineties, it is difficult to create an excessively strong sense of national identity because of the strength of local identity. However, rather than the two forms of identity being opposed to each other, Italy represents an integrative point of reference within which conflicting 'localisms' are able to live together.[6]

Limited national consciousness is perhaps less of a problem in the present day and age than the lack of civic awareness associated with it. Indeed, the experience of identity at different levels (European, national and local) is particularly relevant to the current period of European integration, globalization and even the development in Italy of a multi-ethnic society. Yet, the negative impact of extra-EU immigration on a significant number of Italians suggests that intolerance of outsiders is deep-set and that the road to peaceful multi-ethnic cohabitation in Italy will be tortuous. Most worryingly, this is an area uniting traditionally opposed defenders on the Italian Right of 'local' autonomy and 'Italian' sovereignty. Silvana Patriarca suggests that the continued search among Italian intellectuals, politicians and journalists for a greater sense of national consciousness, as evident in newspaper and journal features and history publications, though partly motivated by the need to find an antidote to recent separatist positions, represents a neo-patriotic and potentially nationalistic stance in opposition to the development of a multi-ethnic society in Italy and to some extent even European integration.[7]

At the dawn of the twenty-first century, therefore, Italy's future appears undecided. Independent of political leanings, her people display a mixture of civic attitudes, many of which are undoubtedly founded on the values of solidarity and public-mindedness, alongside enduring mistrust of the state, clientelistic attitudes and racial intolerance. What is more critical at this juncture is the ability and willingness of politicians to discourage or take advantage of residual elements of backwardness, such as mistrust of the state, in their relationship with the electorate. There is no doubt that Berlusconi's business and media powers – representing a highly contested conflict of interests that is unprecedented in any Western democracy – pose a threat to Italy's future in that sense.

Besides the key role to be played by state institutions and the political class in determining the road that is taken, the strong mediating powers of tradition at the root of Italian society represent the other crucial factor. As much as it has been demonstrated, for example, that under certain conditions family and friendship ties are conducive to broader forms of solidarity, or are justified in the face of inadequate institutional presence, in many cases and circumstances survival strategies founded on such social resources continue to stand in the way of healthy civic development. The question remains whether it is possible to discard the more harmful elements of backwardness without destroying the more positive elements of Italian tradition that continue to figure among Italy's most valued cultural resources.

Notes

1. Nelken, 'A legal revolution? The judges and Tangentopoli', 201.
2. Parker, 'Political Identities', 119.
3. Data taken from Carlo Buzzi, Alessandro Cavalli and Antonio de Lillo (eds), *Giovani verso il Duemila. Quarto rapporto Iard sulla condizione giovanile in Italia* (Bologna: Il Mulino, 1997), chapters 5 and 6.
4. John Dickie, 'The notion of Italy', 26.
5. Galimberti and Paolozzi, *Il volo del calabrone*, 265.
6. Ilvo Diamanti, 'L'Italia: un puzzle di piccole patrie', in Buzzi, Cavalli and de Lillo (eds), *Giovani verso il Duemila*, 145–70(151).
7. Silvana Patriarca, 'Italian neopatriotism: debating national identity in the 1990s', *Modern Italy*, 6(1), 2001, 21–34.

Appendix I: Chronology

1859–70	Unification of Italy
1859	Casati Law on education
1861–65	Phenomenon of brigandage in Southern Italy
1865	Introduction of Italian criminal and police codes
1869	Riots against grain tax in Emilia and Romagna
1874	Vatican declaration of *non-expedit*
1877	Coppino Law on education
1880–87	Italy affected by world agricultural crisis – start of mass emigration
1881	Franchise extended to 2 million
1887	Introduction of protectionist tariffs allowing industrial development in North-West
1888–90	Tariff war with France
1891	Vatican lifts *non-expedit* for local elections; Papal encyclical, *de Rerum Novarum*
1892	PSI founded
1893	Rebellion of *Fasci Siciliani*
1894	Closure of Socialist and Anarchist associations
1896	Defeat of Italian army at Adowa, Ethiopia
1897–98	Widespread demonstrations and riots against economic crisis and *malgoverno*
1898	Eighty-five people killed during military repression of riots in Milan (8 May); introduction of voluntary accident insurance for certain worker categories
1899	Fiat founded
1900	Anarchist assassination of King Umberto I
1901–14	Period of almost uninterrupted rule of Giolitti with openings to Socialists and Catholics
1902	Legislation passed prohibiting children under the age of twelve from working
1906	CGL founded
1907	Maximum number of daily working hours established
1910	Maternity fund for female workers established
1911–12	Libyan war
1912	Franchise extended from 3 to 8 million; voluntary pension fund established

1913	Voluntary accident insurance extended to farm workers
1914	Red Week (June)
1915	Italy enters the First World War on the side of Britain, France and Russia
1917	Austrians defeat Italians at Caporetto
1918	Italian victory at Vittorio Veneto
1919–20	*Biennio Rosso* of strikes and land occupations; D'Annunzio's occupation of Fiume
1919	Introduction of universal male suffrage and electoral system of proportional representation; PPI founded; launching of *Fascio di Combattimento* by Mussolini; *Popolari* and Socialists become major parties following general election; unemployment reaches peak of 2 million; introduction of compulsory old-age, unemployment and disability insurance; trade unions achieve minimum wage, eight-hour working day and recognition of factory commissions; Sacchi Law increases areas in which women can be employed
1920	Occupation of engineering and metal factories and shipyards; launch of second Fascist movement
1921	PCI and PNF founded
1922	Occupation by Fascists of major Northern cities; Alliance of Labour Strike; March on Rome (28 October) – Mussolini becomes prime minister
1923	Acerbo electoral law; Gentile education reform; restrictions on female employment in the professions
1924	Fascists gain majority control of Chamber of Deputies following general election; political crisis following the abduction and murder by Fascists of Matteotti
1925–26	Creation of legal and institutional basis of Fascist dictatorship
1925	Palazzo Vidoni Pact confirms Fascist monopoly over union representation and abolishes elective factory councils; 'Battle for Wheat' launched; founding of ONMI and OND
1926	Opposition parties and trade unions declared illegal; Ministry of Corporations founded; ONB founded
1927	Fascist Labour Charter established; *Quota 90* followed by blue-collar wage reductions – many exporter companies go bankrupt; EIAR set up for political control of radio broadcasts
1929	Lateran Pacts between Vatican and Italian government; introduction of compulsory oath of allegiance to Fascist regime for school and university teachers
1930	Young Fascists founded; introduction of Fascist criminal code; wage and salary cuts and start of period of redundancies in the wake of the world depression
1931	Introduction of Fascist police code

1932	Creation of Fiat *Balilla* (people's car)
1933	Setting up of IRI; industrial value added overtakes value added in agriculture; introduction of 10 per cent ceiling on female employment in state firms; institution of 'Mother and Child Day' (24 December)
1932–33	Compulsorization of Fascist Party membership for appointments and promotions within public employment and the professions
1934	Creation of mixed corporations; introduction of 40-hour week; further wage and salary cuts; introduction of family allowance; new legislation protecting working mothers
1935–36	Ethiopian military campaign
1936	Italian intervention in Spanish Civil War; Rome–Berlin Axis; Italian emigration figures reach a historic low (with the exception of two World Wars) as a result of Fascist opposition and US restrictions of 1921 and 1924
1937	GIL created; Bottai founds Schools Charter; introduction of marriage loans
1938	Introduction of race laws
1939	Pact of Steel between Italy and Germany; invasion of Albania
1940	Italy joins Second World War on the side of Germany; invasion of Greece fails
1941	Italy joins German invasion of the Soviet Union and loses East African empire to the British; introduction of bread rationing
1942	Defeat of Axis forces in North Africa; new civil code reiterates female inequality
1943	Anti-war strikes in Milan and Turin; Anglo-Americans invade Sicily; meeting of Fascist Grand Council leading to Mussolini's dismissal from government; Badoglio announces Armistice with Anglo-American powers; German occupation of Northern and Central Italy; Mussolini creates Italian Social Republic; armed partisan Resistance against Nazis and Fascists begins
1944	Nazis shoot 335 civilians at Ardeatine caves, Rome, in reprisal for partisan attack; Italian army kills over 90 civilians during anti-council demonstration in Ragusa, Sicily; Anglo-Americans liberate Rome
1945	Liberation of Italian territory from Nazis and Fascists completed; Mussolini executed by partisans (28 April); introduction of *scala mobile*
1946	Referendum in favour of Republic and general election of Constituent Assembly – first ever female vote
1947	*Mafia* massacres eleven peasants at Portella delle Ginestre, Palermo, during May Day celebrations
1948	Founding of democratic Constitution of Italian Republic; victory of Christian Democrats at general election; attempt on Togliatti's

	life provoking widespread demonstrations followed by state repression of Left and partisan movement
1949	Italy joins NATO; Vatican excommunicates individuals espousing Communist doctrine
1950	Founding of CISL, after split of all-party union confederation; creation of the *Cassa per il Mezzogiorno*; agrarian reforms; new law on working mothers
1953	*Legge 'Truffa'* electoral reform; ENI founded
1954	RAI television broadcasts begin
1955	Defeat of CGIL at Fiat union elections; eradication of malaria completed
1956	Constitutional Court set up
1957	Italy founder member of European Common Market
1958–63	Most dynamic period of post-war economic boom
1960	Violent demonstrations against MSI congress at Genoa; police killings of demonstrators in Sicily and several Northern cities
1961	Peak in post-war emigration; students of technical schools granted access to university
1962–63	Attempted modernization of Catholic Church by Pope John XXIII; state becomes more tolerant towards union activities; relaxation of television and cinema censorship; establishment of single middle school ending previous class-based discrimination in education
1963	Papal encyclical, *Pacem in terris*; formation of first Centre–Left government
1964	*Piano Solo* military coup planned (but never put into practice)
1967–71	Widespread industrial strikes and student occupations of schools and universities
1968	Police kill 2 workers during strike at Avola, Sicily
1969	Police kill 2 workers during strike at Battipaglia, near Naples; 'Hot Autumn' of industrial strikes; Piazza Fontana bombing kills 16 people and marks start of period of 'Strategy of Tension'
1969–72	Founding of feminist movements
1970	Introduction of divorce; Workers' Statute passed; first regional elections throughout Italy
1971	New legislation on working mothers
1972	Italy converted from country of net emigration to net immigration
1974	Referendum retains divorce; bomb in Brescia kills 6 people; *Italicus* train bombing kills 12 people; international oil crisis sets off high inflation
1975	New family law leads to greater equality between the sexes; control of RAI passes from government to parliamentary commission
1976	Deregulation of state broadcasting monopoly opens way for private radio and television; earthquake in Friuli

1976–79	Period of 'national solidarity' (historic compromise)
1977	Transfer of administrative powers to the regions; creation of *1977* youth movement
1978	Kidnapping and murder of Aldo Moro by Red Brigades; legalization of abortion; creation of national health system
1979	Italy enters European Monetary System
1980	Terrorist bombing of Bologna station killing 85 people; Fiat lays off 14,000 workers – march of 40,000 against protest strike; earthquake hits Naples hinterland killing 6,000 people
1981	Interior Ministry police demilitarized and granted the right to form union; referendum retains abortion
1982	*Mafia* kills prefect of Palermo, General Alberto Dalla Chiesa
1984	Terrorist bombing of Naples to Milan train near Bologna kills 15 people; legislation limits the *scala mobile* (confirmed by referendum the following year)
1987	Italy becomes fifth world economic power overtaking Great Britain; referendum restricts nuclear power
1991	PCI dissolved and refounded as PDS
1992	Start of 'Operation Clean Hands' judicial offensive against political corruption; Christian Democrats and Socialists do badly in general election; rise to prominence of Northern League; *Mafia* kills judges Giovanni Falcone and Paolo Borsellino; Italian economy faces uncontrollable public and foreign deficits; Italy forced to leave European Monetary System; Socialist prime minister, Amato, introduces programme of economic austerity measures
1993	Referendum brings change in electoral system; Christian Democrat and Socialist parties collapse under weight of judicial investigations; *scala mobile* abolished
1994	Berlusconi launches *Forza Italia*; victory of Berlusconi's 'Freedom Pole' alliance at general election
1996	Italy re-enters European Monetary System; victory of 'Olive Tree' Centre-Left alliance at general election
1997	Italy qualifies to join the single European currency (Euro); earthquake in Umbria
1998	Mudslide in Campania kills over 200 people
2000	Death of Craxi in exile
2001	Berlusconi's 'Freedom Pole' alliance wins general election
2002	Italy adopts the Euro

Appendix II: Glossary

ammonizione Literally 'warning'. This was an instrument allowing the Italian police to place restrictions on the movements of criminals and suspected criminals during the Liberal and Fascist periods.

assistenzialismo Term referring to the widespread handing out of welfare payments in post-war Italy in return for political support.

attendismo Wait-and-see policy. This term is applied particularly to the attitude of large sections of the civilian population in Nazi-occupied Italy between 1943 and 1945.

autoriduzione Literally 'self-reduction'. The term refers to the tactic adopted during the worker agitation of the late sixties and early seventies of co-ordinated reduction in factory output. The term also indicates the practice encouraged by the social movements of the seventies of paying for services, such as public transport, at an unofficial reduced rate.

Biennio Rosso Literally 'Red Two Years', referring to the years 1919 and 1920, which were characterized by continuous social, political and economic unrest and a dramatic growth in the trade union movement and mass parties, particularly in the Socialist camp.

bracciante Landless rural labourer.
(plural: *braccianti*)

Camorra Term referring to Neapolitan crime organizations.

Carabinieri Italian military police force.

carabiniere Italian military policeman.
(plural: *carabinieri*)

Cassa per il 'Fund for the South' created in 1950 to encourage econ-
Mezzogiorno omic development in Southern Italy.

clientelism (Italian: In the context of nineteenth- and twentieth-century
clientelismo) Italy, the term refers to the acquisition by a 'client' of resources (for example, work) as a result of his or her ties with a 'patron', usually of a higher social standing, who had access to or control over the resources in question.

comparaggio	Italian term for the practice of god-fathering, which in Southern Italy often implied the creation of patron–client relationships.
confino	Similar to *domicilio coatto* (see below), an instrument empowering the Fascist police to exile criminals and anti-Fascists to remote parts of Italy, particularly to the South and the islands.
Cosa Nostra	Term referring to the Sicilian *Mafia*.
Destra Storica	Term referring to the Right or Moderate Liberal Party governing Italy between 1861 and 1876.
domicilio coatto	Internal exile. An instrument empowering the Italian police to exile habitual criminals and political offenders to remote parts of Italy, particularly the South and the islands, during the Liberal period.
dopolavoro	Literally 'afterwork', referring to the *Opera Nazionale Dopolavoro* (National Afterwork Organization) set up by the Fascist regime for the organization of adult leisure and recreational activities.
Duce	Meaning 'leader' or 'chief', the term was used to refer to the head of government and founder of Italian Fascism, Benito Mussolini.
eccidio proletario	Literally 'proletarian massacre', referring to the not infrequent killing of workers and peasants by the police, *Carabinieri* or army during strikes and demonstrations.
familism (Italian: *familismo*)	This much disputed term refers to strategies of survival and social and economic advancement based on the primacy of the family unit rather than the individuals within it or society at large.
fascio (plural: *fasci*)	Literally 'bundle'. The term referred to a loose grouping of people and was adopted mainly by the Fascists. The local headquarters of the Fascist movement were known as *fasci di combattimento* (combat groups). Fascist women's organizations were named *fasci femminili* and youth groups, *fasci giovanili*.
gabelloto (plural: *gabelloti*)	Farm estate foreman considered a key figure in the rise of the *Mafia*.
latifondista (plural: *latifondisti*)	Large estate owner in the South of Italy.
latifondi/latifundia	Large farming estates of Southern Italy that were eventually dismantled after the Second World War.
lega (plural: *leghe*)	Literally 'league', usually referring to the organizations of members of specific trades and professions or local trade union organizations (often called *leghe di resistenza*).

lottizzazione	The parcelling out among political parties of positions of power within the social, economic and cultural institutions of post-war Italian society.
mafioso (plural: *mafiosi*)	Member of a *Mafia* organization.
malgoverno	Literally 'bad government'. The term is particularly applied to the corruption historically characterizing Italian politics and administration as a result of the predominance of the practices of clientelism (see above) and *trasformismo* (see below).
meridionalista	Name historically given to politicians, historians, sociologists and economists preoccupied with Southern Italy's underdeveloped status compared with the rest of the country.
mezzadria	Sharecropping system.
mezzadro (plural: *mezzadri*)	Sharecropper.
Mezzogiorno	Term often used in Italian for Southern Italy
omertà	'Conspiracy of silence' characterizing social behaviour of rural and Southern Italy.
paese reale *paese legale*	Term indicating the historic difficulty experienced by the majority of Italians (*paese reale* – real Italy) in identifying with their government and institutions (*paese legale* – legal Italy).
partitocrazia	Term referring to the rule by party characterizing government and social, economic and cultural life in Italy.
patronage	In the context of this study, the term indicates the control over resources by 'patrons', traditionally members of the ruling élite, dominating social, economic and political transactions in nineteenth- and twentieth-century Italy. Such resources were handed down to individual 'clients', often in return for votes.
podestà	Government-appointed municipal chief replacing the office of mayor during the Fascist period.
questione meridionale	Literally 'Southern question', referring to the historical phenomenon of the underdevelopment of Southern Italy in comparison with the rest of the nation.
ras	The name for Ethiopian chieftains adopted to refer to local Fascist leaders.
Risorgimento	The name given to the process of unification of Italy during the nineteenth century.
scala mobile	Sliding scale set up in 1945 to safeguard real wages against the effects of inflation.

247

Sinistra Storica	Term referring to the Left Liberal Party succeeding the Right in government in 1876.
squadrismo	Term referring to the organizing of violent squads of Fascists to terrorize and eliminate the enemies of the Fascist movement.
squadrista (plural: *squadristi*)	Fascist squad member.
tangente (plural: *tangenti*)	Bribe.
Tangentopoli	Literally 'Bribesville', referring to the city of Milan, centre of the corruption scandals of the early nineties.
trasformismo	Literally 'transformism', the practice through which politicians gave their support to unstable government majorities in return for favours rather than on the basis of party affiliation.
ventennio	Literally 'twenty-year period', referring to the period of Fascist rule in Italy (October 1922–July 1943).

Select bibliography

General history texts

Absalom, Roger. 1995. *Italy since 1800. A Nation in the Balance?* London: Longman.

Beales, Derek. 1981. *The Risorgimento and the Unification of Italy*, 2nd edn. London: Longman.

Blinkhorn, Martin. 1984. *Mussolini and Fascist Italy*. London: Methuen.

Bongiovanni, Bruno and Nicola Tranfaglia (eds). 1996. *Dizionario storico dell'Italia unita*. Bari: Laterza.

Clark, Martin. 1996. *Modern Italy, 1871–1995*, 2nd edn. London: Longman.

De Felice, Renzo. 1965–97. *Mussolini il fascista*. Turin: Einaudi.

De Grand, Alexander. 2000. *Italian Fascism. Its Origins and Development*. Lincoln, NE: University of Nebraska Press.

Duggan, Christopher. 1994. *A Concise History of Italy*. Cambridge: Cambridge University Press.

Ginsborg, Paul. 1990. *A History of Contemporary Italy: Society and Politics, 1943–1988*. London: Penguin.

Ginsborg, Paul. 1998. *L'Italia del tempo presente. Famiglia, società civile, Stato, 1980–1996*. Turin: Einaudi.

Gooch, John. 1989. *The Unification of Italy*, 2nd edn. London: Routledge.

Hearder, Harry. 1983. *Italy in the Age of the Risorgimento, 1790–1870*. London: Longman.

Lanaro, Silvio. 1992. *Storia dell'Italia repubblicana. L'economia, la politica, la cultura, la società dal dopoguerra agli anni 90*. Venice: Marsilio.

Lyttelton, Adrian. 1973. *The Seizure of Power: Fascism in Italy, 1919–1929*. London: Weidenfeld & Nicolson.

Mack Smith, Denis. 1988. *The Making of Italy, 1796–1870*, 2nd edn. London: Macmillan.

Mack Smith, Denis. 1997. *Modern Italy. A Political History*. New Haven, CT: Yale University Press.

Morgan, Philip. 1995. *Italian Fascism, 1919–1945*. Basingstoke: Macmillan.

Pollard, John. 1998. *The Fascist Experience of Italy*. London: Routledge.

Riall, Lucy. 1994. *The Italian Risorgimento: State, Society and National Unification*. London: Routledge.

Robson, Mark. 1992. *Liberalism and Fascism, 1870–1945*. London: Hodder & Stoughton.

Sassoon, Donald. 1997. *Contemporary Italy: Politics, Economy and Society Since 1945*, 2nd edn. London: Longman.

Seton-Watson, Christopher. 1967. *Italy from Liberalism to Fascism, 1870–1925*. London: Methuen.

Whittam, John. 1995. *Fascist Italy*. Manchester: Manchester University Press.

Specialist works covering all or most of the period analysed in this book

Economy and society
Balcet, Giovanni. 1997. *L'economia italiana. Evoluzione, problemi e paradossi*. Milan: Feltrinelli.
Cento Bull, Anna and Paul Corner. 1993. *From Peasant to Entrepreneur: The Survival of the Family Economy in Italy*. Oxford: Berg.
Crainz, Guido. 1994. *Padania. Il mondo dei braccianti dall'Ottocento alla fuga dalle campagne*. Rome: Donzelli.
Galimberti, Fabrizio and Luca Paolozzi. 1998. *Il volo del calabrone. Breve storia dell'economia italiana del Novecento*. Florence: Le Monnier.
Sori, Ercole. 1979. *L'emigrazione italiana dall'Unità alla seconda guerra mondiale*. Bologna: Il Mulino.
Zamagni, Vera. 1993. *The Economic History of Italy, 1860–1990. Recovery after Decline*. Oxford: Clarendon Press.

The South and the Southern question
Arlacchi, Pino. 1983. *Mafia, peasants and great estates. Society in traditional Calabria*. Cambridge: Cambridge University Press.
Behan, Tom. 1995. *The Camorra*. London: Routledge.
Bevilacqua, Piero. 1993. *Breve storia dell'Italia Meridionale*. Rome: Donzelli.
Blok, Anton. 1988. *The Mafia of a Sicilian Village, 1860–1960: A Study of Violent Peasant Entrepreneurs*, 2nd edn. Cambridge: Polity Press.
Chubb, Judith. 1989. *The Mafia and Politics: The Italian State under Siege*. Ithaca, NY: Cornell University Press
Farrell, John. 1997. *Understanding the Mafia*. Manchester: Manchester University Press.
Hess, Henner. 1998. *Mafia and Mafiosi: The Structure of Power*, 2nd edn. New York: New York University Press.
Lupo, Salvatore. 1993. *Storia della mafia: dalle origini ai giorni nostri*. Rome: Donzelli.
Schneider, Jane (ed.). 1998. *Italy's Southern Question. Orientalism in One Country*. Oxford: Berg.
Tullio-Altan, Carlo. 1986. *La nostra Italia, arretrattezza socioculturale, clientelismo, trasformismo e ribellismo dall'Unità ad oggi*. Milan: Feltrinelli.

Law and order maintenance
Fried, Robert C. 1963. *The Italian Prefects: A Study in Administrative Politics*. New Haven, CT: Yale University Press.
Tarantini, Domenico. 1975. *La maniera forte. Elogio della polizia. Storia del potere politico in Italia: 1860–1975*. Verona: Bertani Editore.
Viola, Gianni. 1978. *Polizia, 1860–1977. Cronache e documenti della repressione in Italia* Verona: Bertani Editore.

Working-class movement
De Grand, Alexander. 1989. *The Italian Left in the Twentieth Century: A History of the Socialist and Communist Parties*. Bloomington, IN: Indiana University Press.

Horowitz, Daniel L. 1963. *The Italian Labour Movement.* Cambridge, MA.: Harvard University Press.

Neufeld, Maurice F. 1974. *Italy: School for Awakening Countries. The Italian Labor Movement in its Political, Social, and Economic Setting from 1800 to 1960.* Westport, NY: Greenwood Press.

Education and culture

Baranski, Zygmunt G. and Rebecca J. West (eds). 2001. *The Cambridge Companion to Modern Italian Culture.* Cambridge: Cambridge University Press.

Barbagli, Marzio. 1982. *Educating for Unemployment. Politics, Labour Markets and the School System. Italy 1859–1973.* New York: Colombia University Press.

Bondanella, Peter. 2001. *Italian Cinema: From neorealism to the Present,* 3rd edn. New York: Continuum.

De Fort, Ester. 1995. *Scuola e analfabetismo nell'Italia del'900.* Bologna: Il Mulino.

Forgacs, David. 1990. *Italian Culture in the Industrial Era 1880–1980. Cultural Policies, Politics and the Public.* Manchester: Manchester University Press.

Forgacs, David and Robert Lumley (eds). 1996. *Italian Cultural Studies. An Introduction.* Oxford: Oxford University Press.

Lumley, Robert. 1996. *Italian Journalism.* Manchester: Manchester University Press.

Pivato, Stefano and Anna Tonelli. 2001. *Italia Vagabonda. Il tempo libero degli italiani dal melodramma alla pay-tv.* Rome: Carocci.

Tarozzi, Fiorenza. 1999. *Il tempo libero. Tempo della festa, tempo del gioco, tempo per sé.* Turin: Paravia.

Tosi, Arturo. 2001. *Language and society in a changing Italy.* Clevedon: Multilingual Matters.

Family, women and demography

Barbagli, Marzio. 1984. *Sotto lo stesso tetto. Mutamento della Famiglia in Italia dal XV al XX Secolo.* Bologna: Il Mulino.

Bell, Rudolph. 1979. *Fate and Honour, Family and Village.* Chicago IL: University of Chicago Press.

Caldwell, Lesley. 1991. *Italian Family Matters: Women, Politics and Legal Reform.* London: Macmillan.

Kertzer, David I. and Richard P. Saller (eds). 1991. *The Family in Italy from Antiquity to the Present.* New Haven, CT: Yale University Press.

Livi-Bacci, Massimo. 1977. *A History of Italian Fertility during the Last Two Centuries.* Princeton, NJ: Princeton University Press.

Schneider, Jane and Peter. 1996. *Festival of the Poor: Fertility Decline and the Ideology of Class in Sicily, 1890–1980.* Tucson, AZ: University of Arizona Press.

Political culture and national identity

Bedani, Gino and Bruce Haddock (eds). 2000. *The Politics of Italian National Identity. A Multidisciplinary Perspective.* Cardiff: University of Wales Press.

Dickie, John. 2001. 'The notion of Italy', in Zygmunt G. Baranski and Rebecca J. West (eds). *The Cambridge Companion to Modern Italian Culture.* Cambridge: Cambridge University Press, 17–33.

Ginsborg, Paul. 1995. 'Italian Political Culture in Historical Perspective', *Modern Italy*, 1(1), 3–17.

Levy, Carl (ed.). 1996. *Italian Regionalism. History, Identity and Politics*. Oxford: Berg.

Tullio-Altan, Carlo. 1986. *La nostra Italia. arretrattezza socioculturale, clientelismo, trasformismo e ribellismo dall'Unità ad oggi*. Milan: Feltrinelli.

Tullio-Altan, Carlo. 1999. *Gli italiani in Europa. Profilo storico comparato delle identità nazionali europee*. Bologna: Il Mulino.

Statistical works
ISTAT. 1986. *Sommario di statistiche storiche 1926–1985*. Rome: ISTAT.

Mitchell, B.R. 1978. *European Historical Statistics*. London: Macmillan.

Chapter 1: Italian society in the wake of the Risorgimento, 1860–1914

Barbagli, Marzio. 1991. 'Marriage and the family in Italy in the early nineteenth century', in John A. Davis and Paul Ginsborg (eds). *Society and Politics in the Age of the Risorgimento*. Cambridge: Cambridge University Press, 92–127.

Barbagli, Marzio. 1991. 'Three Household Formation Systems in Eighteenth and Nineteenth Century Italy', in David I. Kertzer and Richard P. Saller (eds). *The Family in Italy from Antiquity to the Present*. New Haven, CT: Yale University Press. 250–70.

Bell, Donald Howard. 1986. *Sesto San Giovanni: Workers, Culture and Politics in an Italian Town, 1880–1922*. New Brunswick, NJ: Rutgers University Press.

Cardoza, Anthony L. 1979. 'Agrarians and Industrialists: the Evolution of an Alliance in the Po Delta, 1896–1914', in John A. Davis (ed.). *Gramsci and Italy's Passive Revolution*. London: Croom Helm, 172–212.

Cardoza, Anthony L. 1982. *Agrarian Elites and Italian Fascism: The Province of Bologna, 1901–1926*. Princeton, NJ: Princeton University Press.

Davis, John A. (ed.). 1979. *Gramsci and Italy's Passive Revolution*. London: Croom Helm.

Davis, John A. 1979. 'The South, the Risorgimento and the Origins of the "Southern Problem"', in John A. Davis (ed.). *Gramsci and Italy's Passive Revolution*. London: Croom Helm, 67–103.

Davis, John A. 1988. *Conflict and Control. Law and Order in Nineteenth-Century Italy*. Basingstoke: Macmillan.

Davis, John A. and Paul Ginsborg (eds). 1991. *Society and Politics in the Age of the Risorgimento*. Cambridge: Cambridge University Press.

Dickie, John. 1999. *Darkest Italy. The Nation and Stereotypes of the Mezzogiorno, 1860–1900*. Basingstoke: Macmillan.

Dunnage, Jonathan. 1997. *The Italian Police and the Rise of Fascism. A Case-Study of the Province of Bologna, 1897–1925*. Westport: Praeger.

Gribaudi, Gabriella. 1997. 'Images of the South', in Jonathan Morris and Robert Lumley (eds). *The New History of the Italian South*. Exeter: University of Exeter Press, 83–113.

Jensen, Richard Bach. 1991. *Liberty and Order: The Theory and Practice of Italian Public Security Policy, 1848 to the Crisis of the 1890s*. New York: Garland.

Lyttelton, Adrian. 1979. 'Landlords, peasants and the limits of Liberalism', in John A. Davis (ed.). *Gramsci and Italy's Passive Revolution*. London: Croom Helm, 104–35.

Macry, Paolo. 1997. 'The Southern Metropolis: Redistributive Circuits in Nineteenth-Century Naples', in Jonathan Morris and Robert Lumley (eds). *The New History of the Italian South*. Exeter: University of Exeter Press, 59–82.

Macry, Paolo. 1997. 'Rethinking a stereotype: territorial differences and family models in the modernization of Italy', *Journal of Modern Italian Studies*, 2(2), 188–214.

Miller, James. 1990. *From Elite to Mass Politics. Italian Socialism in the Giolittian Era, 1900–1914*. Kent, OH: Kent State University Press.

Morris, Jonathan and Robert Lumley (eds). 1997. *The New History of the Italian South*. Exeter: University of Exeter Press.

Moss, David. 1995. 'Patronage revisited: the dynamics of information and reputation', *Journal of Modern Italian Studies*, 1(1), 58–93.

Riall, Lucy. 1998. *Sicily and the Unification of Italy*. Oxford: Clarendon Press.

Snowden, Frank M. 1986. *Violence and Great Estates in the South of Italy. Apulia, 1900–1922*. Cambridge: Cambridge University Press.

Tilly, Louise A. 1992. *Politics and Class in Milan, 1881–1901*. Oxford: Oxford University Press.

Chapter 2: Social fragmentation and violence in Italy, 1915–25

Alberghi, Pietro. 1989. *Il Fascismo in Emilia Romagna. Dalle origini alla marcia su Roma*. Modena: Mucchi.

Bell, Donald Howard. 1986. *Sesto San Giovanni: Workers, Culture and Politics in an Italian Town, 1880–1922*. New Brunswick, NJ: Rutgers University Press.

Cardoza, Anthony L. 1982. *Agrarian Elites and Italian Fascism: The Province of Bologna, 1901–1926*. Princeton, NJ: Princeton University Press.

Casali, Luciano (ed.). 1982. *Bologna 1920*. Bologna: Cappelli.

Clark, Martin. 1988. 'Italian Squadrismo and Contemporary Vigilantism', *European History Quarterly*, 18(1), 33–49.

Corner, Paul. 1975. *Fascism in Ferrara, 1915–1925*. Oxford: Oxford University Press.

Corner, Paul. 1990. 'Italy', in Stephen Salter and John Stevenson (eds). *The Working Class and Politics in Europe and America, 1919–1945*. London: Longman, 154–71.

Dunnage, Jonathan. 1997. *The Italian Police and the Rise of Fascism. A Case-Study of the Province of Bologna, 1897–1925*. Westport: Praeger.

Kelikian, Alice A. 1979. 'From Liberalism to Corporatism: the Province of Brescia during the First World War', in John A. Davis (ed.). *Gramsci and Italy's Passive Revolution*. London: Croom Helm, 213–38.

Kelikian, Alice A. 1986. *Town and Country under Fascism. The Transformation of Brescia, 1918–26*. Oxford: Clarendon Press.

Molony, John N. 1977. *The Emergence of Political Catholicism in Italy. Partito Popolare 1919–1926*. London: Croom Helm.

Roberts, David D. 1979. *The Syndicalist Tradition and Italian Fascism*. Manchester: Manchester University Press.

Snowden, Frank M. 1979. 'From sharecropper to proletarian: the background to fascism in rural Tuscany, 1880–1920', in John A. Davis (ed.). *Gramsci and Italy's Passive Revolution*. London: Croom Helm, 136–71.

Snowden, Frank M. 1986. *Violence and Great Estates in the South of Italy: Apulia, 1902–1922*. Cambridge: Cambridge University Press.

Snowden, Frank M. 1989. *The Fascist Revolution in Tuscany, 1919–1922*. Cambridge: Cambridge University Press.

Spriano, Paolo. 1975. *The Occupation of the Factories*. London: Pluto Press.

Steinberg, Jonathan. 1986. 'Fascism in the Italian South: The Case of Calabria', in David Forgacs (ed.). *Rethinking Italian Fascism: Capitalism, Populism and Culture*. London: Lawrence & Wishart, 83–109.

Thompson, Doug. 1991. *State control in Fascist Italy. Culture and conformity, 1925–1943*. Manchester: Manchester University Press.

Williams, Gwyn. 1975. *Proletarian Order: Antonio Gramsci, Factory Councils and the Origins of Italian Communism, 1911–1921*. London: Pluto Press.

Chapter 3: The experience of Fascism, 1925–39

Abse, Tobias. 1996. 'Italian workers and Italian Fascism', in Richard Bessel (ed.). *Fascist Italy and Nazi Germany. Comparisons and contrasts*. Cambridge: Cambridge University Press, 40–60.

Aquarone, Alberto. 1969. 'Italy: the crisis and the corporative economy', *Journal of Contemporary History*, 4 (4), 37–58.

Berghaus, Günter (ed.). 1996. *Fascism and Theatre. Comparative Studies on the Aesthetics and Politics of Performance in Europe, 1925–1945*. Oxford: Berghahn.

Bessel, Richard (ed.). 1996. *Fascist Italy and Nazi Germany. Comparisons and contrasts*. Cambridge: Cambridge University Press.

Bordoni, Carlo. 1974. *Cultura e propaganda nell'Italia fascista*. Messina–Florence: G. D'Anna.

Bosworth, R.J.B. 1998. *The Italian Dictatorship. Problems and Perspectives in the Interpretation of Mussolini and Fascism*. London: Arnold.

Bosworth, R.J.B. and Patrizia Dogliani (eds). 1999. *Italian Fascism. History, Memory and Representation*. Basingstoke: Macmillan.

Caldwell, Lesley. 1986. 'Reproducers of the Nation: Women and the Family in Fascist Policy', in David Forgacs (ed.). *Rethinking Italian Fascism. Capitalism, Populism and Culture*. London: Lawrence & Wishart, 110–41.

Cannistraro, Philip. 1975. *La fabbrica del consenso: Fascismo e mass media*. Bari: Laterza.

Collotti, Enzo and Lutz Klinkhammer. 1996. *Il fascismo e l'Italia in guerra*. Rome: Ediesse.

Corner, Paul. 1979. 'Fascist agrarian policy and the Italian economy in the inter-war years', in John A. Davis (ed.). *Gramsci and Italy's Passive Revolution*. London: Croom Helm, 239–74.

Corner, Paul. 1990. 'Italy', in Stephen Salter and John Stevenson (eds). *The Working Class and Politics in Europe and America, 1919–1945*. London: Longman, 154–71.

De Grazia, Victoria. 1981. *The culture of consent. Mass organization of leisure in fascist Italy*. Cambridge: Cambridge University Press.

De Grazia, Victoria. 1992. *How Fascism Ruled Women: Italy, 1922–1945*. Berkeley, CA: University of California Press.

De Luna, Giovanni. 1995. *Donne in oggetto: l'antifascismo nella società italiana, 1922–39*. Turin: Bollati Boringhieri.

Dogliani, Patrizia. 2000. 'Sport and Fascism', *Journal of Modern Italian Studies*, 5(2), 326–43.

Duggan, Christopher. 1989. *Fascism and the Mafia*. New Haven, CT: Yale University Press.

Forgacs, David (ed.). 1986. *Rethinking Italian Fascism: Capitalism, Populism and Culture*. London: Lawrence & Wishart.

Gentile, Emilio. 1995. *La via italiana al totalitarismo. Il partito e lo Stato nel regime fascista*. Rome: La Nuova Italia Scientifica.

Ipsen, Carl. 1996. *Dictating Demography: The Problem of Population in Fascist Italy*. Cambridge: Cambridge University Press.

Koon, Tracy. 1985. *Believe, Obey, Fight: Political Socialization of Youth in Fascist Italy, 1922–1943*. Chapel Hill, NC: University of North Carolina Press.

Levy, Carl. 1996. 'From Fascists to Post-Fascists: Italian roads to Modernity', in Richard Bessel (ed.). *Fascist Italy and Nazi Germany. Comparisons and contrasts*. Cambridge: Cambridge University Press, 165–96.

London, John. 1999. 'The Uncertainty of Fascist Aesthetics: Political Ideology and Historical Reality', *Renaissance and Modern Studies*, 42, 49–63.

Mack Smith, Denis. 1976. *Mussolini's Roman Empire*. London: Longman.

Mason, Tim. 1995. *Nazism, Fascism and the Working Class*. Cambridge: Cambridge University Press.

Newby, Wanda. 1991. *Peace and War. Growing up in Fascist Italy*. London: Picador.

Passerini, Luisa. 1987. *Fascism in Popular Memory*. Cambridge: Cambridge University Press.

Piva, Francesca and Gianni Toniolo. 1987. 'Sulla disoccupazione in Italia negli anni trenta', *Rivista di Storia Economica*, 4(3), 345–83.

Roberts, David D. 1979. *The Syndicalist Tradition and Italian Fascism*. Manchester: Manchester University Press.

Salvemini, Gaetano. 1969. *Under the Axe of Fascism*, 2nd edn. New York: Fertig.

Sarti, Roland (ed.). 1974. *The Axe Within: Italian Fascism in Action*. New York: New Viewpoints.

Tannenbaum, Edward R. 1972. *Fascism in Italy. Society and Culture, 1922–1945*. London: Allen Lane.

Thompson, Doug. 1991. *State control in Fascist Italy. Culture and conformity, 1925–1943*. Manchester: Manchester University Press.

Toniolo, Gianni. 1980. *L'economia dell'Italia fascista*. Bari: Laterza.

Treves, Anna. 1976. *Le migrazioni interne nell'Italia fascista: Politica e realtà demografica*. Turin: Einaudi.

Vannutelli, Cesare. 1974. 'The living standard of Italian workers, 1929–39', in Roland Sarti (ed.). *The Axe Within: Italian Fascism in Action*. New York: New Viewpoints, 139–60.

Venè, Gian Franco. 1988. *Mille lire al mese. Vita quotidiana della famiglia nell'Italia fascista* Milan: Mondadori.

Wagstaff, Christopher. 1996. 'Cinema', in David Forgacs and Robert Lumley (eds). *Italian Cultural Studies. An Introduction*. Oxford: Oxford University Press, 216–32.

Willson, Perry. 1993. *The Clockwork Factory: Women and Work in Fascist Italy*. Oxford: Clarendon Press.

Willson, Perry. 1996. 'Women in Fascist Italy', in Richard Bessel (ed.). *Fascist Italy and Nazi Germany. Comparisons and contrasts*. Cambridge: Cambridge University Press, 78–93.

Wolff, Richard J. 1990. *Between Pope and Duce: Catholic Students in Fascist Italy*. New York: Peter Lang.

Chapter 4: War, civil conflict and the end of dictatorship, 1940–50

Abse, Tobias. 1996. 'Italian workers and Italian Fascism', in Richard Bessel (ed.). *Fascist Italy and Nazi Germany. Comparisons and contrasts*. Cambridge: Cambridge University Press, 40–60.

Baranski, Zygmunt G. and Robert Lumley (eds). 1990. *Culture and Conflict in Post-war Italy*. London: Macmillan.

Barkan, Joanne. 1984. *Visions of Emancipation: The Italian Workers' Movement since 1945*. New York: Praeger.

Battaglia, Roberto. 1957. *The Story of the Italian Resistance*. London: Odhams Press.

Bedani, Gino. 1995. *Politics and Ideology in the Italian Workers' Movement. Union Development and the Changing Side of the Catholic and Communist Subcultures in Post-war Italy*. Oxford: Berg.

Bosworth, R.J.B. 1998. *The Italian Dictatorship. Problems and Perspectives in the Interpretation of Mussolini and Fascism*. London: Arnold.

Bosworth, R.J.B. and Patrizia Dogliani (eds). 1999. *Italian Fascism. History, Memory and Representation*. Basingstoke: Macmillan.

Clark, Martin. 1988. 'Italian Squadrismo and Contemporary Vigilantism', *European History Quarterly*, 18 (1), 33–49.

Collotti, Enzo and Lutz Klinkhammer. 1996. *Il fascismo e l'Italia in guerra*. Rome: Ediesse.

Cooke, Philip. 1995. 'Il partigiano Johnny. Resistenza e mondo contadino nelle Langhe', *Italia Contemporanea*, 198, 63–76.

Cooke, Philip (ed.). 1997. *The Italian Resistance. An Anthology*. Manchester: Manchester University Press.

Cooke, Philip (ed.). 2000. Special issue on the Italian Resistance, *Modern Italy*, 5(2).

Dalla Casa, Brunella and Alberto Preti (eds). 1995. *Bologna in guerra, 1940–1945*. Milan: Franco Angeli.

Deakin, Frederick W. 1962. *The Brutal Friendship. Mussolini, Hitler and the Fall of Italian Fascism*. London: Weidenfeld & Nicolson.

Delzell, Charles F. 1961. *Mussolini's Enemies: The Italian Anti-Fascist Resistance*. Princeton, NJ: Princeton University Press.

Domenico, Roy Palmer. 1991. *Italian Fascists on Trial, 1943–48*. Chapel Hill, NC: North Carolina Press.

Dondi, Mirco. 1999. *La lunga liberazione*. Rome: Editori Riuniti.

Dunnage, Jonathan (ed.). 1999. *After the War: Violence, Justice, Continuity and Renewal in Italian Society*. Market Harborough: Troubador.

Ellwood, David. 1985. *Italy, 1943–1945*. Leicester: Leicester University Press.

Ellwood, David. 1992. *Rebuilding Europe: Western Europe, America and Postwar Reconstruction*. London: Longman.

Forgacs, David. 1996. 'Cultural consumption, 1940s to 1990s', in David Forgacs and Robert Lumley (eds). *Italian Cultural Studies. An Introduction*. Oxford: Oxford University Press, 273–90.

Fraddosio, Maria. 1996. 'The Fallen Hero. The Myth of Mussolini and Fascist Women in the Italian Social Republic (1943–5)', *Journal of Contemporary History*, 31(1), 99–124.

Galli della Loggia, Ernesto. 1996. *La morte della patria*. Bari: Laterza.

Harper, John L. 1986. *America and the Reconstruction of Italy, 1945–1948*. Cambridge: Cambridge University Press.

Lamb, Richard. 1993. *War in Italy, 1943–1945. A Brutal Story*. Harmondsworth: Penguin.

Lepre, Aurelio. 1989. *Le illusioni, la paura, la rabbia. Il fronte interno italiano (1940–1943)*. Rome: Edizioni Scientifiche Italiane.

Lewis, Norman. 1967. *The Honoured Society. The Mafia Conspiracy Observed*. Harmondsworth: Penguin.

Lewis, Norman. 1983. *Naples '44*, 2nd edn. London: Eland.

Marcus, Millicent. 1986. *Italian Film in the Light of Neorealism*. Princeton, NJ: Princeton University Press.

Newby, Wanda. 1991. *Peace and War. Growing up in Fascist Italy*. London: Picador.

Pavone, Claudio. 1991. *Una guerra civile. Saggio storico sulla moralità nella Resistenza*. Turin: Bollati Boringhieri.

Quartermaine, Luisa. 2000. *Mussolini's Last Republic: Propaganda and Politics in the Italian Social Republic (R.S.I.) 1943–45*. Exeter: Elm Bank Publications.

Rusconi, Gian Enrico. 1995. *Resistenza e postfascismo*. Bologna: Il Mulino.

Slaughter, Jane. 1997. *Women and the Italian Resistance, 1943–1945*. Denver, CO: Arden Press.

Woolf, Stuart J. (ed.). 1972. *The Rebirth of Italy 1943–1950*. London: Longman.

Chapter 5: Social, cultural and economic transformation in post-war Italy, 1950–80

Allum, Percy A. 1973. *Italy–Republic without Government?* London: Weidenfeld & Nicolson.

Allum, Percy A. 1973. *Politics and Society in Post-war Naples*. Cambridge: Cambridge University Press.

Baldi, Stafano and Raimondo Cagiano de Azevedo. 2000. *La popolazione italiana. Storia demografica dal dopoguerra ad oggi*. Bologna: Il Mulino.

Banfield, Edward. 1958. *The Moral Basis of a Backward Society*. London: Collier-Macmillan.

Barbagli, Marzio. 1990. *Provando e riprovando. Matrimonio, famiglia e divorzio in Italia e in altri paesi occidentali*. Bologna: Il Mulino.

Barkan, Joanne. 1984. *Visions of Emancipation: The Italian Workers' Movement since 1945*. New York: Praeger.

Bedani, Gino. 1995. *Politics and Ideology in the Italian Workers' Movement. Union Development and the Changing Side of the Catholic and Communist Subcultures in Post-war Italy*. Oxford: Berg.

257

Brögger, Jan. 1971. *Montevarese: A study of peasant society and culture in Southern Italy.* Oslo: Universitetsforlaget.

Caldwell, Lesley. 1995. 'The Family in the Fifties: A Notion in Conflict with a Reality', in Christopher Duggan and Christopher Wagstaff (eds). *Italy in the Cold War. Politics, Culture and Society, 1948–1958.* Oxford: Berg, 149–58.

Catanzaro, Raimondo (ed.). 1991. *The Red Brigades and Left-Wing Terrorism in Italy.* London: Pinter.

Chubb, Judith. 1982. *Patronage, power and poverty in Southern Italy. A tale of two cities.* Cambridge: Cambridge University Press.

Clark, Martin. 1988. 'Italian Squadrismo and Contemporary Vigilantism', *European History Quarterly*, 18(1), 33–49.

Crainz, Guido. 1998. *Storia del miracolo italiano. Culture, identità, trasformazioni fra anni cinquanta e sessanta.* Rome: Donzelli.

Dagrada, Elena. 1996. 'Television and its Critics: A Parallel History', in David Forgacs and Robert Lumley (eds). *Italian Cultural Studies. An introduction.* Oxford: Oxford University Press, 233–47.

Davis, John A. 1973. *Land and Family in Pisticci.* London: Athlone Press.

Della Porta, Donatella. 1995. *Social movements, political violence, and the state: A comparative analysis of Italy and Germany.* Cambridge: Cambridge University Press.

Drake, Richard. 1995. *The Aldo Moro Murder Case.* Cambridge, MA: Harvard University Press.

Duggan, Christopher and Christopher Wagstaff (eds). 1995. *Italy in the Cold War. Politics, Culture and Society, 1948–1958.* Oxford: Berg.

Ferraresi, Franco. 1996. *Threats to Democracy. The Radical Right in Italy after the War.* Princeton, NJ: Princeton University Press.

Flores, Marcello and Alberto De Bernardi. 1998. *Il Sessantotto.* Bologna: Il Mulino.

Foot, John. 1999. 'Immigration and the city: Milan and mass immigration, 1958–98', *Modern Italy*, 4(2), 159–72.

Forgacs, David. 1996. 'Cultural consumption, 1940s to 1990s', in David Forgacs and Robert Lumley (eds). *Italian Cultural Studies. An Introduction.* Oxford: Oxford University Press, 273–90.

Franziosi, Roberto. 1994. *The Puzzle of Strikes: Class and State Strategies in Post-war Italy.* Cambridge: Cambridge University Press.

Furlong, Paul. 1994. *Modern Italy. Representation and Reform.* London: Routledge.

Goddard, Victoria A. 1996. *Gender, Family and Work in Naples.* Oxford: Berg.

Golden, Miriam. 1988. *Labour Divided. Austerity and Working Class Politics in Contemporary Italy.* Ithaca, NY: Cornell University Press.

Gundle, Stephen. 1996. 'Fame, Fashion, and Style: the Italian Star System', in David Forgacs and Robert Lumley (eds). *Italian Cultural Studies. An Introduction.* Oxford: Oxford University Press, 309–26.

Gundle, Stephen. 2000. 'The "civic religion" of the Resistance in post-war Italy', *Modern Italy*, 5(2), 113–32.

Hine, David. 1993. *Governing Italy. The Politics of Bargained Pluralism.* Oxford: Clarendon Press.

Kertzer, David I. 1980. *Comrades and Christians. Religion and Political Struggle in Communist Italy.* Cambridge: Cambridge University Press.

King, Russell. 1985. *The Industrial Geography of Italy*. Beckenham: Croom Helm.

Lewis, Norman. 1967. *The Honoured Society. The Mafia Conspiracy Observed.* Harmondsworth: Penguin.

Liguori, Maria Chiara. 1996. 'Donne e consumi nell'Italia degli anni cinquanta', *Italia Contemporanea*, 205, 665–89.

Low-Beer, John R. 1978. *Protest and Participation. The new working class in Italy.* Cambridge: Cambridge University Press.

Lumley, Robert. 1990. *States of Emergency: Cultures of Revolt in Italy from 1968 to 1978.* London: Verso.

Mapelli, Vittorio. 1999. *Il sistema sanitario nazionale*. Bologna: Il Mulino.

McCarthy, Patrick. 1997. *The Crisis of the Italian State. From the Origins of the Cold War to the Fall of Berlusconi and Beyond*. Basingstoke: Macmillan.

McCarthy, Patrick (ed.). 2000. *Italy since 1945*. Oxford: Oxford University Press.

Meade, Robert C. 1990. *Red Brigades: The Story of Italian Terrorism*. London: Macmillan.

Moss, David. 1989. *The Politics of Left-Wing Violence in Italy, 1969–85*. London: Macmillan.

Pivato, Stefano. 2000. 'Sport', in Patrick McCarthy (ed.). *Italy since 1945*. Oxford: Oxford University Press, 171–82.

Portelli, Alessandro. 1997. *The Battle of Valle Giulia: Oral History and the Art of Dialogue*. Madison, WI: University of Wisconsin Press.

Putnam, Robert. 1993. *Making Democracy Work: Civic Traditions in Modern Italy*. Princeton, NJ: Princeton University Press.

School of Barbiana. 1973. *Letter to a Teacher*. Harmondsworth: Penguin.

Silverman, Sydel. 1975. *Three Bells of Civilization. The Life of an Italian Hill Town*. New York: Columbia University Press.

Spotts, Frederic and Theodor Wieser. 1986. *Italy: A Difficult Democracy. A Survey of Italian Politics*. Cambridge: Cambridge University Press.

Tarrow, Sidney. 1989. *Democracy and Disorder: Protest and Politics in Italy, 1965–1975*. Oxford: Clarendon Press.

Trigilia, Carlo. 1990. 'Work and politics in the Third Italy's industrial districts', in Frank Pyke, Giacomo Becattini and Werner Sengenberger (eds). *Industrial Districts and Inter-firm Co-operation in Italy*. Geneva: International Institute for Labour Studies, 160–84.

Tunesi, Simonetta. 2000. 'Italian environmental policies in the post-war period', in Patrick McCarthy (ed.). *Italy since 1945*. Oxford: Oxford University Press, 118–32.

Wagstaff, Christopher. 1996. 'Cinema', in David Forgacs and Robert Lumley (eds). *Italian Cultural Studies. An Introduction*. Oxford: Oxford University Press, 216–32.

Wagstaff, Christopher. 2001. 'The Media', in Zygmunt G. Baranski and Rebecca J. West (eds). *The Cambridge Companion to Modern Italian Culture*. Cambridge: Cambridge University Press, 293–309.

Walston, James. 1988. *The Mafia and Clientelism. Roads to Rome in post-war Calabria*. London: Routledge.

Willan, Philip. 1991. *Puppetmasters. The Political Use of Terrorism in Italy*. London: Constable.

Chapter 6: Affluence and moral crisis: Italian society in the eighties and nineties and Conclusion: Italian society at the dawn of the twenty-first century

Alexander, David. 1991. 'Pollution, policies and politics: the Italian environment', in Filippo Sabetti and Raimondo Catanzaro (eds). *Italian Politics. A Review*, Vol. 5. London: Pinter, 90–111.

Allum, Percy A. and Ilvo Diamanti. 1996. 'The Autonomous Leagues in the Veneto', in Carl Levy (ed.). *Italian Regionalism. History, Identity and Politics*. Oxford: Berg, 151–69.

Andall, Jacqueline. 1990. 'New migrants, old conflicts: the recent immigration into Italy', *The Italianist*, 10, 151–74.

Baldi, Stafano and Raimondo Cagiano de Azevedo. 2000. *La popolazione italiana. Storia demografica dal dopoguerra ad oggi*. Bologna: Il Mulino.

Barbagli, Marzio. 1990. *Provando e riprovando. Matrimonio, famiglia e divorzio in Italia e in altri paesi occidentali*. Bologna: Il Mulino.

Barbagli, Marzio. 1998. *Immigrazione e criminalità in Italia*. Bologna: Il Mulino.

Bedani, Gino. 1995. *Politics and Ideology in the Italian Workers' Movement. Union Development and the Changing Side of the Catholic and Communist Subcultures in Post-war Italy*. Oxford: Berg.

Bull, Martin and Martin Rhodes (eds). 1997. *Crisis and Transition in Italian Politics*. London: Frank Cass.

Buzzi, Carlo, Alessandro Cavalli and Antonio de Lillo (eds). 1997. *Giovani verso il Duemila. Quarto rapporto lard sulla condizione giovanile in Italia*. Bologna: Il Mulino.

Cartocci, Roberto. 1994. *Fra Lega e Chiesa*. Bologna: Il Mulino.

Cavalli, Alessandro and Antonio de Lillo. 1988. *Giovani anni 80. Secondo rapport lard sulla condizione giovanile in Italia*. Bologna: Il Mulino.

Cento Bull, Anna. 1996. 'Ethnicity, Racism and the Northern League', in Carl Levy (ed.). *Italian Regionalism. History, Identity and Politics*. Oxford: Berg, 171–87.

Cento Bull, Anna. 2000. *Social Identities and Political Cultures in Italy. Catholic, Communist and 'Leghist' Communities between Civicness and Localism*. Oxford: Berghahn.

Dagrada, Elena. 1996. 'Television and its Critics: A Parallel History', in Forgacs and Lumley (eds). *Italian Cultural Studies. An Introduction*. Oxford: Oxford University Press, 233–47.

Della Porta, Donatella. 1995. *Social movements, political violence, and the state: A comparative analysis of Italy and Germany*. Cambridge: Cambridge University Press.

Della Porta, Donatella. 1995. 'Political Parties and Corruption: Reflections on the Italian Case', *Modern Italy*, 1(1), 97–114.

Farrell, Joseph. 1995. 'Berlusconi and Forza Italia: New Force for Old?', *Modern Italy*, 1(1), 40–52.

Farrell, Joseph and Carl Levy. 1996. 'The Northern League: Conservative Revolution?', in Carl Levy (ed.). *Italian Regionalism. History, Identity and Politics*. Oxford: Berg, 131–50.

Forgacs, David. 1996. 'Cultural consumption, 1940s to 1990s', in David Forgacs and Robert Lumley (eds). *Italian Cultural Studies. An Introduction*. Oxford: Oxford University Press, 273–90.

Frei, Matt. 1998. *Italy. The Unfinished Revolution*. London: Arrow.

Furlong, Paul. 1994. *Modern Italy. Representation and Reform*. London: Routledge.

Gilbert, Mark. 1995. *The Italian Revolution. The End of Politics, Italian Style?* Boulder, CO: Westview Press.

Ginsborg, Paul *et al*. 2000. 'Italy in the present tense: a roundtable discussion', *Modern Italy*, 5(2), 175–91.

Goddard, Victoria A. 1996. *Gender, Family and Work in Naples*. Oxford: Berg.

Gundle, Stephen and Noëlleane O'Sullivan. 1995. 'The Crisis of 1992–1994 and the Reform of Italian Public Broadcasting', *Modern Italy*, 1(1), 70–81.

Gundle, Stephen and Simon Parker (eds). 1996. *The New Italian Republic: from the Fall of the Berlin Wall to Berlusconi*. London: Routledge.

Gundle, Stephen. 1996. 'Fame, Fashion, and Style: the Italian Star System', in David Forgacs and Robert Lumley (eds). *Italian Cultural Studies. An Introduction*. Oxford: Oxford University Press, 309–26.

Hine, David. 1993. *Governing Italy. The Politics of Bargained Pluralism*. Oxford: Clarendon Press.

Ieri, Paolo. 1988. 'The nuclear power issue: a new political cleavage within Italian society', in Raffaella Y. Nanetti, Robert Leonardi and Piergiorgio Corbetta (eds). *Italian Politics: A Review*, Vol. 2. London: Pinter, 71–89.

ISTAT. 1990. *Le regioni in cifre*. Rome: Istituto Nazionale di Statistica.

ISTAT. 1996–99. *Rapporto sull'Italia*. Bologna: Il Mulino.

Koff, Sondra Z. and Stephen P. Koff. 2000. *Italy. From the First to the Second Republic*. London: Routledge.

LaPalombara, Joseph. 1987. *Democracy Italian Style*. New Haven, CT: Yale University Press.

Locke, Richard M. 1995. *Remaking the Italian Economy*. Ithaca, NY: Cornell University Press.

Lumley, Robert. 1996. 'Peculiarities of the Italian Newspaper', in David Forgacs and Robert Lumley (eds). *Italian Cultural Studies. An Introduction*. Oxford: Oxford University Press, 199–215.

McCarthy, Patrick. 1997. *The Crisis of the Italian State. From the Origins of the Cold War to the Fall of Berlusconi and Beyond*. Basingstoke: Macmillan.

McCarthy, Patrick (ed.). 2000. *Italy since 1945*. Oxford: Oxford University Press.

Mapelli, Vittorio. 1999. *Il sistema sanitario nazionale*. Bologna: Il Mulino.

Mershon, Carol and Gianfranco Pasquino (eds). 1995. *Italian Politics. Ending the First Republic*. Boulder, CO: Westview Press.

Mignone, Mario B. 1995. *Italy Today. A Country in Transition*. New York: Peter Lang.

Moss, David. 1995. 'Patronage revisited: the dynamics of information and reputation', *Journal of Modern Italian Studies*, 1(1), 58–93.

Padoa Schioppa Kostoris, Fiorella. 1993. *Italy. The Sheltered Economy. Structural Problems in the Italian Economy*. Oxford: Clarendon Press.

Parker, Simon. 1996. 'Political Identities', in David Forgacs and Robert Lumley (eds). *Italian Cultural Studies. An Introduction*. Oxford: Oxford University Press, 107–28.

Parker, Simon. 1999. 'The end of Italian exceptionalism? Assessing the transition to the Second Republic', *The Italianist*, 19, 251–83.

Patriarca, Silvana. 2001. 'Italian neopatriotism: debating national identity in the 1990s', *Modern Italy*, 6(1), 21–34.

Pivato, Stefano. 2000. 'Sport', in Patrick McCarthy (ed.). *Italy since 1945*. Oxford: Oxford University Press, 107–82.

Putnam, Robert. 1993. *Making Democracy Work: Civic Traditions in Modern Italy*. Princeton, NJ: Princeton University Press.

Pyke, Frank, Giacomo Becattini and Werner Sengenberger (eds). 1990. *Industrial Districts and Inter-firm Co-operation in Italy*. Geneva: International Institute for Labour Studies.

Rhodes, Martin (ed.). 1997. *Southern European Welfare States. Between Crisis and Reform*. London: Frank Cass.

Scobie, H.M., S. Mortali, S. Persuad and P. Docile. 1996. *The Italian Economy in the 1990s*. London: Routledge.

Spotts, Frederic and Theodor Wieser. 1986. *Italy: A Difficult Democracy. A Survey of Italian Politics*. Cambridge: Cambridge University Press.

Stille, Alexander. 1995. *Excellent cadavers. The Mafia and the death of the first Italian Republic*. London: Jonathan Cape.

The Italian experience of immigration, special issue of *Modern Italy*, 4(2), 1999.

Tullio-Altan, Carlo. 1999. *Gli italiani in Europa. Profilo storico comparato delle identità nazionali europee*. Bologna: Il Mulino.

Tunesi, Simonetta. 2000. 'Italian environmental policies in the post-war period', in Patrick McCarthy (ed.). *Italy since 1945*. Oxford: Oxford University Press, 118–32.

Wagstaff, Christopher. 1996. 'Cinema', in David Forgacs and Robert Lumley (eds). *Italian Cultural Studies. An Introduction*. Oxford: Oxford University Press, 216–32.

Wagstaff, Christopher. 2001. 'The Media', in Zygmunt G. Baranski and Rebecca J. West (eds). *The Cambridge Companion to Modern Italian Culture*. Cambridge: Cambridge University Press, 293–309.

World Trade Organization. 1985–1998. *International Trade Statistics*, Annual Reports.

Index

abortion
  increased acceptance 103
  legalization 181, 182
Acerbo, Giacomo (1888–1969) 63
agriculture
  land reclamation 78–9
  modernization 8–9, 78–9, 200; role of
    Mafia 17
  reform 150–1
  regional variations 7, 12
Allied bombings 119–20
Allied occupation 126
Amato, Giuliano (*b*1938) 201
AN – Alleanza Nazionale 218–19, 223–4
  youth support 237
anarchists 50, 52
Andreotti, Giulio (*b*1919) 213
anti-Fascism 86–7
  creation 110
  motivations 121
  and post-war violence 131–2
  repression 85
anti-Interventionists 39–40
anti-Semitism 108 *see also* Jews
Ardeatine caves 130, 224
Arditi del Popolo 56, 61–2
attendismo 129–30
autarchy 73, 74
Autunno Caldo see 'Hot Autumn'
Avanguardia Nazionale 186
Aventine Secession 67

Badoglio, Pietro (1871–1956) 122
  post WWII government 135–6
Berlusconi, Silvio (*b*1936) 218, 220,
    226–8, 236
  forms government 219
  media powers 239
Bicycle Thieves (De Sica, 1948) 144

Biennio Rosso (Two 'Red' Years) 48, 49,
    54
  gains rolled back 65, 66
  violence 31–2
birth control & family planning 30,
    101, 162, 182
birthrate/fertility levels 30
  baby boom 159
  decline 102, 161, 206–7
braccianti (day labourers) 7, 12, 13, 20,
    24, 29, 47, 49, 51, 58, 61, 77
brigandage/brigands 4, 5–6
Brigate Rosse (Red Brigades) 178, 187–90

Camorra (Naples) 18, 178, 213 *see also*
    organized crime
  exploit economic patronization 155
  resurgence 133
Caporetto (battle, 1917) 40, 44
  impact 45
Casati Law (1859) 24
  South, benefits 26
Cassa per il Mezzogiorno 151, 155
  dismantled 200
Casti Connubi (Papal encyclical, 1930)
    101
Catholic Action (*Azione Cattolica*) 21,
    141, 164, 170
Catholic Church
  and anti-Left strategy 158
  and Fascist family policies 101
  female employment 31
  influence diminishes 170, 183
  and mass culture 99–100, 166
  non-expedit 6; lifted 21
  peasant leagues 50
  peasant rebellions, supports 6
  reform 167–8, 170
  undermining state authority 163